# THE BATTLE FOR SOCIAL SECURITY

## From FDR's Vision to Bush's Gamble

Nancy J. Altman

WILEY

John Wiley & Sons, Inc.

Published by John Wiley & Sons, Inc., Hoboken, New Jersey.
Published simultaneously in Canada.

For general information on our other products and services or for technical support, please
contact our Customer Care Department within the United States at (800) 762-2974, outside
the United States at (317) 572-3993 or fax (317) 572-4002.

Wiley also publishes its books in a variety of electronic formats. Some content that appears in
print may not be available in electronic books. For more information about Wiley products,
visit our web site at www.wiley.com.

ISBN-13   978-0-471-77172-2
ISBN-10   0-471-77172-4

Printed in the United States of America

10  9  8  7  6  5  4  3  2  1

*For Chip, my extraordinarily wonderful husband
and partner for life*

# Contents

## CHAPTER 1

# From the Poorhouse to Free Parking

At 8:46 A.M. on Tuesday, September 11, 2001, American Airlines Flight 11 crashed into the North Tower of the World Trade Center. At that moment, Beatrice M. Disman, the New York Regional Commissioner of the Social Security Administration, was entering a conference room at the program's headquarters in Baltimore, Maryland. A few minutes later, she was handed a note, which she quickly scanned. Bolting from the room and grabbing a phone, she hurriedly called her New York office, located a short walk from the World Trade Center—close enough that many of her colleagues had seen the plane hit the tower. She reached the assistant regional commissioner, who told her, "We're evacuating." Disman responded that she was returning to New York immediately.

By Thursday, September 13, two days after the attack, Social Security was in overdrive. The families of virtually every worker who perished that day were entitled to benefits under the program. The daunting task facing Social Security was to identify those families, contact them, and help them secure the financial protection their loved ones had earned for them.

The Social Security Administration was among the first insurers to meet with employers and victims' families. Its employees worked with the New York Police Department, the Fire Department, and the Port Authority to find the families of every firefighter and police officer who had died. Social Security employees were at the Family Assistance Centers established at Pier 94 and Liberty State Park. They set up a special Web page, informing the families of the victims how to apply for benefits, as well as displaying the 800 number and a link to Social Security's office locator.

By Sunday, September 16, public information spots about Social Security were running on every major network affiliate in New York City, on the local television stations, and on Spanish-language stations. In addition, Social Security distributed press releases and fact sheets to national media outlets and advocacy organizations. Lines of communication were established with local hospitals and the New York City Labor Council.

Program representatives called the families of every missing employee of those companies located in the World Trade Center. Social Security caseworkers spoke with the families of each missing firefighter and each missing police officer. The program contacted a number of the city's largest financial service corporations, which might have had people in the World Trade Center on the day of the attack. The program's employees phoned the union that represented the restaurant workers in the World Trade Center. To make sure Social Security reached foreigners who might be eligible for benefits, its representatives called over 60 consulates. All of these steps were taken on top of Social Security's normal workload.

Social Security employees worked 15-hour days, seven days a week to get benefits to the families as quickly as possible. Long though the hours were, the program's employees were eager to work. When Disman asked her managers to find people willing to help on the weekend, the response was overwhelming. The employees did not want to leave their long shifts to go home and rest. The people in the World Trade Center were their friends and neighbors, and the Social Security representatives knew that they were throwing an economic lifeline to the families when they needed help the most.

A stay-at-home dad lost his wife in the World Trade Center on September 11. In the midst of his grieving, he could see no way to remain at home with his child or support the child at the level they had been living. Unaware of the valuable Social Security benefits his wife had earned for her family through her work, he reluctantly put the family home on the market after that tragic day. The call from Social Security, from out of the blue, was a godsend. He hung up the phone and called his real estate agent. He could keep his home, after all.

Social Security recognized that it was vital to get benefits to the families quickly. In anticipation of natural disasters and other tragedies, the

Social Security Administration had long-standing emergency procedures in place. In response to the attack, it invoked those existing procedures, which included, among other emergency measures, waiving the standard requirement of a death certificate, instead relying on airplane manifests and employer work records as proof of death.

On October 3, 2001, three weeks after the terrorist attack, Social Security checks were mailed and electronically transferred, as they are every month, to program beneficiaries. Included among the 47 million people receiving Social Security benefits in October were the stay-at-home dad, his young child, and thousands of other members of families who lost loved ones on September 11.

In the chaotic aftermath of that tragic day, millions of Americans reached into their pockets to contribute to the Red Cross and other charitable organizations assisting the families of the 9/11 victims. But the most immediate, sustained, and generous support for those families came from Social Security. Today, virtually all working Americans continue to contribute to the 9/11 families every payday. The money withheld from every worker's paycheck for Social Security goes into the program's Old Age and Survivors Insurance Trust Fund, out of which those victims' families receive benefits. Virtually every child who lost a parent in the terrorist attack will receive a Social Security check every month until his or her late teens. So will the children's surviving parents who care for them.

Just as the actions of the brave police and firefighters in response to the terrible events of September 11 filled all of us with gratitude and pride, so Social Security's response to the attack on America might have led us to celebrate this vital institution and recognize its value in our modern, insecure world. Instead, as Social Security was diligently finding and assisting the families of the victims, President George W. Bush had the program in his crosshairs.

Four months and 9 days before September 11, President Bush established a Social Security commission. The president instructed it to report back to him with changes that "must include individually controlled, voluntary personal retirement accounts." Three months and 10 days after September 11, the commission filed its report with the President.

The commissioners offered three alternatives in response to the President's directive to develop private account proposals. Just like the proposal President Bush unveiled once he was safely reelected, all three alternatives diverted a substantial percentage of the current Social Security payroll tax to fund individual accounts.

Only two of the three alternatives put forward by the commission addressed the long-range deficit that was projected in the Social Security program. Both recommended fundamentally altering Social Security through a technical adjustment to the benefit formula, just as the President himself proposed in a press conference on April 29, 2005. Although President Bush talks about strengthening Social Security, his proposals would profoundly weaken the system and radically transform it from a program of social insurance into a program of individual self-help.

Social Security provides a specified percentage of a worker's earnings in the event of death, disability, or old age. In contrast, the President's indexing proposal would cause Social Security benefits inexorably to erode into a very minimal, almost flat benefit, largely unrelated to earnings. Americans would be on their own to supplement the meager benefit with whatever they could accumulate in their own individual accounts. In his late night monologue, comedian Jay Leno succinctly and accurately summarized President Bush's Social Security plan as "Good luck, Grandma. You're on your own."

For the first time in the 70-year life of Social Security, a President has proposed undoing this program that provides security to so many. The President seeks to focus public attention only on the part of Social Security dealing with retirement. But Social Security is not just a retirement program; it is, more accurately, a family protection program. Social Security is the nation's largest children's program. Over 5 million children live in homes where part or all of the family income comes from Social Security. Over 3 million children receive Social Security as dependents of deceased, disabled, or retired workers—including virtually all the children who lost parents on September 11, as well as the children of fallen and disabled U.S. soldiers in Iraq, Afghanistan, and elsewhere.

All parts of the program are interwoven. One single benefit formula generates payment amounts for all beneficiaries: retirees, disabled workers, spouses, widows, widowers, and children. The retirement strand of the program cannot be removed without unraveling the entire fabric.

In the current debate, President Bush has attempted to convince Americans that Social Security is outmoded and fundamentally flawed—created long ago, designed for the last century, and unworkable for an aging population. But knowledge of the program and its vivid history reveals that Bush's assault is just another battle in a long-standing ideological war. A small minority, outside the mainstream, has always believed that all but the neediest individuals should be completely on their own and has long fought a campaign against Social Security.

Some of the most powerful and wealthy families in America considered President Franklin Delano Roosevelt a traitor to his class because he championed Social Security and other progressive programs and policies. President George W. Bush's grandfather, Prescott Bush, once remarked of Roosevelt: "The only man I truly hated lies buried in Hyde Park."

Opponents of Roosevelt fought against Social Security in 1935. The program was a major campaign issue in the waning days of the election of 1936. At the time of the election, Social Security had been enacted just the year before and no taxes had yet been collected or benefits paid. Nevertheless, Republican Presidential candidate Alf Landon and his supporters did everything they could in the closing weeks of the campaign to undermine support for the program. In words that sound astoundingly like those uttered by President Bush today, a *Time* magazine article of the day summarized the position that Landon and his supporters had espoused concerning Social Security in the just-completed election: "Said Republicans: 'Wage earners, you will pay and pay in taxes…and when you are very old, you will have an I.O.U. which the U.S. Government may make good if it is still solvent.'"

Even Roosevelt's landslide reelection victory did not stop the diehards. A small intransigent group continued to oppose Social Security in the decades following its enactment. When Social Security started projecting deficits in the mid-1970s, opponents of the program saw an opportunity to spread doubt and anxiety.

Just like today, the overblown rhetoric of "crisis" and "bankruptcy" was swirling around Social Security in the late 1970s and early 1980s. In 1978, a candidate running hard for a congressional seat in west Texas spoke to a group of real estate agents about Social Security in a campaign stop at Midland Country Club. "[Social Security] will be bust in 10 years unless there are some changes," the candidate claimed, adding: "The ideal solution would be for…people [to be] given the chance to invest the money the way they feel." The candidate's name: George W. Bush.

Throughout its storied history, Social Security has had its foes, but it has also had its champions. At every stage, people who have believed in the common good and the values of family and community have worked to give Social Security life and vigor. Some are famous names from history, but others are unsung heroes. One outstanding leader in the creation and development of Social Security is Arthur Altmeyer, a serious, bespectacled, scholarly man, called "Mr. Social Security" by President Roosevelt. Another is the gregarious, energetic Wilbur Cohen, about whom Senator Paul Douglas quipped, "…an expert on Social Security is a person who knows Wilbur Cohen's telephone number."

One more invaluable hero is the dignified and personable Robert M. Ball, who the late Senator Daniel Patrick Moynihan said was "as wise a counsellor as any Senator will know." Still another is Robert J. Myers, a tall, shy, soft-spoken actuary, whom Moynihan labeled "a national treasure." These people and many others have played crucial roles in Social Security's dramatic history, a story that includes riveting accounts of dedication and conflict, of perseverance and close calls, of visionaries and determined opponents.

The work of all these supporters and defenders has always been backed by Social Security's most important champion, the American people. Through its many challenges, Social Security has always emerged victorious, because Americans have remained committed to this essential program. The large majority of Americans have supported Social Security because it embodies the best of American values, including reward for work, compassion, fairness, foresight, and prudent, conservative management. This unflagging support has permitted Social Security to eradicate much of the economic insecurity of the past and to transform society.

Before the enactment of Social Security, people worked as long as they could hold jobs. But this was an insecure state of affairs. The fast pace of many jobs "wears out its workers with great rapidity," a commentator noted in 1912. "The young, the vigorous, the adaptable, the supple of limb, the alert of mind, are in demand," he explained. "Middle age is old age."

Once a job was lost, an older worker could seldom find a new one. Older people almost never had sufficient savings to last until death. The dilemma of saving for one's own retirement was described in 1934:

> A man's productive, wage-earning period is rarely more than 45 years. Under present conditions he must earn enough in this period to contribute toward the support of aged parents, rear and educate children, maintain his family at a standard of living more or less consistent with American ideals, and save enough in the form of insurance or absolutely safe investment to provide a modest income until death, if he survives his working period. This last

item of his budget is the one least urgent, least stressed by advertising propaganda, and most easily disregarded among the many
financial demands.

Other than the reference to supporting one's parents—a job largely taken
over by Social Security—the description of the difficulty of saving for
retirement could have been written today.

Those unable to work almost always moved in with their children.
Those who had no children or whose children were unable or unwilling
to support them typically wound up in the poorhouse. The poorhouse
was not some ancient Dickensian invention; it was a very real means of
subsistence for elderly people in the world immediately preceding Social
Security.

When Social Security became law, every state but New Mexico had
poorhouses (sometimes called almshouses or poor farms). The vast
majority of the residents were elderly. Most of the "inmates," as they were
often labeled, entered the poorhouse late in life, having been independent wage earners until that point. A Massachusetts Commission reporting
in 1910 found, for example, that only 1 percent of the residents had
entered the almshouse before the age of 40; 92 percent entered after
age 60.

A higher percentage of men wound up in the poorhouse, even though
women's life expectancies were longer than men's, just as they are today.
The reason for this surprising result, according to a 1919 Pennsylvania
commission, was that women's traditional work around the house was
useful even as they aged. Consequently, the commission discovered,
"Children or relatives will make greater sacrifices in order to keep an old
mother at home and prevent her going to a poorhouse, than they would
for an aged father or other male relative."

The poorhouse was a fate to be dreaded. Even in as progressive a state
as New York, the conditions were abysmal. In 1930, the New York State
Commission on Old Age Security found that "worthy people are thrown
together with whatever dregs of society happen to need the institution's
shelter at the moment; sick people are thrown together with the well, the
blind, the deaf, the crippled, the epileptics; the people of culture and
refinement, with the crude and ignorant and feeble-minded."

"Privacy, even in the most intimate affairs of life, is impossible; married
couples are quite generally separated; and all the inmates are regimented
as though in a prison or penal colony," the commission reported. It noted

that "private possessions, other than the clothes on the back, are almost out of the question, since individual bureaus, closets, tables or other articles of furniture, outside of a bed, are generally not provided."

The poorhouse was always lurking in the background, haunting people as they aged. It was a powerful, ubiquitous image in the general culture. The early Monopoly boards, beginning with the game's invention in 1903, contained a square labeled "Poorhouse." Today, in a world with Social Security, that same exact square reads "Free Parking."

Poorhouses and destitute senior citizens were a fact of life well before the Great Depression. Surveys by Wisconsin and New York, published in 1925 and 1929 respectively, found that almost half the population aged 65 and older had "insufficient subsistence income." A writer in 1912 described the inevitable fate most Americans faced as they aged:

> After the age of sixty has been reached, the transition from non-dependence to dependence is an easy stage—property gone, friends passed away or removed, relatives become few, ambition collapsed, only a few short years left to live, with death a final and welcome end to it all—such conclusions inevitably sweep the wage-earners from the class of hopeful independent citizens into that of the helpless poor.

What follows is the story that changed that inevitable ending.

## CHAPTER 2

# Social Security's Grandfather

John R. Commons was a brilliant, creative scholar with a self-deprecating sense of humor and a warmth of manner. Rumpled in appearance, serious in expression, and intellectual though he was, he was not the stereotypical absent-minded professor. He was a pragmatist, a man of action, who, underneath his soft-spoken exterior, cared deeply about others.

Commons's name matched his values. He greatly respected common men and women. He believed in the concept of the "commons," the idea—reflected in the name of one of America's oldest parks, the Boston Common, referred to informally by many Bostonians as "the Commons"—that we are interdependent and united in our humanity.

Born in 1862 near the Ohio-Indiana border, he was the grandson of farmers and the son of an unsuccessful businessman, who, according to Commons, "could not fit himself to the Money and Credit economy." Commons graduated from Oberlin College in 1888, "by the indulgence of my professors," he wryly claimed.

By the time he graduated, he had witnessed a dramatic national transformation. The United States was in the process of becoming the world's leading industrial nation, producing the most steel, iron, coal, timber, gold, and silver of any country in the world. Between 1870 and 1900, the automobile, telephone, electric light bulb, typewriter, Linotype, phonograph, cash register, air brake, and refrigerator car all were invented, and all led to new industries. Businesses became larger, factories became commonplace, and the need for labor exploded.

The number of people living in cities had grown at a frenetic pace. In a 20-year period, Chicago tripled in size. When Commons was born, only 9 cities had populations over 100,000; in another decade, he would live in a country where 38 cities were that large, including 3 with populations over a million.

Many of these new city dwellers came from rural areas. In 1920, for the first time in the nation's history, more Americans would live in cities than in the country. As people moved from farms, they left a self-sufficient life of growing their own food and living with extended family to a world of groceries, rent, and streets full of strangers.

This was also a period of enormous immigration. From Commons's eighteenth birthday to the start of the first World War, 34 years later, over 20 million immigrants arrived on American shores. They generally left most of their relatives thousands of miles behind. The newcomers typically came with nothing more than the clothes on their backs and the suitcases in their hands.

For the first time in the country's history, millions of people were totally dependent on wages. Not surprisingly in an era before minimum wage and maximum hours laws, the United States witnessed frequent and sustained strikes—36,000 of them between 1881 and 1905—as workers organized into unions to improve their working conditions.

Employers retaliated by obtaining court orders against strikers on the grounds of criminal trespass, threats to property rights, and unlawful conspiracy. Those union leaders who defied the court orders were sent to prison for contempt. When those tactics failed to break the strikes, some employers hired Pinkerton Detective Agency guards and other private security forces who often resorted to back-alley violence.

Newspapers across the nation trumpeted the labor strife in sensational, front-page headlines. In 1886, during Commons's sophomore year at Oberlin, newspapers were full of stories about the Haymarket Square riot, where what started as a peaceful picket line at the McCormick Reaper factory in Chicago ended with 11 people killed, more than 100 injured, and 8 people convicted of inciting to violence.

Troubled by the social upheaval that was engulfing the country, Commons decided to study economics in order to help improve working conditions and prevent the underlying causes of the violence. Upon graduation from Oberlin, he applied to Johns Hopkins University to do graduate work in economics. He was drawn to the school in part because he had read an editorial attacking one of Hopkins's professors, Richard T. Ely, for his "socialist" views. An independent thinker himself (Commons voted for the Prohibitionist candidate for president in 1884 and the Communist party candidate for governor when he lived in New York a decade later), Commons was attracted to other similarly open-minded thinkers.

Professor Ely was the perfect teacher for Commons. Having graduated from Columbia University in 1876, at a time when the United States had no doctoral programs, Ely, like most of the intellectuals of his generation, studied in Germany, where he learned about the worker security reforms undertaken there. Urbanization, industrialization, and widespread worker unrest occurred earlier in Europe than in the United States. The bloody worker uprising in Paris in 1848—dramatized in the musical *Les Misérables*—was but one stark example of the worker protests, repression, and violence sweeping that continent. The lead Europe had with worker unrest also gave the continent a head start in developing solutions.

By the time Ely arrived in Germany, a number of European governments had already tried inducing private savings as a way of dealing with economic insecurity. These voluntary programs proved useless. Over time, it became clear that workers either could not or would not increase their savings enough, even with incentives, to protect themselves against the new economic risks. In 1850, for example, France established its National Old Age Insurance Institution, a voluntary program, where benefits were directly related to contributions. Not even workers making average wages took part. To the extent the program was used at all, it was almost exclusively the upper middle class who took advantage of it.

Germany was the first nation to take the bold step of enacting compulsory, universal social insurance. In 1883, Chancellor Otto von Bismarck instituted a landmark national health insurance program for wage earners. Over the next few years, Germany added programs of workers' compensation and retirement, disability, and survivors' benefits, and the rest of Europe followed Germany's lead.

Professor Ely studied these programs in depth and passed along his firsthand knowledge to his students. Commons became Ely's research assistant, and the two men grew close. Ely believed that, in addition to classroom work, students should gain experience in the real world, so on Ely's suggestion, Commons became a case worker with the Charity

Organization Society. The charity's director, John M. Glenn, instructed Commons to help a Civil War veteran obtain a pension.

Military pensions for veterans dated back to the Revolutionary War. The Civil War was such a bloody, violent conflict that it produced the largest proportion of people disabled, widowed, or orphaned in all of American history. The destructiveness led Congress to authorize relatively generous benefits for soldiers who had been disabled in the war and for survivors of soldiers who had been killed.

As Civil War veterans aged, pressure mounted to expand the program. The Republican party platform in 1888 contained a plank stating that "any man who honorably wore the Federal uniform" should be protected with a pension, so that he would never be subjected to the terrible fate of becoming "the inmate of an almshouse, or dependent upon private charity."

The idea proved popular. In 1890, Congress expanded Civil War pensions to cover any veteran who was disabled, regardless of cause. Sixteen years later, Congress expanded the program once more to provide benefits to veterans simply on the basis of old age.

The soldier whom Commons sought to help was disabled from tuberculosis. Although Congress had recently expanded the program to include disabilities not related to military service, the law on the books did not magically translate to cash in his pocket. When Commons was assigned the case, he found the soldier "in the third story of a rattle-shack tenement, his wife doing all she could to care for him." The ailing veteran and his overworked wife had neither the energy nor the resources to take on a government bureaucracy.

Commons spent a year at the task. He visited the pension office, spoke with lawyers, and worked with the Democratic congressman from Baltimore, Representative Harry W. Rusk, who proved challenging because of his sympathies for the confederacy. Ultimately, after arduous effort and seemingly endless hours, Commons succeeded, and the veteran got the benefit he had earned with his war service. Commons, for his part, got the benefit of an education. For the rest of his life, he was to combine teaching and scholarship with efforts to make government work more compassionately for the people it served.

After two years of study, Commons left Johns Hopkins for a teaching position at Wesleyan University. He lasted one year. The next few years proved no more fruitful. Struggling to find himself, he went through a succession of jobs, teaching at various universities and colleges, as well as taking positions with government and private research organizations. Finally, in 1904, his mentor, Professor Ely, who had left Hopkins and joined the faculty of the University of Wisconsin in Madison, helped secure him a faculty appointment there.

Commons's start in Madison was marked by two other commencements, one in the university, one in the state government. The brand-new university president, Charles R. Van Hise, told the faculty in his inaugural address that he expected them to spend equal time on teaching, scholarship, and assisting the state government, a close neighbor just down the road in the small town of Madison. Also commencing was a new era in Wisconsin's political history. After two terms as governor, the progressive Robert M. La Follette gained control, for the first time, of both houses of the legislature.

Commons could not have written a better script for himself. The combination of teaching, writing, and working with a progressive government to put his ideas about worker security into action was exactly what he felt destined to do. Feeling "born again...after five years of incubation," Commons knew instantly that he had found a permanent home.

He proved to be a popular professor. Early on, he began a tradition of regular Friday night dinners, first in restaurants and then in his home, where professors and students mingled and discussed the leading issues of the day. The tradition lasted until his retirement in June 1934, and generations of students became known to him and each other as "Friday Niters."

The Friday Niters represented early-twentieth-century networking at its best. Professors and students forged close friendships over these casual evenings. Graduates working in Madison remained regulars; others were sure to drop in on the weekly gatherings when they returned for visits. Friday Niters shared information about jobs and generally helped each other succeed.

Commons became a nationally recognized scholar. In his first year at Wisconsin, he began work on the *History of labour in the United States*, which, with the help of younger colleagues and students, developed into a four-volume classic still used today.

His instant success as a teacher and scholar were matched by his instant access to state government. Fortuitously, Commons had met Governor La Follette two years before coming to Madison. In Commons's first few months at the university, La Follette contacted him to draft strong legislation reforming Wisconsin's civil service. After that, Commons began to develop his own ideas for legislation.

In 1906, the Russell Sage Foundation financed a survey of Pittsburgh's social conditions. Commons's supervisor from Baltimore's Charity Organization Society, John M. Glenn, was now head of the foundation, and he asked Commons to oversee the labor side of the survey.

The survey included the case of Adam Rogalas, a Russian immigrant who had worked for the Iron City Grain Elevator Company. On October 17, 1906, Rogalas was killed at work when the supports of the floor above gave way, dumping heavy bags of stored grain on him. He left behind his pregnant wife and four children aged ten, six, five, and two. After the accident, Mrs. Rogalas earned what she could by taking in laundry. Pittsburgh's welfare laws provided her with groceries valued at $6.00 a month, a pittance for a family of six. She supplemented her earnings by begging outside the Catholic church on Sundays.

She found a lawyer who agreed to sue the employer for damages of $20,000. After a year's wait and a short trial, the judge ruled that the evidence did not support a finding that the employer had been negligent. The Grain Elevator Company won the case and paid Mrs. Rogalas nothing.

The Rogalas family's fate, and similar reports of other innocent workers killed or injured at work, caused Commons to turn his energy toward legislation providing compensation for workplace injuries and death. Maryland had enacted a workers' compensation program in 1902, but two years later the courts had held it unconstitutional. Commons began drafting his own version for Wisconsin.

Around that same time, while attending a meeting in Atlantic City of the American Economic Association, Commons bumped into Henry W. Farnam, the renowned economics professor from Yale University. The two friends decided to take a walk on the unseasonably mild December day. As they strolled along the boardwalk, Farnam turned to Commons and remarked, "Curious isn't it, that you, a radical, and I, a conservative, find ourselves working together."

The two men were of strikingly different temperaments and political beliefs. Farnam was a conservative patrician from New England; Commons was a midwesterner with a more liberal philosophy. Notwithstanding these differences, both labor economists shared a deep concern about worker security.

Both understood that even the most skilled, hardworking, and frugal workers could not adequately protect themselves and their families from economic risk. They agreed that hardworking Americans who lost their wages through no fault of their own should not be forced into poverty and reliance on charity. Rather, government should assist workers in preventing that fate through the provision of social insurance. They believed that worker unrest was caused by a deep sense of insecurity. If workers had greater security, they would not be tempted to join radical political movements, both men agreed.

Their joint concern had led them, together with Professor Ely, to found the American Association for Labor Legislation. The AALL was modeled on the International Association for Labor Legislation, an organization based in Europe and dedicated to producing uniform labor laws across the European continent.

The three economists thought that the AALL would fill the important role of studying labor conditions and labor legislation in the United States and publicizing the findings. The AALL was concerned with all aspects of worker security—the freedom to unionize, the need for a legislated minimum wage and maximum hours, the importance of the health and safety of the workplace, and the necessity of social insurance covering industrial accidents, health, old age, disability, death, and unemployment. The organization studied these issues and assisted in the dissemination of legislative efforts to achieve them.

The membership at the first AALL meeting, on February 15, 1906, consisted of 23 people, including academics and representatives of business, labor, social work, and charitable organizations. Within seven years, the membership had expanded to 3,348, and included a broad cross-section of people concerned about worker security. The membership encompassed the political spectrum and included such notables as Louis Brandeis, Samuel Gompers, Woodrow Wilson, and Jane Addams.

In 1910, the AALL decided to become politically active and changed its stated objectives from "encourag[ing] the study of labor legislation" to "encourag[ing] the study of labor conditions in the United States with a view to promoting desirable labor legislation." One of AALL's first focuses of legislative action was its effort to convince state governments to establish programs providing workers with compensation when they were injured in the workplace.

In 1911, the workers' compensation legislation, which Rogalas's story inspired Commons to draft, was enacted by Wisconsin and subsequently upheld by the courts. Wisconsin became the first state to compensate workers who were injured on the job. The AALL publicized the Wisconsin bill and sought to convince other states to enact similar statutes.

Shortly after the bill's enactment, Arthur Altmeyer, an office boy working in his uncle's law firm, happened to see a pamphlet describing Wisconsin's newly enacted Workmen's Compensation Act. The moment he learned that the principal author of the legislation was the renowned professor John R. Commons, Altmeyer resolved, he later explained, "that I was going to go under Professor Commons and study labor legislation." That fall, Altmeyer enrolled as a freshman at the University of Wisconsin.

Altmeyer began to attend Commons's Friday night get-togethers. He overlapped one year with another Friday Niter, Edwin Witte, a graduate student also studying with Commons. The two students, who shared a similar passion for improving the lives of workers, became friends. Sharing the same passion but living 1000 miles away was an outspoken, confident, and compassionate woman who was pushing for better working conditions in New York. Frances Perkins, a tireless advocate for worker rights, was secretary of New York's chapter of the National Consumers League.

The National Consumers League had been founded in 1899 by Jane Addams, Florence Kelley, and other women associated with Hull House, perhaps the most famous residence of the settlement movement, where middle class volunteers lived in poor neighborhoods and sought to assist their low-income neighbors. The league's main goal was to expose scandalous working conditions and push for a minimum wage and maximum hours for women and children. It had the word "consumers" in its name because the founders believed that acceptable working conditions should be a prerequisite for consumer purchases.

On a sun-drenched Saturday, on March 25, 1911, Perkins was having tea in Washington Square in New York City, near her Consumers League office. Suddenly, she heard screams of "Fire! Fire!" She leaped up and joined a throng of others rushing toward the shouts. To her horror, she saw deadly, swelling flames engulfing the Asch Building, whose top three floors housed the Triangle Shirtwaist Factory. For 15 terror-filled minutes, she watched 146 workers—mainly women between the ages of 13 and 23—perish as they desperately tried to escape the fire. The workers had been, as usual, locked in to ensure that they would not leave their sewing machines and, as a result, were trapped inside. Perkins witnessed young women praying on the window ledges of the factory before they leaped to their deaths.

The widespread publicity about the fire revealed that the factory had complied fully with all city regulations. Public outcry caused the state legislature, which included freshman senator Franklin Roosevelt, to create the New York State Factory Investigation Commission to study the safety of working conditions inside factories. Headed by state senator Robert Wagner and Assemblyman Al Smith, and staffed by Frances Perkins, who left the Consumers League to take the job, the commission expanded its investigation to include wage rates and other conditions of employment. Originally authorized for only one year, the commission remained in existence until 1915.

During those years, the AALL was achieving great success in its efforts to encourage the enactment of workers' compensation legislation around the country. By 1915, 30 states had enacted workers' compensation statutes. With its efforts to obtain legislation going so well, the AALL added health insurance to its agenda. In 1913, the AALL set up a committee to study the issue, and in 1915, it published a model bill.

At first, the AALL appeared to be as effective in the area of health insurance as it had been in the field of workers' compensation. In 1915, the Republican governor of California, Hiram Johnson, established the California Social Insurance Commission and instructed it to study the issue of health insurance. The governor appointed Barbara Nachtrieb Armstrong, one of the first female law graduates in the country, to be the executive secretary of the commission. The commission proposed that California enact health insurance for its citizens. Governor Johnson endorsed government health insurance, as did the governors of Massachusetts and Nevada.

In 1916, Congress held hearings on the issue. That same year, the Social Insurance Committee of the American Medical Association (AMA) recommended compulsory government-run health insurance, and the American Hospital Association and the National Association of Manufacturers established internal committees to study the subject. In 1917, the House of Delegates of the AMA passed a resolution supportive of government health insurance plans. By that time, AALL's model bill had been introduced in the legislatures of 12 states, the New York Senate had passed the proposed legislation, and 8 states had appointed study commissions.

California, because of limitations in its state constitution, required a two-thirds vote of each house of the legislature plus a majority vote of the population on a state ballot referendum in order to enact health insurance. A health insurance bill received the necessary vote of the California legislature in 1917 and was placed on the November 1918 ballot. Former president Theodore Roosevelt, Senator William Borah (R-Idaho), and a number of leading newspapers all came out in favor of government-sponsored health insurance.

As part of the effort, the state commissions in Illinois and Ohio asked Commons to survey the attitudes of the various groups regarding government health insurance and to prepare a report summarizing his findings. He coauthored the paper with Altmeyer, who was now a graduate student in economics and Commons's research assistant. Their paper, "The Health Insurance Movement in the United States," was appended to the reports of both the Illinois and Ohio commissions.

When Commons and Altmeyer began the paper, government health insurance looked like it would be enacted quickly without enormous struggle, just as workers' compensation legislation had been. But the reformers were to learn that the entrenched interests would not stay quiet for long. By the time the paper was published, the movement was in free fall.

The more physicians learned about the proposal, the more they opposed it, fearing it would lead to government control of medical practice. Breaking with the position taken by the AMA, a number of state medical associations came out in opposition. Similarly, the National Association of Manufacturers' Committee on Industrial Betterment, which had supported the legislation in 1916, repudiated that support in mid-1917. Insurance companies opposed it, as did the Pharmaceutical Manufacturers' Association.

Perhaps most damaging, the American Federation of Labor (AFL), a group that might have been considered a natural ally, was against government-provided health insurance. The AFL's leader, Samuel Gompers wanted gains for workers to come through collective bargaining and feared that government-provided benefits would weaken the incentive of workers to join unions. Gompers felt so strongly about the issue that he resigned his membership in the AALL.

A coalition consisting of many of these groups unleashed a massive advertising campaign against government-provided health insurance. Playing on anti-German and anti-Russian sentiment generated by World War I, they released ads claiming that the proposals were, at one and the same time, symbols of Prussian autocracy and Soviet communism.

In November 1918, California voters marched to the polls with images of Lenin and the German kaiser intertwined with thoughts of government-provided health insurance floating through their heads. Californians defeated the ballot referendum, which would have established a statewide health insurance plan. Six months later, the New York Assembly defeated the bill that had been passed by the State Senate. In 1920, the AMA formally reversed its position, putting itself on record as opposing government health insurance. That sounded the death knell. Every health insurance proposal in the country was dead.

That same year, the nation ratified the Eighteenth Amendment, granting women the right to vote. Witte, who had stayed in Madison to work in government while lecturing part-time at the university, was now the top administrator of Wisconsin's Industrial Commission. The commission, which was created as part of Commons's 1911 legislation establishing workers' compensation, consisted of a board of experts appointed by the governor. The board's job was to advocate and implement labor legislation.

In 1920, Witte approached Altmeyer to be the commission's chief statistician. Altmeyer accepted the offer. Meanwhile, the AALL and the National Consumers League continued to lobby for worker legislation.

The AALL shifted its focus from health insurance to the concerns of unemployment and old age, while the Consumers League continued to work for minimum wage and maximum hour legislation. In this area, too, Commons and Wisconsin were leaders. Commons drafted a minimum wage bill that was introduced in the Wisconsin legislature in 1911—the first of its kind in the nation.

By 1923, 11 states, the District of Columbia, and Puerto Rico had enacted minimum wage laws protecting women and children. But in that year, progress came to a screeching halt. By a 5 to 3 decision, the Supreme Court, in *Adkins v. Children's Hospital*, struck down the District of Columbia's minimum wage law. The Court found that the law, which required a minimum wage for women and children employed in Washington, D.C., had interfered with the right of employers and employees to enter into contracts freely. The Court held that the due process clauses of the Fifth and Fourteenth Amendments, which prohibit the federal government and the states, respectively, from depriving people "of life, liberty, or property, without due process of law," guaranteed this freedom of contract. Because the Fifth Amendment applies to the federal government and the Fourteenth Amendment applies to states, the Court's decision effectively struck down minimum wage laws everywhere.

The year before the Supreme Court issued its opinion in the *Adkins* case, Witte accepted the position of chief of the Wisconsin Legislative Reference Library, which required him to research and draft legislation, and Altmeyer took over Witte's position as secretary of the State Industrial Commission. The new job caused Altmeyer to travel frequently to Washington, D.C., as well as to conferences where he met colleagues from other state governments. His counterpart in New York was Frances Perkins. When Al Smith had become governor of New York in 1918, he had appointed Perkins to be the first woman to serve on the New York State Industrial Board.

In 1926, Smith appointed Perkins to the position of chairman of the board. Two years after that, on November 8, 1928, as Smith met defeat in his run to be president, Franklin Roosevelt became governor of New York. He appointed Perkins to be his industrial commissioner, the top position in the state's Labor Department, where she remained for four years.

Then, in late February 1933, Roosevelt's secretary called Perkins and asked her to come to Roosevelt's New York City home at 8:00 P.M. That evening, the newly elected President of the United States invited Perkins to become his secretary of labor. In accepting, she became the first woman cabinet officer in the history of the United States.

Perkins moved to Washington and contacted her colleague from Wisconsin, Arthur Altmeyer, who agreed to join her at the Department of Labor. The legacy of John Commons, in the person of Arthur Altmeyer, traveled from the shores of Lake Mendota in Madison to the banks of the Potomac and the New Deal.

CHAPTER 3

# Essential Insurance, Poor Welfare

Not quite spring but not still winter, Washington was cold and blustery on that eventful Saturday, March 4, 1933, when the thirty-second President of the United States was to be inaugurated. Dark clouds sporadically released icy cold rain on the spectators wrapped in blankets and overcoats for protection against the raw, gusty day. A half million citizens, hoping to get a glimpse of their new president, lined Pennsylvania Avenue, crammed onto the temporary bleachers, or pressed against the ropes that were retrieved from storage and set up every four years. Thousands of other onlookers, packed in on all sides, were gathered in front of the steps of the east portico of the domed Capitol building, where a columned platform had been erected. American flags and red, white, and blue bunting were everywhere.

It was not just the sky that was dark and cold. By the beginning of 1933, about 15 million Americans were unemployed—almost 40 percent of the workforce. Of these, between 1 and 2 million people were traipsing the country in vain, looking for any kind of work. Hundreds of thousands of others who had lost homes and savings were camped just outside of Washington, in New York's Central Park, and in and around other cities, in shacks, tents, and cardboard boxes—shantytowns angrily nicknamed "Hoovervilles."

Millions more were underemployed, working just two or three days a week, one or two weeks a month. Even those still employed full time saw their earnings cut by a third. People were hungry for any kind of work, no matter how little it paid. When New York advertised for 100 men to shovel snow for 50 cents an hour, 1,000 men lined up at the employment office at dawn, some dressed in expensive overcoats and homburg hats. A mother of six picketed in protest at being excluded, on account of her sex, from the temporary snow-shoveling job.

Nor did people have savings on which they could fall back. By 1933, 11,000 of the nation's 25,000 banks had failed. Millions of people lost every penny of savings. People who still had savings began to panic and made runs on banks, jeopardizing those that were still solvent. To stop more bank failures, 38 states took the extreme step of declaring an indefinite bank "holiday" and ordered banks to be closed. In today's world of instant, around-the-clock banking, many Americans have experienced the frustration and slight panic of an evening out, an empty wallet and no ATM in sight. That feeling of unreachable money was the experience of every American in all but 10 states, with the significant twist of uncertainty over when, or even whether, they would see their hard-earned dollars again.

People who lost their jobs or saw their hours and pay reduced, whose savings were lost or frozen, were almost always breadwinners for others. Most workers were married with children. Routinely, elderly parents lived in the household, too. In reality, the statistics about unemployment represented the fortunes of three generations: the workers themselves, their children, and their elderly parents.

As Franklin Roosevelt took the oath of office on that cold, rainy day in March, workers who were laid off could not expect help from employers or even unions. By 1931, only a few private unemployment funds existed in all of the United States:. These consisted of just 14 company plans, 3 plans run by international unions, 45 plans run by local unions, and 16 plans administered jointly by employers and unions. Taken together, these plans covered less than one-third of 1 percent of the workforce.

At the start of the Great Depression, unemployed workers could not look to government either. No state had adopted a program of unemployment insurance. Workers in Wisconsin were a bit more fortunate, because that state enacted unemployment insurance on January 28, 1932. But even those workers would have to wait until July 1934 when the new law would become effective. Or perhaps they would wait forever. Some employer was guaranteed to bring a lawsuit, testing the constitutionality of the enactment.

Spurred by the huge numbers of unemployed, bills offering some help had been introduced in Ohio and 21 other state legislatures by the time of that overcast March inauguration day, so some assistance might eventually arrive. But state-by-state enactments had built-in disadvantages. Some states might not enact unemployment programs. States that did necessarily imposed higher costs on employers and provided incentives for businesses to relocate. During the election of 1932, the same truck could be seen every day headed out of Wisconsin. Painted in big letters on its side were the words: "Forced to leave Wisconsin by La Follette's program of unemployment compensation." Governor La Follette lost his bid for reelection.

Even harder than being unemployed in the midst of the Depression was being unemployed and old. By 1934, over half of the elderly in America were impoverished. If you were old, unable to work, and your children were unable to support you, the poorhouse was generally all that remained between you and life on the street. Records of almshouses in 121 urban areas revealed that between 1929 and the end of 1933, the populations in those institutions jumped by almost 75 percent.

It was unlikely that you would have any other assistance from the government. So-called outdoor relief (i.e., assistance provided outside a poorhouse) was generally given only to people whose physical condition made removal to a poorhouse impossible. Even then, government welfare programs rarely provided cash; instead, welfare agencies paid storekeepers directly for groceries and merchandise.

In response to the suffering, a number of states passed laws providing noninstitutional assistance to the needy elderly. These laws imposed strict limitations, however, requiring recipients to prove lengthy residency, generally 15 years or more, few assets, and no financially competent relatives. Even then, because state treasuries were depleted, most states were unable to fund these programs adequately. By 1935, only about 3 percent of the elderly were receiving benefits, and those benefits averaged only about 65 cents a day, well below the level generally recognized as necessary for subsistence. Some states had statutes but no funds appropriated for benefits. A U.S. Bureau of Labor Statistics report that canvassed the state programs found "sharply curtailed benefits and refusal to take on new pensioners, even the discontinuance of the system altogether.... In...other jurisdictions...a waiting list as large or larger than the number of actual beneficiaries."

Chances of getting a benefit from a private pension were remote. They were relatively rare and unreliable. Like today, these were voluntary arrangements that employers could terminate at will. Unlike today, they were unregulated and often were unfunded. They generally imposed onerous requirements for qualification, such as working continuously for the same employer for at least 20 years and not leaving before retirement. And even then, courts often permitted employers to arbitrarily retract the pension promise, finding that the pension was merely a gift and therefore the promise could be broken without penalty.

For all these reasons, activists in the American old-age assistance movement were hostile to employer-sponsored pensions, viewing them simply as employer devices to control workers and believing them to be inherently insecure. By 1933, the hostility appeared justified. Between 1929 and 1932, almost 10 percent of all existing pension plans were discontinued, closed to new employees, or suspended. Those that remained were in shaky financial shape.

Government employees held the best chance of getting a pension, but even that was no guarantee. Starting with New York City in 1894, about half the public school teachers in the country were covered under state or local pension programs by 1933. Nevertheless, a 1920 study of these arrangements found: "Of the nearly one hundred teachers' retirement systems now in operation in the United States, only a few can escape total collapse unless fundamentally altered." Congress had enacted a pension program for its civilian workforce on May 22, 1920. But at the time of Roosevelt's inauguration, the federal government employed only 63,000 civilian workers and the pension program had been around for only 13 years.

Nor were those who had served their country in wartime any better off. The handful of still-living Civil War veterans had pensions, but veterans of World War I were not so lucky. Out of concern for the cost of a pension program for those veterans, Congress initially offered them only a modest contributory insurance program. In 1924, after four years of intense lobbying by the then-new American Legion, Congress authorized "bonuses" to World War I veterans. The "bonus bill," passed over

President Coolidge's veto, provided for additional benefits to veterans based on length of service, to be paid in 1945.

As the Depression deepened, veterans' groups argued that bonuses payable in two decades did not help veterans starving today. And the claim of starvation was not hyperbolic. Starting around 1931, looting of grocery stores—food riots, as the looting came to be called—began to occur with some frequency around the country.

In that year, Congressman Wright Patman (D-Tex.), reintroduced legislation that he had sponsored in the prior Congress. The bill provided for the immediate payment of the World War I bonuses. Patman's proposal was very popular but very expensive; Congress enacted a compromise bill, which President Hoover promptly vetoed.

Over the spring and summer of 1932, a "Bonus Army" of between 15,000 and 25,000 unemployed veterans and their families, impoverished by the Depression, descended on Washington in hopes of securing benefits. They set up tents and camped in and around the nation's capital. In response, the House of Representatives resuscitated and passed the Patman bill on June 15, 1932.

Hoping the Senate would follow the House's lead, around 12,000 soldiers of the so-called Bonus Army milled around outside the Senate chambers. Despite the intimidating size of the crowd, the Senate defeated the legislation by a vote of 62 to 18. Senator Hiram Johnson (R-Calif.), the former governor of California who had supported health insurance, was one of the few senators who voted for passage. He reportedly said to a colleague immediately after the vote:

> This marks a new era in the life of our nation.... The time may come when this folderol—these trappings of government—will disappear, when fat old men like you and me will be lined up against a stone wall.

Notwithstanding Johnson's grim prediction, many veterans simply left the city after the vote, but others, with no home to return to, remained. Rumors circulated that the Bonus Army included Communists. Anxious to get rid of the remaining veterans, President Hoover announced that they all had to leave by July 24. Four days after the deadline, on July 28, Hoover decided to clear Washington of the remainder of the Bonus Army.

At first, Hoover relied on local police to do the job. But the veterans refused to leave, and some fought back with bricks and rocks. After a police officer suffered a fractured skull, the jumpy police opened fire, killing two veterans. At this point, the police retreated, and the Washington, D.C. government asked Hoover for help.

Hoover called in the army under the command of General Douglas MacArthur. The future five-star general saw his job as quelling the "incipient revolution in the air," as he told his adjutant, Major Dwight Eisenhower. Aided by Major George Patton, McArthur undertook his assignment with gusto.

At the Ellipse, under the shadow of the Washington Monument and the White House, the general amassed an overpowering force of cavalry with sabers, infantry with fixed bayonets, and six tanks with machine guns. Then the rout began. Mounted soldiers charged into gathered crowds, indiscriminately swinging swords. Infantry, with bayonets fixed, hurled tear gas. The crowd, which included children and babies in mothers' arms as well as onlookers who had innocently wandered downtown to enjoy the summer day, fled in panic. As soldiers pursued the retreating Bonus Army across the Anacostia Bridge and away from the city, troops led by MacArthur, Eisenhower, and Patton set fire to the remains of the encampments. One of the routed Bonus Army veterans was ex-Sergeant Joseph Angelo, who 14 years earlier, on the fields of France, had saved Patton's life when he had pulled the wounded future general into a foxhole.

Given the conditions and people's sense of desperation, the country was ripe for demagogues. Huey Long had been elected governor of Louisiana in 1928 and U.S. Senator in 1930—although he did not show up and take the oath of office until 1932, after he had made certain that one of his cronies, Oscar K. "OK" Allen, would succeed him in the governorship. In February 1934, under the slogan, "Every Man a King," Long proposed a radical, Robin Hood-type scheme called "Share Our Wealth." It called for confiscating the wealth of the nation's rich and using the money to pay every family an annual income of $5,000.

Long's proposal proved immediately popular. By 1935, every state had Share Our Wealth clubs. After just one year, there were 27,000 clubs nationwide, consisting of 4.7 million members.

Well-known author Upton Sinclair decided in 1933 to run for governor of California. He promised to institute a program called "End Poverty in California," or EPIC, which called for replacing capitalism with a cooperative Socialist society. For a time, it appeared that he might win. A powerful coalition of Republicans, Hollywood studios, and ad agencies raised money and campaigned against him. The coalition produced and circulated fake newsreels of crazed down-and-outers descending on California to "launch the Sinclair revolution." In the end, Sinclair was defeated, but 27 out of the 80 members of the state legislature were newly elected legislators who had run on the EPIC platform.

These were the conditions and mood of the country facing President Roosevelt as he took the oath of office. He wasted no time getting to work. His record-setting First Hundred Days were aimed specifically at the emergency of the Depression. Congress enacted more than a dozen historic pieces of legislation intended to put people back to work, promote economic recovery, and reform the banks and stock exchanges.

Once legislation was enacted to deal with the current emergency, Roosevelt planned to propose measures that protected workers in all economic circumstances, good and bad. As governor of New York, he and his state industrial commissioner, Frances Perkins, had pushed for progressive legislation, which included state-supported old-age pensions, unemployment insurance, and a minimum wage for women and children. In addition, both were familiar with the legislation enacted in Wisconsin, the state on the cutting edge of the worker protection movement.

But before the administration developed a proposal, Congress began its own deliberations. In February 1934, Senator Robert F. Wagner (D-N.Y.) and Representative David J. Lewis (D-Md.) introduced legislation on unemployment insurance. In March, a subcommittee of the House Ways and Means Committee held hearings on the Wagner-Lewis bill. Secretary Perkins testified in support, and on March 24, President Roosevelt sent the chairman a letter, which the administration released to the public, endorsing the bill in principle and urging action before the close of the session in June.

The Wagner-Lewis bill targeted its help on the unemployed. But the unemployment figures told only part of the story. Hidden in the shadows of the numbers were impoverished, aged parents dependent on their adult children. Although official Washington was not focused on the plight of the elderly, ordinary people were.

Five months before the Wagner-Lewis bill was introduced, a doctor from Long Beach, California, Francis E. Townsend, found himself at age 66 unemployed with no savings. Dr. Townsend had an idea, which he sent to the *Long Beach Press-Telegram*, a local newspaper. His idea, published on September 30, 1933, was that the federal government should provide every person aged 60 or older a pension of $200 per month, a princely sum in the 1930's. The only requirement, in addition to being retired and not a criminal, was that the recipient had to spend every penny within 30 days of receipt.

The idea spread around the country at a rate astonishing to believe in that pre-Internet world. A year after Townsend wrote his letter to the newspaper, *Time* magazine reported in its October 15, 1934, issue: "By last week the flow of money…was enough to pay the wages of 50 people.…There were Townsend Clubs in every State except Delaware.…Between 2,000,000 and 5,000,000 people had put their names to petitions begging their Congressmen to vote the Plan into effect at once." In some congressional districts, a candidate's position on the Townsend plan determined the outcome of the election.

Even in the short time between the publication of Townsend's letter and the consideration of the Wagner-Lewis bill, supporters of the Townsend proposal were exerting considerable pressure on the administration. The president began to indicate informally that he thought old-age insurance should be added to the Wagner-Lewis bill. In a related development, Senator Clarence Dill (D-Wash.) and Representative William Connery (D-Mass.) introduced legislation designed to help states provide old-age assistance to the needy elderly. The administration took no position on this proposal. Nevertheless, the Dill-Connery bill passed the House and had considerable support in the Senate.

As these developments were unfolding in Congress, President Roosevelt became convinced that there were severe weaknesses in both the Wagner-Lewis bill and the Dill-Connery legislation. In addition, Roosevelt was beginning to believe that the country was ready for and needed a more sweeping set of changes.

The president decided that his administration should take some time to develop a comprehensive measure while Congress adjourned for the summer and escaped the hot, sticky Washington weather. His goal was to have a well-crafted proposal ready when Congress returned the following January 1935. The legislation could then, he reasoned, be introduced at the start of the new Congress and quickly enacted.

Roosevelt made his thinking known in May 1934, in private meetings with supporters of both the Wagner-Lewis proposal and the Dill-

Connery legislation. Neither measure was acted on, and both died when Congress adjourned.

In a cabinet meeting, it was agreed that an interagency committee appointed by the president would develop a wide-ranging social insurance package. On June 8, 1934, near the end of the legislative session, Roosevelt sent a message to the Seventy-third Congress summarizing the accomplishments to date and outlining future goals. He stated, "I place the security of the men, women and children of the Nation first," noting, "People want…some safeguard against misfortunes which cannot be wholly eliminated in this man-made world of ours."

Roosevelt alerted Congress that he planned to propose a comprehensive program of social insurance. He emphasized that it was not "an untried experiment" and reminded members, "This seeking for a greater measure of welfare and happiness does not indicate a change in values. It is rather a return to values lost in the course of our economic development and expansion."

On June 29, the president promulgated Executive Order No. 6757, which established an interagency, cabinet-level task force, the Committee on Economic Security (CES). The author of both the president's June 8 message to Congress and the June 29 executive order was the second assistant secretary of labor, Arthur Altmeyer.

Roosevelt intentionally made CES an interagency committee to ensure that all aspects of the legislation were considered. CES consisted of five high-ranking members of the administration: Secretary of Labor Perkins, Secretary of the Treasury Henry Morgenthau, Secretary of Agriculture Henry A. Wallace, Attorney General Homer Cummings, and the Federal Emergency Relief administrator, Harry Hopkins. The membership was logical and predictable, with the exception of Agriculture Secretary Wallace, who, at the last minute, replaced Commerce Secretary Daniel C. Roper, even though industrial workers would be more the focus of CES's work than agricultural workers. In making the last-minute change in the executive order, Roosevelt may have been responding to Wallace's greater interest in the subject.

Roosevelt asked his secretary of labor and close, longtime confidante Frances Perkins to chair the cabinet-level group. It was natural for the Department of Labor to take the lead, Perkins had a passionate interest in social insurance, and, as a result of her long relationship with the president, she had his trust and confidence. Inclusion of another longtime associate from New York, Treasury Secretary Morgenthau, ensured that the Treasury Department would participate directly in a thorough exploration of all financing options.

The participation in CES's deliberations by the Department of Justice, through the inclusion of Attorney General Cummings, was crucial because of the anticipated threat to the program from a court challenge. The inclusion of lawyers in the deliberations on how to structure the legislation was imperative to ensure the best possible chance against the inevitable lawsuit that would follow passage of the legislation by Congress.

In 1934, as CES's work was getting under way, it was a very real question whether the federal government had the power under the Constitution to undertake what Roosevelt envisioned, regardless of how it was structured. Although the breadth of federal undertakings today obscures the fact, the Constitution not only defines the structure of the federal government, but also limits its reach. Article 1, section 1, permits Congress only those "legislative powers herein granted." All other powers are reserved to the states, except for those powers forbidden to be exercised by any level of government.

In order to exercise its power constitutionally, Congress must have an explicit grant of authority in the Constitution. The Supreme Court had developed a pattern of interpreting every authorization as narrowly as possible, sometimes straining the common-sense meaning to limit the power of the government. The leading treatise on constitutional law at the time most of the judges were educated reflected its perspective in its title. *Constitutional Limitations* was the way in which it was generally referred (although its actual title was the more cumbersome name, *A Treatise on the Constitutional Limitations which Rest Upon the Legislative Power of the States of the American Union*).

Even nonlawyers understood that the New Deal legislation was likely to face trouble in the courts. Three Republicans had preceded Roosevelt in office, and the judiciary reflected that fact. The courts were dominated by conservative Republicans at every level. Most of those sitting on the bench had been educated in the nineteenth century and mirrored that era's economic and legal perspective in their thinking. They embraced the dominant nineteenth-century beliefs in laissez-faire economics, Social Darwinism, and strict limits on the power of the central government.

A majority of the justices on the Supreme Court shared this conservative outlook. Although three justices, Louis D. Brandeis, Benjamin Cardozo, and Harlan Fiske Stone, held a more expansive view, four others, Willis Van Devanter, James C. McReynolds, George Sutherland, and Pierce Butler—derisively referred to as the Four Horsemen of Reaction—held very narrow views regarding federalism and economic regulation and were thought to be a dependable bloc of votes against the New Deal legislation. Chief Justice Charles Evans Hughes and Justice Owen Roberts held the two swing votes.

In addition to the attorney general, the secretary of labor, the secretary of the treasury, and the secretary of agriculture, Roosevelt appointed Federal Emergency Relief Administrator Harry Hopkins to the cabinet-level CES. Roosevelt did so in part because, as head of the government's relief agency, Hopkins understood best the current needs of the country, and in part because Hopkins had a close relationship with the president. The inclusion of the head of the relief agency was no indicator of the manner in which Roosevelt thought the program should be structured, however.

Early on in the deliberations over Social Security, Hopkins raised with Roosevelt the possibility of combining the long-term program with short-term relief efforts. After all, Hopkins argued, the populations to be served overlapped and insurance would not provide an adequate level of benefits for a number of years. Roosevelt was firm in his opposition to the suggestion. As Frances Perkins reported, "Although Hopkins was eloquent, the President at once saw that this would be the very thing he had been saying he was against for years—the dole."

Roosevelt understood that welfare and social insurance were intrinsically different. Humans have always sought security from life's dangers. Generally, the most effective action against life's insecurities has been collective in nature. Collective action to ensure physical security has taken the form of armies, police forces and militia. Collective action to ensure economic security has taken two separate forms, each quite distinct from the other.

One form of collective action that developed historically was welfare. The antecedents to modern welfare programs can be traced from biblical prescriptions, such as the commandment that "thou shalt not wholly reap the corners of thy field, neither shalt thou gather the gleanings of thy harvest. And thou shalt not glean thy vineyard...; thou shalt leave them for the poor." In England, the practice of voluntary tithing to the church to help the poor evolved into compulsory tithing, then into the English poor laws, and then to America's welfare laws, which were transplanted from England by the colonists. These programs, modern and ancient, involve arrangements among financially unequal parties—those materially better off providing assistance to those less advantaged, the poor.

In contrast, a second, equally rich, but fundamentally different tradition of providing economic security came in the form of a pooling of resources and risk among equals. As far back as the Middle Ages in England and elsewhere in Europe, individuals who had a common trade or craft banded together to form mutual aid societies or guilds, which, in addition to regulating the craft, provided a variety of wage-replacement benefits to its members. Another antecedent to modern social insurance, appearing in the mining districts of central Europe as early as the sixteenth century, were the customary funds, which provided benefits for sickness and accidents.

Welfare programs are designed for people who are already poor. Social insurance prevents workers from becoming poor in the first place. Welfare programs are essential as long as there is poverty, but they have inescapable, inherent weaknesses.

Welfare, by definition, provides a benefit based on need. The benefit is generally an amount designed to provide the recipient with just enough to get by, as judged by the provider. Eligibility is determined by an examination of the potential recipient's income and assets to ensure that he or she is really in need. Past earnings are irrelevant as long as the person has no accumulated assets. Obviously, if the potential recipient is earning income above the subsistence level, he or she is not in need of the community's help. Moreover, if the person has savings upon which to draw, he or she is, again, not in need of the assistance of others.

For those people who can earn no more than the community-determined subsistence level, means-tested welfare removes financial incentives to work. Wages reduce the means-tested assistance, leaving recipients where they began. Work, in that situation, is like running on a treadmill. The work effort gets people no further along financially. Over the years, welfare reformers have attempted to modify welfare programs to include what they described as work incentives. At most, the modifications softened somewhat the inherent financial disincentives to work. Further, welfare discourages savings. If potential recipients must exhaust their savings before they are eligible to receive welfare, they are penalized for their thrift.

Insurance has none of these shortcomings. Insurance is a matter of right for those who are eligible. Eligibility is based on achieving insured status, irrespective of need. If the insurance is designed to replace wages, as Social Security is, work is encouraged. Under Social Security and other wage-replacement pensions, the higher one's prior earnings, the higher the benefit received. Moreover, if the retirement program is not complete in itself but simply provides a base on which to build, as Social Security does, it encourages savings. Unlike welfare, savings do not disqualify a person from receipt of benefits. Rather, they permit an additional source of income from which to draw when one is no longer receiving a paycheck.

By definition, then, welfare discourages work; wage-related insurance encourages it. Welfare discourages savings; social insurance providing a floor of protection encourages workers to save. To qualify for welfare, recipients must prove something negative about themselves—that they do not have enough to get along on their own. In contrast, beneficiaries of social insurance must prove something positive—that they have worked enough to qualify for benefits.

President Roosevelt was committed to structuring Social Security as social insurance, not welfare. The commitment, however, did not emerge as the result of an intellectual exercise and deep study of the objective advantages of insurance over welfare. Rather, Roosevelt preferred insurance because he understood what it meant to be dependent.

Frances Perkins witnessed Roosevelt undergo "a spiritual transformation during the years of his illness....The man emerged completely warmhearted, with humility of spirit and with a deeper philosophy. Having been in the depths of trouble, he understood the problems of people in trouble." Roosevelt understood clearly that people would be uplifted in spirit if they worked hard and joined together to provide a common pool of funds from which to draw when working days were over. He understood how demeaning it was for people to have to prove to some other person that they could not support themselves without help, and how crippling in spirit to feel oneself to be helpless and a failure.

That benefits for the elderly be structured as insurance, not welfare, was a deeply held, long-standing view of the president. In 1931, in his annual message to the legislature, then-Governor Roosevelt stated that the welfare bill enacted in the prior session "may be justified only as a means intended to replace to a large extent the existing methods of poorhouse and poor-farm relief," but it should not be expanded, for to do so would "smack of the…dole." Rather, he continued, "Our American aged do not want charity, but rather old age comforts to which they are rightfully entitled by their own thrift and foresight in the form of insurance."

He believed that "the next step to be taken should be based on the theory of insurance by a system of contributions commencing at an early age. In this way," he explained, "men and women will, on arriving at a period when work is no longer practicable, be assured not merely of a roof over head and enough food to keep body and soul together, but also enough income to maintain life during the balance of their days in accordance with the American standard of living."

President Roosevelt recognized that to get immediate assistance to people in need—to alleviate the immediate suffering caused by the Depression—there was no alternative to welfare. But for the long term—once the Depression was history and the economic health of the country was restored—the president wanted a system of insurance in place to guarantee for posterity that people would have a reliable, stable source of income from which they could draw in old-age. Acutely conscious of the debilitating quality of fear, he wanted all workers to have the peace of mind and security that they would be insured against their dependency on wages.

His goal was for a program that would be permanent, available in good economic times as well as bad. According to Perkins, the president "insisted that [Social Security and welfare], however much they might apply to the same people, should be kept separate because relief appropriations should be curtailed…as soon as there was a revival of business and employment opportunities. The systems of…insurance ought to continue as a permanent part of our economy."

Understanding the difference, President Roosevelt instructed the Committee on Economic Security to design insurance for the long run, not simply welfare to address the current economic crisis. Consistent with the goal of formulating a program of insurance, he wanted the program to be self-supporting and actuarially sound.

Roosevelt was interested in comprehensive reform. His vision, as Altmeyer was to describe it, was "of every child being issued an 'insurance policy' on the day he was born to protect him against all the major economic misfortunes which might befall him during his lifetime." As Roosevelt told Frances Perkins:

> I see no reason why every child, from the day he is born, shouldn't be a member of the social security system. When he begins to grow up, he should know he will have old-age benefits direct from the insurance system to which he will belong all his life. If he is out of work, he gets a benefit. If he is sick or crippled, he gets a benefit. ...
>
> And there is no reason why just the industrial workers should get the benefit of this. Everybody ought to be in on it—the farmer and his wife and his family.

Roosevelt wanted a broad system of insurance protection, carefully crafted, able to command congressional support and withstand judicial scrutiny. And he wanted it fast.

His goal was to have a proposal ready to be introduced on the day Congress returned to town in January. Accordingly, the executive order establishing CES ordered it to "report to the President not later than December, 1934," approximately five months from the date the executive order was signed.

Frances Perkins assigned Altmeyer the job of implementing the executive order. For the crucial job of executive director, Altmeyer thought of his friend and colleague from Wisconsin, Edwin Witte. Witte had extensive experience as a manager in government and had spent a number of years in charge of drafting Wisconsin's many labor statutes.

On July 24, on Secretary Perkins's authorization, Altmeyer telephoned Witte to offer him a job, just as Witte had done for him so many years before in Wisconsin. When Witte received Altmeyer's call, he cleared his calendar, worked out leaves from his positions at the university and the state government, and arrived in Washington two days later. The speed with which he came was warranted. The job was massive, and the clock was ticking.

## CHAPTER 4

# Bold Woman, Cautious Men

The Washington that Ed Witte encountered in the summer of 1934 was a city in transition. It was, as it had been since its creation, a small, sleepy southern town. With the election of Franklin Roosevelt, though, it was becoming an exciting, youthful, dynamic center of power.

Between 1930 and 1940, 180,000 people moved to Washington, an increase in population of almost 50 percent in a single decade. Even more dramatic, between Roosevelt's inauguration in March 1933 and the end of the following year, the federal civilian workforce grew from 63,000 to 93,000 employees, an increase of 50 percent in less than two years.

The people flooding Washington were coming to design, staff, implement, and defend the ambitious undertakings of the new administration. They were needed everywhere. New agencies were being created and the existing ones expanded.

The majority of those coming to assist in the "new deal for the American people," which Roosevelt had promised in his speech accepting the 1932 Democratic nomination, were young, energetic, hardworking, well educated, and very smart. They came from college campuses, law schools, and graduate programs in economics. They arrived from large cities and small towns. Some came because they were inspired by Roosevelt's words; others, because more traditional jobs had been wiped out by the Depression.

The new administration benefited from prejudice elsewhere. Norman Altman, a Phi Beta Kappa graduate of Cornell University and a high-ranking student at Harvard Law School, where he had been a member of the *Harvard Law Review*, sought employment in corporate law firms. After months of seeing his Christian classmates with inferior academic records receive multiple offers from Wall Street law firms while he and his Jewish classmates failed to secure a single one, Altman turned his sights toward Washington. He spent the next years at the Securities and Exchange Commission in its formative stage, and at the Department of Labor, developing regulations for the Fair Labor Standards Act.

Women and African Americans, too, found opportunity in the new administration, where discrimination was less conspicuous and rampant. An African American graduate of Harvard College decided, in the last year of his doctoral program in economics, to accept an offer to be assistant to Harold Ickes, secretary of the interior. This young black man, Robert Weaver, remained in government and developed an expertise in housing. In 1966, he became President Lyndon Johnson's secretary of housing and urban development.

The hiring could be thought of in terms of ever-widening concentric circles. At the centers were the president's closest advisers. Roosevelt's "brain trust," a group of advisers from academia, hired the extremely able men and women they knew who, in turn, hired younger colleagues and their brightest students. The Committee on Economic Security staff represented a good example of this concentric-circle hiring.

CES needed a few research assistants to respond to inquiries made by members of Congress and the senior people on the project, as well as to answer the voluminous mail that started pouring in from the public as soon as the formation of CES was announced. Supporters of the Townsend plan were particularly prolific letter writers. At the height, mail from Townsendites averaged about 1,500 letters a day.

Altmeyer had hired his Wisconsin friend and colleague Ed Witte. Now Witte needed a research assistant. In thinking about whom to hire, Witte remembered a former student from Wisconsin, Wilbur Cohen, who had taken his courses, had been a regular at Professor Commons's Friday night get-togethers, and had just graduated. Cohen impressed Witte greatly with his intellect, energy, hard work, and drive. Having graduated in June without a job, Cohen jumped at the chance Witte offered him.

When Cohen reported to work on August 11, 1934, Witte was still in the process of getting CES under way. Witte's first priorities included securing headquarters for CES staff, consulting with people in and out of the administration about their views regarding CES's work, organizing the technical board of government experts, and hiring a staff.

Harry Hopkins helped Witte secure offices for the CES staff in the same building that housed Hopkins's Federal Emergency Relief Administration—the Walker-Johnson building at 1734 G Street, N.W., a converted apartment house next to the Corcoran Gallery of Art, about a block west of the White House. Witte originally thought that the work could be done by about 25 people. This turned out to be an underestimate. At its height, CES employed about 100 people.

CES borrowed from every department of the executive branch to assist in the work. It drew economists, lawyers, statisticians, stenographers, typists, analysts, as well as equipment. In addition, it brought in experts from around the country, some onto the staff and some simply as consultants.

President Roosevelt had presented CES with a daunting task: an enormously broad mandate and very little time to complete it. In accordance with the president's directive, Secretary Perkins set an ambitious agenda. She instructed the staff "to report upon all the possible alternatives," which included "every experiment in social insurance in every country" in the world. She wanted recommendations that were sound policy but that also were politically achievable, that fit the nation's needs and culture, and that were backed by solid research and analysis.

The staff was to consist of a number of working groups, including, among others, one concentrating on unemployment compensation, one on old-age security, and one on health insurance. The goal of the working groups was to provide CES and, ultimately, the president with a range of choices about how to structure the various programs, as well as background information and recommendations.

By the time Witte arrived in Washington, Bryce Stewart, an expert in the field of unemployment compensation, was already being considered to head the unemployment compensation working group and Edgar L. Sydenstricker, a well-respected health expert, was under consideration to head the health insurance working group. Both men were highly qualified, so Witte offered them the positions and they both accepted.

Finding a head for the old-age working group proved more challenging. Witte and everyone else he spoke to thought the natural choice to serve as head of the working group on old-age security was Murray W. Latimer. A well-recognized expert on industrial pensions, he was the author of the most complete, exhaustive, and authoritative treatise written on the subject of industrial pensions in North America. Mild-mannered, intelligent, earnest, and calm in manner, Latimer was an ideal person to work with Witte in what was sure to be a high-stress five months of long hours and late nights.

But Latimer had, on July 21, just become chairman of the newly created Railroad Retirement Board. The board had the job of administering the brand-new national pension system for railroad workers, a law President Roosevelt had signed two days before promulgating the executive order establishing CES.

The railroads, having established in the nineteenth century some of the first private pension plans in the country, were on the forefront of old-age security. Even in 1925, two companies alone—the Pennsylvania Railroad System and the New York Central Lines—accounted for 40 percent of all employees covered by private pensions.

Not immune from the current economic crisis, the railroads had been suffering record losses, and as a result were forced to lay off their employees in large numbers. The financing of the industry's pension plans had always been shaky, but now with the aging of its workforce and the general economic conditions, the entire system of plans was on the verge of collapse. Many plans had already terminated; others failed to pay promised benefits. Because failed plans were particularly disruptive in the vital business of transportation, the federal government decided to step in. One supporter during the congressional debate had suggested that, in addition to taking over retirement responsibilities from the railroads, the system could be "a trail blazer" for a government-run program covering the entire population.

Latimer had been enlisted to help draft the proposal that became the Railroad Retirement Act, the statute that he was now so engaged in implementing. Bryce Stewart, the person tapped to head the CES working group on unemployment compensation, had worked with Latimer on the drafting as had J. Douglas Brown, a professor of economics and director of the industrial relations section at Princeton University,

Because Latimer was so hard at work getting the retirement program for railroads up and running, he was not in a position to chair the working group, and so recommended Brown. On the basis of Latimer's recommendation and Brown's well-established reputation, Witte asked the

Princeton professor to chair the CES working group on old age. A quiet, careful, philosophical, scholarly man, Brown was able to get along with those in the university, with labor leaders who had worked their way up the ranks, and, later when he became dean of the faculty at Princeton, with wealthy donors. He, like Latimer, would fit in well working with Witte.

After some consideration, Brown finally declined the offer, because, he told Witte, the position was incompatible with his responsibilities at Princeton. Though Brown never said so, the president of the university, Harold Willis Dodds, a staunch Republican who hated Roosevelt, may have refused to give Brown a leave of absence. Dodds once famously said, "Each one of us requires the spur of insecurity to force us to do our best," and may have not wanted to be a party, even indirectly, to efforts to increase the security of workers. Brown did agree to serve as a consultant to the working group and was an integral member, spending a few days every week in Washington until the project was complete. Nevertheless, Witte had to keep looking for someone to chair the group.

Having failed to land his first two choices, Witte turned to Professor Barbara Nachtrieb Armstrong, who was already in Washington working as a consultant to CES. The first female law professor in the United States, Armstrong was on leave from the University of California at Berkeley. In addition to her law degree, she also held a doctorate in economics and for 10 years had taught half-time in the Berkeley economics department.

Immediately after graduating from the law school at Berkeley in 1915, she had been appointed by then-Governor Hiram Johnson to be the executive secretary of the California Social Insurance Commission. In 1932, she published a landmark treatise, *Insuring the Essentials: Minimum Wage Plus Social Insurance—A Living Wage Program*. The book was an exhaustive survey of developments in the United States and around the world with respect to minimum wage, workers' compensation, health insurance, retirement insurance, disability insurance, survivors' insurance, unemployment insurance, and means-tested welfare for the elderly. The concluding chapter, entitled "Looking Forward," offered Armstrong's predictions of future trends and her policy recommendations.

Armstrong was new to the Washington political scene, having only recently been recruited to work as a consultant to CES. She had been vacationing at Lake Tahoe when she received a telegram stating that President Roosevelt wanted her to come to Washington to be a consultant to CES. The telegram requested that Armstrong meet with a Mr. Eliot in

San Francisco. Thomas Eliot, the general counsel for CES and the associate solicitor of the Department of Labor, was in San Francisco to oversee a collective bargaining election of the longshoremen under the National Emergency Act.

The only Mr. Eliot that Armstrong knew was on the Berkeley summer school faculty. Her first reaction was that the telegram was some kind of joke. Ernestine Black, a close friend and a reporter with the Hearst papers, was vacationing with Armstrong. Literally stopping Armstrong from throwing the telegram in the garbage can, Black asked to read the message, looked it over, and counseled, "This is the real thing.... Now you go down and get interviewed."

After meeting with Eliot, Armstrong accepted the position as consultant to CES on the issues of old-age security and unemployment insurance Just weeks after Armstrong arrived in Washington, Witte, having failed to land Latimer or Brown as chair of the old-age working group, offered Armstrong the position, which she accepted.

Shortly after Armstrong agreed to become chair, the Supreme Court of the District of Columbia declared the Railroad Retirement Act unconstitutional and blocked its enforcement. The government appealed immediately, but Latimer, with time on his hands now that his Railroad Retirement Board was under injunction, joined Brown as a consultant on the working group.

The staff was coming together. It was crucial that an actuarial team be put in place for the work to proceed. The decision was made to hire two actuaries who would spend about three months in Washington and then would be on call. They would be assisted by a Committee of Actuarial Consultants, consisting of the profession's top people who could not be induced to come to Washington full time.

In addition to these senior people, CES needed junior actuaries to carry out some of the work. Professor Henry Lewis Rietz, one of the actuarial consultants, remembered his former research assistant at the University of Iowa. A recent graduate, Robert J. Myers, was a gifted mathematician who appreciated the discipline's predictability and logic. Rietz wrote to Myers, who was now living at home in Philadelphia, "The Committee [on Economic Security] is looking for a junior actuary for a temporary job in Washington, D.C., and I am writing to you because you are my nearest graduate to Washington." Noting that "my principal qualification seemed to be that I lived near Washington," Myers took the train to the nation's capital and joined the staff on September 23, 1934.

By this time, the work of the CES staff was in full swing, and Witte was engaged in an impressive amount of plate-spinning. In addition to assembling and managing a staff, ensuring that it carry out the heavy workload at high standards under extremely tight deadlines, Witte also had to satisfy Altmeyer, Perkins, the other members of the cabinet-level CES, and ultimately the president. On top of that, he had to deal with the public.

In addition to the stacks of mail being sent by supporters of the Townsend plan, physicians started protesting immediately upon the announcement that CES was to study national health insurance. Telegrams and letters flooded in. The *Journal of the American Medical Association* editorialized about the exclusion of physicians from CES's team of staff and consultants. The editor of the journal, a well-known AMA spokesman, sent a copy of the editorial to Perkins with a letter suggesting forcefully that "it would be highly desirable that the medical profession is adequately represented in any studies of the need for sickness insurance."

As if all of that were not enough pressure, Barbara Armstrong was doing her part to keep Witte's blood pressure elevated. A quick-witted, committed, strong-willed, energetic, fiery personality—Latimer called her "peppery"—among an otherwise mild-mannered, soft-spoken staff of economists and actuaries, she was a splash of red in an otherwise black-and-white photograph. She and Witte instantly clashed on policy matters and in personality.

At Witte's first meeting with Secretary Perkins, the secretary had asked him to prepare, by September 1, just a few weeks away, a preliminary report outlining the major aspects of the economic security problem and providing tentative recommendations of the staff. Witte told her that the deadline would be difficult to meet but he would do his best. As Armstrong's very first assignment, before she had been named head of the old-age security study, Witte asked her to write a general memorandum explaining the issues in the areas of old-age security and unemployment insurance and recommending what should be done.

Armstrong's view was that the way to reduce poverty was to ensure people a living wage through a legislatively set minimum, when people were able to work, and then provide compulsory, government-run insurance to protect those workers when they were unable to work as a result of unemployment, ill health, disability, or old age. She also believed that these programs could be operated sensibly only on an exclusively federal level.

Witte did not necessarily disagree with any of that as a philosophical matter. However, cautious and careful by nature, thrust from Wisconsin into the center of Washington politics, Witte was sensitive to what he perceived to be the concerns of those to whom he reported. His view, which he believed Perkins and the president shared, was that the biggest problem facing the country was unemployment. Old-age security was important but of secondary concern to unemployment insurance. Moreover, since old-age insurance would have a long start-up period, old-age welfare would have to meet the immediate needs, so this form of help should be given serious attention. As a bottom line, Witte believed that if other proposals were to make unemployment insurance more difficult to enact, it was not clear that the risk was worth it.

Witte saw his job as developing legislation that would pass Congress and be held constitutional. His view was that jointly-run federal-state programs were most likely to stand up to these challenges and would be more acceptable to those for whom he worked. The Democratic platform in 1932 had referred to federal-state partnerships, and the president himself consistently expressed the view that social insurance should be a combined federal-state effort. Roosevelt, having come from state government, was a strong believer in the strength of federalism. He was a proponent of the concept of the states as laboratories to test various approaches, which, if successful, could be replicated elsewhere.

And the states were beginning to take action in the area of unemployment insurance. Wisconsin had already enacted a system of unemployment compensation, Ohio and a number of other states appeared poised to act, and Congress was unlikely to want to halt that activity. Additionally, the Wagner-Lewis bill that Congress had considered seriously in its last session would have created a joint federal-state undertaking.

At base, Witte was cautious; Armstrong was bold. He worked in the political world, where compromise was a way of life. She came from the academic world, where reason is valued above all else, and what is right is nonnegotiable. Conflict, perhaps, was inevitable.

According to Armstrong, Witte talked to her privately about her report and tried unsuccessfully to convince her to change it. He hinted to her vaguely that someone higher up wanted certain results, but to no avail. Her position was clear and unwavering.

Witte presented the preliminary report at a staff meeting, in advance of giving it to Perkins. At the meeting, the first one Armstrong attended, she sat in horror as Witte distributed and then began to describe her memorandum, but with his recommendations substituted for hers. She interrupted, saying "Just a minute, Mr. Chairman." When Altmeyer, who was chairing the meeting, recognized her, she continued, "I see my name is on this report. This is *not* my report. This is just the opposite of everything that I recommended and said." Then, turning to face Witte, she continued: "How dare you leave any person's name on something that you have altered to make it say what that person didn't say and did not believe?"

Witte sat in stunned silence. Everyone else at the meeting looked uncomfortable and stared down at the table. In Armstrong's mind, "That was the beginning of war."

Years later, Witte explained that the speed with which Secretary Perkins wanted the report required him to prepare a composite document. He took the factual backgrounds from the memoranda prepared by the various staff members and put them together with his own recommendations to form the main body of the report. He signed the document and indicated where his recommendations disagreed with those made by other members of the staff. He then appended the recommendations of the other staff members to the back of the report. Apparently, Armstrong saw her name on the report—perhaps the initial letter of her last name resulted in her memorandum being first—and mistakenly believed Witte was purposely and duplicitously trying to pass off his own recommendations as hers.

Fortunately for both of them, Armstrong was soon the head of the old-age security working group, while most of Witte's time and energy were spent on unemployment compensation, the substantive area he knew best and believed most likely to make its way into law. Altmeyer and Witte were, of course, both from Wisconsin, and both had worked on the recently enacted Wisconsin legislation.

There were numerous details to work out in the unemployment proposal. A fundamental question was whether the president should propose a solely federal program or propose that the federal government either compel or induce states to establish their own programs. If Roosevelt were to propose a combined federal-state program, what was the most effective way for the federal government to spur states to act?

There were two basic alternatives under discussion. The federal government could offer matching grants to states that enacted programs of unemployment insurance. Alternatively, it could impose a tax on payrolls for a federal unemployment insurance program but offset the taxes paid at the federal level, if states were imposing taxes at the state level for the same purpose. Each approach had its own set of advantages and disadvantages.

Other questions abounded. Should taxes be imposed just on employers or jointly on employers and employees? How should the level of taxation be determined, and what should the benefits be? With what federal requirements should states be required to comply?

There were countless variations in design to consider. In general terms, the staff divided into two broad camps, those who favored the approach that Wisconsin had adopted in its state statute, under which employers paid according to their experience, and those who preferred the approach that Ohio had included in its pending legislation, which imposed a uniform rate of taxation. These points of view were vigorously and extensively debated.

The old-age security group, faced with similar myriad questions and options, was left to work on its own, undisturbed by Witte or others. The nucleus of the working group consisted of Armstrong, Latimer, and Brown, who got along very well both personally and in terms of their policy views. Assisting them was Otto Richter, an actuary on loan from the American Telephone and Telegraph Company. Bob Myers was assigned to work for Richter.

As with unemployment compensation, CES would have to recommend to the president whether old-age insurance should be exclusively federal or a combined federal-state effort. Armstrong, Brown, and Latimer were united from the outset that the only sensible, workable approach was a program that was national in scope, compulsory, and contributory. The administrative complexity of states keeping track of employment and benefits for a mobile workforce, of retirees having to contact a dozen states and cash a dozen checks each month, the financial necessity of full reserves for each state program—an amount that would exceed federal securities available for investment—and other similar problems made it clear, they believed, that a federal program was the only way to go.

The firmness of their joint conviction that a unitary, compulsory federal program was the only right option was clear, but there was, of course, the question of the constitutionality of such an arrangement. This uncertainty led to the second confrontation in a staff meeting, this time between Armstrong and Thomas Eliot, the general counsel for CES.

Prior to coming to Washington, Armstrong had secured from her Berkeley colleague, Professor Dudley O. McGovney, a brief arguing that the approach the working group favored could withstand judicial scrutiny. On her first day in Washington, Armstrong telephoned another constitutional law scholar, Douglas B. Maggs, a professor at Duke Law School, who sent her a similar opinion. In addition, Armstrong met with Alexander Holtzoff, an assistant to the attorney general, who was assigned to CES. He agreed with Armstrong about the constitutionality of her proposal and wrote a memorandum asserting that the unitary federal approach stood the best chance of being upheld in the courts.

At the meeting following the one in which she erupted at Witte, Armstrong said that her working group had decided that a federal program of old-age insurance was to be the centerpiece of their work. As soon as she finished, Eliot, the general counsel, said, "But you can't do that, because it's unconstitutional."

"What makes you think so, Mr. Eliot?" Armstrong retorted.

He replied, "To begin with, it's my job to know these things because I'm general counsel of this committee."

She interrupted him and the two began to argue. After some more back-and-forth, Armstrong announced that she had briefs from McGovney and Maggs defending the constitutionality of her approach and that she had discussed the matter with Holtzoff, who was of the same opinion.

To this, Eliot responded, "Well, at least you'll have to admit that none of those people are comparable to Thomas Reed Powell at Harvard."

Armstrong acknowledged, "Well, I agree with you that Thomas Reed Powell is the dean of constitutional law men in American law schools…"

"Well," Eliot cut in, triumphantly, "he says that it can't be done, that it's unconstitutional. Now I guess that disposes of the constitutionality question. Shall we go on to other things?"

Armstrong was furious. The meeting took place on a Friday. At 6:00 P.M. that evening, she was on the train to Boston. What Eliot did not know was that Armstrong and Powell were friends; They had gotten to know each other through mutual friends when he had been in California with his wife.

Armstrong arrived at Powell's house, they sat in his library, and she explained what had happened. He laughed and told her, "Well, of course, I never said such a thing or thought such a thing. What do you want me to do?" She asked him to say what he had just said in a letter to Eliot, explaining what he did think. She would hand-carry the letter, she told him, to Washington.

Powell agreed and wrote:

Dear Tom:

Somewhere you picked up the impression that I believed that it would be unconstitutional to have a compulsory old age insurance system in this country. Of course, until the Supreme Court has a specific law and passes upon it, no one can be sure of this. But to the extent that I am supposed to be a constitutional law authority, I say of course we can have it.

Sincerely yours,

Thomas Reed Powell

P.S.: I have no doubts whatsoever.
        T.R.P.

At the next staff meeting, Armstrong slid the note across the table to Eliot and asked him whether he wanted to read it out loud or should she. He turned pale, asked how she had gotten it, and mumbled that she should read the note, which she happily did. The Harvard professor's missive settled the matter for CES. It could not resolve, however, the underlying question of the constitutionality of the arrangement that Armstrong thought best for the country.

Eliot and Armstrong, together with Holtzoff from the Department of Justice, were the only lawyers engaged in the project. They were an island in a sea of economists, actuaries, health policy experts, and other nonlawyers. The legal issues were complicated and nuanced. No one could know with any certainty how the Supreme Court would rule.

The central question was whether Article I of the Constitution authorized Congress to enact social insurance. One possible grant of authority lay in Article 1, section 8, clause 3, which authorizes Congress to "regulate Commerce...among the several states." As of 1934, however, the

Court had developed a very narrow, formalistic interpretation of the so-called commerce clause.

Today, the courts view even intrastate commerce as within congressional power under the commerce clause, because the operation of local commerce affects interstate commerce. In contrast, in the 1930s, courts deemed local commerce to be beyond the reach of Congress. Moreover, the courts had ruled that certain economic activity—manufacturing, agriculture, and mining, for example—was not commerce at all, but pre-commerce and therefore not within the power of Congress to regulate.

In 1916, Congress had wanted to limit the use of child labor in factories, but lacked the power to do so directly, because manufacturing was not considered "commerce…among the several states." In an effort to circumvent the Court's limitation, Congress enacted a statute that barred the transportation in interstate commerce of goods produced by child labor. In 1918, the Supreme Court ruled that Congress could not do indirectly what it was prohibited from doing directly and held the Child Labor Act unconstitutional.

But President Roosevelt was not trying to regulate directly the employment relation by mandating that employers provide insurance to their employees. Instead, he planned to tax the employers and employees, collect the money in a fund, and pay benefits from it. It was a similar end, but a different mechanism, and that made an important difference. The Constitution included another possible source of authority, Article 1, section 8, clause 1, which states: "The Congress shall have Power to lay and collect Taxes…to…provide for the general Welfare of the United States." Today, courts interpret that language expansively. In the 1930s, however, the limits of this taxing and spending clause had not been well tested, and the government lawyers could anticipate a number of possible arguments.

In response to the Supreme Court's 1918 decision declaring the federal regulation of child labor unconstitutional, Congress enacted the Child Labor Tax Law of 1919, which taxed employers who employed child labor. The Supreme Court struck this down as well, concluding that the payment by employers, although structured as a tax, was really a penalty on employers who failed to comply with its regulations. Congress was not trying to raise revenue with this tax, the Court reasoned, but to stop a labor practice that it lacked power to control.

Social insurance appeared to be distinguishable, however. In the case of social insurance, Congress would truly be seeking to raise revenue to finance the program. Even so, the Constitution requires that Congress spend the funds "to provide for the general Welfare." Because the Court had not had much opportunity to interpret this phrase, its decisions contained little guidance.

The framers of the Constitution held sharply divergent views of the phrase's meaning. Alexander Hamilton interpreted the phrase broadly. In Hamilton's view, anything Congress deemed to be for the public good was within the general welfare provision. In contrast, James Madison's view was that the phrase simply was shorthand for the various enumerated powers, not a separate grant of additional power. In other words, Congress could spend only for specific objectives entrusted to it by some other provision of the Constitution. If that were the correct interpretation, government lawyers would be back where they started, looking to the commerce clause for authority.

One slight glimmer of light in this bleak picture was that the courts had upheld some federal spending schemes on the procedural ground that no taxpayer was injured sufficiently by spending from general revenue to have standing to challenge the expenditure, and the direct recipients of the program could show no injury, either. The problem for CES was that if the spending was linked to an earmarked tax, a taxpayer could challenge both the tax and the spending of the receipts as a package. President Roosevelt had been very explicit that he wanted the government insurance directly tied to earmarked contributions.

Adding to CES's constitutional woes, even if the Supreme Court could be convinced that Congress had the power to do what it wanted under some express grant of authority, the enactment could still be unconstitutional if it were trumped by another part of the Constitution. The Tenth Amendment, for example, provides "The powers not delegated to the United States by the Constitution...are reserved to the States." Prior to 1934, the Court had ruled that Congress could exercise an express power if and only if it did not invade traditional powers of the states. Controlling the terms and conditions of employment in manufacturing was considered a traditional state power. In addition, the due process clauses of the Fifth and Fourteenth amendments, which the Court used to strike down minimum wage statutes, represented another obstacle to social insurance legislation.

Notwithstanding all these potential arguments against the legislation, the administration had received some helpful, encouraging hints from some important people in the months before CES was established. The daughter of Justice Louis Brandeis, Elizabeth Brandeis Raushenbush, had been a student of Professor Commons and had married another of his protégés, Paul Raushenbush, the author of Wisconsin's unemployment compensation legislation. The couple lived in Madison, were regulars at Commons's Friday night gatherings, and knew Altmeyer and Witte well. In December 1933, she and her husband visited her parents at their home on California Avenue in Washington, D.C. Brandeis pointedly asked his son-in-law if he was familiar with *Florida v. Mellon*, and, if not, the justice instructed, he should read it.

The case, decided in 1927, involved the federal estate tax. During the 1920s, Florida advertised that it had no inheritance tax, as an inducement to attract wealthy elderly people to settle there. Other states, seeing their inheritance tax bases shriveling, appealed to Congress. Succumbing to the pressure, Congress amended the federal estate tax to provide that any taxes paid to a state government could be offset against the federal liability. Florida brought suit, arguing that it was being coerced into enacting an inheritance tax.

The Supreme Court found that the state had no standing to sue, because, in its view, states were free to choose whether to enact the tax or not. Raushenbush understood immediately what his father-in-law was signaling. The case gave a road map for the design of federal social insurance. He called Altmeyer and related the conversation.

Then, the following spring, just a short time before CES got under way, Secretary Perkins attended a tea at the home of her friend Lucy Stone. Stone's husband, Justice Harlan Fiske Stone, happened to be home, and he and Perkins chatted. Perkins mentioned that she had hopes of developing a program of social insurance but she was concerned she coyly confided, because "Your Court tells us what the Constitution permits." The justice drew her aside and whispered, "The taxing power of the Federal Government, my dear; the taxing power is sufficient for everything you want and need."

None of this resolved the constitutionality of the various approaches, of course. Neither Eliot nor Armstrong nor any of the constitutional law experts—nor, for that matter, not even an individual justice himself—could know for certain how the Supreme Court would rule. Nevertheless, the clash with Eliot at the second staff meeting gave Armstrong the free rein she wanted.

Armstrong, Brown, and Latimer all believed that the ability to work independently from Witte and the rest of the staff, without supervision or attention, was good, especially given the obvious antipathy between Witte and Armstrong. They believed it was good, that is, until November.

The president's executive order, promulgated in June, had provided for an advisory council as a way of generating broad support, but by November, nothing had been done to create it. Part of the problem was that the administration did not want too big an advisory council, which could be unwieldy and might become a runaway body, taking a position inconsistent with the administration's view and generating some embarrassing press. At the same time, numerous experts around the country were vitally interested in the subject and wanted to be included in the process. The resolution was to appoint a relatively small advisory council, but simultaneous with its first meeting in November, hold a conference where a much larger group could be invited.

The council was to consist of equal numbers of business and labor representatives with other members representing the public. The group's membership, announced on November 5, consisted of five prominent business people, including Gerard Swope, the president of General Electric, Walter Teagle, the president of Standard Oil, and Marion Folsom, treasurer of Eastman Kodak; five prominent labor leaders, including William Green, the president of the American Federation of Labor; and ten prominent members of the public, including Raymond Moley, a close adviser to President Roosevelt, John Winant, the governor of New Hampshire, and, as chair, Frank Graham, the president of the University of North Carolina.

Care was taken with the selection process to have balance— Republicans as well as Democrats, some geographical diversity, agriculture as well as industry, and so on. Nevertheless, when the names were announced on November 5, there were complaints that no direct service providers were included and no Catholics. Consequently, the 20-person council quickly grew to 23.

CES scheduled the first advisory council meeting for November 15. The day before, on November 14, the administration planned to host the National Conference on Economic Security, to which about 150 of the leading experts in the field were invited. Two of the most prominent experts, who had done more than anyone to focus attention on the plight of the elderly, were Isaac M. Rubinow and Abraham Epstein. Rubinow, about 20 years older than Epstein, had immigrated to the United States from Russia at the age of 18, as had Epstein. Trained as a doctor, Rubinow became frustrated with simply attending to the medical symptoms caused by his patients' extreme poverty. He decided to work to alleviate the poverty itself.

He earned a doctorate in economics, qualified as an actuary, and authored several books, including an early classic, *Social Insurance*, published in 1913. When Roosevelt signed the executive order establishing the Committee on Economic Security, he was engrossed in reading Rubinow's 1934 work, *The Quest for Security*. At the time, Rubinow was terminally ill, so he could not participate in the staff work of CES or attend the national conference. When Roosevelt learned of Rubinow's cancer, the president inscribed and autographed his own copy of Rubinow's book and sent it to the author.

Epstein was also an economist and author, but was more of an activist. In 1927, he formed the American Association for Old Age Security, which lobbied for old-age security legislation. In 1933, he broadened the focus of his organization to include unemployment insurance, so he changed its name from the American Association for Old Age Security to the American Association for Social Security. That was the first use that anyone could recall of the phrase "Social Security." Epstein was invited to speak at the national conference.

The National Conference on Economic Security convened on November 14 at the Mayflower Hotel in Washington. The printed program of the conference listed unemployment insurance as a subject for discussion but did not mention old-age insurance. Late that afternoon, the participants, as well as the advisory council and members and staff of CES traveled to the White House, just a few blocks away, for an address by the president. The president's remarks were prepared by Witte, Altmeyer, and Perkins. Although afterward, all three claimed that the speech was misinterpreted, Roosevelt's words came as a bombshell to CES's working group on old-age insurance. Roosevelt said:

> On some points it is possible to be definite. Unemployment insurance will be in the program....I do not know whether this is the time for any Federal legislation on old age security.

Armstrong, Brown, and Latimer were apoplectic. Deciding to "fix…that little wagon," Armstrong called her old friend Max Stern, a reporter with the Scripps-Howard newspaper chain. After Armstrong filled him in about the president's remarks, Stern agreed to create a "backfire." Next, Brown called his friend Louis Stark, who was a reporter with the *New York Times*. A lead article by Stark and an editorial appeared in the next day's *Times* harshly criticizing the president for his "turndown" of old-age pensions. A similar story was put out over the Associated Press wire.

The elderly of the nation, many of whom supported the Townsend plan, had been following news stories about the work of CES closely. They reacted immediately and vociferously. Letters, phone calls, and telegrams poured into the White House.

The president, who was by this time vacationing in Warm Springs, Georgia, voiced his displeasure in a phone call to Secretary Perkins. Witte, visibly upset, soon burst into the office shared by Armstrong and Brown and asked if they knew how and why the speech received such negative press. They both feigned ignorance.

Perkins immediately issued a press release stating that the president strongly supported old-age insurance. Two days later, in a written address to the National Conference of Mayors, Roosevelt stated plainly that old-age insurance would be included in his recommendations to Congress. That settled the question.

Health insurance fared less well. From the moment it was announced that CES would be studying national health insurance with the goal of proposing legislation to Congress, physicians around the country sent to members of Congress, the White House, and CES truckloads of letters and telegrams expressing opposition to any form of health insurance.

Even Roosevelt's own physician lobbied him, telling the president that physicians were very concerned. A close friend of First Lady Eleanor Roosevelt had convinced her that hospitals would not be able to handle the influx that would be generated by the program, and medical care in the country would decline. A concerned Eleanor passed those thoughts along. The father-in-law of the Roosevelts' son James—the prominent neurosurgeon Dr. Harvey Cushing—weighed in as well, telling the president that he should listen carefully to doctors and not force any proposal on them.

CES itself was sharply divided. Hopkins, Morgenthau, and Wallace were pushing Roosevelt to propose national health insurance. Perkins, backed by Altmeyer and Witte, was concerned that the AMA's opposition could jettison the entire package of reforms, including the unemployment compensation piece.

No major groups, not even organized labor, could be counted on to lobby hard against the AMA. The current president of the AFL, William Green, was on the advisory council to CES. Nevertheless, the organization continued to reflect the view of its first president, the late Samuel Gompers, who had believed that gains made by workers should come from collective bargaining, not from the government.

When confronted with conflicting advice, Roosevelt's instincts invariably were to try to accommodate everyone. A story, perhaps apocryphal, relates a scene in the Oval Office, with Roosevelt at his desk, Eleanor seated nearby. First Senator A enters and says, "Mr. President, it is imperative that you do x." Roosevelt responds, "You are right, Senator." Senator A leaves, and immediately following, Senator B walks into the office. Senator B says, "Mr. President, you must *not* do x." Roosevelt responds, "You're right, Senator." Senator B departs. Eleanor, who has been watching all of this, turns to her husband and says, "Franklin, Senator A said x, and you said he was right; then Senator B said the exact opposite, and you said *he* was right. Now they both can't be right." Without missing a beat, Franklin replies, "You're right, too, Eleanor."

Faced with such strong and conflicting pressure, Roosevelt sought to delay making a decision and keep options open, hoping that somehow a compromise agreeable to all could be found. He set up a Medical Advisory Committee comprised of leading physicians. Personally overseeing the selection of members, Roosevelt tried to make it inclusive, appointing to it the president of the AMA and several prominent doctors, including his son's father-in-law, Dr. Cushing.

Roosevelt had hoped that the appointment of the Medical Advisory Committee would quiet the public uproar, but it did not. At the urging of Perkins, the president invited Cushing to a private luncheon on November 14 at the White House, where Roosevelt assured Cushing that he planned to proceed slowly and carefully. Later that afternoon, in the address to the National Conference on Economic Security that would cause such an uproar with respect to old-age security, Roosevelt said about health insurance:

> Whether we come to this form of insurance *sooner or later on*, I am
> confident that we can devise a system which will enhance and not
> hinder the remarkable progress which has been made and is being
> made in the practice of the professions of medicine and surgery in
> the United States.

The Medical Advisory Committee seized the opening and requested
more time. Instead of the December deadline, which remained operative
for the rest of the CES work, Roosevelt agreed to delay recommendations
concerning health insurance until March 1. This action, together with
Roosevelt's public and private remarks, ended the controversy for the
moment.

The old-age piece of the enterprise got a further boost on December
8, when Armstrong and Richter briefed CES's advisory council, which
had been established in November and included representatives of business, labor, and the public. The business representatives were effusive
with their praise for the proposal of the old-age working group, thanking
the pair and telling them that it was the soundest, most well-devised program that they had ever seen from a government committee. Even the
labor representatives found no objection to taxing employees equally with
employers. Bill Green, the president of the AFL, believed, as Brown later
recalled, "that workers 'should not pay a cent' for unemployment insurance. His simple justification was that everyone got old, but that it was the
employer who laid men off. There never was any objection from the labor
movement against equal contributions to old age insurance."

Armstrong recalled leaving the meeting. "Well, we went out of that
meeting walking on air, Mr. Richter and I. As a matter of fact, we skipped
the whole way across Washington, DC. It's a wonder we weren't picked
up for 'drunken and disorderly conduct.'"

Following the national conference and the advisory council meeting, it
was definite that the president's legislative package would include insurance programs covering old age and unemployment. In addition, because
of the crisis confronting the country, CES decided to propose separate,
additional programs of welfare for the elderly and for dependent children.
Further, the members decided to propose continuation of federal emergency relief for the unemployed.

Having determined the contours, CES still had to decide on the
details. By November, although an enormous amount of work had been
done on the staff level, CES members themselves had not reviewed the
staff policy recommendation with care nor resolved many policy deci-

sions. Numerous drafts and memoranda sketching various aspects of the proposals had been circulated, but during the months that the staff had been working so diligently, CES had met only twice, once in August and once in October.

In the CES meeting on November 9, just before the national conference, the members decided that unemployment compensation should be a combined federal-state program. The president's speech on November 14 reflected that decision. At the next meeting on November 16, though, at the strong urging of Secretary Wallace supported by the Treasury Department representative, CES reversed itself. Within the day, CES members called Perkins urging that the group reconsider the issue once more. At the next meeting, they switched back. Unable to put the matter to rest, CES wound up holding four meetings on this one question.

By this time, the December 1 deadline had come and gone. The president had made clear to the entire cabinet that any proposed legislation to be introduced at the beginning of the new Congress had to be to him by Christmas day, no later. Perkins knew the question had to be resolved for good. During Christmas week, she scheduled a meeting of CES at her house at 8:00 P.M. She told the others that she was turning off the telephones for the evening and that they would stay all night, if necessary. At 2:00 A.M., with deep reservations, they concluded that CES would propose to the president a federal-state system for unemployment insurance. They reviewed all decisions one last time and instructed the staff to finalize the draft report.

They decided to recommend a federal tax on employers based on a percentage of payroll to finance the proposed unemployment insurance program; the federal tax would be offset by unemployment taxes paid to the state. Part of what persuaded them was the concern about the constitutionality of the proposal. If Congress enacted a federal tax that could be offset by state programs, and the federal part were held unconstitutional, some of the states that had enacted programs might continue them on their own. However, if the state programs were designed to rely on federal subsidies for part of their funding, the states might not have the resources allocated to continue the programs without the federal funds. For purposes of uniformity, some aspects of the qualifying state programs were specified. However, the group resolved the hotly debated Wisconsin versus Ohio approach by giving the states flexibility.

Though Roosevelt had agreed to postpone the issuance of the health insurance part of the report until March 1, members of the working group on health insurance proposed that the January report at least include a statement announcing that a plan on health insurance would be forthcoming and specifying some general principles concerning health insurance. CES and Roosevelt gave the staff the go-ahead. When the medical community received the January report containing the statement and principles on health insurance, doctors went to code blue. Medical journals ran negative editorials; letters and phone calls once again flooded Washington. The AMA called an emergency meeting and passed a resolution stating its "unyielding opposition" to national health insurance.

With respect to old-age security, CES proposed three separate programs. The cabinet-level group proposed means-tested welfare, which the members anticipated would diminish in importance as the insurance program matured. CES also proposed that the government sell voluntary annuities as supplements to the compulsory program. As its core proposal in the area, CES proposed compulsory retirement insurance, the program now known as Social Security.

With respect to the compulsory insurance, CES agreed to the staff recommendation that the program be exclusively federal. In response to the concerns about constitutionality, the working group proposed this paragraph be included in the final report:

> In its consideration of the advantages of old age insurance, the staff is fully aware of the limitations imposed upon the Federal Government by our Constitution which would affect the adoption of such a program. The staff is convinced, however, that it should first seek out the most constructive proposals for old age security adapted to American economic and social conditions and then, and only then, test as far as possible whether such proposals can be made effective within our legal system. Since law is a living science, it is reasonable to assume that if a sound program of old age security can be projected, our system of constitutional law will evolve in time to support that program.

Honest as the sentiment expressed was, those who reviewed it recognized the adverse use opposing counsel could make of the paragraph in the inevitable litigation and wisely struck it.

The thorniest problem confronting CES regarding old-age insurance was its financing. It was agreed that contributions from both employers and employees had many advantages over other taxes, but there was substantial disagreement over the rate at which to set the taxes and whether general revenues should be used for part of the funding.

All pension programs, private as well as public, must confront whether and how to advance fund promised benefits. Prior to the enactment of the Employee Retirement Income Security Act of 1974 (ERISA), which regulates private pensions, employers were free to not fund pension benefits at all, but simply to pay them from current income as the benefits became due. Congress determined, in 1974, that this current funding of benefits was not acceptable in the case of private plans for rank and file workers. Because private employers run the risk of lacking sufficient monies to pay the promised benefits when they become due or of going out of business altogether, Congress mandated that private pensions be advance-funded and that the contributed funds be held in trust for workers.

The government, in contrast, has a continuous flow of workers, is in no danger of going out of business and, most important, has the power to tax and so can always satisfy pension promises. Moreover, because standards of living tend to go up over time, there is a strong argument for paying benefits out of current income. As the nation's productivity increases, the pension obligations become easier to pay. A shortcoming of current funding (colloquially referred to as pay-as-you-go) is that the rate of contribution is not stable. It rises and falls as the number of workers in relation to the number of retirees changes.

CES fully and clearly understood that the funding issues were down the road. As with the start-up of any pension program, CES recognized that in the early years of Social Security there would be relatively few beneficiaries receiving relatively low benefits and relatively large numbers of contributors.

Today's misleading refrain, that Social Security is unsustainable because there used to be 16 workers paying in for every beneficiary—a statistic plucked from 1950—never played any part in anyone's thinking about the long-term funding of Social Security. CES ignored, as irrelevant, early worker-to-beneficiary ratios. In the early days, CES members knew that even a very low rate of taxation would result in more than enough revenue. They were concerned not with the early start-up years, but later years, over the long run.

CES recognized that, as the system matured, coupled with the well-understood projected aging of the population and increases in longevity, current funding of benefits would require either substantially higher payroll taxes down the road or government contributions, something the president was firmly against. The third alternative was to set relatively high tax rates initially and build a reserve that could be invested to generate income. This alternative had a number of drawbacks, though. First, the country was in the midst of the Great Depression and taxes are deflationary. Moreover, it was believed that the projected reserve would grow larger than the amount of available government bonds.

CES was concerned about a deflationary tax at the time the country was struggling to escape the Depression, but did not want ultimate tax rates to rise to unacceptably high levels. Balancing these interests, CES decided that the best alternative was for future government payments. The program would be self-financing with equal employer and employee contributions until sometime after 1965, when, CES recommended, general revenue would make up the shortfall. In other words, CES decided on partial advance funding and partial pay-as-you-go, with any future deficit to be made up by general revenue.

Just days before the report was due to go to Roosevelt, Secretary of the Treasury Morgenthau objected to any scheme that would require payments out of general revenue at any time, notwithstanding that he or his representative had attended all CES meetings, and he had signed off on the report. Nevertheless, Morgenthau announced that if the general revenue remained in the proposal sent to the president, he would insist on a qualifying statement to the report stating his opposition to the method of financing. Perkins was determined to have a unanimous report. It took her personal phone call and considerable discussion to convince Morgenthau to sign the report without dissent. The report was submitted to President Roosevelt on January 15.

The president issued a press release announcing that on January 17, he would be sending to Congress a special message dealing with the proposed legislation. Then, on the afternoon of January 16, Roosevelt sent for Perkins. He explained that he had been studying one of the tables in the report and saw the use of general revenue after 1965. He asked if that was a mistake. When he was informed that it was no mistake, he told Perkins that he could not support the program because of the general revenue financing.

It is lost to history whether Roosevelt truly discovered the deficit himself by a perusal of various tables appended to the report, as he claimed and as contemporaneous accounts state, or whether Morgenthau, despite his assurance to Perkins not to object, nevertheless raised his concern privately with the president. In any event, Roosevelt insisted that the report be changed. He asked that the actuarial table showing the general revenue be removed and the report rewritten so that the CES recommendation concerning tax rates and benefit schedules be presented as simply one possible approach that Congress might or might not adopt. He indicated that the administration's recommendation on funding would be made as part of Morgenthau's testimony when hearings were held.

All members of CES were contacted, the report was rewritten along the lines the president requested, and the revised report was submitted to Roosevelt on January 17, still bearing the date of January 15. The president's message, together with the revised report, was submitted to Congress later that day. In less than six months, CES had produced legislation and 10 large volumes of reports and studies to support its decisions. Now it was Congress's turn.

CHAPTER 5

# A Teeny-Weeny
# Bit of Socialism

Inside the Oval Office and on Capitol Hill, the normally mundane question of who should introduce the president's proposal sparked heated discussions. Secretary Perkins's thought was that Senator Robert Wagner and Representative David J. Lewis—the cosponsors of the previous Congress's Wagner-Lewis unemployment compensation bill—should have the honor of introducing the legislation. However, as word got out, a number of members of Congress said they wanted to be the ones to drop the administration's Economic Security Act of 1935 in the hopper.

To complicate matters further, the Committee on Economic Security thought a special ad hoc committee, with members from both the tax and labor committees, would expedite the process of consideration. As a revenue measure, the bill customarily would be referred to the tax-writing committees, the Ways and Means Committee in the House and the Finance Committee in the Senate.

When the chairman of the Ways and Means Committee, Representative Robert L. Doughton (D-N.C.), got wind of the plan, he was furious. He let the president know that he wanted to introduce the bill, and he wanted his committee to have exclusive jurisdiction—although he had never spoken about social insurance in a speech or expressed any interest whatsoever in the subject up to this point, as far as anyone could remember.

It took a meeting of the president, the Democratic leadership, chairmen of several committees of Congress, and a handful of other members to sort it all out. When Perkins consulted Roosevelt about it before the meeting, he instructed her, "We will have to put it through the Ways and Means Committee. It is the only thing to do. You will hurt Bob Doughton's feelings. You will hurt Pat Harrison's [chairman of the Senate Finance Committee] feelings if you don't."

So, on January 17, 1935, the Economic Security Act of 1935 was introduced once by Wagner, once by Doughton, and once by Lewis. Doughton was not furnished his own copy of the legislation, so his staff hastily got a copy of the bill that Wagner introduced in the Senate earlier in the day. Doughton put his own name on the Wagner bill and dropped it in the hopper. But there was a problem. Lewis had already introduced the measure in the House, and normally bills are numbered in the order that they are introduced. In this case, the clerk of the House was persuaded to do otherwise. Doughton's bill jumped the line and was given the lower number. The lower-numbered bill, the so-called Doughton bill, became the one that the Ways and Means Committee considered.

Senator Harrison chose, in the end, to defer to his colleague Senator Wagner, and let him have the honor of introducing the bill in the Senate. This saved Perkins the unpleasant task of breaking it to Wagner that the bill was going to be called the Harrison-Doughton bill.

The competition did not end there, though. When the House bills were introduced, Speaker of the House Joseph W. Byrns (D-Tenn.) referred them to the Ways and Means Committee. The chairman of the Labor Committee, Representative William P. Connery, Jr., who had introduced an old-age assistance bill in the prior two Congresses, objected to the referral and moved that the bill be sent to his committee instead. After a brief but angry debate, the motion was defeated.

Twenty-four hours before Roosevelt's bill was introduced three times, a brand new congressman beat him to the punch. Representative John Steven McGroarty (D-Calif.) introduced his own Social Security bill, based on the Townsend plan. He described it to the press this way:

> Why, this will mean permanent prosperity. It will empty the poorhouses and the jails. It will cure 90% of our problems. You can't laugh it down. This won't debunk. It's the simplest thing in the world. These professional economists can't see it. It comes from the brain of a little country doctor. God always picks a man like that.

Talk of the Townsend plan was everywhere. Just the week before, Dr. Townsend himself was in Washington stirring up support for the plan and stirring up pressure on Congress. He spoke about his plan to an audience that included about 20 congressmen. The plan sounded spectacular, as he described it:

> Give all the aged a pension and the task of spending it every month, before they could receive more. Purchasing power will be restored. Business will boom. Prices will go up, of course. But what's the difference? Everyone will have plenty of money. There will be no more poverty. Everyone will be working.

The congressmen in the audience were either too polite, too politically scared, or too naive to point out that this free lunch was not quite as good as it sounded. In fact, a number of the congressmen even joined the Townsend club the doctor was organizing that night.

Even the president found himself cautiously tiptoeing around the idea. At his speech before the National Conference on Economic Security— the same speech in which he said he was not sure whether this was the time for legislation on old-age security—he went on to explain:

> Organizations promoting fantastic schemes have aroused hopes which cannot possibly be fulfilled. Through their activities they have increased the difficulties of getting sound legislation.

The reason for Roosevelt's oblique reference was obvious. By mid-October, Townsend had acquired 2 million signatures on petitions urging congressional action on his plan. Now in January, just three months later, he was claiming to have 25 million signatures. The number of Townsend clubs had climbed to 25,000 across the country.

The plan's popularity was not hard to fathom. As its promoters liked to say, it was supported by the 10 million people over age 60, the 10 million who had parents over age 60 whom they were supporting, and the remaining millions who planned to become 60 some day. A congressman from Oregon who attended the Townsend rally put the politics plainly:

> About 120,000 people in my district have signed a Townsend petition. When I first heard of this I laughed at it. Then I got the smile off my face. It's like a punching bag—you can't dodge it. If we don't pass it this session we'll have to meet it when we get back home.

This was the political climate facing the members of the Seventy-fourth Congress. The question was, would they pass the Townsend plan, the Roosevelt plan, or pass nothing at all?

Initial reaction to the Roosevelt proposal was favorable. Members of both parties praised the legislation as sound and conservative. Most newspapers printed favorable editorials, saying the same. The little criticism there was tended to complain that the proposal did not go far enough. By February, though, the opposition became organized and press reaction turned negative.

Understanding the nation's great need for this legislation and perhaps hoping to forestall opposition, Roosevelt, both in his January 17 message to Congress and in direct conversation with key members, consistently urged speedy action. In deference to the president, the congressional leadership decided to hold hearings in both the Senate and the House simultaneously. The Ways and Means Committee was scheduled to hold its first hearing on January 22, five days after the bill had been introduced. When the committee learned that the Senate Finance Committee had also scheduled its first hearing on that day, it hastily moved up its start by one day, so that it could be on record first.

Hearings lasted about a month. Covering the proceedings for CES was the executive director's young assistant, Wilbur Cohen. This was his first taste of what would become a lifelong passion for Congress and the legislative process. The administration led the witness list in the House and was second behind Senator Wagner in the Senate. The testimony by administration witnesses was straightforward, with no surprises. That is, until Treasury Secretary Morgenthau appeared.

In its deliberations the prior December, CES had agreed, as a fundamental principle, that old-age insurance should be universal, in order to provide everyone with the important protection and to establish a broad insurance pool over which to spread the risk. The cabinet-level group had recommended to the president that all workers be covered, with the only exceptions being federal workers covered by the relatively new civil service retirement system, railroad workers covered by the recently enacted Railroad Retirement Act, and state and local workers, with respect to whom there were constitutional questions involving state sovereignty.

Morgenthau had a representative at all CES deliberations and had signed its report to the president. He had not been reticent, even at the eleventh hour, about objecting to the proposed financing scheme contained in the report. But he had never breathed a word of objection to the decision to propose nearly universal coverage.

Nevertheless, at the hearing, Morgenthau forcefully asserted that the Treasury Department believed it would be extremely difficult to collect payments from agricultural workers, domestic workers, and employers with only a few employees. With Secretary Perkins seated next to him at the witness table, her eyes widening and her jaw dropping, he urged Congress to restrict coverage of the legislation to those involved in "commerce and industry," about 60 percent of the workforce. As the members of the committee nodded their heads in agreement, Perkins sat frozen in shock and disbelief.

While Morgenthau's testimony caused quite a stir within the administration, the greatest press attention was reserved for the testimony of Dr. Townsend and his supporters. Townsend's appearance was widely publicized in advance. His appearances drew the largest crowds and received front-page coverage in all the newspapers.

Testifying before Congress for the first time, Townsend did not so much attack the old-age insurance provisions of the administration bill as simply assert that his plan should be substituted for it. After Townsend's appearance, every member of Congress was deluged with mail in support of his plan.

Meanwhile, the Committee on Economic Security's working group on health insurance produced a draft report, notwithstanding the torrent of opposition that resulted simply from the mere mention in the January report that the health insurance recommendations would be out in March. In addition to the report, the staff drafted legislative language on health insurance in the form of an amendment to the Social Security bill now pending before Congress.

CES was divided whether to advise the president to follow the course of action the staff proposed or hold off, in order not to endanger the rest of the Social Security bill. The five members remained as sharply split as they had been months before. Recognizing the impasse, they decided to present the pros and cons to the president without forming a consensus and to suggest that he decide without the benefit of a unified recommendation of his advisers.

Roosevelt believed that proposing national health insurance would fuel the opposition and could bring the entire reform package down. He recognized that the country wanted and needed unemployment compensation, old-age insurance, and the various welfare programs. The risk of losing everything was too great. He decided not to offer an amendment on health insurance and not to release the CES report on that subject.

Once the month-long hearings on the president's bill ended, the Ways and Means Committee immediately went into executive session to begin its mark up of the legislation. Roosevelt and his advisers thought they would have an easy time in the House. Their real focus and attention would be required only when the bill got to the Senate. They miscalculated.

By this time, the opposition had coalesced. On the left, people complained that the old-age proposal did not go far enough, that it was not generous enough and was too conservative in its structure. On the right, people complained that the bill went too far.

The Republicans on the committee had, by now, lined up solidly against the old-age part of the bill. Prominent Republicans said they wanted to rely exclusively on welfare to deal with the problem of the elderly. They claimed that by structuring the program as insurance, the government would be competing with private insurance companies. They asserted that the payroll tax would be too burdensome on business and would harm economic growth They argued that the measure would destroy private pensions. They attacked the proposal as unconstitutional. And a few Democrats agreed with them.

No constituency seemed to support the administration's approach. The bill's natural allies in Congress were being pressured relentlessly by Townsend supporters. The House members were highly susceptible to the pressure because a mobilized single-issue constituency in a small district could make the difference in a close election. In reality, not more than a handful of members truly supported the Townsend plan. Most could see the naïveté of its design. If enacted, benefits would cost half the national income. At the same time, politicians were afraid to cast a vote against it. And a vote for the president's plan did not get much support among the bill's natural constituency, the elderly. Senior citizens wanted the Townsend plan, and they gave their representatives no credit for a vote in favor of a more moderate measure.

Labor was not playing any active role in favor of the bill, either. Some in the labor movement feared that social insurance would reduce the incentive of workers to unionize. Bill Green president of the AFL and a member of the 1934 advisory council, testified before both committees. His testimony before the Senate consisted of a carefully crafted statement, detailing a laundry list of amendments that he thought would improve the bill. Reporters interpreted his testimony as an attack on the bill by organized labor. The next day, in testimony before the Ways and Means Committee, Green tried to correct the record by talking extemporaneously, saying that organized labor supported the bill but simply thought the suggested changes would strengthen it. But the damaging impression made the day before was hard to undo.

About a week before the Ways and Means Committee was to report the bill out of committee, Representative Claude A. Fuller (D-Ark.) canvassed the members of the committee and found that a motion to strike the old-age insurance piece of the bill would carry by one vote. The president, who had been taking a low-key approach up to this point, let the senior members of the committee know that he believed the old-age insurance provisions were the most important part of the legislation, and it was important to him that the entire bill be reported out intact. Perkins, too, took steps to mobilize supporters of the bill.

Representative Frederick M. Vinson, who would be appointed chief justice of the Supreme Court by President Truman in 1946, devised a compromise. Some of the Democratic members were concerned that the voluntary annuities in the bill would unfairly compete with the insurance companies. Vinson worked out a deal in which the lead supporters of the president's proposal would vote to strike the voluntary annuities, if, in exchange, the hesitating members would support the compulsory old-age insurance. When the votes were taken, the voluntary annuities were struck from the bill by a nearly unanimous vote of the committee; the compulsory insurance withstood a motion to strike by just a handful of votes.

Somewhere in the middle of the deliberations, someone on the committee moved that the name of the bill be changed from the Economic Security Act of 1935 to the more alliterative Social Security Act of 1935. The motion carried by voice vote. No one today knows what inspired the name change. By the time the bill's name was modified, the phrase "Social Security" had been popping up in newspaper accounts about the Townsend plan and other forms of old-age proposals. Nor does anyone today know which member proposed the change. Years later, Ed Witte and Tom Eliot, who had both been present at the markups, tried to recall, but were only able to narrow the possibilities down to three different members.

Whatever inspired whomever to propose the name change, the name stuck. Though "Social Security" was the name of the entire bill, it has become closely associated with the old-age program, and not at all with unemployment compensation or any of the welfare programs that were enacted as part of the same bill. It was a phrase used only in the United States until 1940, when the International Labor Organization, a Geneva-based agency of the United Nations, issued a major report called "Approaches to Social Security," and the rest of the world began to use the name, too.

With its new moniker, the Social Security Act of 1935 was favorably reported out of committee on April 5. On the final vote, all the Democrats present voted for passage. Every Republican voted against the bill. In a minority report, the Republicans stated that they favored the welfare provisions, would be willing to give the unemployment insurance a trial, but were flatly opposed to old-age insurance, which they said would "impose a crushing burden upon industry and labor," would "establish a bureaucracy in the field of insurance in competition with private business," and would "destroy" private pensions.

The House took up the Social Security bill on April 11. Representative Joseph Patrick Monaghan rose, on April 18, to offer as an amendment the Townsend-plan bill, which had been introduced by Representative McGroarty in January, the day before the president's bill was dropped in the hopper. Ordinarily, a vote in Congress, when not taken by voice, is recorded, with each member signifying "aye" or "nay." Historically, a vote was taken by calling the roll, which is still the procedure in the Senate. Today the House of Representatives records each vote electronically.

The Monaghan amendment—a vote on the Townsend plan—used a special procedure, called a division. This method has members stand if they support the measure. The presiding officer counts those standing. Then they sit and those opposed stand and are counted. No record of individual votes is made. The Townsend-plan amendment was rejected by a vote of 206 to 56, though without an official record of who voted which way. Nevertheless, reporters sitting in the House gallery noted who voted for the amendment and the names were printed in the newspaper. Those voting for the Townsend plan were overwhelmingly conservative Republicans who were seeking to defeat Social Security.

Next, Chairman Connery rose to offer an amendment. While Ways and Means had been busy with the administration bill, Chairman Connery had held his own set of hearings in the Committee on Labor on a more liberal and more comprehensive bill, which had been sponsored by Representative Ernest Lundeen (Farmer-Laborite-Minn.). The Lundeen bill was all-encompassing social insurance that would cover all workers and farmers who were unable to work as the result of ill health, old age, maternity, industrial accident, or disability. On March 15, the bill had been favorably reported out of committee on a 7 to 6 vote, with the chairman casting the deciding vote. The bill was pending on the House calendar, but its backers were unable to obtain a rule from the Rules Committee to permit it to come to the House floor for consideration. Unable to get a rule for the bill, Chairman Connery offered his committee's marked-up Lundeen bill as an amendment. The House rejected it by a vote of 158 to 40.

The last vote of the day came on an amendment offered by the ranking minority member of the Ways and Means Committee, Representative Allen Towner Treadway (R-Mass.). His amendment was to strike old-age insurance from the bill—to strike Social Security from the Social Security bill—and keep only the provisions providing welfare for the elderly, not social insurance for retirement.

He argued that "business and industry are already operating under very heavy burdens" and that old-age insurance would cause more unemployment. Representative Thomas A. Jenkins (R-Ohio) rose in support of the amendment, rhetorically asking "Why talk about wanting to relieve the depression, why talk about charity, why talk about all these other things when you are placing a financial lash upon the backs of the people whose backs are breaking under a load of debts and taxes?" Social Security, he said, is "compulsion of the rankest kind." The amendment was defeated by a vote of 125 to 49.

The next day, on April 19, Treadway again rose, this time to move to recommit the bill to the Ways and Means Committee with instructions to strike the old-age and unemployment insurance provisions and to increase the federal contribution for old-age welfare. Knowing that he was going to lose, he announced that he would "vote most strenuously in opposition to the bill at each and every opportunity." He added that he was disgusted "at the attitude of business in that it has not shown the proper interest in protecting itself by stating its case before Congress."

Representative John Taber (R-N.Y.) speaking in support of the Treadway motion, charged, "Never in the history of the world has any measure been brought here so insidiously designed as to prevent business recovery, to enslave workers and to prevent any possibility of the employers providing work for the people." Representative Daniel Reed (R-N.Y.), who in 1952 would become chairman of the Ways and Means Committee, also spoke: "The lash of the dictator will be felt and 25 million free American citizens will for the first time submit themselves to a fingerprint test." Representative James W. Wadsworth (R-N.Y.), added his thoughts, "This bill opens the door and invites the entrance into the political field of a power so vast, so powerful as to threaten the integrity of our institutions and to pull the pillars of the temple down upon the heads of our descendants."

The motion to recommit failed by a vote of 253 to 149. Every Republican but one voted to recommit. In all, approximately 50 amendments were offered. The Democratic leadership had made clear it wanted all amendments defeated, and they were. On April 19, 1935, the Social Security Act of 1935 passed the House of Representatives by a vote of 371 to 33. Altmeyer speculated that the lopsided nature of the final vote, notwithstanding the strong opposition of the Republicans, had little to do with an eleventh-hour change of heart and everything to do with the power of the Ways and Means Committee. At that time, it was also the Committee on Committees and, as such, controlled which members served on what committees.

Now the action moved to the Senate. The administration had assumed from the beginning that the Senate would pose the most serious obstacle to passage of the bill. The Finance Committee included some of the most conservative members in that body. The committee delayed its markup until May, two and a half months after the conclusion of its hearings and almost a month after the House passed the bill.

The section of the bill providing a federal-state matching program of welfare for the aged contained a requirement that states provide benefits at a level that was "a reasonable subsistence compatible with decency and health." In the hearings, Senator Harry F. Byrd (D-Va.) had badgered Witte into acknowledging that this requirement would give the federal government the right to determine what "decency and health" was in every state. The southern senators on the committee objected to the language and it was dropped during markup. Altmeyer speculated that what motivated the hostility to the provision was that African Americans had a significantly lower standard of living than European Americans in those states, and the southern members wanted no federal interference in the way the states treated their African American populations.

As in the House, the major opposition was to the old-age insurance part of the legislation. In the committee hearings, Senator Thomas P. Gore (D-Okla.), who believed that the proposal unwisely sought to substitute Social Security for what he perceived as the laudable individual struggle for existence, had asked Perkins, "Isn't this Socialism?" When she strongly reacted, "Oh, no," he smiled gently, leaned forward in his chair, and, as if Perkins were a child who was not being totally candid, rhetorically asked, "Isn't this a teeny-weeny bit of Socialism?"

In unfortunate timing, just days into the Finance Committee markup, the U.S. Supreme Court held that the Railroad Retirement Act, which created a national pension system for railroad workers, was unconstitutional. On a 5 to 4 decision, the Court found that Congress did not have power under either the interstate commerce clause or the taxing power of the Constitution to enact the program. The opinion gratuitously added that the law also violated the due process clause of the Fifth Amendment for, among other faults, treating all railroads as one single employer and levying the same tax, irrespective of the age of the individual railroad's workforce.

This was an extremely troubling development for supporters of Social Security. The similarity of both the subject matter and the provisions of the Railroad Retirement Act naturally brought into sharp focus the question of the constitutionality of the Social Security Act. The Railroad Retirement case was supposed to be the easier for the government, because railroads, unlike manufacturing, had long been held to be instrumentalities of interstate commerce and already were highly regulated by Congress.

A member of the committee asked the attorney general for an opinion on the constitutionality of the proposed legislation in light of the Supreme Court decision. The opinion came back that the legislation could be distinguished. Not surprisingly, many members of the committee were not persuaded and used the constitutionality of the measure as a focus of their attack.

Working from the version of the bill that passed the House, Senator Wagner moved to restore the voluntary annuities that had been struck from the House bill, a move strongly opposed by Senator Augustine Lonergan (D-Conn.). The motion carried by one vote, with the chairman casting the deciding vote. After the vote, the chairman assured Lonergan that he would not oppose a motion to strike the provision if it were offered on the Senate floor.

Just as in the Ways and Means Committee, it appeared that a majority was prepared to vote to strike the compulsory old-age insurance part of the bill. The night before the vote, Senator William H. King (D-Utah) contacted Witte and told him that he was opposed to both the old-age insurance program and the unemployment insurance program. After some discussion, Senator King said that he would support the unemployment provisions if Witte would prepare an argument against the old-age insurance part for King to use in his opposition.

Witte wrote the best argument he could against the old-age provisions and sent it to King a few hours later. The next day, King read Witte's statement but was vague about the source, leaving the impression it was written by an opponent of the proposal whom the senator frequently quoted.

When King concluded this persuasive attack, the chairman, unaware of its true origin, asked Witte, who was in attendance, if he wished to respond. Witte, of course, knew better than anyone else in the room the response to what he had written. Judging his audience, he emphasized what he believed would be most persuasive to the members. While acknowledging the shortcomings King had pointed out, Witte stated emphatically his belief that "the probable alternative was a modified Townsend plan." Immediately after Witte concluded his remarks, the chairman, who knew how to assess his committee perfectly, put the question to a vote. The committee defeated the amendment to strike the old-age program, with all those perceived as doubtful voting to retain it.

The most serious threat to the old-age program was brought by Senator Bennett Champ Clark (D-Mo.). Many insurance companies were concerned that the old-age proposal would dry up their pension business. Walter Forster, of the well-known insurance brokerage firm of Towers, Perrin, Forster and Crosby, developed an amendment that would provide employers the ability to opt out of Social Security if they provided equivalent private pensions to their employees. Senator Clark offered the amendment in committee.

The Clark amendment had superficial appeal, just as similar opting-out and privatizing proposals do today. And like its contemporary counterparts, the Clark amendment was a secret killer. It would have made the old-age insurance piece unworkable because it would have undercut its universality and uniformity, keys to it working effectively. As with any insurance, one of the concerns was with adverse selection. The most prosperous companies and employees would opt out, while the struggling companies would stay in, making the contribution base narrow and insecure.

Chairman Harrison was a master in managing his committee to get the results he wanted. If he wanted an amendment to pass, he would declare it adopted, unless someone was able to object quickly. If he was uncertain of the outcome, he would manage to delay the vote until he had a better fix on who was leaning which way. The Clark amendment was defeated on a tie vote in committee, with several members who might have voted for it not in attendance. The controversial votes out of the way, the senators voted by voice to report the bill out of committee. Social Security was safe, but only for the moment. Supporters of the Clark amendment were determined to take the fight to the Senate floor.

Eliot, as one of the drafters of the legislation, had attended all committee sessions. One member of the committee, Senator Henry W. Keyes (R-N.H.), had gone to college with Eliot's father. Just before the committee went into executive session for the first time, the elder Eliot remarked to his son, "If I were a betting man, I would wager that in the committee meetings, Harry Keyes will not say ten words." So Eliot decided to count.

Sure enough, every morning, when Keyes had walked into the committee room, he would smile and bow politely to everyone, not uttering a sound. When the chairman polled the members on an issue, most would answer "aye" or "nay"; Keyes would simply nod or shake his head. Eliot began to think the man was incapable of speech.

The work of the committee was now complete, and Chairman Harrison began to wrap up. He launched into a long and flowery speech, along the lines of today's Academy Awards acceptance speeches, thanking everyone involved. In the middle of his litany of appreciation, as the chairman paused to take a breath, Keyes quickly looked up and in a loud voice interrupted, "I move we adjourn."

The bill was reported to the full Senate on May 13, but consideration was delayed for several weeks so that the Senate could complete other business. Then, just as the Social Security bill was supposed to be called up, Huey Long staged his longest filibuster. Seeking to prevent his political enemies in Louisiana from access to lucrative jobs under the National Industrial Recovery Act, his filibuster was an attempt to force the Democratic leadership to retain a provision in that legislation. The provision in question, which required Senate confirmation for senior officials in the National Recovery Administration, had been added to the pending legislation the day before, but the administration opposed it. Consequently, the leadership wanted the amendment reconsidered and defeated.

As Long began his filibuster, the galleries were packed with Shriners, members of the fraternal organization known as the Shrine, in town for a convention. Their heads festooned with the organization's trademark red fez with black tassel, they had visited the Senate expressly in hopes of catching a glimpse of Long, and they were not disappointed. Long announced that he would lecture about the Constitution, a document, he alleged, that was now "ancient and forgotten lore," thanks to the president's New Deal. One by one, hour after hour, he read each provision, discussed its origin, and analyzed its meaning, an activity cowboy-humorist Will Rogers lauded as being educational for the senators, remarking "A lot of 'em thought he was reviewing a new book."

As night descended, people entered the galleries in evening clothes, word having spread about the entertainment on the floor. As Long carried on, he looked around the nearly empty chamber, seeing a few members dozing at their desks, and asserted to Vice President John Nance Garner, who was presiding over the session, that every member should be forced to listen to him until excused. Garner dryly retorted, "That would be unusual cruelty under the Bill of Rights."

After having read and analyzed the entire Constitution, Long offered, Dear-Abby style, "I will accommodate any senator on any point on which he needs advice." Getting no takers, he offered the same to reporters sitting in the galleries. The reporters, eager for copy and happy to be entertained, obliged with questions. Speak about Frederick the Great, talk about Judah P. Benjamin, tell us about the Confederate secretary of state from Louisiana, the reporters requested, and Long willingly responded, happy to indulge their whimsical requests. When even the reporters ran out of questions, Long began reciting recipes for fried oysters and other Louisiana fare.

Finally, at 4:00 A.M.., after 15 hours and 30 minutes, Long announced that he was yielding the floor to speak to the leadership and headed hastily to the bathroom. While he was gone, the amendment at issue was tabled, the bill was passed, and the path was clear to begin the debate on Social Security.

By far the greatest lobbying and most bitter debate was over the Clark amendment, allowing employers with private pensions to opt out of Social Security. The only other amendment of note was Longeran's motion, defeated in committee and now offered on the floor, opposing voluntary annuities. The amendment easily prevailed, without even a recorded vote. On June 17, supporters moved adoption of the Clark amendment, this time on the Senate floor. Debate lasted two days. Opponents asserted that the person behind the amendment, Walter Forster, was concerned only about earning commissions. There was some merit to the charge. Forster was not an employer with a pension plan and was not working for any in his lobbying efforts; rather, he made his living drafting and selling pension plans. Forster told a friend privately that he had spent $50,000 entertaining members in connection with his lobbying effort.

Inside and outside the chamber, heavy lobbying was taking place. Forster and two lobbyists for the Equitable Life Assurance Society buttonholed members entering and leaving the chamber, while representatives of the administration were doing the same. Tom Eliot, Charlie West, a former congressman, and "Tommy the Cork" Corcoran, the famed wonder-boy power broker, were each assigned four wavering senators to convince. None of West's assigned members went with the administration. Eliot's split, two and two. Tommy the Cork got all four of his.

Organized labor also let friendly senators know that they opposed the Clark amendment. Inside the chamber, senators supporting and opposing the amendment tried to persuade uncommitted senators to vote with them. When the vote was taken, nearly every Republican senator voted for the Clark amendment and half the Democratic senators did. It passed by a vote of 51 to 35.

Senator Daniel O. Hastings (R-Del.) moved, as the last amendment before final passage, to strike the old-age insurance provisions, arguing that Social Security would "end the progress of a great country and bring its people to the level of the average European." Twelve of the 16 Republicans present voted for the amendment. Later that day, the Senate passed its version of the Social Security Act of 1935 by a vote of 77 to 6.

The next day, both chambers appointed conferees to reconcile the House and Senate versions. As is customary, the conferees were the senior members of each committee who had voted for the bill. Unfortunately for the administration, two of the three Democratic conferees representing the Senate had opposed the old-age insurance provisions, but had voted for passage of the omnibus package. This meant that a majority of the Senate conferees were hostile to Social Security.

After a month of wrangling over differences, the conference committee had resolved every disagreement but one, the Clark amendment. In mid-July, the conferees, unable to reach agreement on this one remaining point, requested instructions from their respective bodies. On July 17, both Houses instructed their conferees to hold firm. The House of Representatives stated firmly that it would never pass a bill with the Clark amendment; the Senate made clear it would not enact the bill without it.

Time was running out on Social Security, at least for this session. Congress was within weeks of adjournment, and the conferees were deadlocked, perhaps irreconcilably. The House conferees kept raising problems with the drafting of the Clark amendment. They were pointing out problem after problem, different ways the language could permit inadequate retirement plans to qualify for exemption, and the Senate conferees were scrambling to come up with answers.

Finally, the conferees assigned three staffers the job of focusing all their energies on redrafting the Clark amendment to make it work. The three were Leonard Calhoun, a lawyer who had been brought to Washington by Senator Clark, Tom Eliot, and a third staffer named Bill Woodward. The three men worked around the clock, as hard as they could. As they became more and more immersed in the details, they became more and more bogged down.

Without realizing it, the conferees had, in effect, asked the three staffers to draft a pension reform bill. If a private plan was to substitute for Social Security, it would have to be reasonably secure, fair to its workers, and adequate in the benefits it provided. The problems are numerous, including issues about eligibility requirements, portability, vesting, adequate funding, and the impact of bankruptcy. Decades later, Congress would need 10 years of hearings and study to develop pension reform legislation. The three staffers were asked to complete the drafting in a matter of days.

After two weeks of excruciatingly long and frustrating hours of work, the three reported back that it would take many months more of intense effort—well beyond the end of the congressional session—to work out all the difficulties. At that point, a compromise was reached. The Senate conferees agreed to report the bill without the Clark amendment in exchange for the appointment of a special joint committee to develop a more workable proposal that would meet the concerns of both sides. The understanding was that, if a workable proposal could be drafted, it would be introduced and passed in the next session.

The House accepted the conference report and passed the measure on August 8. The Senate acted on August 9. The enactment was, in its general design, consistent with the work that had emerged from the Committee on Economic Security. Social Security met the president's requirement that the program be social insurance, not welfare. The basic structure of the old-age insurance provisions of the Social Security Act, enacted in 1935, remains in place today.

CES intended that Social Security be universal, covering every worker in the country on a mandatory basis. This was and is important to the functioning of the program because Social Security is based on the insurance principle of risk that is widely pooled. But the year was 1935, and the United States had never before in its history taken on a job that would reach every worker. Though he might have raised his objection sooner, Secretary Morgenthau was understandably concerned about the capacity of the government to undertake such a technically complicated, administratively difficult, and broad-reaching job. The decision by Congress to start with just a portion of the workforce and expand from there caused the principle of universal coverage to be an intention and hope, but not the reality in 1935.

Social Security did not have in 1935, and never has had, wealth as a restriction on receipt of benefits. Rather, Social Security was, and remains, a program of social insurance. The insurance is payable irrespective of other assets. No one would ever say that a wealthy person with fire insurance should not be permitted to collect under the policy, if the insured property burns down, simply because he or she is wealthy and does not need the insurance proceeds. Similarly, Social Security has from its inception been designed to be payable to anyone who is insured, when an insured event occurs.

In order to receive benefits, workers must be insured, a status they achieve by working the requisite amount of time in employment that is covered by Social Security. "Insured status" is another fundamental concept that began in 1935. Workers who were—and today are—insured receive benefits as the result of an insured event. In 1935, the insured event was aging and retirement. In future years, insured events would be expanded to include death and disability.

If a worker was insured and the insured event occurred, the level of benefits a worker qualified for was related to the wage level on which contributions were made, and that remains true today. Those who contributed more in absolute dollars to the system—workers with higher wages—received higher benefits in absolute dollars. At the same time, those who had less income out of which to contribute—lower-income workers—received benefits that replaced a higher percentage of those wages. These results were achieved through the use of an ingenious benefit formula. The benefit formula enacted in 1935 was changed in 1939, and never went into effect. Nevertheless, its progressive design is similar in concept to what is used today. Under the 1935 formula, all wages, up to the maximum wage base, for all years worked were to be added together. (Today, average, not cumulative, wages are used.) Those wages then were to be plugged into this benefit formula:

- The first $3,000 of wages on which Social Security contributions were made produced a monthly benefit equal to $\frac{1}{2}$ of 1 percent of those wages.
- For total lifetime earnings in excess of $3,000 but under $45,000 on which Social Security contributions were paid, a benefit equal to $\frac{1}{12}$ of 1 percent was earned.
- All covered earnings above $45,000 produced a benefit equal to $\frac{1}{20}$ of 1 percent, up to a maximum benefit of $85.

To see how this translates, consider the case of three hypothetical workers:

- Worker A, at age 65, had lifetime earnings of, and paid Social Security taxes on, $3,000.
- Worker B, at age 65, had lifetime earnings of, and paid Social Security taxes on, $45,000.

- Worker C, at age 65, had lifetime earnings of, and paid Social Security taxes on, $115,000.

Here is how the benefits, if the formula had remained law, would have worked:

- Worker A would receive a Social Security benefit of $15 per month (½ of 1% of $3,000).
- Worker B would receive a benefit of $50 per month (½ of 1% of $3000, or $15 plus ½ of 1% of $42,000 ($45,000–$3,000) or $35.00) (i.e., $15 + $35 = $50).
- Worker C would receive a benefit of $85 per month (½ of 1% of $3,000, or $15 plus ½ of 1% of $42,000, or $35 plus ¹⁄₂₀ of 1% of $70,000 ($115,000–$45,000 or $35) ($15 + $35 + $35 = $85).

Notice that:

- Worker A, the low earner, gets $15.
- Worker B, the middle earner, gets $50.
- Worker C, the high earner, gets $85.

Notice also that:

- Worker B, the middle-income worker, has lifetime earnings that are 15 times larger than Worker A, the low-income worker, but the benefit is just a little over three times larger.
- Worker C, the high-income worker, has earned almost 37 times more than Worker A, the low-income earner, but has a benefit only between five and six times larger.
- Worker C, the high-income worker, earned more than 100 percent over what Worker B, the middle-income worker made, but has a benefit, less than 50 percent larger.

A weighted benefit formula was adopted for a number of compelling reasons. At the same time that Social Security was enacted, a program of means-tested assistance for the elderly passed Congress. Social Security's benefit levels had to be high enough to provide a benefit that was, after a lifetime of working and contributing, higher than what the beneficiary would be able to get from the local welfare office. At the same time, benefits had to be large enough for all workers so that they received a reasonable return on their contributions. Fairness demanded that those who paid more received higher benefits. The twin goals of equity and adequacy were achieved by using a weighted benefit formula. A weighted formula permitted adequate benefits to be paid to low-wage workers and fair benefits to high-wage workers without the entire system being too expensive.

The benefit formula has been modified numerous times since 1935. Today benefits are an average of lifetime earnings, not an accumulation of them. Also, the amounts of earnings are higher in nominal and real terms. But the original structure—three categories of wages with each higher bracket of wages replaced at a lower percentage amount—is the same today. The formula continues to meet the dual program goals in place from the beginning, that benefits be fair for every contributor, providing more for those who contributed more, while also adequate for low-income earners least likely to have savings or private pensions.

The 1935 enactment, just like today's program, required workers and employers to contribute an equal amount to finance benefits. The amount to be contributed, then as now, was a uniform percentage of wages up to a maximum wage level. Starting on January 1, 1937, workers would be required to contribute 1 percent of wages up to a maximum taxable wage level of $3000, and their employers were required to match the amount. The tax rate was scheduled to rise every three years by a combined employer-employee rate of 1 percent, until it reached 6 percent in 1949. Even an initial contribution rate of 1 percent would build a substantial reserve. The solution to the financing question, raised by Secretary Morgenthau at the last minute, was that Social Security would not use general revenue, but rather would be self-supporting, as the president had insisted.

The designers of Social Security intended that the monies collected should be dedicated to the program. This was tricky because of the constitutional challenge that was sure to come. The lawyers wanted to blur the connection between taxing and spending, hoping in that way to uphold the arrangement by denying potential plaintiffs standing to sue. As a compromise between the designers and the lawyers, Title II of the Social Security Act created "an account in the Treasury of the United States to be known as the 'Old-Age Reserve Account.'" Title VIII of the Social Security Act imposed taxes on employers and employees. These taxes were paid into the general fund. But the legislation went on to authorize an annual appropriation from the general fund to the Old-

Age Reserve Account in the exact amount as the proceeds from the Title VIII tax.

Not surprisingly, many doubted whether this obvious attempt to keep the courts from ruling on Social Security's constitutionality would successfully fend off a court challenge. The minority report to the House Ways and Means Committee stated that Title II and Title VIII "are interdependent, and neither is of any consequence without the other." The report continued: "This separation is a separation in words only. There is no separation in spirit or intent. These two titles must stand or fall together."

The Republican-drafted report pointed out what everyone knew, but hoped the courts would not pierce through. The design was not very subtle, but it was the best the lawyers could do. The court challenge was unquestionably coming, and the courts were likely to invalidate the statute. The most immediate threat was not the courts, however, but the 1936 election. The courts might not have to act if a Republican president and a Republican-controlled Congress mooted the question by repealing the legislation.

But the election was a year away and a court action, even farther away, because the taxes did not go into effect until 1937. Now was the time to celebrate a valiant effort. President Roosevelt signed the Social Security Act of 1935 on August 14. His statement at the signing ceremony was thoughtful and prophetic, as well as optimistic, given the threats still lying ahead:

> We can never insure one hundred percent of the population against one hundred percent of the hazards and vicissitudes of life, but we have tried to frame a law which will give some measure of protection to the average citizen and to his family against the loss of a job and against poverty-ridden old age.
>
> This law, too, represents a cornerstone in a structure which is being built but is by no means complete.

CHAPTER 6

# Dirty Tricks

*My First Days in the White House* was not a memoir, at least not yet. Dashed off in six weeks, in the spring of 1935, Huey Long wrote it as part of a calculated strategy. Long planned to arrive at the Democratic National Convention the following year as both the head of the Louisiana delegation and as a presidential candidate. He knew, of course, that Roosevelt would win the nomination, though Long thought he might pick up several southern states in addition to Louisiana.

Immediately after the convention, he planned to allege that the Democratic party, like the Republican party, was dominated by big business, that the American people were being sold out. Part of his attack would be that Social Security was not generous enough; the nation needed his more radical and lavish Share Our Wealth plan.

He would then dramatically announce that he was forming a third party. In May, Long talked to Townsend about his third-party plans. He also recruited Floyd B. Olson. A strong supporter of Robert La Follette in his run for the presidency in 1924, Olson became governor of Minnesota in 1930, running as a candidate of the Farmer-Labor party. In that election, he bragged, "I am not a liberal, I am what I want to be—I am a radical."

Also included in the discussions was Milo Reno, a farm activist from Iowa, who organized "farm holidays," strikes for higher prices. Originally a supporter of Roosevelt, he had become dissatisfied with the president's agricultural policies. Long also figured on the support of the well-known author Upton Sinclair, who had run so well in California.

Huey Long was willing to recruit any Roosevelt hater, no matter what his political views. He courted the governor of Georgia, Eugene Talmadge. Bedecked in trademark red suspenders, Talmadge was a colorful politician, entertaining and outrageous, like his friend Huey. Talmadge hated Roosevelt—referring to him as "that cripple in the White House"—and he hated the New Deal. He claimed to oppose the New Deal because of its cost and paternalistic policies, but his rhetoric displayed a more malevolent concern. About Social Security, he claimed: "In Georgia the white folks would get about $30,000 a month. The Negroes would get $2,250,000. If that plan was in effect in Georgia, there wouldn't be a plow-hand, hoehand, or washwoman in the State." Talmadge let Long know that he was ready to join him in his effort to stop Roosevelt.

Long recruited all these people, but he knew he would be the one calling the shots. He or a candidate who fronted for him would run in the general election, siphoning just enough votes to throw the election to the Republican candidate. The new Republican president, he reasoned, would cause so much economic hardship that the country would be ripe for radical leadership in 1940, and he would be waiting, poised to step in.

He had reason to believe his scheme would work. He had the absolute, complete support of radio preacher Father Charles E. Coughlin. Originally a supporter of Roosevelt, Coughlin coined his trademark assertion that the choice in 1932 was between "Roosevelt or ruin." But Couglin had grown to hate the president. Roosevelt *and* ruin, he now said. In a typical radio address, he excoriated the "great betrayer and liar, Franklin D. Roosevelt," who, Coughlin said, "promised to drive the money changers from the temple," but, instead, drove "the farmers from their homesteads and the citizens from their homes in the cities." And a lot of people listened. Coughlin's *Golden Hour of the Little Flower*, broadcast over CBS radio, had a larger share of the listening audience than today's Howard Stern, Rush Limbaugh, Paul Harvey, and Larry King put together. Coughlin claimed he received 400,000 letters of support after each week's Sunday broadcast.

In addition to his radio show, he published the *Social Justice Weekly*, which had a circulation of 1 million readers. On November 11, 1934, Coughlin had established the National Union for Social Justice—his own political action committee, long before those organizations became commonplace and regulated.

Long had other substantial financial support, as well. Some of the largest corporations and banks secretly came to him, some offering him as much as $2 million for his cause to remove Roosevelt from the White House. When Long pointed out to one businessman that he was more radical than the president, the contributor bitterly replied, "We're not for you either." Long just smiled and took the money.

And the campaign he was planning would be expensive. He had attention-grabbing, grandiose ideas. For his 1930 run for the Senate, Long commissioned the building of a sound truck, the first, he claimed, ever used in an American campaign. The truck would precede him at every stop, blaring his arrival and generating huge crowds. For his presidential run, he had purchased two additional sound trucks. In addition, with the goal of covering all 48 states, he had also purchased a "sound plane," a private plane he would travel in, which, as he neared his destination, would announce that Huey Long was onboard and would soon be delivering a speech.

The administration was concerned, and for good reason. Jim Farley, a close Roosevelt adviser, commissioned a secret poll of Long's national strength. It revealed that if Long himself were the candidate, he could tip a close election. He was attractive not just in the South, but in industrial centers and rural areas nationwide.

Long planned to head to New York to sign a contract for his book right after the end of the congressional term. The last day of the session was fast approaching. The leadership set the date of adjournment for Saturday, August 26. The last "must" item on the legislative calendar was funding to get Social Security started. The Third Deficiency Bill appropriated funds primarily to finance the first 10 months of the program's operation, to tide it over until a regular appropriation could be enacted the following session.

The Social Security Act of 1935 had created a three-person bipartisan Social Security Board. On August 23, nine days after the passage of the act and three days before the scheduled adjournment, the president had appointed, and the Senate had confirmed as the first board members, Arthur Altmeyer, John G. Winant, the former three-term Republican governor of New Hampshire, as chairman, and Vincent E. Miles, a Democratic national committeeman from Arkansas.

Even before the Social Security bill was enacted, Altmeyer had begun to work on a budget for the new agency, as well as a structure and a pro-

cedure for choosing personnel. The chairman of the House Appropriations Committee was a plain-speaking, straight-shooting Texan named
James P. "Buck" Buchanan. He was powerful, and his committee generally deferred to him. He held an informal hearing on the appropriation,
by himself, without other members present. He called just one witness,
Arthur Altmeyer.

When Altmeyer was finished explaining his proposed budget,
Buchanan leaned back, put his feet up on the table, and responded, "I
don't understand a damned thing you're saying, and I don't believe you do
either." He then took a deep breath, looked hard at Altmeyer, and finally
continued, "But I'll give you the money anyway." Altmeyer confessed
years later that the budget was "based entirely upon conjecture."

The bill passed the House on a voice vote and was sent to the Senate.
The hearing in the Senate was less colorful but equally satisfactory in its
outcome. Viewing the bill as a routine matter that would pass quickly, the
Senate leadership scheduled it for the last day of the legislative session.
Since the appropriation bill was the only urgent item on the agenda, the
Senate convened at 6:00 P.M., with the agreed-upon adjournment time of
midnight.

The end of a legislative session tends to be chaotic, with last pieces of
legislation rushing through and members attaching their favorite pet
projects. This one was no different.

The Third Deficiency Bill, containing Social Security's financing, was
before the Senate, the last obstacle to going home. Senator James "Jimmie"
Byrnes (D-N.C.), angry that the Agricultural Adjustment Administration
was offering cotton farmers loans on what he thought were miserly terms,
rose to offer an amendment statutorily mandating better terms. The senators representing wheat farmers rose in support and proposed a similar
adjustment for the wheat farmers. Together they voted to attach their
amendments to the deficiency bill.

This was a problem. Because the bill now contained a provision different from the House bill, it would have to go back to the House for
approval before it could be signed into law, and the hour was growing late. Buchanan, the no-nonsense House chairman, would have to
approve.

When a contingent of senators sought him out, he told them to forget
it. He was upset with all the pork the Senate was adding. When warned
that the deficiency bill funding Social Security might fail, he was unmoved,

responding "We got along for 143 years without a Social Security Board." It was now 9:00 P.M. In response to reporters' questions about being the one to block funds to cotton and wheat farmers, he replied, "Those damned amendments would cost more than $500 million a year. If we are going to make wheat and cotton loans, why not make loans on everything including sorghum molasses and onions? Would I accept the Senate amendments? Hell, no!"

The White House proposed a compromise—something not requiring legislation—that seemed acceptable to all parties. The way seemed clear for the deficiency bill. Majority leader Joseph T. Robinson asked unanimous consent to reconsider the vote on the bill, so the amendment for the cotton and wheat farmers could be struck, now that a compromise had been reached.

Long immediately jumped up, shouting "I object." He continued, "You've done worse than make a legislative trade. You've stopped the wheat people so they can't have their day in court. This may be my swan song." When the majority leader responded that there was no time to pursue the matter more fully before the designated adjournment at midnight, Long told him to change the adjournment date and stay in session. Long informed Robinson, "I have nothing to do," adding mischeviously, "I'm just having a high-heeled good time."

And so the filibuster began. Two months earlier, Long had held the floor for 15 hours and 30 minutes. This time he only had to hold the floor a few hours, until the Senate adjourned *sine die* at midnight, a short sprint around the track for this filibuster marathoner.

Progressive senators started beseeching Long to relent, pointing out that Social Security and other worthy causes would suffer. Robinson even asked for a quorum call, so senators could talk to Long privately. Long responded to all of them, "All I care is what the boys at the forks of the creek think of me."

Finally, close to midnight, Senator Lewis B. Schwellenbach (D-Wash.) was yielded time and asked, "[W]hether or not, because of his selfish desire to get publicity for himself, the Senator from Louisiana has not defeated the hopes, aspirations and the desires of the people of this country?" Before Long could respond, the presiding officer, Vice President Garner, learned that the House had just adjourned. Garner banged his gavel and brought the session, and the filibuster, to a close. Altmeyer sat, watching helplessly, in the Senate gallery.

Congress immediately left town. An appropriation for the newly formed Social Security Board would have to wait until January. With his filibuster, Long gained press attention and improved his standing with the farm vote. In defending his action, Long asserted that the "abortion" of an act—Social Security—was "signed, sealed, and delivered, and," referring to the president, "that feller's got enough money to polish the North Star if he wants to." Then he added darkly, "This is his last term."

He hopped a train to New York, signed a contract for his book, *My First Days in the White House*, and returned to Louisiana. On Sunday, September 8, in the Baton Rouge capitol building he had helped create, Huey Pierre Long was shot at close range by Dr. Carl Weiss, a brilliant but troubled young doctor. Two days later, Long died at home. His last words were "God, don't let me die. I have so much to do."

Without their most charismatic leader, the other enemies of the president soldiered on. Many of the same businessmen who were so eager to back Long threw money at anyone who might keep Roosevelt from a second term. A group of disaffected Democrats—funded by the du Ponts and newspaper magnate William Randolph Hearst—had formed the American Liberty League in August 1934. The group was headed by John W. Davis, the Democratic presidential candidate who was defeated in 1924, and Al Smith, the Democratic candidate defeated in his bid for the presidency in 1928.

Davis was a conservative lawyer, who would later successfully defend the steel industry against the federal government's attempt to seize it during the Korean War and unsuccessfully argue for retention of the "separate but equal" doctrine in *Brown v. Board of Education*. His hostility to the New Deal and Roosevelt's policies was not surprising. Smith's shift to the right in opposition to his former ally Roosevelt, in contrast, was a dramatic lurch from his earlier progressive days. Roosevelt, in a conversation with Perkins, summed up the startling transformation: "I just can't understand it. Practically all the things we've done in the federal government are like the things Al Smith did as governor of New York."

The American Liberty League wanted desperately to defeat Roosevelt. In 1935, the league spent twice as much in this pursuit as the Republicans. Among other efforts to discredit the president, the league prepared and widely distributed pamphlets comparing Roosevelt to Stalin, Hitler, and Mussolini. Some of Roosevelt's initiatives were fascist; others were communist. Social Security was, the pamphlets proclaimed, "the end of democracy."

On January 25, 1936, the Liberty League held a banquet for 2,000 at the Mayflower Hotel in Washington, D.C. Al Smith—the "unhappy warrior," according to Senate majority leader Robinson, who had been Smith's running mate in 1928, when Smith was "the happy warrior"— gave the keynote address that night. It was a bitter, over-the-top attack, comparing the Roosevelt administration to "Karl Marx or Lenin." Pierre du Pont remarked, "It was perfect," but the speech played poorly elsewhere. Smith and the league were widely denounced.

A week later, the du Ponts tried again to undercut Roosevelt, this time through the racist Eugene Talmadge. An anti-Roosevelt convention—nicknamed the Goober convention and the Dixie Democrats—was convened in Macon, Georgia, in February. The assembly was organized by Talmadge and the Southern Committee to Uphold the Constitution, "a hybrid organization," according to the *Baltimore Sun*, "financed by northern money, but playing on the Ku Klux Klan prejudices of the south." On every conventioneer's chair was a pamphlet containing a variety of photographs of the president and his wife meeting with or walking with African Americans.

Thomas Dixon, the author of the book that was made into the movie *Birth of a Nation* and another book glorifying the Ku Klux Klan, was the first speaker. Standing under a gigantic Confederate flag, he attacked the Roosevelt administration for its anti-lynching bill, which he called "the most brazen attempt to outrage states' rights by placing Federal bayonets at our backs!" Talmadge, rising to roars of "Give it to 'em, Gene," was, for him, restrained, though he did refer to the administration as "a collection of cheats, racketeers and madmen." He made clear that he was interested in becoming president.

Meanwhile, the Republican party was in complete disarray. It had been in turmoil since after the 1932 election. The party was divided over how to deal with such a popular president: whether to attack his policies or go along with them. Most Republican members of Congress went along with Roosevelt's emergency legislation and tried to appear constructive in their criticism of the rest of his legislative agenda. As the 1934 midterm election approached, they received thousands of letters instructing them to support the president, which reinforced their political instinct not to appear obstructionist to Roosevelt's legislative program.

In contrast, former President Herbert Hoover, through his hand-picked national chairman, Everett Sanders, vehemently attacked the New Deal. Historically, ex-presidents and defeated presidential candidates generally retired from active politics. Hoover, though, wanted another shot at beating Roosevelt, hoping that the new president and his New Deal would self-destruct. He believed he was the victim of circumstances, that his policies had been sound, and he wanted vindication. In February 1933, just before leaving office, Hoover and several key advisers had rented office space a short stroll from the White House.

Republicans in Congress blamed Hoover for running an inept campaign and tried to keep their distance. On February 25, 1934, the congressional and senatorial campaign committees took the extraordinary step of adopting resolutions that separated them from the national committee. To make matters worse, western, rural Republicans representing the farm belt and eastern Republicans representing industrial business interests were at odds over policy.

In June 1934, the simmering unrest in the Republican party broke out into the open. The occasion was the meeting of the Republican National Committee at the Palmer House in Chicago. The purpose of the meeting was to find a way to retire the debt from the 1932 campaign and position the party for the upcoming fall campaign by drafting a platform and selecting a new national committee chairman.

Some of the dissension could be seen in positions taken by various state chairmen and committees. The Republican state chairman in New York, for example, urged that the president's policies be given time to see if they worked, free from attack. The Illinois Republican state committee accused the president of betraying democracy.

The showdown came over whom to pick as a new chairman. Henry Prather Fletcher, supposedly a compromise candidate, was selected. A Rough Rider in the Spanish-American War, Fletcher had supported the more progressive Teddy Roosevelt in his bid against William Howard Taft in 1912. But he was Hoover's pick in 1930 to head the Tariff Commission, and it was well known that he was close to Hoover, as well as the two conservative Republican presidents before him.

And the platform that was adopted sided with the Roosevelt bashers. It asserted, "A small group in Washington, vested with temporary authority, is seeking covertly to alter the framework of American institutions. In place of individual initiative they seek to substitute complete government control of all agricultural production, of all business activity." It charged, "American institutions and American civilization are in greater danger today than at any time since the foundation of the republic."

The Democrats had a field day. General Hugh Johnson, the colorful director of the National Recovery Administration, proclaimed, "These pirates have reached way back into the dark ages of the Old Deal and pulled out Mr. Fletcher." In a play on Fletcher's surname, the same as that of Horace Fletcher, a trendy nutritionist of the day who advocated chewing each bite of food precisely 32 times, a practice that became known as Fletcherizing, Johnson lampooned, "They are going to Fletcherize their social program—you know—you take almost nothing into your mouth and then you chew it and chew it and chew it until it really is nothing." Then back to the pirate image, he thundered, "Social program from that crew under the Jolly Roger! You might just as well try to pick fleas out of a sand pile with a pair of boxing gloves on your fingers!"

The 1934 midterm election was a disaster for the Republicans. Generally, when a party lost the presidential election, it made a comeback at midterm. In 1922, for example, the Democrats gained 75 seats in the House of Representatives, cutting the Republican margin of control from 168 to 18. In 1930, the Democrats gained 53 seats in the House and had taken over control. In fact, the last time a party out of power lost seats in the midterm election was before the Civil War—until 1934. When all the votes were counted, the Democrats had picked up 10 seats in the Senate, leaving the Republicans with just 25 senators. In the House of Representatives, the Democrats had increased their control, as well. The Republicans had 14 fewer House seats than before the election. Fletcher summed up election day succinctly: "When you're licked, you're licked."

The gubernatorial results were equally dismal for the Republicans. No Republican governor was reelected, except one: Alfred M. Landon of Kansas. That glimmer of bright light gave the little-known governor his first public prominence. A few days after the election, the *Kansas City Journal-Post*, in a story recapping the election, mentioned Landon as a possible presidential candidate. After that, his name popped up regularly on lists of who might be the Republican standard bearer in 1936.

The *Kansas City Star* decided to make Landon's candidacy happen. Its managing editor had gone to college with Landon. Another editor, also a Landon friend, was a shrewd political operative. Together with the paper's president and editor-in-chief, they counseled the broad-shouldered, gray-haired governor and cultivated the quiet campaign. Another supporter and adviser was William Allen White, the widely-reprinted progressive editor of the *Emporia Gazette*, whom Landon had backed when White had run for governor as an independent a decade before.

At the end of 1935, about a dozen states had managed to balance their budgets, but Landon was the governor who announced the feat in a well-timed radio address. William Randolph Hearst hated Roosevelt and was on the lookout for a candidate who could beat him. After the radio address, Hearst dispatched a team to investigate Landon's background. When the report came back clean, Hearst followed up with a mob of reporters to generate publicity.

Landon did not have an uncontested stroll to the nomination. On his right, Hoover was running hard, despite his denials that he was a candidate. He toured the country, giving more speeches than at any time since his defeat in 1932, and hoped for a deadlocked convention that would turn to him.

Landon also was competing with two senators. The oldest candidate, and also the most liberal, was 30-year veteran of the Senate, William E. Borah (R-Ida.). After the devastating 1934 election, he had counseled, "I should like to see the Republican Party reorganized....I don't think there is any room in this room for an old conservative party." He complained, "There was a vast amount of reaction against the New Deal, but what were the people offered?...People can't eat the Constitution."

The other senator was Arthur H. Vandenberg (R-Mich.), another bright spot from the 1934 election. Not only was he reelected , but he was credited with carrying a number of Michigan representatives to victory on his coattails. He had positioned himself in the middle, supporting some parts of the New Deal, opposing others. Some saw him simply as an opportunist.

Also running was dark horse candidate, publisher Frank Knox, who had founded New Hampshire's *Manchester Leader* in 1912, then purchased the *Union* and one other rival newspaper. In 1931, he had acquired Chicago's *Daily News*. Since the 1934 election, he had been successfully raising money for the GOP.

But none of these other candidates could match the Hearst publicity machine. Hearst ran stories about the "Kansas Coolidge" and the "Great Economizer," and the rest of the nation's newspapers joined the frenzy. Landon's small-town, quiet life made good copy. Hearst had Damon

Runyon, author of *Guys and Dolls*, write a piece, "Horse and Buggy Governor." The title was a clever, veiled reminder of a widely-reported attack Roosevelt had leveled at the Supreme Court, where he charged that the country had "been relegated to the horse-and-buggy definition of interstate commerce" as a result of the Court's misguided rulings. Hearst instructed another writer to make the Landons "the best-loved family in America." A remarried widower, with a three-year old daughter, Nancy, and two-year-old son, Jack, Landon and his family made appealing reading.

Even as early as December 1935, Landon had a sizable lead. A Gallup poll showed Landon with 33 percent of party support; Borah next, with 26 percent; Hoover with 12 percent; with Knox garnering 8 percent and Vandenberg just 3 percent.

Landon decided to campaign in no primaries, although others entered slates in his name. He took the public stance that he was busy working for Kansas. If he were to be nominated, the party would have to come to him. Campaigning for the nomination through radio addresses, he stayed in Kansas. The decision to skip the primaries was easier to make in 1936, of course, since primaries were much less important than today in securing a party's nomination.

Senators Borah and Vandenberg were busy in Washington, now that the second session of the Seventy-fourth Congress had convened. On January 3, 1936, Roosevelt delivered his State of the Union Address to the 600 people seated on the floor of the House of Representatives, to the 600 people in the galleries, and, for the first time in history, to millions more listening on the radio. He was forced to spend much of the speech discussing the disturbing developments in Europe and Asia. His message on domestic policy was one of consolidating gains and continued forward progress.

Soon after the State of the Union, the Senate Finance Committee appointed a subcommittee to consider a revised Clark amendment, which, in the prior session, almost prevented passage of Social Security. The subcommittee held a few meetings, but nothing more happened.

After a few weeks, Thomas Eliot, now general counsel for the Social Security Board, telephoned Senator William H. King (D-Utah.), the acting chairman of the Senate Finance Committee. King had been one of the strongest supporters of the Clark amendment in the last session. Eliot reminded King that he and the other two staffers, after failing to come up with compromise language the summer before, had pledged to write a new Clark amendment when Congress resumed. Eliot then asked, "When do you want the amendment? We haven't heard from you."

King laughed sheepishly and told Eliot, "Oh! Mr. Forster was in the other day. You can forget the amendment. Mr. Forster said he'd made a terrible mistake." King then explained that last summer, when the Social Security Act was being debated, Forster had been concerned that "the passage of the old-age insurance bill would ruin his business of selling private pension plans." To Forster's surprise and delight, he discovered that "the passage of the Social Security Act has got everybody thinking about pension plans," King explained. "He doesn't want any Clark Amendment." King ended the conversation by telling Eliot not to worry about drafting any language. "You can forget it forever," he informed Eliot.

As King had accurately related to Eliot, the insurance brokers who had originated and championed the amendment were no longer interested. Prior to the enactment of Social Security, most people saw retirement on an adequate income as an impossible dream. With the promise of Social Security, it became a realistic goal. At the same time, most people saw that the promised benefits were inadequate, if they wanted to maintain their standards of living in retirement. Consequently, they began to think about methods to supplement the promise. The insurance brokers were selling more retirement plans than ever before.

While the legislative session percolated along, the primary season began. By this time, Landon had added a campaign manager, John D. M. Hamilton. Hamilton was much more conservative than Landon, but had served in Washington in several Republican National Committee positions, knew the national scene, and was an experienced politico.

Even without active campaigning, Landon began winning primaries. He won the Massachusetts primary with no campaigning, and the wins kept rolling in. "Missouri Delegates are Pledged to Landon," trumpeted the headlines, and "Landon to Get 90 New York Votes, Leaders Hint."

The one stumble, to those not in the political know, appeared to be the California primary, which could have put Landon over the top but instead seemed to go to Hoover. People who followed the race closely, however, realized that Hoover, not wanting an embarrassing loss in his home state, had run a slate of delegates pledged in name to Republican state chairman Earl Warren, but understood to be "uninstructed"—free to go for any candidate.

Hearst had run a delegation pledged to Landon, but Landon neither embraced nor repudiated the slate, and Hoover supporters made Hearst the issue. Hearst, who had served in the House of Representatives as a Democratic congressman from New York from 1902 to 1906, was portrayed as an East Coast Democrat seeking to dominate California. Many saw the California vote as a referendum on Hearst, not a test of Landon's popularity.

Sure enough, when the Republicans held their convention in Cleveland on June 9, Alfred Mossman Landon was nominated on the first ballot. No other candidates were even named; all withdrew, for the sake of party unity. Two of the other candidates, Knox and Vandenberg, both in the running for vice president, gave seconding speeches, with Vandenberg declaring "I belong to but one bloc, and it has but one slogan—Stop Roosevelt!" After some confusion when it appeared that Vandenberg would be tapped, Landon picked Knox to be his running mate.

At the end of the month, the Democrats held their convention in Philadelphia. Although Roosevelt met some opposition in the primaries, none of his foes traveled to Philadelphia, and the president was renominated with no opposition. The day before the convention was to open, Al Smith and several other prominent Democrats signed an open telegram that urged convention delegates to nominate a "genuine Democrat," not Roosevelt. The message warned, "If you fail, then patriotic voters of all parties will know unhesitatingly to what standard they must rally in order to preserve the America of the great leaders of the past."

The convention itself had no acrimonious floor debates or even roll call votes. Roosevelt's acceptance speech was stirring, with numerous memorable lines. "Dante tells us," he reminded the cheering throng, "that divine justice weighs the sins of the cold-blooded and the sins of the warm-hearted in different scales. Better the occasional faults of a Government that lives in a spirit of charity than the consistent omissions of a Government frozen in the ice of its own indifference." In words still remembered today, he told his supporters, "This generation of Americans has a rendezvous with destiny."

Three days before the Democratic conventions, Huey Long's coalition made clear that it was still together and still working to deny Roosevelt a second term. In Chicago, Gerald L. K. Smith, a Huey Long crony who took over the Share Our Wealth organization, announced that he and Townsend had established "a loose working agreement" with Coughlin.

Coughlin then went on the radio to deliver an address entitled "Why I Can Support Neither the New Deal nor the Old Deal." Asked afterward about a third party, Coughlin explained that canon law forbade him from forming a third party, but he had been in discussions with a third-party candidate who would get the priest's endorsement.

That same day, William Lemke, an obscure, balding, freckle-faced congressman from North Dakota, announced that he was running for president as a candidate of the newly formed Union party. A former Republican who supported Roosevelt in 1932, he had become disillusioned with the president. In particular, he wanted more done to help farmers whose farms were being foreclosed.

A month later, Cleveland was host to the second Townsend National Convention. Almost 5,000 delegates arrived, more than the number at the Republican and Democratic conventions combined. Townsend spoke first, describing his plan to the already converted, and then sat down to thunderous applause, cheers, and whistles. Next, Gerald L. K. Smith spoke. "We must make our choice in the presence of atheistic Communistic influences!" he roared to the crowd. "It is Tammany or Independence Hall! It is the Russian primer or the Holy Bible!"

The next day, it was Father Couglin's turn. Employing his usual rhetoric about the "great betrayer and liar" who broke his promise to "drive the money changers from the temple," he roared to sustained applause, "I ask you to purge the man who claims to be a Democrat from the Democratic Party, and I mean Franklin Double-Crossing Roosevelt." About "poor Mr. Landon, the creature of three newspaper editors," he simply said, "He doesn't know whether he's coming or going."

The last to speak was the Union party candidate, Congressman Lemke. He knew his audience. He promoted the Townsend plan for the benefit of Dr. Townsend, he cursed the "money-changers" for Coughlin, and for Smith, the successor to Huey Long, the Kingfish, he promised that if president, he would "make every man a king."

Every party platform that year addressed Social Security. Father Coughlin's Union party called for "reasonable and decent security for the aged," in a nod to the Townsend supporters. The Communist party and the Socialist party platforms both called, with varying degrees of specificity, for liberalization of old-age pensions. The Prohibition party platform proudly pointed out that it was the first in the nation to push for old-age benefits and urged their extension to "other disabilities."

The Democratic party platform, in accordance with Roosevelt's request, was organized around the first sentence of the Declaration of Independence: "We hold these truths to be self evident." One of those truths was that government had "certain inescapable obligations," including "[p]rotection of the family and the home." Under this broad obligation came the provision of social security.

The platform reminded the reader, "We have built foundations for the security of those who are faced with the hazards of unemployment and old age." On that foundation, the document continued, should be added "economic security for all our people." Social Security benefits, the platform exhorted, must "keep step with the ever-increasing capacity of America to provide a high standard of living for all its citizens."

Unlike the platforms of the other parties, the Republican platform was cagily drafted. It appeared to support the idea of social insurance. It acknowledged collective responsibility, proclaiming "Society has an obligation to promote the security of the people, by affording some measure of protection against…dependency in old age." At the same time, the platform claimed, "The New Deal policies, while purporting to provide social security, have, in fact, endangered it." It then asserted that the legislation was "unworkable." It criticized Social Security for limiting its coverage to industrial workers and failing to cover agricultural workers, professionals, and domestic workers. It also complained about the "so-called reserve fund," which it claimed "will contain nothing but the Government's promise to pay, while the taxes collected in the guise of premiums will be wasted by the Government in reckless and extravagant political schemes."

In place of Social Security, it proposed an alternative that consisted of four basic principles. First, the program should be "a pay-as-you-go policy, which requires of each generation the support of the aged and the determination of what is just and adequate." Second, everyone over age 65 should be eligible for the benefit, which should "provide a minimum income sufficient to protect him or her from want." Third, the program should be a joint federal- state undertaking. And fourth, the program should be funded by "a direct tax widely distributed."

On a superficial read, the alternative looked progressive. It covered all the elderly and was financed through a more progressive tax. It was immediately praised by newspaper editorials and liberal commentators. *The Nation* editorialized that "it is encouraging to see the G.O.P. coming out emphatically...for old-age...insurance, though it would leave the burden primarily on the states." It went on to gush that the proposal "was in advance of the Democratic Party in insisting that revenues for social insurance should be derived from general taxation."

The expert on social insurance though, and for that matter, the careful reader recognized that, notwithstanding its artful wording, the Republicans were not proposing insurance at all. The word "insurance" was never used in connection with the Republican proposal. It appeared only in the discussion of the Social Security Act, which the platform claimed was "unworkable." Rather, the Republicans were proposing welfare. Eveline M. Burns, who taught economics and social work at Columbia University and had worked on the employment opportunities working group of the Committee on Economic Security, fired off a letter to the editor of *The Nation*. "Careful study of the Republican plank reveals that...it nowhere suggests giving aged people security *as a right*," she pointed out. "Instead," she continued, "there is to be a system of state-operated old-age pensions payable to people *in need*."

And so the general campaign started. Through much effort and many tough battles, the Union party managed to get on the ballot in 34 of the 48 states. By election day, Lemke had campaigned in all but one of those 34 states and had traveled 30,000 miles. Townsend claimed he had 10 million Towsendites who would vote for Lemke. Smith claimed 6 million Share-Our-Wealthers who would do the same. Coughlin, for his part, promoted Lemke's candidacy throughout 1936, going so far as to threaten to cancel his radio program if Lemke did not receive over 9 million votes. Some in the press predicted that Lemke and his running mate, Boston labor lawyer Thomas Charles O'Brien, would affect the outcome of the race.

The first polls after the nominating conventions showed unexpected strength for Landon, which worried the Democrats. The Republicans had a big advantage in that most of the press was conservative and pro-Republican. On the other hand, Roosevelt had the ability, by virtue of his position as president, to make news.

The years 1935 and 1936 saw the worst weather in United States history. The Great Plains was experiencing the most severe drought in recorded history, with 60-mile-per-hour winds that created a swirling dust bowl so intense that people could not see their hands in front of their faces. Then, around Labor Day, 1935, the strongest hurricane in U.S. history struck the Florida Keys. A brutally cold and wet winter in the West was followed by severe flooding, setting record high-water marks, in the mid-Atlantic states and New England, during spring 1936.

Roosevelt traveled in a special train to tour the damaged areas and announce emergency relief. Just before Labor Day, he toured the drought-ravaged midwestern and western states and held a meeting in Des Moines with governors, including, of course, Kansas's governor, Alf Landon. After three days back in the White House, he was traveling again, this time to the South, a long-planned trip to counteract Talmadge and the Dixie Democrats.

As the president's motorcade traveled from Asheville, North Carolina to Charlotte, it began to rain. Secret Service agents started putting up the convertible's top, but Roosevelt, seeing supporters standing along the route, instructed that the top be kept down. Even as the rain became heavy, Roosevelt kept the top down, much to the delight of the crowds. Twice, when Roosevelt traveled through the part of the country hit by drought, the skies had grown dark and it had rained. This time, for the "luckiest politician," as *Time* magazine dubbed him, the rain stopped just as he was about to speak and a dramatic rainbow filled the sky.

Landon, too, was busy traversing the country by special train. For most people, Landon was an unknown commodity at the time of his nomination. Few outside of Kansas had heard of him before he made his run for the presidency. Saying that he did not want to "write the Republican platform in advance," he issued bland and vague policy statements prior to securing the nomination. In a May 7 radio address on Social Security, he said, "I'm for it. Every big industrial nation has had to move in that direction," and added that, while in the past, the nation was able to get by on individual savings and family support, old-age security now required the national government "to take a hand."

The Hearst-run *Washington Herald* clarified Landon's position in a May 28 editorial, stating that Landon believed that Social Security "must be along AMERICAN lines," unlike Roosevelt's program, which will "reduce millions of Americans to the condition of 'STATE PARASITES.'" The editorial further made clear that Landon would never support legislation "based on COLLECTIVIST DELUSIONS or that is plainly UNCONSTITUTIONAL."

Landon's speech accepting the Republican nomination lacked specifics. About Social Security, he said: "We shall amend the Social Security Act to make it workable....But it must be kept in mind that the security of all of us depends on the good management of our common affairs."

But as the election drew closer, Landon made the repeal of Social Security a central theme of his campaign. The new law had three features ripe for exploitation in a political campaign. First, employee and employer taxes were to begin a few months after the election, on January 1. The first monthly benefits, however, were not scheduled to start for six years, until 1942. The lag gave older workers time to achieve insured status, but created a political vulnerability. This feature permitted Landon and the Republican party to focus on the tax and hint that the benefit payments were uncertain, because a future Congress had the power to repeal their payment.

In addition, the Social Security contributions were scheduled to accumulate and be invested in federal Treasury bills. Republicans argued that this arrangement encouraged deficit spending, something they were complaining about more generally. And finally, keeping track of everyone's wage records was a massive endeavor, much larger than any similar project ever undertaken by the government. The necessary record keeping allowed Republicans to conjure images of the United States transformed into an Orwellian world of Big Brother. These complaints were either not voiced at all or mentioned only in passing when the legislation was before Congress, but they played prominently in the months leading up to the election.

As the election drew nearer, Landon's rhetoric grew shrill. On a campaign swing through Wisconsin, in Milwaukee's municipal auditorium, he gave a blunt and hard-hitting major address. In words that sound astonishingly like today's Bush administration, Landon argued:

> The worker's cash comes into the treasury. What is done with it? The law requires the Treasury to buy Government bonds. What happens when the Treasury buys Government bonds? Well, at present, when there is a deficit, the Treasury gives some nice new bonds in exchange for the cash which the Treasury gives the Treasury. Now, what happens to the cash that the Treasury gives the Treasury? The answer is painfully simple. We have good spenders at Washington, as they spend the cash the Treasury gives the Treasury....The workers asked for a pension and all they have received is just another tax.

Landon denounced Social Security as "a fraud on the workingman" and "a cruel hoax." And intimating that Social Security would undermine freedom, he promised that "the Republican party will have nothing to do with any plan that involves prying into the personal records of 26 million people." He concluded that Social Security was "unjust, unworkable, stupidly drafted and wastefully financed."

Attacks on Social Security became stock lines in the stump speeches of Landon and other Republicans. Landon told crowds that he favored a much more modest welfare program over the universal work-based contributory insurance. He questioned whether workers would ever really see any benefits. And he argued that the trust fund was a sham, the Treasury bonds, just worthless pieces of paper, mere IOUs.

The Milwaukee speech was the last straw for Republican John G. Winant, the chairman of the Social Security Board. Distressed by the party platform and the increasingly inflammatory rhetoric of the candidate and his supporters, the former Republican governor of New Hampshire felt he could not keep quiet any longer.

"Utopia John," as Roosevelt liked to call him, understood the value and need for Social Security. He viewed the program as appropriately nonpartisan and asserted in a speech on the first anniversary of the program's enactment, "The Social Security Act, in my judgment, is the most humane document written into law in this century."

A loyal Republican who had supported Coolidge and Hoover, Winant himself was frequently mentioned as a possible Republican candidate for president. He knew that speaking out in the heat of the election was political suicide. Fully aware of the political cost, however, he chose to break ranks with his party over the issue.

Winant was a man of principle and felt he had no choice but to resign and join the election fray. Years later, as Winant was returning home after serving as ambassador to Great Britain during World War II, Churchill said of him, "[H]ow gladly he would give his life to see the good cause triumph. He is a friend of Britain, but he is more than a friend of Britain—he is a friend of justice, freedom and truth." Winant heard the call of justice and truth in the fall of 1936, as well.

Two days after Landon's Milwaukee address, Winant tendered his resignation to Roosevelt so that he would be free to campaign. He felt he could not speak out, even for the purpose of education, while he remained a member of the Social Security Board, and he feared that his silence would be interpreted as quiet support for Landon's position. In his letter of resignation, he explained:

> Having seen...the cruelties of the depression, I have wanted to help...in lessening the hardships, the suffering, and the humiliations forced upon American citizens because of our previous failure as a nation to provide effective social machinery for meeting the problems of dependency....The Social Security Act is America's answer to this great human need....While I retain this position [as chairman of the Social Security Board] I am not free to defend the Act.

Roosevelt responded that the letter of resignation "greatly distresses me." He wrote that he "hesitated to accept" the resignation because he "did not wish to lose the benefit of [Winant's] devoted and disinterested service in the administration of the social security program." The president reluctantly concluded, "It is, therefore, with the deepest regret that I yield to your wish and accept your resignation."

Once his resignation was accepted, Winant began traveling the country, speaking on the radio and delivering speeches in support of Social Security. The attacks by Landon and his allies continued unabated. In a speech in St. Louis, Landon asked, "Imagine the field opened for federal snooping. Are there 26 million going to be fingerprinted? Are their photographs going to be kept on file in a Washington office? Or are they going to have identification tags put around their necks?"

The images of freedom curtailed and dog tags around the neck became the orchestrated attack. Hamilton, now the chairman of the Republican National Committee, held up dog tags as he spoke in Boston and confided that at least Washington was going to make them out of stainless steel so that they would not stain the skin. Knox asserted that Social Security "puts half the working people of America under federal control." Radio ads threatened that workers in the future would only have identification numbers, not names, as far as the government was concerned.

Industrialist Henry Ford issued a statement denouncing Social Security:

> Under some social security systems abroad a man cannot quit his job, or apply for another, or leave town and go to another even to get a better job because that would break the 'economic plan.' Such a restriction of liberty will be almost a necessity in this country too if the present Social Security Act works to its natural conclusion.

Conservative newspapers, particularly the Hearst chain, joined the chorus. The closer the election, the more outrageous the charges. The day before the election, the Hearst papers carried front-page stories, with a bold-type question: "Do You Want A Tag And A Number In The Name Of False Security?" The paper carried a picture of a man, bare from the waist up, with only a dog tag on a chain around his neck. The picture, entitled "Snooping-Tagging," bore the caption: "Each worker would be required to have one for the privilege of suffering a pay cut under the Social Security Act, which is branded as a 'cruel hoax.'"

As Winant responded to the attacks against Social Security, he tried to maintain some semblance of neutrality, carefully speaking for the program, not against Landon. But a week before the election, Landon and the Republicans undertook a tactic that so repulsed the serious, idealistic Winant, he abandoned his lifelong Republican ties and publicly announced his support for Roosevelt.

Days before the election, the Republican National Committee mailed millions of pamphlets, posters, and pay envelope inserts, all attacking Social Security, to employers across the country. The materials, designed to frighten, were extremely misleading. The pamphlets and posters portrayed a supposed judge saying "You're Sentenced TO A WEEKLY PAY REDUCTION *for* ALL YOUR WORKING LIFE. YOU'LL HAVE TO *SERVE THE SENTENCE* UNLESS YOU HELP REVERSE IT NOVEMBER 3." Numerous employers nationwide distributed the pamphlets and displayed the posters on company bulletin boards and on factory walls.

That was bad enough, but worse was coming. On the Friday before the election, workers all over the country opened their pay envelopes and withdrew with their money what looked like an official government notice. It was captioned "Notice—Deductions from Pay Start Jan. 1," and at the bottom of the insert were the words, in big, black letters, "Social Security Board, Washington, D.C." Included with a worker's pay, the notices stated:

> Effective January, 1937, we are compelled by a Roosevelt "New Deal" law to make a 1 per cent deduction from your wages and turn it over to the government. Finally, this may go as high as 4 per cent. You might get this money back...but only if Congress decides to make the appropriation for this purpose. There is NO guarantee. Decide before November 3—election day—whether or not you wish to take these chances.

Reading the notice, a worker was left with the clear impression that Social Security was merely a gimmick to raise taxes, not a contributory retirement program.

Reports started coming into both the Democratic and Republican headquarters about workers tearing Roosevelt campaign buttons from their shirts and throwing them on the ground, stripping Roosevelt bumper stickers off cars, and ripping Roosevelt posters off walls. Republicans got an excited call from a campaign headquarters in Ohio: "The labor vote has stayed unimpressed and adamant until now that the Social Security issue is brought home to them. This state is all agog over payroll reduction." Democratic local offices placed concerned calls with similar reports. Campaign workers in Michigan and Pennsylvania, as well as Labor's Nonpartisan League, all phoned in panicked messages that Roosevelt had better act quickly to counter the dirty trick.

The Social Security Board had already prepared 50 million explanatory pamphlets about Social Security, in anticipation of the assignment of Social Security numbers to every covered worker. The board released the pamphlets immediately, and, with the help of unions, they were distributed at factory gates and elsewhere. In addition, the board had prepared explanatory movies that were released to movie theaters. One film played continuously on Times Square on election day.

Three days before the election, on Saturday, October 31, President Roosevelt addressed a packed crowd at Madison Square Garden and denounced what he called "the current pay-envelope campaign against America's working people." Calling the tactic an act of "desperate men with their backs to the wall," he roared, "It is an old strategy of tyrants to delude their victims into fighting their battles for them."

He pointed out, "Every message in a pay envelope, even if it is the truth, is a command to vote according to the will of the employer. But," he continued, "this propaganda is worse—it is deceit." He then catalogued all the misrepresentations in the Republican materials, everything "[t]hey carefully conceal," ending each point, "That omission is deceit." He concluded the litany of deceits with an observation that, like every other point he made, remains true today: "They do not tell him that the insurance policy that is bought for him is far more favorable to him than any policy that any private insurance company could afford to issue. That omission is deceit."

He ended with a most serious indictment: "But they are guilty of more than deceit. When they imply that the reserves thus created against both these policies will be stolen by some future Congress, diverted to some wholly foreign purpose, they attack the integrity and honor of American

Government itself. Those who suggest that, are already aliens to the spirit of American democracy."

President Roosevelt was reelected on November 3, 1936, by a landslide. He received 61 percent of the popular vote and 90 percent of the Electoral College, carrying every state but Maine and Vermont. Republicans lost 14 seats in the House of Representatives and 8 seats in the Senate. The third-party Lemke-O'Brien ticket, inspired by Huey Long, received fewer than 900,000 votes. As he promised, Father Coughlin gave up the radio, although, as it turned out, only temporarily.

Social Security had been vindicated. But the Supreme Court and the threat it posed to Social Security lay in wait.

## CHAPTER 7

# Ready, Set, Start Again

While Roosevelt, Landon, and all the other candidates standing for election in November 1936 were frenetically crisscrossing the country, spending endless hours in search of votes, Arthur Altmeyer was spending endless hours on Social Security. From the moment of its enactment, he had fewer than 17 months to get up and running what would be, when it opened its doors, the largest insurance program undertaken anywhere in the history of the world.

An unprecedented endeavor, Social Security would affect the daily lives of millions of Americans. The Social Security Board had to be ready to keep track of all the wages of each of the 26 million employees working in covered employment when contributions started rolling in after January 1, 1937. It had to be ready to receive the workers' wage reports from 1.7 million employers.

Although the statute delayed the payment of monthly benefits until January 1, 1942, it provided for the lump-sum refunds of contributions to workers who reached 65 without having worked long enough to qualify for benefits and to the estates of deceased workers. Those benefits started in less than a year and a half, as well. The unemployment compensation part of the program would require enormous cooperation between the federal government and every state. Everything would require meticulous record keeping. And this was 1935—years before the world's very first electronic computer would be constructed.

Forget computers. The board had no desks or filing cabinets. No secretaries. Thanks to Huey Long's filibuster, no money.

The morning after Long's last filibuster, as he headed to New York in search of a publisher, Altmeyer headed to the Oval Office in search of funding. Meeting with Roosevelt and Altmeyer were the congressional leadership and the comptroller general—the head of the General Accounting Office (today, the Government Accountability Office), an independent congressional watchdog that, among other tasks, ensures the proper spending of government funds. The purpose of the meeting was to figure out a way to scrounge up some money for Social Security until Congress returned in January and appropriated funds for it.

The first comptroller general in GAO's history, John R. McCarl, a Republican appointed by President Warren G. Harding, came to Social Security's rescue. Making an analogy to the Committee on Economic Security, which had been established properly as a research project of the Federal Emergency Relief Administration, McCarl pointed out that another research project could be established to study and develop the method of implementing Social Security.

Sitting in his high-backed red leather chair, which Secretary Perkins had donated to the money-strapped Social Security Board, Altmeyer knew that getting the right people in place was crucial. He was determined to be uncompromising in securing those people.

A few staff members of the Committee on Economic Security transferred to the new Social Security Board. Witte went back to Wisconsin, but his assistant, Wilbur Cohen, shifted over to the new organization. Bob Myers made the move as well, although he had to wait for the Social Security Board to receive its regular appropriation in January. In the interim, he accepted a job with the Railroad Retirement Board, created under new legislation enacted after the Supreme Court held the 1934 act unconstitutional. Even as he accepted the job, he knew that his career would be with Social Security.

Except for the few carryover people from CES, everyone would be new hires. In theory, Altmeyer and the board were spared political patronage appointments, because all appointees, other than lawyers and other experts, were to come through the civil service system. In theory. This was, after all, political Washington, a company town, where the company was the federal government and the currency was who you knew.

During those first months, Altmeyer was constantly dodging bullets. With the country still in the midst of the Great Depression, constituents turned to members of Congress for help finding jobs, and here was this brand-new, gigantic agency. The temptation for members of Congress was irresistible. Altmeyer, for his part, was resolute in his determination not to bend to political pressure. The classic irresistible force met the immovable object.

The first volley was fired by the entire Democratic membership of the House Ways and Means Committee. The members commanded Altmeyer to meet with them to discuss personnel. At the meeting, Altmeyer calmly explained that he would be happy to consider anyone whom a member recommended, but, of course, all prospective applicants had to take the civil service exam and go through the standard procedure. Altmeyer then followed up the meeting with one-on-one appointments with each member.

Despite his most diplomatic efforts, Altmeyer nevertheless found himself repeatedly fending off pressure. Ways and Means Committee member Fred M. Vinson, who later became chief justice of the Supreme Court, was particularly persistent in pushing Altmeyer to hire someone Altmeyer believed was completely unqualified. Altmeyer tried gently to convince Vinson of the candidate's incompetence, but to no avail. Finally, one day as the two were walking down a corridor, together with the chairman of the committee, Vinson forcefully asked Altmeyer point blank whether he was going to appoint the person in question or not. Altmeyer, feeling cornered and flustered, blurted, "I will have to act as my conscience dictates."

Hearing this, the tall, husky Vinson turned on the mild-mannered, slender Altmeyer, shoved him against the wall, shook his fist, and screamed, amid a stream of profanities, "I have a conscience too!" Taken aback but unflinching in his determination, Altmeyer did not hire the candidate.

The powerful chairman of the Senate Appropriations Committee, Senator Carter Glass (D-Va.), not to be outdone, aggressively pushed one of his constituents on Altmeyer. Hoping to get off the hook, Altmeyer told Glass that the constituent, a pleasant but unqualified woman, was not an expert and so would have to go through the Civil Service Commission. To Altmeyer's dismay, the commission ducked the decision, saying she actually was an expert, and tossed the problem back to Altmeyer.

With the decision once again back on his desk, Altmeyer declined to hire the woman. Senator Glass, in retaliation, attached a rider to the board's appropriation bill, requiring Senate confirmation of all experts and attorneys above a threshold salary level. It took a year, but the identical provision was dropped from the next appropriation bill at the insistence of the House conferees.

Not long after, the chairman of the Senate Appropriation's subcommittee having jurisdiction over the Social Security Board insisted that he be consulted about the managers of Social Security's field offices located in his state. In particular, he wanted a political protégé appointed. The protégé actually was qualified, but there was another problem. The other senator from the state also wanted to be consulted and he insisted the candidate not be appointed. To make matters worse, the second senator was backed by the governor. And to make matters impossible, James Farley, the chairman of the Democratic National Committee and close adviser to the president, told Altmeyer he wanted to keep the governor and senator happy.

Caught in the crossfire, Altmeyer met with Roosevelt. The president, in his characteristic manner, threw back his head, laughed, and said, "Cheer up! The good Lord in his wisdom may solve your difficulty by calling the old boy to his reward." Though the Lord did not solve Altmeyer's problem, the electorate did. The senator and the governor both lost in the next election.

Much worse and considerably uglier, someone told the members of the Ways and Means Committee that Altmeyer was stacking the agency with Jews. A member of the committee called Altmeyer and berated him for hiring "too damned many New York Jews." Soon after, the chairman of the committee told Altmeyer that he had great respect for "members of your race" but he and his committee colleagues were concerned by the large numbers being hired. Chairman Doughton was shocked, though not embarrassed, when Altmeyer told him that he actually was Christian, not Jewish.

Members complained to the president, as well. Roosevelt asked Altmeyer what the facts were. Altmeyer told him that no statistics were kept, but the number of Jews was actually quite small, much less than 5 percent. When Roosevelt heard the response, he laughed and said that the percentage was smaller than the number of Jews at Harvard. That seemed to end the matter.

Altmeyer was standing up to extremely powerful members who had control over his budget and the program over which he had administrative responsibility. He made it a point, whenever he went against what one of these members wanted, to meet personally with the member and explain exactly why he took the action he took. If the person fit another position and qualified through the civil service system, Altmeyer would offer the applicant that job. He never compromised, but he tried to be responsive. Most of the time, this attitude helped. But even when it did not, Altmeyer always chose the best people. The program was too important to do otherwise.

The job facing the Social Security Board would require the smartest, most capable people around. It was unprecedented. The board estimated that there were about 26 million covered workers, employed by about 1.7 million employers, and every year, about 2.5 million new workers would be added. There were, according to board calculations, hundreds of thousands of workers with the surnames Smith, Jones, Brown, Miller, and dozens of other common family names, all of whose records would have to be kept straight, their wage histories following them through all geographical and job moves.

All these workers would have to be somehow identified in a manner guaranteed not to produce duplications, and each of the more than 26 million workers would have to be contacted. The identifying information would be kept on file at Social Security's headquarters in Baltimore. In this pre-computer age, when all records were paper, a filing system had to be developed so that the files of each one of the 26 million plus workers could be found quickly. Each record would have to be updated with new wage information; earned benefits would have to be calculated when workers retired or the contributions repaid, if workers died.

To develop a centralized system of record keeping, Altmeyer turned to the established insurance companies for help. He was shocked to find that their systems were completely inadequate. John G. Winant sought to hire a top executive of the Equitable Life Insurance Company to assist in the complicated work. The executive agreed to accept the offer, but only if President Roosevelt himself asked. When Roosevelt's assistant, Marvin H. McIntyre, made the call for the president, the offended executive turned down the job.

On the recommendation of several insurance companies, Altmeyer hired Harry Hoff, an expert on office layout and management. Hoff studied the problem intensely for several months, and then, looking very solemn, he came to Altmeyer and requested a meeting with the board. At the meeting, Hoff announced that he had concluded, after careful and sustained analysis, that the job was impossible. He recommended that the board notify Congress that the government could not run the Social Security program, after all.

Altmeyer and the others at the meeting politely but firmly told Hoff to get back to the drawing board. After several more months of work, Hoff developed a system that met the approval of Altmeyer and the other members of the board. It is the numerical system still in place today.

The enormous job of keeping track of workers had led Landon to ask during campaign appearances, "Are there 26 million going to be finger-printed?...Or are they going to have identification tags put around their necks?" Although the board never contemplated the use of dog tags, Landon and his supporters might have gotten the idea because the Addressograph Corporation had made a prototype stainless steel tag on a chain and had pitched its use to the staff. Rejecting that and all the other far-out ideas, the board decided to issue cards.

Identical to those issued today, the cards were designed by an artist from Albany, New York, and bore numbers consisting of three digits, followed by two digits, followed by four digits. This system permitted a billion permutations, enough numbers to take care of the working population for the foreseeable future.

Although the numbers appear random, they are not. It was imperative that no two people inadvertently be assigned the same number. This was tricky because the numbers would be assigned not from one centralized location, as they are today, but from locations around the country.

To solve the problem, each state was subdivided and assigned digits. These numbers are the first set of three numbers, called area numbers. Numbers beginning 001 to 049 are New England's numbers. From there, the numbers flow geographically south and west, with the highest state numbers being 575 to 576, for workers in Hawaii. After Hawaii, the next set of numbers goes to the District of Columbia, then the Virgin Islands, Puerto Rico, Guam, American Samoa, and the Philippines. The first three digits originally represented the location where a worker applied for a card. Now numbers are assigned centrally, so the numbers are based on the address of the applicant.

The next numbers—the middle set of two numbers, called group numbers and the final set of four numbers, called serial numbers—were all about filing. In these days before computers, paper files of each individual worker's wage record had to be stored and then retrieved quickly when needed for updating records or calculating benefits. Consequently, a storage and retrieval system was a driving force and a primary concern in devising the system. In today's computer age, the breakdown of Social Security numbers into a middle set of two numbers and a final set of four numbers is significant only as a reminder of the mind-boggling job facing Social Security in 1936.

Although northernmost parts of Maine are farther north than New Hampshire, the first area numbers, 001 to 003, were assigned to New Hampshire. The thought was that Winant, now returned to the Social Security Board after the campaign, could be given the number 001-01-0001, as an honor. He declined, though, and that number eventually went to Grace D. Owen, a woman in Concord, New Hampshire, who happened to apply early in the morning on the first day possible, but that is the end of the story.

Before Owen could be assigned her number, Social Security needed a distribution system. The board had a numbering system and the 26 million workers were out there. But how to match workers and numbers? Social Security had not yet set up field offices. Without computers, it would be impossible to handle the program centrally. After several false starts, the board decided that the most feasible solution was to use the U.S. postal system with its 45,000 post offices. Letter carriers delivered applications for numbers, helped people fill out the forms, answered questions about the program, returned the forms to typing centers where the cards could be produced, delivered the cards to the workers, and transmitted the applications of workers together with their newly-assigned Social Security numbers to Baltimore. In just three short weeks, the job was largely done.

Altmeyer was concerned initially that the pre-election charges by Republican of regimentation, together with employer hostility to Social Security, would present problems in the number distribution, but using the post office might have helped. In musing about social insurance in 1934, Roosevelt had remarked, "The system ought to be operated through the post offices. Just simple and natural—nothing elaborate or alarming about it." He was speaking, of course, in a different era, when people sat on their porches, knew their letter carriers by name, and received their mail dependably in rain, snow, sleet, and hail.

By June 30, 1937, the index of workers covered over an acre of floor space and contained what had now grown to about 30 million workers' names and numbers. It was so efficient, that, despite its size, a clerk could locate an individual's name and number literally in seconds. J. Douglas Brown, who helped to write the original legislation and served on a number of advisory councils thereafter, was amazed by the efficiency of the operation. Brown reminisced about members of the various advisory councils on which he served playing a game he called "How unique is your name? Let's check with Baltimore," Social Security's headquarters, where all records were kept. Brown remembered, "Reinhard Hohaus [an actuary who served on several of the councils] would always win....My name always lost." Hoff had done a spectacular job in designing the system and he knew it. Once, when he developed kidney stones, he was quick to tell Altmeyer that kidney stones were an ailment suffered by Caesar, Napoleon, and other men of genius, like himself.

By the time Grace D. Owen of Concord, New Hampshire was assigned 001-01-0001 as her Social Security number, the 1936 election was history. The electorate had resoundingly rejected the assault on Social Security. But the Supreme Court was soon to decide whether the new program was constitutional. The National Labor Relations Act, which had been signed into law a month before Social Security, was facing challenges in the courts, as well. And Roosevelt intended to propose a minimum wage and maximum hours bill. On this subject, the Supreme Court had been unwilling to let even the states act, and was likely to be even more restrictive with the federal government.

Recent history did not look promising. Between January 1935 and May 1936—less than a year and a half—the Supreme Court invalidated 11 pieces of federal legislation, including 2 that were integral parts of Roosevelt's New Deal program to restore the country to economic health. This contrasted with the first 140 years of U.S. history, during which the Supreme Court invalidated an average of 1 federal statute every other year. The district courts, taking their direction from the signals sent by the Supreme Court, issued during the same period 1600 injunctions against federal officials seeking to carry out New Deal laws.

On Monday, May 27, 1935, a day New Dealers referred to as Black Monday, the Supreme Court struck down the National Industrial Recovery Act, as well as two other New Deal enactments. The following Friday, at the president's regular twice-weekly press conference, Roosevelt uttered his famous line charging that the country had "been relegated to the horse-and-buggy definition of interstate commerce," giving rise to the Runyon title about Landon, "The Horse and Buggy Governor."

Roosevelt set forth a detailed explanation of the probable reach of the holding that the National Industrial Recovery Act was unconstitutional. The president stated "that the implications of this decision could, if carried to their logical conclusion, strip the Federal Government of a great many other powers." He added, "We thought we were solving [the economic problems facing the nation], and now it has been thrown right straight in our faces." When asked if there was a solution other than a constitutional amendment, the president responded cryptically, "Oh, yes, I think so. But it has got to come in the final analysis."

The issue of the courts and the Constitution did not stop with Black Monday. The Supreme Court held the Agricultural Adjustment Act unconstitutional on January 6, 1936; after the ruling, Senator Hugo Black (D-Ala) charged, "This means that 120 million are ruled by five men." When the Court, on May 18, 1936, ruled unconstitutional the Bituminous Coal Conservation Act regulating coal companies, the *United Mine Workers Journal* bitterly declared, "If we understand correctly the decision...labor has no rights under the Constitution." Republicans were concerned about some of the decisions, as well. In response to a June 1, 1936, ruling striking down a New York minimum wage statute drafted to meet the objections of the Court in the earlier *Adkins* case, the District of Columbia minimum wage law that the Court had invalidated in 1923, Herbert Hoover said, "Something should be done to give back to the states the powers they thought they already had." Nevertheless, for the most part, Republican ire was saved for Roosevelt and the Democrats, not the courts.

At the Republican National Convention in the summer of 1936, Herbert Hoover had roused the crowd by asserting "The American people should thank Almighty God for the Constitution and the Supreme Court." He continued, "Fundamental American liberties are at stake," and asked the cheering delegates, "Is the Republican Party ready for the issue? Are you willing to cast your all upon the issue? Will you, for expediency's sake, also offer will-o'-the-wisps which beguile the people? Or have you determined to enter in a holy crusade for freedom which shall determine the future and the perpetuity of a nation of free men?" The Supreme Court had been the focus of the first plank of the Republican platform, which read: "We pledge ourselves…to resist all attempts to impair the authority of the Supreme Court."

At the Democratic convention later that summer, the keynote speaker, Senator Alben Barkley of Kentucky, responded, "Over against the hosannas of Hoover for the tortured interpretations of the Constitution of this nation, I place the tortured souls and bodies" of American workers and their families. The Democratic platform joined the issue. "The Republican platform proposes to meet many pressing national problems solely" through state action. In contrast, the Democrats "have sought and will continue to seek to meet these problems through legislation within the Constitution. If," however, this will not work, it continued, the Democrats will propose a "clarifying amendment."

Roosevelt's advisers had discussed with him whether to make the Constitution and the Supreme Court a campaign issue in 1936. Roosevelt's attorney general, Homer Cummings, urged him to do so. Jim Farley counseled against it, arguing that "although the lawyers go on about the Supreme Court," the president would never be able to "get sufficient excitement among the people about it." Felix Frankfurter, then a professor at Harvard Law School, disagreed with both, arguing that an amendment was the wrong approach entirely. He believed that the individuals on the Supreme Court and their constitutional interpretation were the problem, not the underlying document itself.

With the election behind him, Roosevelt thought about what his advisers had said. Like Frankfurter, he was not drawn to the lengthy, cumbersome amendment process. Moreover, all of the proposed constitutional amendments, according to his attorney general, were either too narrow or too broad in their reach. He wanted to find a quicker, easier solution that would uphold the New Deal programs without inadvertently creating unforeseen problems that an amendment might.

The question of the Supreme Court was on his mind in January following the election, when the new Seventy-fifth Congress convened. On Senator Arthur Vandenberg's mind was Social Security. Although Landon had lost the election, Vandenberg continued to believe that the Republicans were right about Social Security. He disliked the accumulation of funds and he disliked the insurance approach. In early January, Vandenberg introduced a concurrent resolution calling for changing the law so that funds would not accumulate and so that new groups of people would receive benefits. The Senate Finance Committee scheduled a February 22 hearing on his resolution.

Meanwhile, Roosevelt's thoughts about the Supreme Court were starting to gel into a plan. Article III of the Constitution creates a "supreme Court" and provides that its justices "shall hold their Offices during good Behaviour," but leaves to Congress the job of deciding the actual number of justices. In 1937, the number of justices was nine, but it had not always been so. In fact, the number was initially set at six, then reduced to five, then back to six, then increased to seven, then to nine, then to ten, then reduced back to seven, then restored once again to nine. And the reasons for the changes had been plenty political.

As early as January 1935, Attorney General Cummings had talked to Roosevelt about adding more justices to the Supreme Court to make a liberal majority. Some months later, Roosevelt had mentioned, at a cabinet meeting, what he described as the "distasteful idea" of adding justices as one of several options. Then, a month after that, Cummings had written the president a letter about the idea, and Roosevelt had encouraged him to pursue it.

In the course of his research, Cummings discovered that, in 1913, Supreme Court Justice James C. McReynolds, then President Wilson's attorney general, had argued in his annual report for the Department of Justice that the president should have the ability to appoint additional judges when older judges failed to retire. McReynolds had asserted that some judges "have remained upon the bench long beyond the time when they were capable of adequately discharging their duties." As a solution, McReynolds had continued: "I suggest an act providing when any judge of a Federal court below the Supreme Court fails to avail himself of the privilege of retiring now granted by law, that the President be required, with the advice and consent of the Senate, to appoint another judge, who shall preside over the affairs of the court and have precedence over the older one."

Cummings and Roosevelt saw in the McReynolds proposal the solution to the problem. The Supreme Court then sitting was the oldest in the Court's history. In particular, the so-called Four Horsemen of

Reaction—Willis Van Devanter, James C. McReynolds, George Sutherland, and Pierce Butler—were 78, 75, 75, and 71, respectively. In contrast, two of the three most liberal justices—Louis D. Brandeis, Benjamin Cardozo, and Harlan Fiske Stone—were considerably younger. Only Brandeis was over 70. With respect to the two swing votes on the court, Chief Justice Charles Evans Hughes and Justice Owen Roberts, Hughes was over 70; Roberts was not.

Roosevelt particularly relished the fact that the idea had originated with one of the Four Horsemen—one of the four conservative sitting justices. The president held a gleeful press conference and sent a special message to Congress on February 5, 1937, proposing legislation that would grant new power to the president with respect to the judiciary. Specifically, he sought the power to nominate an additional judge to a federal court whenever there was a sitting judge, having served at least 10 years, who did not retire or resign within six months of turning 70. If enacted, this power would give the president the immediate opportunity to appoint six new Supreme Court justices, which would bring the liberals a majority on the Court whether the conservatives chose to retire or not.

Lacking candor about motive, Roosevelt's message to Congress focused on the heavy workload of the federal courts, the need for "younger blood," and the "delicate subject" of "aged or infirm judges" unable to carry out their responsibilities. The message pointed out that the size of the Supreme Court had been changed legislatively seven times in the past. No mention did he make of seeking to change the outcome of cases.

Immediately following the press conference that was held an hour before the president sent his message to Congress outlining his proposal, the news was out over the ticker tape. Stock prices fell. Newspapers carried banner headlines. The New York Times intoned, "Cleverness and adroitness in dealing with the Supreme Court are not qualities which sober-minded citizens will approve."

The immediate reaction among politicians was mixed. When Representative Maury Maverick (D-Tex.) was handed a copy of the president's message with a copy of the bill stapled to it, he ripped the message off, signed his name to the bill, and dropped it in the hopper. Reporters who took their own informal polls of members agreed that the measure would pass easily.

But some important Democrats signaled unease. Senator George W. Norris (D-Neb.), a strong supporter of the New Deal, said simply, "I doubt the wisdom of the remedy suggested." Senator Henry F. Ashurst (D-Ariz.), chairman of the Senate Judiciary Committee—the Senate committee that would consider the legislation—hesitated, making clear his discomfort, before he was finally persuaded to sponsor the bill. And the House Judiciary Committee chairman Hafton Sumners (D-Tex.) said noncommitally, "We'll take their baby out and look at it." After a decent period of looking at the baby, the conservative Sumners told colleagues, "Boys, this is where I cash in my chips."

Hoover accused the president of seeking "to pack the court." Other Republicans, though, kept relatively quiet, happy to let the Democrats battle each other. A Gallup poll taken about a week after Roosevelt's plan was announced showed the country disapproving but not overwhelmingly. Thirty-eight percent supported the plan, 44.8 percent opposed it, with 17 percent undecided, according to the reported results.

A week later, just as the Senate Finance Committee was getting ready to hold its hearing on Senator Vandenberg's Social Security resolution, poll results were actually slightly more favorable to the president. Opposition had gone up a point, but the percentage favoring Roosevelt's plan went up six percentage points, thanks to some of the undecideds making up their minds. Nevertheless, the press had turned even more negative, and senators spoke against the scheme on the floor of the Senate.

Columnist Dorothy Thompson, wife of author Sinclair Lewis, wrote: "No people ever recognize their Dictator in advance....Since the great American tradition is freedom and democracy you can bet that our dictator, God help us! will be a great democrat through whose leadership alone democracy can be realized." She concluded that people will not "call him 'Fuhrer' or 'Duce.' But they will greet him with one great big, universal, democratic, sheeplike blat or 'O.K., Chief! Fix it like you wanna, Chief! Oh Kaaay!'" Representative Samuel Pettengill (D-Ind.) stated his opposition simply: "A packed jury, a packed Court and a stacked deck of cards are on the same moral plane. . . . It is more power than a good man should want or a bad man should have."

On the other hand, organized labor, fearing an adverse ruling on the National Labor Relations Act, supported the president. The argument before the Supreme Court over the constitutionality of the labor legislation was held on February 10, 1937. Hearings on the president's plan were set for March.

Meanwhile, on February 22, the Senate Finance Committee held a hearing on Vandenberg's resolution calling for revision of the Social Security Act. Altmeyer was called to testify. Vandenberg expressed his opposition to having reserves build up in Social Security. In terms identical to the debate today, Altmeyer explained that if Social Security was not the holder of Treasury bonds, the bonds presumably would be held by private investors. Vandenberg was unpersuaded.

At the conclusion of the hearing, Altmeyer approached Vandenberg and spoke to him privately. Altmeyer suggested that if Vandenberg were concerned that the Social Security reserves would encourage Congress to engage in deficit spending in the rest of the government, the Senator could propose that some of the fund assets be invested in private securities. Vandenberg reacted in feigned horror, "That would be socialism." Instead, Vandenberg asked Altmeyer if he would object to the appointment of a congressional commission to study the question. Altmeyer countered that the Congress suggest people, and the Social Security Board set up its own advisory committee.

They compromised that the Finance Committee would set up a Special Committee on Social Security, consisting of three members, Chairman Harrison, Senator Harry Flood Byrd (D-Va), and Vandenberg. The Special Committee, together with the Social Security Board, would appoint an advisory council, which would report jointly to the board and the Finance Committee.

By now, the court-packing scheme was starting to reach its climax. On March 9, the president addressed the nation about the issue in one of his famous and familiar fireside chats. He spoke of "the need to meet the unanswered challenge of one-third of a Nation ill-nourished, ill-clad and ill-housed." He painted a picture of the federal government "as a three-horse team.... Two of the horses are pulling in unison today; the third is not." And he reassured listeners, "You who know me will accept my solemn assurance that in a world in which democracy is under attack, I seek to make American democracy succeed."

His chat helped. A Gallup poll right before his address showed opposition to the plan close to 50 percent and support at under 42 percent. After the radio talk, opposition had fallen back to 44 percent and, for the first time since the proposal was announced, support for the plan was higher than the opposition, at almost 46 percent.

The chairman of the House Judiciary Committee, Hafton Sumners—the Texan who had looked at the baby and cashed in his chips—opposed the president's proposal and had it bottled up and not moving. That meant that the administration would have to start in the Senate, instead.

On March 22, the Senate Judiciary Committee began its hearings on Roosevelt's judicial reorganization proposal. The hearings were lively. Supporters of the president included a long list of noted legal scholars. The star witness for the opposition was Chief Justice Hughes.

The sitting chief justice did not appear in person, of course. Senator Burton K. Wheeler (D-Mont) had written to him, posing specific questions. Wheeler read Hughes's response out loud for the record. The chief justice restricted his remarks to the narrow question of efficiency—the ostensible reason Roosevelt gave for proposing his plan. The letter made the points that the Court was up-to-date with its docket and a Supreme Court of 16 justices would be unwieldy.

In keeping with the best of Hollywood, Hughes provided a blockbuster surprise ending. The Chief Justice wrote, "On account of the shortness of time I have not been able to consult with the members of the Court generally...I have been able to consult with Mr. Justice Van Devanter and Mr. Justice Brandeis, and I am at liberty to say that the statement is approved by them." Here was Justice Brandeis, one of the liberal members of the Court, a reliable vote to uphold New Deal enactments, giving aid and comfort to those opposed to the president.

The Supreme Court offered another surprising twist on March 29. The Court does not disclose in advance whether opinions will be announced on any given day. Court-watchers know what opinions are left towards the end of the term, but, for the most part, they must just come and see what unfolds. Nevertheless, those watching suspected something was up. Senator Wagner, author of the National Labor Relations Act, was seated in the dignified marble-friezed room in the brand-new Supreme Court building. Three high-ranking Justice Department lawyers were sitting in the front row.

Electricity ran through the crowd as the chief justice read the summary of the decision in *West Coast Hotel Co. v. Parrish*, ending with the words "Our conclusion is that the case of *Adkins v. Children's Hospital*, supra, should be, and it is, overruled. The judgment of the Supreme Court of the state of Washington is affirmed." Elsie Parrish, a chambermaid working for the Cascadian Hotel of Wenatchee, Washington, was entitled to her $14.50 for her 48-hour workweek, as promised by Washington state's minimum wage law, rather than the mere $12 her employer had been paying her.

The Washington state minimum wage law was almost identical to the New York minimum wage law that the Court had held unconstitutional less than 10 months before. The Court had struck down the New York law by a vote of 5 to 4, but now the nearly identical Washington law was upheld by the same vote count. The only vote that changed was that of Justice Owen J. Roberts.

But the Court was not done. It had another surprise for the country two weeks later. On April 12, the Court was back in session, prepared to hand down more opinions. Again, the courtroom was packed. People had stood in line since daybreak to get a coveted seat. The chief justice's wife, apparently tipped off by her husband, sat in the front row of the family section, off to the side. And then the chief justice silently nodded to the justice in the farthest seat to the right. Justice Roberts picked up papers and began, "In this case we are to decide whether the National Labor Relations Act…" "The silent intake of spectators' breaths," according to Time magazine, "all but caused a vacuum in the courtroom." The Court held that the act was within the legislative power of Congress.

Supreme Court deliberations are kept secret, so no one can know for certain what caused the Court's seemingly abrupt reversal—dubbed by pundits "the switch in time that saved the Nine." Most people assumed the switch was in direct response to Roosevelt's attempt to pack the Court.

After retiring from the bench, Roberts wrote a memorandum on the matter, that was published posthumously in 1955. As it turned out, the Court voted to uphold Washington's minimum wage law on December 19, well before the president proposed his legislation to "pack" the Court. (Roberts' reversal—the deciding vote—surprised the other justices, causing one to remark, "What is the matter with Roberts?") The Court delayed announcement of the opinion because Justice Stone, one of the liberal justices, was very ill. On February 6, five days after Stone's return to work on February 1, the Court took a pro forma second vote making official, though still undisclosed, the secret the Court had been holding since December. Whether a principled decision on the merits or the pressure exerted by a determined president just reelected in a landslide, the outcome was the same: The constitutional crisis had been averted.

Whatever the motivation behind the switch, the Supreme Court was not done with its gifts for the president. On May 18, Justice Van Devanter, a member of the conservative bloc, announced that he would be retiring at the end of the term. Roosevelt would be able to strengthen the liberal bloc for the start of the new term. That summer the president nominated, and five days later the Senate confirmed, Senator Hugo Black to fill the vacancy.

For most of the country, the constitutional crisis seemed to be resolved with Roberts's switched vote. "Why shoot the bridegroom after a shotgun wedding?" was the general sentiment. But Altmeyer and the other supporters of Social Security were not ready to celebrate. The Social Security Act of 1935 was still the subject of lawsuits. On April 14, two days after the Court's stunning opinion upholding the National Labor Relations Act, the U.S. Court of Appeals for the First Circuit held Social Security to be unconstitutional. In extraordinarily fast action, the Supreme Court granted a writ of certiorari, agreeing to hear the case, on April 26. The Court held arguments just nine days later, on May 5.

On May 24, one week before the June 1 end of the term, the Supreme Court was back in session, ready to hand down more opinions. Altmeyer and Winant, together with Frank Bane, the Social Security Board's executive director; R. Gordon Wagenet, the Unemployment Compensation director; Murray Latimer, the chairman of the Railroad Retirement Board; as well as Tom Eliot, now general counsel for the Social Security Board; and 23-year-old Wilbur Cohen, sat in the courtroom waiting anxiously. Also in attendance were Senate majority leader Robinson, a handful of other senators, and several lawyers from the Justice Department.

The suspense did not last long. As soon as the distinguished liberal Justice Benjamin N. Cardozo began to deliver the Court's opinion, every person in the room knew the outcome. A half century later, Cohen recalled "as if it were yesterday," leaving the courtroom and walking down the marble steps across from the Capitol building "in an euphoric glow."

Although Altmeyer and the other Social Security officials were relieved by the Court's decision, their day-to-day work was unchanged. By that time, more than 30 million Social Security numbers had been issued;

around $150 million in taxes had been collected; about a dozen benefit claims had been paid; and approximately 150 local field offices had been opened around the country.

In addition to assembling a nonpartisan, highly qualified staff, Altmeyer set clear lines of authority and a well-defined mission for the organization. He emphasized that Social Security was there to serve the public. With respect to the joint federal-state unemployment insurance program, the federal government was to be considered a partner to the states, not the police, simply enforcing federal rules.

When claimants began to come in for benefits, they were applying for payments they had earned with their labor, Altmeyer stressed. Social Security employees were to help them get the benefit, even helping them to fill out forms. Social Security representatives, Altmeyer explained, were there to inform beneficiaries of the program what their rights were, not to impose obstacles.

A federal statute had long been on the books that prohibited federal officials from assisting people who were making claims against the government. Citing the statute, the GAO at first objected to the policy being set by Altmeyer, but after a lengthy meeting, the GAO withdrew its objection.

To back up the broad policy being set, Altmeyer established an extensive training program. Employees were required to go through rigorous instruction upon being hired. All employees—those in the headquarters in Baltimore and those out in the field, those in positions dealing with the public and those who were not—were to be trained. In addition to special training for particular positions, Altmeyer wanted every employee, whether professional or clerical, higher paid or lower, to understand the law, its history, the conditions that gave rise to it, the philosophy underlying it, and the goal of service. In the days before computers, data was stored on punch cards. Social Security employed many people to carry out the tedious job of punching workers' data on the cards. To emphasize the importance of every job, Altmeyer was fond of saying, in an unartful, though well-meaning way, those punch-card operators were not punching cards; they were punching people.

By this time, the Finance Committee and the Social Security Board had jointly named the advisory council for which Vandenberg had pushed. It consisted of 25 members, an equal number of business and labor representatives and almost twice as many members representing the general public. Several of the names were familiar from 1934. Ed Witte, the cautious executive director with whom Armstrong had battled three years before, was named as a representative of the public. So was Professor J. Douglas Brown—Witte's second pick, after Latimer, for working group chair, who worked so well with Armstrong. Other familiar names from 1934 were three business representatives: Marion Folsom of Eastman Kodak, M. Albert Linton of the Provident Mutual Life Insurance Company, and Gerard Swope, president of General Electric.

The Democratic members of the Ways and Means Committee were furious when they found out about the advisory council and when they learned it was the handiwork of Vandenberg. Congress was controlled by the Democrats. Vandenberg had run for president in 1936 and was likely to try again in 1940. Why was he getting this political advantage? Although Vandenberg had voted for final passage of the Social Security Act in 1935, he had sided with most of the other Republican Senators in the vote immediately preceding its passage, a losing effort, to strike the old-age insurance provisions—a much more telling indicator of his view. Why was he getting to call the shots? Why had Altmeyer gone along with an obviously partisan ploy?

The Democratic members ordered Altmeyer to come to Capitol Hill and defend his action. Though Altmeyer tried to explain that he felt he had no choice, since an advisory council was used in 1934 and was widely considered a mark of good government—the proverbial mom and apple pie that everyone is for—the Democrats remained unmollified.

Altmeyer was caught in a squeeze play. The Democratic House members wanted no council. Vandenberg was pushing Altmeyer aggressively to schedule a meeting. To make matters worse, the Republicans were already seeking to capitalize on the council, before it had even met. Hamilton, Landon's campaign manager and now the chairman of the Republican National Committee, was making speeches in which he bragged that the Republicans in Congress had "forced the Democratic Social Security Board to start action to adopt the Republican proposal" to get rid of the "needless 47 billion dollar reserve."

The Republican National Committee had begun slipping material to friendly columnists. As they had done in the prior campaign, the Republicans were, through the columnists, charging that the tax was taking money from the poor to feed a wasteful government. To add heat to the already bubbling political cauldron, organized labor was beginning to grumble publicly about the taxes on wages.

Not knowing what to do, Altmeyer took no steps to convene the council but instead met with Harrison, the chairman of the Senate Finance Committee, to seek guidance. After several discussions, the two men decided that Altmeyer should proceed with the council but should consult the president first.

But Roosevelt was busy with other matters. While Altmeyer was trying to sort out the conflicting pressures, Roosevelt was feeling pressure of his own. Although the Supreme Court was no longer knocking down his legislation, his court-packing scheme was still pending in Congress. Trying to save face, Roosevelt agreed to a compromise that would permit him to name just two additional justices, a compromise the Democratic leadership in Congress had been pushing him to accept for weeks. The compromise would have worked in April. But now opposition had solidified. There were no guarantees the leadership could prevent an embarrassing defeat for the president.

On June 14, the Senate Judiciary Committee filed its report on the president's plan. "We recommend the rejection of this bill as a needless, futile and utterly dangerous abandonment of Constitutional principle," it read, adding that the measure should be "emphatically rejected" by the full Senate. On July 2, Majority Leader Robinson called up Roosevelt's original Court reorganization plan and immediately moved to substitute the compromise. Anticipating a long debate and perhaps a filibuster, the House took a two-week recess.

For the first three days of the Senate debate, supporters of the president held the floor. Unable to present their case, the opponents continually interrupted Robinson and the others with sharp questions. Robinson got so flustered, he actually reached in his pocket, pulled out a cigar, and lit a match, before he realized where he was. Throwing down the match, he relinquished the floor and hurried into the Democratic cloakroom.

The arguments rose to a fever pitch. Farley, the postmaster general and Roosevelt's close political adviser, thought he was speaking off the record when he told reporters that senators better support the president if they wanted patronage from him. He made the mistake of mentioning two senators by name. When a reporter printed the remark, the two senators, who had been quiet on the bill, now felt compelled to speak up. One of them, who was sick in bed, announced that he was disobeying his doctor's orders to speak and began, "I think this cause is worthy of any man's life."

The words turned out to be prophetic. Robinson played hardball, enforcing little-known rules and getting favorable rulings from the presiding officer. He seemed on the verge of prevailing for the president. In the middle of the debate, as he was being challenged for his aggressive tactics, he felt chest pains and went home. During the night, he got out of bed to check some point in a bound edition of the *Congressional Record*. The next day, July 14, he was found on the floor dead, with his reading glasses and the *Congressional Record* on the floor beside him.

A week after Robinson's fatal heart attack, the Senate sent the Court reorganization bill back to committee by a vote of 70 to 20. The committee stripped the bill of everything controversial and returned it to the floor, where it quickly passed the Senate and the House. Roosevelt signed it into law on August 26.

In September, the court-packing battle done, Altmeyer met with Roosevelt about the advisory council. Roosevelt listened and thought. He had, the year before, been in a bruising presidential campaign where Social Security had been a dominant issue. A major political vulnerability was the long lag time between the start of taxes and the start of monthly benefits.

Tax collections had begun in January. An increase in the rate was scheduled for January 1, 1940, 10 months *before* the next presidential election. Monthly benefits were not to begin for another two years after that, in 1942, *following* the next election. Not good politics, as any politician could see.

If the law was unchanged, he or whoever else ran for president could be open to the same political charge that the program was merely a gimmick to raise taxes; a future Congress could always, if it so chose, repeal the benefits. Moving the benefits up so they started before the election made obvious political sense. Moreover, Roosevelt, from the beginning, had desired more comprehensive social insurance. He also favored making the program universal, by covering the rest of the working population.

Perhaps Vandenberg and the Republicans had handed the Democrats an opportunity. Vandenberg was concerned with the buildup of the reserve, but if the reserve was to be eliminated, only two options were possible. Congress could reduce the income to the program. That would mean cutting the already low taxes that workers were already paying. The Republicans were not pushing for this option. The other alternative was to increase the outgo by increasing and expanding benefits.

Roosevelt told Altmeyer to assemble the advisory group. The group should report before the new Congress convened in January 1939, about 15 months away, so that amendments could be enacted and benefits could begin by January 1, 1940, well before the next presidential election. In addition to considering questions of the reserve and financing, Altmeyer and Roosevelt agreed, the council should also be asked to make recommendations concerning extending the program to include benefits for spouses, survivors, and disabled workers. The council should also examine the issue of extending coverage to agricultural workers, domestic employees, and the self-employed.

Roosevelt instructed Altmeyer to pull together an unpublicized group—essentially the Committee on Economic Security, except with Altmeyer in place of Cummings, now that the Supreme Court had upheld the constitutionality of Social Security. Its job would be to prepare for any administrative difficulties in anticipation of these changes.

The advisory council held its initial meeting toward the end of 1937, on November 5 and 6. Nominated by Swope, Doug Brown became chairman of the council. It met every few months, with a smaller executive group, chaired by Brown, working together between meetings.

The council's members represented a wide range of views. On the left, Harvard professor Alvin Hansen, a Keynsian economist, focused on Social Security's effect on the economy. On the right was M. Albert Linton, who had advised Landon during the campaign and now provided advice to Vandenberg.

The council issued interim reports on coverage and financing. Its final report was published on December 10, 1938. As was to happen many times in the future, conservatives and liberals on the council came to the same conclusions for completely different reasons. Hansen, concerned that the economy was still in a depression, wanted to reduce taxes and increase benefits to stimulate the economy. Linton was opposed to the buildup of a reserve, because he believed it led to deficit spending by the government. Both men for their own set of reasons, and everyone with views in between, agreed that it made sense to increase benefits for those near retirement, balanced by reductions in the ultimate levels when the program reached maturity.

Consistent with this desired outcome, the council proposed changing the benefit formula, so that it would not be based on total wages over a lifetime of work but rather average wages over a lifetime. The council also proposed permitting a few years of low or no earnings to be eliminated for purposes of calculating the average. This led to a number of important improvements. First, older workers close to retirement would be eligible for higher benefits, since high wages averaged over a few years would produce higher benefits than the sum of those wages. Also, workers who had years of work mixed with years out of the workforce would receive higher benefits than under the 1935 law. The council also agreed to advance two years the start of the payment of monthly benefits from the politically unappealing January 1, 1942, to the much more politically friendly January 1, 1940.

The council proposed that benefits be expanded to include monthly payments for dependent family members in addition to benefits for the workers themselves. Wives reaching age 65 should receive an amount equal to half that earned by their husbands, unless they themselves had earned, through their own work, a benefit larger than the 50 percent amount. A widow and her dependent children each, the council recommended, should receive benefits equal to 50 percent of the primary amount earned by the deceased husband. For elderly widows, the percentage proposed was 75 percent. (Today the percentage for surviving elderly spouses is 100 percent of the worker's earned benefit; children and the parent caring for them, such as the 9/11 families each receive a benefit equal to 75 percent of the worker's, benefit, up to a family maximum, and today all benefit rules are gender-neutral.) The council unanimously agreed with the importance of adding disability benefits, but it split over whether these benefits should be added immediately or studied further.

To pay for part of the cost of these expansions, the council recommended that the size of the individual worker's benefit be reduced over the long run and that the relatively expensive refund of contributions upon the death of a worker be eliminated in favor of a more modest death benefit. The council also proposed that coverage of Social Security be extended to farm workers, domestic workers, and employees of nonprofit organizations. Coverage should also, it recommended, be extended to self-employed and all governmental employees, after the administrative and legal issues were studied and resolved.

The council discussed in detail the financing and reserve issue. Because of concern about the Supreme Court, the drafters in 1935 had provided that Social Security's income was to be paid to the general fund of Treasury, and benefits were to be paid from an earmarked account that was funded from an annual appropriation from general revenues. The council recommended establishing a trust fund to hold both the contributions and reserve. With the constitutionality of the act now established, no barrier existed to a trust fund, which would be the holder of Social Security's assets and through which income and outgo would flow.

Instead of the partial reserve contemplated in 1935, the council recommended converting Social Security to greater reliance on pay-as-you-go, with only a contingency reserve. It recommended that the costs of the program should eventually include contributions from general revenue, although no specific recommendations were made concerning when this should happen, how it should be legislated, or how large the contribution should be.

In an attempt to put to rest claims that the Treasury bonds in which the Social Security funds were invested were somehow not real and in some way represented a misuse of funds, the appendix to the advisory council report contained a strongly worded statement:

> The special securities issued to the old-age reserve account are general obligations of the United States Government, which differ from other securities of the Government only in the higher rate of interest they bear and in the fact that they are not sold in the open market....
>
> The United States Treasury uses the moneys realized from the issuance of these special securities by the old-age reserve account in the same manner as it does moneys realized from the sale of other Government securities....The members of the Council, regardless of differing views on other aspects of the financing of old-age insurance, are of the opinion that the present provisions regarding the investment of the moneys in the old-age reserve account do not involve any misuse of these moneys or endanger the safety of these funds.

The advisory council concluded its work and signed its report on Saturday, December 10, 1938. The following Monday, the Social Security Board announced that the council had completed its work, and its report would be transmitted to the Senate Finance Committee on December 15.

Immediately, after the council completed its work that Saturday, Brown called a press conference to explain the council's recommendations. As is typical, because the press conference occurred before the report had been transmitted to the Finance Committee, the report was embargoed until the official release date of December 15, and the front of each copy of the report was stamped with the date, December 15, when journalists could begin to write stories quoting from the report.

The press conference was well attended, with between 100 and 150 reporters covering the event. Brown went over every recommendation, repeatedly stressing several broad themes, including the importance of protecting families. "Every ten minutes I'd say, 'We must protect the family unit,'" he recalled years later. He then returned to Princeton. To his surprise, he received an angry phone call from an editor whom he had worked with at the *New York Times*. The editor informed Brown, "You told us this release date was [December 15]. The *Tribune* already has it. It's on the street." Vandenberg had leaked a preliminary copy of the report to the Republican *Herald-Tribune*, and the paper had scooped its rivals. Notwithstanding any bad feelings about the breach of the embargo date by the *Tribune*, numerous newspapers throughout the country ran favorable editorials about the council's recommendations.

On December 30, 1938, the Social Security Board transmitted the council's recommendations to the president, with only minor modifications, together with some of its own unrelated proposals. On January 16, 1939, Roosevelt sent the administration's legislative recommendations, based on the council's report, to Congress.

The Townsend movement, though not as powerful as it had been in 1935, remained a powerful force nonetheless. Almost 9 percent of Americans over age 65 were paid members of a Townsend club. Moreover, the Townsendites employed a strategy of endorsing political candidates who expressed support for the Townsend plan. In 1938, 147 Townsend-backed House candidates won election. These included many Republicans who opposed social spending generally, but not where the elderly were concerned. Moreover, 3 of the 147 were members of the House Ways and Means Committee.

To make the politics even more intricate, Vandenberg was considering another run for president. No one knew whether Roosevelt would be a candidate in 1940. A third term was without precedent. Many, including

Vandenberg himself, said publicly that they did not think Roosevelt should run again.

On February 1, the House Ways and Means Committee began hearings on both the administration's recommendations and other bills concerning old-age security. Altmeyer was the lead witness and was called back to respond to testimony by proponents of the Townsend plan. Though a number of Republican members used the hearings as a platform to criticize the scheduled buildup of reserve fund assets, the questioning was generally friendly. The major difficulty for Altmeyer was acoustical.

The committee hearing room had terrible acoustics and no microphones. Exacerbating the problem, Chairman Doughton was hard of hearing. All through Altmeyer's lengthy testimony, which ran over 13 separate sessions, the chairman kept interrupting to say "Speak up, young man, speak up!" even though Altmeyer was shouting at the top of his lungs.

The Ways and Means Committee generally accepted the administration's proposal, though it chose not to expand coverage. In an election-savvy move, the committee added the politically desirable change of eliminating the payroll tax increase scheduled for January 1, 1940, an election year. It did retain the other scheduled increases contained in the 1935 act.

Prior to reporting the bill to the floor, the committee reported out the Townsend proposal without recommendation. The House debated the Townsend bill for four hours. On June 1, the House rejected it by a vote of 302 to 97. The next day, the administration's bill was reported out. The Republicans on the committee supported the bill, but added a minority report taking credit for eliminating "the staggering and illusory" reserve. The minority report also criticized the elimination of the return of contributions on death, although it clarified, "We do not wish to be understood as opposing the liberalization of the present old age insurance provisions."

Debate on the floor began on June 6 and lasted four days. Representative Robert W. Kean (R-N.J.), concerned about Social Security reserves being used for current expenses, proposed that the assets be invested in one-year marketable Treasury bonds, rather than nonmarketable longer-term ones. The amendment lost on a voice vote. On June 10, the Social Security Amendments of 1939 passed the House of Representatives by a vote of 364 to 2. The Senate Finance Committee began its hearings two days later. The bill passed the Senate on July 13 and was signed into law on August 11.

The Social Security Amendments of 1939 made extremely significant improvements. At the same time, they retained the basic structure and principles established in 1935. The program remained compulsory social insurance, with the goal, though not yet the reality, of universality. Benefits were earned by working in covered employment. Workers were eligible as a matter of right, as a consequence of work, not as a matter of need.

Benefits remained progressive through the use of a weighted benefit formula, similar to what was done in 1935. Now though, benefits were based on average wages, not cumulative wages, which in the early years resulted in larger benefits for those close to retirement. Today, that same benefit structure provides larger amounts for workers, mainly women, who have years outside of paid employment and years of part-time work.

Social Security remained self-financing. With the constitutionality of the program no longer in doubt, Congress established a trust fund that would hold Social Security's assets and through which income and outgo would flow. The creation of a trust fund was a significant legal step. Trusts are one of the oldest creations of English law, much older than corporations. For the last 1,000 years, the formation of a trust has established a legal relationship where one person or group of people, the trustees, have legal control over property held in trust for the benefit of other people, the beneficiaries. A trust's purpose is to ensure that assets are used prudently and exclusively in the best interest of trust beneficiaries. The creation of the Social Security trust was a meaningful, as well as symbolic, decision by the government to hold and protect assets contributed to Social Security in accordance with well-established principles of trust law.

Another change Congress made was to enact the Federal Insurance Contributions Act. This enactment removed the wage contribution and payroll tax from the Social Security Act and instead placed them in the Internal Revenue Code. Although most Americans tend to refer to the payments by the act's acronym, FICA, it is good to pause and reflect on the name of the statute chosen in that era before spin doctors: the Federal Insurance Contributions Act.

Perhaps the most important contribution of the 1939 amendments was to extend Social Security's protection to families. The benefits for dependent widows, spouses, and children added in 1939 have never been well publicized, as important as they are. These were the benefits that the victims of the 9/11 terrorist attack qualified for through their work. It was with respect to these benefits that the Social Security Administration worked so tirelessly in the immediate aftermath of the attack, so that the victims' families could begin to receive them less than a month later, in October 2001. They are also received by the families of the fallen American soldiers in Iraq and Afghanistan.

About a month after the Social Security Amendments of 1939 became law, Vandenberg—the senator who had set the whole amendment package in motion by his insistence on an advisory council—announced that he was once again running for president. On October 2, 1939, he was featured on the cover of *Time* magazine. The story praised him for "exposing the 'dangers' of the Social Security's so-called…reserve fund of the future."

About five weeks before the amendments were enacted, the Social Security Board, as part of a government reorganization plan, was brought within a newly created agency, the Federal Security Agency, later to be renamed the Department of Health, Education and Welfare. By that time, over 300 field offices were established.

As part of the hiring for the new field offices, the Social Security Board had sent a letter to a man who had done well on a civil service exam two years before, upon graduating Phi Beta Kappa with honors from Wesleyan University with bachelor's and master's degrees. He was offered a job as field assistant in the Newark, New Jersey, field office of Social Security. On January 1, 1939, Robert M. Ball reported to work. His first assignment was to travel to Washington, D.C. in order to participate in the six-week training program Altmeyer had established. Upon his graduation from the training program, on February 18, 1939, as a member of the fifty-seventh class to be trained, Ball returned to New Jersey to begin his work as a GS-3, with a salary of $1620—the lowest-level job at the lowest pay given an employee with a college degree.

The 1939 amendments, with their extension to families and their changes to the benefit formula, have often been called Social Security's second start. Five months after Congress enacted those amendments, on January 31, 1940, the first monthly benefit check, numbered 00-000-001, was paid to Ida May Fuller of Vermont. In that first year, over 222,000 people—including almost 55,000 children—received Social Security benefits. What was destined to become America's most successful domestic program had begun.

CHAPTER 8

# Dr. Win-the-War
# Replaces
# Old Dr. New Deal

It was a bracing December Sunday in Washington, D.C. The Redskins were playing their final game of the season at home in Griffiths Stadium against division rival Philadelphia, before a crowd of 27,102 fans. Among the season ticket holders in the stands were two regulars, Bob Myers and his wife, Rudy.

Eight minutes into the game, the public address announcer interrupted his play-by-play commentary to broadcast, "Admiral W. H. P. Bland is asked to report to his office at once." This was not unusual; in high-powered Washington, people were always being paged in those days before cell phones.

A few minutes later, another request: "The Resident Commissioner of the Philippines, M. Joaquim Eilzaldo, is urged to report to his office immediately." Again, the crowd did not stir; the fans were preoccupied watching quarterback Sammy Baugh, deep in Eagles territory, marching the home team toward what would be the first of three touchdowns that afternoon.

Soon, though, the interruptions became too numerous to ignore. "Joseph Umglumph of the Federal Bureau of Investigation is requested to report to the FBI office at once." "Capt. R. X. Fenn of the United States Army is asked to report to his offices at once." "Mr. J. Edgar Hoover is asked to

137

report to his office." The announcements continued through the game with increasing frequency and urgency.

It appeared that every cabinet officer, military officer, diplomat, and other high-ranking official in Washington was in Griffiths Stadium and was being instructed to head for his office immediately. Bob and Rudy Myers knew something was up but could not guess what it might be. It was only when they returned home and turned on their radio did they learn that Japan had bombed Pearl Harbor. The date was Sunday, December 7, 1941.

As on September 11, 2001, the events of that day turned the nation in a dramatically new direction. The decade prior to Pearl Harbor was a time of concern about worker security and a period of legislative action to address those concerns. In the four years immediately preceding the start of World War II, President Roosevelt had signed into law the National Labor Relations Act, the Social Security Act, the Fair Labor Standards Act, and the 1939 amendments to the Social Security Act. With the bombing of Pearl Harbor, the focus of the country shifted instantly.

From December 7 onward, the prosecution of World War II dominated every other concern. Signaling the switch, President Roosevelt remarked, at his very first press conference following the attack, that "old Dr. New Deal" would now have to be replaced by "Dr. Win-the-War."

"We are determined to pay whatever price we must to preserve our way of life," the president proclaimed on January 5. Spelling out the details, he proposed an enormous jump in the budget, almost tripling from fiscal year 1941 to fiscal year 1942, then more than doubling again in fiscal year 1943. More than 90 percent of it was to be spent on the war effort. The amount was much greater than the total value of all stock on the New York Stock Exchange, more than half the nation's income, equal to all the products produced by all American factories just a few years before, in 1939. The proposed level of spending reverberated around the world. As *Time* magazine described it, "In Britain there was a wave of elation. In the Axis countries there was a stunned silence—and then an uneasy denial that the program (its staggering figures were not revealed to the people) could be carried out."

To pay for the massive new spending, Roosevelt asked for increased taxes, as every citizen's shared responsibility in helping to win the war. "When so many Americans are contributing all their energies and even their lives to the Nation's great task," he said, " I am confident that all Americans will be proud to contribute their utmost in taxes."

The president was concerned that his tax program be fair, in addition to simply raising revenue. "Tax programs too often follow the line of least resistance," Roosevelt cautioned, explaining that he sought "a well-balanced program which takes account of revenue requirements, equity, and economic necessities."

Calling progressive taxes "the backbone of the federal tax system," Roosevelt proposed increasing income tax rates, as well as reducing the size of personal exemptions and deductions for dependents. He also proposed imposing a new "Victory Tax" of 5 percent on incomes over $624. A weekly wage of just $12 for 52 weeks generated an income of $624. The minimum hourly wage in 1942 was $0.30, or $12 for a 40-hour week.

These proposed changes were groundbreaking. For most of the nation's history, there was no income tax at all. The first income tax was not enacted until 1861. Created to pay for the Civil War, it lasted only 11 years, until 1872. With the advent of industrialization and the great disparity of wealth in the country—a few able to amass enormous fortunes while large numbers lived in abject poverty—many thought it only fair to impose the tax burden more heavily on wealthy tycoons than on impoverished workers.

In 1894, Congress enacted a progressive income tax, but the Supreme Court now found the tax to be unconstitutional, even though the Court had earlier upheld the Civil War tax. In 1909, as support for a progressive income tax grew, proponents in Congress again pushed for one. Conservatives, fearing that they would lose outright, countered with a constitutional amendment granting Congress the power to impose an income tax. The tactic worked. Instead of enacting a tax, Congress passed the proposed amendment overwhelmingly, but the amendment still needed the approval of two-thirds of the states to become law. Sponsors had hoped that the cumbersome amendment process would slow down a federal income tax, perhaps forever. After all, other than the Bill of Rights, the Constitution had been amended only five times before, and the last three amendments had been the Reconstruction Amendments, ratified shortly after the end of the Civil War. The states of the Confederacy had been required to ratify those amendments as a condition of their reentry into the Union.

To the shock and dismay of the conservative sponsors, the constitutional amendment flew through the state legislatures and became part of the Constitution on February 25, 1913. Congress immediately passed a progressive income tax, the Revenue Act of 1913. But the new measure was limited in scope, imposing a tax on less than 1 percent of the population, and those who paid the tax paid only 1 percent of net income.

Franklin Roosevelt was the first president to make serious use of the income tax in peacetime. He started relying on it soon after he took office. To help finance the New Deal, Congress enacted the Revenue Act of 1935. Popularly known as the Wealth Tax, the enactment taxed the wealthy at high rates, including a rate of 75 percent on incomes over $5 million.

Even with the Revenue Act of 1935, only 5 percent of Americans were required to pay income tax. But that 5 percent was not happy. They didn't like the tax and they didn't like the New Deal programs the tax was financing. Some of the wealthiest businessmen in America, according to a *Time* magazine retrospective on the twentieth century, spent the Roosevelt years "in their clubs denouncing 'that man in the White House,' 'that traitor to his class.'" They also spent time looking for ways to avoid the Wealth Tax.

A Roosevelt friend confided to the president that he had heard a New York financier boast, "My fortune is in the Bahama Islands, and is going to stay there as long as that bastard is in the White House." On another occasion, Roosevelt spent an afternoon sailing on the Vanderbilt yacht. Roosevelt's host and friend, Cornelius Vanderbilt, offhandedly remarked that several of his acquaintances were incorporating their yachts to reduce taxation.

In 1937, President Roosevelt requested congressional hearings on a variety of tax-avoidance devices. In response to the efforts to avoid taxation, Congress enacted the Revenue Act of 1938. This addressed some problems, but not all.

What the President was now proposing would dramatically expand the size and reach of the income tax. Roosevelt was acutely aware of his proposal's impact. In addition to taxing lower-income Americans, he wanted to make sure the wealthy paid their fair share. The president pointed out in his January 5, 1942, Budget Message, "The higher the tax rates the more urgent it becomes to close the loopholes." As part of his 1942 tax package to finance the war, Roosevelt sought to close a number of the same loopholes in the tax system he had pursued unsuccessfully in 1937.

Members of Congress were understandably cautious in response to the president's call for a new Revenue Act of 1942. Roosevelt was asking for taxes on top of taxes. In anticipation of what appeared to be the coming war, Congress had enacted two tax increases, one in 1940 and one in 1941. The Revenue Act of 1941, in particular, had itself been a substantial tax increase. Together, the two already-enacted tax measures were projected to cause taxes to triple from 1940 to 1943. On top of these scheduled tax increases, the president was now proposing to have taxes go up another 50 percent.

No one knew what public reaction to all of these new taxes would be. The chairmen of the two congressional tax-writing committees—the members who would have to do the heavy lifting for the president—spoke openly of the need to proceed carefully and not overreach. Chairman Doughton of the Ways and Means Committee remarked, "As Senator George [chairman of the Senate Finance Committee] has so aptly said, we can confiscate only once, but we can tax perpetually, provided we preserve free enterprise."

The big increases in the legislation of 1940 and 1941 were just starting to take effect. The two chairmen wanted to see how Americans reacted when they paid their taxes in 1942, before they enacted the even larger tax increases the president sought.

To help get people used to the idea of paying taxes, Treasury Secretary Morgenthau had Walt Disney prepare a cartoon, called "The New Spirit," featuring Donald Duck. In the eight-minute cartoon, released weeks after the president's message to Congress, Donald listens to a radio intoning "Your country needs you!" With American flags in place of his pupils, Donald asks, "How can I help?" When the radio responds, "By paying your income tax," Donald starts to sputter indignantly. But the radio quickly adds, "Taxes to beat the Axis!" At that, Donald figures out his taxes, writes a check for the $13 he owes, and hand-carries it all the way to Washington.

The cartoon was probably unnecessary. People seemed eager to pay the new tax. "Even hard-boiled Collectors of Internal Revenue, who are not easily fazed, were fazed on 'T' (for Tax) Day," Time magazine reported. "Thousands of little wage-earners, filing their first returns under the new tax law's dwarf-high exemptions...owed no tax at all. Hundreds of them paid up just the same. They sent in checks ranging form $5 to $100— unsolicited gifts to the Government, to help win the war."

At the start of hearings on the president's 1942 proposal for taxes, Secretary Morgenthau testified before the Ways and Means Committee in a packed hearing room with camera bulbs flashing. In defending what would be the largest revenue-raiser in American history, he made clear, "The new taxes will be severe, and their impact will be felt in every American home." But he reminded the members, "War is never cheap; but…it is a million times cheaper to win than to lose."

Congress recognized the need for the new revenue, though specific proposals met some resistance. In the Senate, Vandenberg expressed reservations about the proposed increases in corporate tax rates. An amendment was offered by another member to reduce the excise tax proposed on champagne and sparkling wine. In opposition, Senator Robert M. La Follette, Jr., pointed out that "the Senate apparently is in a mood to tax the bread off the tables of the poor." Finally, on October 21, 1942— a day that U.S. marines were suffering heavy casualties in fierce fighting on Guadalcanal, two weeks before the Allied landing in North Africa— President Roosevelt signed into law the Revenue Act of 1942.

The federal income tax, which theretofore had been imposed only on the wealthiest 5 percent of the population, was now to reach millions of working men and women. Two tax professors said that the income tax had "changed its morning coat for overalls," adding that taxpayers had "spread from the country club…down to the railroad tracks and then over to the other side of the tracks." More precisely, in 1939, 4 million Americans paid federal income tax. By 1945, the number had grown tenfold to 42.7 million.

Two of the president's proposals had dealt specifically with retirement income. First, he had proposed modifying the rules surrounding the taxation of private pensions to prevent a plan from becoming "a tax-avoidance mechanism." With the enactment of the Revenue Act of 1913, the federal government had to determine the appropriate taxation of private pension plans. The tax treatment developed incrementally as issues had arisen from time to time. In making determinations, the government had been forced to choose whether to favor pension arrangements when compared to current cash wages or penalize them. Neutrality was impossible without extraordinarily complicated rules and administration.

By the 1920s, the basic tax treatment of private pensions had been worked out. The government had chosen favorable treatment. Employers were permitted to deduct contributions to pension trusts at the time the contributions were made. The pension trusts into which the contributions were paid were accorded tax-exempt status. Employees did not have to take the payments into income at the time the contributions were made to the trust funds but only at payout, when the employees actually received the benefits.

The tax treatment of these plans was inconsequential in the early days, because so few plans existed and because so few taxpayers were subject to federal income tax. However, with the enactment of the Wealth Tax in 1935, enterprising insurance agents discovered the favorable tax treatment and began to market pension plans aggressively. The National Underwriter Company published two weekly newsletters that provided those in the insurance and financial services with up-to-date tax and business information. On April 23, 1937, the newsletter contained a piece entitled "Pension Trusts are Termed Richest Field Yet Untapped."

Roosevelt did not propose changing the tax treatment of pension plans, because that would have resulted in penalizing the arrangements. Rather, the administration advocated limiting the advantageous tax treatment to those pension arrangements that qualified. Qualification should be contingent, the administration proposed, on satisfying several requirements, which included covering a reasonable portion of low and moderate-income workers, restricting the size of benefits going to higher income employees, and easing plan provisions that worked to prevent employees from collecting on the promised benefit.

The members of the Ways and Means Committee received, according to the chairman, "volumes of communications, letters and telegrams" opposing the proposed pension changes. Walter Forster, the author of the Clark amendment in 1935, was back prowling the halls of Congress. He contended that the pension provisions "were obviously conceived to further certain undisclosed social objectives." He and others argued that the proposed changes would cause many plans to terminate.

In the final bill that emerged from Congress, several of the pension proposals had been dropped. Others were enacted in watered-down form. The tax treatment accorded pension plans in the early years of the federal income tax together with the restrictions put in place as part of the Revenue Act of 1942, form the structure of the tax treatment of private pension plans today.

Despite the restrictions, private pension plans flourished. The cost of living, which had gone up 15 percent since 1939, was projected to increase at least 23 percent more in 1942 alone. In response to the raging inflation, President Roosevelt imposed controls on prices and wages. The wage controls exempted private pension contributions and other forms of deferred compensation. Fringe benefits were one way that companies could compete for workers in the labor market made tight by the demands of the war. The combination of wage controls, high corporate tax rates, high individual income taxes, the excess profits tax and the tight labor market propelled employers to create and expand private pension plans. In 1940, employer contributions to private pension plans were $180 million. By 1945, the money contributed annually had risen to $830 million.

The second retirement income provision in the president's proposal concerned Social Security. In addition to all the other proposals to raise revenue for the war effort, Roosevelt called for expanding the Social Security payroll tax. But he added, "I oppose the use of pay-roll taxes as a measure of war finance unless the worker is given his full money's worth in increased social security."

Roosevelt noted, "From the inception of the social security program in 1935 it has been planned to increase the number of persons covered and to provide protection against hazards not initially included." Consistent with these long-standing goals, he said, "I recommend an increase in the coverage of old-age and survivors' insurance, addition of permanent and temporary disability payments and hospitalization payments beyond the present benefit programs, and liberalization and expansion of unemployment compensation in a uniform national system."

And he showed how this made sense in the current climate. "By expanding the program now, we advance the organic development of our social security system and at the same time contribute to the anti-inflationary program." He explained that the addition of new benefits would bring more monies in the short term, because many workers would be paying in but relatively few would be collecting. The president explained, "Additional employer and employee contributions will cover increased disbursements over a long period of time....The present accumulation of these contributions would absorb excess purchasing power. Investment of the additional reserves in bonds of the United States Government would assist in financing the war."

The proposal was consistent with the advice of Altmeyer, who had been recommending the expansion of Social Security regularly, well before Pearl Harbor. The 1938 advisory council had recommended these same program improvements, in addition to its other suggestions that were enacted. Most recently, in Roosevelt's 1941 State of the Union Address, the president had called for expansion of the coverage of Social Security.

Meanwhile, Dr. Townsend and his supporters continued to agitate for more generous pensions for the elderly. In June 1941, the Senate had formed a special Senate Select Committee to Investigate the Old-Age Pension System. Its charge was to examine the current programs of old-age support and to develop a plan for a minimum pension for all the aged. A number of vocal Towsendites were members of the select committee, including the chairman, Sheridan Downey (D-Calif) and Senator Claude Pepper (D-Fla.).

On August 28, 1941, the committee had reported out a plan that provided for a flat pension for everyone with a Social Security–type, wage-related plan on top. The committee included a minority report advocating expansion of Social Security.

On October 11, 1941, Altmeyer had given the president a draft message on Social Security, as Roosevelt had requested. Because of the pressure of world events and other matters, the president did not act on the draft until after the bombing of Pearl Harbor, when he included its substance in his message to Congress requesting increased taxes to support the war effort.

Despite the president's request, Congress did not consider improvements to Social Security. Much more surprising, not only did Congress not increase the payroll tax, as the president had requested, it delayed the already-scheduled increase, which was to take effect on January 1, 1943. Here was a ready source of income to the government that did not even require a vote. The increase was in the law as a result of the 1935 legislation.

Nevertheless, Senator Vandenberg offered an amendment in the Senate to postpone for one year the scheduled increase in the payroll tax. In response, Roosevelt sent a letter, drafted by Arthur Altmeyer, to the chairman of the Senate Finance Committee and the House Ways and Means Committee objecting to the delay on the dual grounds that the funding was necessary to ensure the long-term self-sufficiency of the program and that the revenue would help to finance the war effort. Despite the letter, the postponement was enacted. At the same time, Vandenberg, who had sought the postponement, agreed to an amendment that authorized general revenues to be used in the event that Social Security lacked sufficient income to pay promised benefits.

Even without the 1943 increase in payroll tax rates, the trust funds continued to grow. As a result of the war, the economy was booming and retirements were delayed. For the remainder of the war years, Congress repeatedly postponed the scheduled payroll tax increase. The increase scheduled for January 1, 1944, was first postponed until March 1 and then until January 1, 1945. The delay until January 1, 1945, was included in the Revenue Act of 1943, which Congress enacted over the president's veto. Roosevelt objected to the bill, which he charged was a tax relief bill "not for the needy but for the greedy." On December 16, 1944, the Social Security payroll tax scheduled for the upcoming January 1 was postponed once again, this time until January 1, 1946.

In just over a two-year period then, between the fall of 1942 and the end of 1944, Congress postponed the payroll tax increase four times. During those same years, no Social Security benefit increases or changes in coverage were enacted. As a result, Social Security grew very slowly. The numbers qualifying for benefits were small and the benefit levels did not keep pace either with inflation or with increases in wage growth.

In his Budget Message of January 3, 1945, Roosevelt again urged Congress to expand Social Security. In his State of the Union Message three days later, the president declared, "An expanded social security program, and adequate health and education programs, must play essential roles in a program designed to support individual productivity and mass purchasing power." He promised, "I shall communicate further with the Congress on these subjects at a later date." On March 26, 1945, the House of Representatives authorized the Ways and Means Committee to spend $50,000 on a study analyzing the need to expand Social Security.

Thursday, April 12, 1945, started out like every other day for most Americans at home and most soldiers in the field. Then in the late afternoon, the news started to spread. People were stunned, speechless, teary, unbelieving. At 3:35 in the afternoon, Central War Time, Franklin Delano Roosevelt breathed his last breath.

The news circled the globe. Winston Churchill paled and sat motionless for five minutes. Generalissimo Chiang Kai-shek left his breakfast untouched and retired to meditate. General Charles de Gaulle drove to the U.S. embassy in Paris and signed the register of bereavement. Even enemy Japan offered its sympathies and expressed respect for Roosevelt's leadership And ordinary people everywhere grieved.

Vice President Harry S. Truman was presiding over the Senate on the afternoon of April 12. As a senator droned on about a water treaty with Mexico, the vice president passed the time writing notes to his wife and daughter. At 4:56 P.M. Eastern War Time, Truman gaveled the session to a close and headed to the office of Speaker of the House Sam Rayburn, with whom he wanted to discuss some pending legislation. When Truman arrived, the Speaker told him that the White House had called and wanted him to go there immediately.

When he entered the White House, Eleanor Roosevelt, dressed in black, told him simply, "Harry, the President is dead." Shocked, Truman was speechless for a moment, then regained his composure and asked, "Is there anything I can do?" Mrs. Roosevelt responded, "Is there anything we can do for you? For you are the one in trouble now."

The war in Europe ended not quite one month later, on May 8, 1945. Three months after that, on August 15, 1945, at noon Japan Standard Time, Emperor Hirohito announced on radio that Japan had surrendered.

On September 6, Truman sent a message to Congress concerning various steps necessary to convert from a wartime economy to a peacetime one. He recommended a specific liberalization of unemployment insurance and promised, "I expect to communicate with the Congress on [extending, expanding, and improving our entire Social Security program] at a later date."

In November 1945, President Truman sent a message to Congress, outlining a national health insurance program, although he was careful to point out that his proposal was not "socialized medicine." Senators Wagner and James Murray (D-Mont.), as well as Congressman John Dingell (D-Mich.), immediately introduced bills embodying the president's proposals. Nevertheless, the only action Congress took in 1945 with respect to Social Security was to postpone yet again the tax increase, scheduled to take effect on January 1, 1946, for one year, to January 1, 1947.

In 1946, Congress held hearings on Social Security improvements, which included consideration of the addition of national health insurance, but the only significant action was to postpone, for the sixth time in the decade, the scheduled Social Security tax increase, this time until January 1, 1948. As part of a reorganization plan, the Social Security Board was renamed the Social Security Administration, and the three-person board was replaced by a single commissioner. Truman named Arthur Altmeyer to that position.

Then, in November 1946, Congress switched to Republican control for the first time since Herbert Hoover was president. Altmeyer, Cohen, Ball, and other Democratic supporters of Social Security held their breaths. What would a Republican-controlled Congress do with Social Security?

CHAPTER 9

# Third Time's the Charm

Those who preferred means-tested welfare to Social Security were winning the war without firing a shot. Preoccupied with World War II and concerned about tax levels, Congress had taken no steps to keep Social Security's benefits up to date with wage growth and inflation. Moreover, as with any pension program in the beginning, relatively few of the elderly had qualified for benefits.

Members of Congress who wanted to help the elderly thought about welfare, not Social Security. More than twice as many senior citizens received means-tested welfare payments as received Social Security in the late 1940s. Social Security covered only about 60 percent of the workforce and, in existence for just about a decade, was still in its infancy. Most elderly either had not worked in covered employment or had worked for too short a time to qualify for benefits.

Because of Social Security's exclusion of agricultural workers, the disparity between the numbers of welfare recipients and Social Security beneficiaries was even more pronounced in rural states. In Oklahoma, 57.5 percent of the elderly received welfare in 1947; only 5 percent received Social Security. North Carolina, South Carolina, Mississippi, Tennessee, Alabama, and Georgia all had about four times as many elderly receiving welfare as drew Social Security checks.

Moreover, the average size of welfare payments was substantially greater than the average Social Security benefits. While welfare payments had doubled in the 1940s, average Social Security benefits had increased only about 10 percent. Even that 10 percent increase—far less than the increase in inflation or wages over the same period—was simply the result of more people qualifying for higher benefits due to wage growth, not a consequence of any affirmative action by the government. Consequently, in 1949, welfare payments averaged $42; Social Security benefits averaged just $25. The disparity in coverage and benefit levels between the two programs caused a Texas congressman to remark, "Old age and survivors insurance means practically nothing to us."

As it had been in 1935 and 1939, Social Security was once again at a crossroads. There were those who believed Social Security did not go far enough and should be revamped, along the lines of the Townsend plan, into a universal program providing generous, flat benefits unrelated to wages. Although the Townsend movement was no longer as strong as it had been in the 1930s, it continued to be a presence, with over 134,000 paid members in 1947. And the movement remained a political factor in elections. In the late 1940s, two-thirds to three-fourths of Townsend-endorsed candidates won.

At the other extreme were those who preferred a targeted, means-tested welfare program to a program of social insurance. In the middle, Arthur Altmeyer and the Truman administration believed that the 1935 and 1939 acts were extremely good first steps, but more was needed. Eventually Social Security should be universal in its coverage, its benefits should be more adequate, and it should cover the costs of health care and the loss of wages due to disability.

By 1947, the economy had made a smooth transition to peacetime. The nation was experiencing virtually full employment. All economic indicators were strong. In a decade, the output of goods and services had risen by two-thirds; incomes were up by 50 percent; and the gross national product had increased 10 percent in the last year alone. Inflation was down, and the recession that some had predicted was nowhere in sight. Millions of veterans were taking advantage of educational benefits and loan guarantees available under the G.I. Bill of Rights, an enactment that was to transform a generation.

Nevertheless, in his 1947 State of the Union Address, President Truman chose to emphasize an ambitious agenda rather than to focus on the economic strength of the country. He advocated an increase in the minimum wage and civil rights for all citizens. With respect to the rest of the world, he urged passage of what would become known as the Marshall Plan—

characterized by some as the most unselfish act by a victor toward a loser in all of history—and sought the opening of America's borders to people displaced by the Nazis. He endorsed keeping the nation strong through universal military service. And he spoke of expanding Social Security and enacting national health insurance.

Despite Truman's call for expansion of Social Security, the program seemed to be headed backwards. Senator Vandenberg, now president pro tem of the Senate, was once again pushing for yet another postponement of the scheduled Social Security tax increase. This time, the administration decided to work with Congress, rather than simply oppose the postponement as it had done unsuccessfully the prior half dozen times. The administration agreed to support a two-year postponement of the scheduled increase of the payroll tax, until 1950, in exchange for Vandenberg's support of an advisory council appointed by and responsible to the Senate Finance Committee. The council, in the pattern of those before it, would consist of representatives of business, labor, and the public, and would be assigned the task of studying the entire program.

The 1938 advisory council had played a positive role in facilitating program improvements.. Consequently, Altmeyer thought it might be effective in the current situation, as well. Moreover, Senator Eugene Millikin (R-Colo.), the Republican chairman of the Senate Finance Committee, was a supporter of Social Security. He wanted neither a Townsend-type program nor means-tested welfare, but rather the continuation of the mainstream, conservatively operated program of social insurance already serving the country.

On July 23, 1947, the Senate passed Senate Resolution 141, which directed the Finance Committee "to make a full and complete investigation of old-age and survivors insurance and all other aspects of the existing social security program, particularly in respect to coverage, benefits, and taxes related thereto." On August 6, Congress froze the payroll tax rate until 1950 with future increases scheduled for 1950 and 1952. On September 28, the Senate Finance Committee appointed 17 people to serve on the advisory council.

The council members were selected by Senator Millikin in consultation with Senator Walter F. George (D-Ga. ), the ranking minority member, and Senator Vandenberg. The 17 members invited to serve on the advisory council were, as a group, knowledgeable about Social Security, constructive in their approach, and well respected in their chosen fields. A number were familiar names from the short history of the program. J. Douglas Brown, now the dean of the faculty of Princeton University, was appointed as a representative of the public. He had been one of the three key people, together with Barbara Armstrong and Murray Latimer, to develop Social Security in 1934, and had chaired the 1938 advisory council.

Marion Folsom, the treasurer of Eastman Kodak Company, who had been a member of the 1934 and the 1938 advisory councils, was appointed as a representative of business. Eastman Kodak had developed among the first profit-sharing, stock bonus, pension, unemployment, and sick benefit programs for its workers. Moreover, Folsom had chaired working groups on Social Security for the National Association of Manufacturers and the Chamber of Commerce.

Another business representative was M. Albert Linton, the president of the Provident Mutual Life Insurance Company. Well-known and respected in the insurance community, he also had participated in the prior two advisory councils. He had advised, among others, Landon and Vandenberg on Social Security matters.

Soon after their appointments, on October 17, the three men met in New York, together with a fourth member, Sumner H. Slichter, an extremely distinguished economics professor at Harvard University. Slichter's economics textbook was used in virtually every college and university introductory course on the subject. He supplemented his professor's salary with work as a consultant to some of the major corporations in the nation. Strong-minded and unpredictable, Slichter had been named associate chairman of the council.

The four talked about the forthcoming work of the council and the need for a well-qualified staff director. Senator Millikin, concerned that the advisory council be independent of Truman, wanted to select an executive director who did not work at the Social Security Administration, in order to reduce the influence of the president and his appointees. Doug Brown proposed Bob Ball.

Ball had started his career in Social Security at a New Jersey field office, and then had transferred to a position in the central office of the Social Security Administration in Baltimore. The year before the Senate had established the advisory council, Karl de Schweinitz, an expert in public welfare, had decided to start an organization, the University-Government Center on Social Security, which would teach college professors and state and federal officials about Social Security, in order to increase public knowledge of the program. Schweinitz had asked Ball to join him. Although Ball's career at Social Security was advancing rapidly, he decided to trade the security of government for the risk and opportunity of the new venture.

In his new position, Ball had worked with Brown and had impressed him. At Brown's suggestion during the course of the informal meeting in New York, the four men decided to recommend Ball as the executive director of the advisory council, and Ball was subsequently offered the position. He took a leave of absence from the University-Government Center and began his new work.

The council quickly agreed that Folsom, Linton, Brown, and Slichter, together with two labor representatives, Nelson Cruikshank of the AFL and Emil Rieve of the Congress of Industrial Organizations (CIO), would form a steering committee. The council met once a month; the steering committee met two weeks prior to the meetings, in order to go over the agenda for the meetings.

Senator Millikin had named as chairman of the advisory council Edward R. Stettinius, who had become prominent as the president of the U.S. Steel Corporation and as secretary of state, where he had presided over the very first meeting of the United Nations. At the time of his appointment to the council, Stettinius an extremely wealthy entrepreneurial capitalist, spent most of his time promoting various investments, including mahogany forests in Africa. A handsome man with a thick shock of prematurely white hair and bushy eyebrows, which he blackened with a pencil to accentuate the striking appearance of his white hair, Stettinius was an extrovert with the personality of a salesman.

He had little interest in the work of the council and was only too happy to let Slichter, the associate chairman, act as chairman in fact, though not in name, in overseeing the work and ensuring the smooth functioning of the council. On the rare occasions that Stettinius did attend meetings of the council, he would sit next to Ball and whisper about whatever happened to be on his mind, such as a new ballpoint pen he was contemplating promoting. (Ballpoint pens had only recently begun to be marketed in the United States. In October, 1945, Gimbels Department Store, which had placed a full page ad in the *New York Times* the day before, had 5000 people at its entrance when it opened its doors on the first day the pens went on sale. In one day, it sold out of its complete stock of 10,000 pens, priced at $12.50 each.)

Every so often, Stettinius would look up, interrupt the council member who happened to be speaking and comment, "That is very interesting," after which he would go back to muttering under his breath to Ball. On a few occasions, Ball and Slichter met with Stettinius and his wife at the luxurious suite at the Mayflower Hotel, where they stayed when in Washington. Ball had never seen such opulence and later remarked about Stettinius, "I was impressed, not with his brain, but with his money."

The structure of advisory council meetings preceded by steering committee meetings where the agenda was set proved to be extremely successful. Ball provided careful and skillful staffing, as he and the rest of the small staff broke the huge task into manageable pieces. Before every meeting, Ball would prepare an issue paper, which provided background information, highlighted key points, elaborated the pros and cons, and offered a staff recommendation. The members of the council recognized how well Ball's working papers facilitated their deliberations. The one time Ball varied from the approach, providing a paper with no staff recommendation, Professor Slichter, the brilliant, independent-minded intellectual, objected, calling the approach taken in the staff material "highly irregular."

The council easily agreed that Social Security should be expanded to include most of the groups not then covered, though they recognized that the administrative problems would be complex and numerous. The major uncovered groups were agricultural workers, farmers, self-employed, professional groups, and workers employed in homes. Each group presented its own particular problems. Self-employed individuals, for example, did not have clear-cut wages that could be ascertained for purposes of insuring against loss. Domestic employees and agricultural workers presented tricky reporting problems.

Despite all the problems, the council became convinced that not only should universality of the program continue to be the goal but also that the Social Security Administration could handle the administrative difficulties associated with coverage of these new groups. Ball and the rest of the staff worked long hours to try to develop workable solutions to all the practical problems.

Much more of a sticking point among the members was how large benefits should be and how quickly workers should qualify for them. The division broke down along business and labor lines, with public representatives generally siding with the otherwise outnumbered labor representatives. A major point of contention was how high to set the maximum taxable wage base, the level dividing covered wages, on which taxes were imposed and benefits calculated, from uncovered wages. The level had never been changed from the original 1935 level of $3000. In 1937, when taxes were first collected, 92 percent of all earnings fell within the $3000 level. Only 3 percent of all workers made in excess of $3000. In the intervening decade, Social Security had come to cover an increasingly smaller percentage of total wages earned in covered employment and of workers who had no wages above the taxable base. Now only 85 percent of all earnings were below the maximum taxable wage base; almost 30 percent of covered workers had wages above the Social Security wage base.

Linton, in particular, was concerned about Social Security crowding out private insurance and objected to raising the wage base above the statutory level of $3000. This was one of the rare points where the commission did not reach unanimity. The labor representatives wanted the maximum taxable wage base raised to $4800. The majority of the members compromised on a maximum taxable wage base of $4200.

In addition to the issue of the wage base, commission members fought about the overall level of benefits. Labor was concerned about the inadequacy of current benefits and wanted those benefits increased. Business, on the other hand, was reluctant to increase current benefits because of how large benefits would be down the road. As part of the 1939 amendments, Congress had modified the benefit formula to include a 1 percent increase in benefits for every year of work in employment covered by the program. In that way, as Social Security matured and workers gained more and more years of covered work, benefit levels were to rise gradually, reaching their ultimate level in around 40 years or so, when workers were able to have a complete career under the program. The business representatives, looking down the road, did not want high benefits today, because built on top of them would be the gradually rising benefits. An intuitive master of *Getting to Yes*, long before the book was a bestseller, Ball broke the impasse by recognizing that if the ultimate level of benefits were made effective today, both sides would get what they wanted. He saw that the road to compromise lay in dropping the 1 percent increment. When Altmeyer first heard about the idea, he expressed some reservation. However, the reworked formula broke the logjam and attracted the support of the full council. Altmeyer over time came to see the wisdom in the change.

Following Ball's recommendation, the council decided to issue four separate reports, combining them into one comprehensive package only at the end. Consistent with Ball's and the council's assessment that modification of the old-age and survivors' program was the highest priority, the first report, issued on April 8, 1948, dealt exclusively with that program. It recommended 22 specific modifications to the program, 20 of them by unanimous vote. The recommendations dealt with coverage of the program, eligibility for benefits, size of benefits, and financing of the changes.

In introducing the recommendations, the report highlighted the strengths of the program and the reasons for its expansion: "The Council has studied the existing system of old-age and survivors insurance and unanimously approves its basic principles." It recapped the goals of the program: "Since the interest of the whole Nation is involved, the people, using the Government as the agency for their cooperation, should make sure that all members of the community have at least a basic measure of protection against the major hazards of old age and death."

The report then described how the protection should be designed: "A properly designed social security system will reinforce the drive of the individual toward greater production and greater efficiency, and will make for an environment conducive to the maximum of economic progress." It described why a needs test would be a mistake and why social insurance was superior:

> The Council favors as the foundation of the social security system the method of contributory social insurance with benefits related to prior earnings and awarded without a needs test. Differential benefits based on a work record are a reward for productive effort...while the knowledge that benefits will be paid—irrespective of whether the individual is in need—supports and stimulates his drive to add his personal savings to the basic security he has acquired through the insurance system.

The council expressed concern that "only about three out of every five jobs are covered by the program," that "only about 20 percent of those aged 65 or over are either insured or receiving benefits under the program," and that the level of benefits was "inadequate."

It recommended extending coverage to most of the then uncovered groups—farm workers; household workers; the self-employed; federal, state, and local workers; and those working for nonprofit organizations. It advocated easing the requirements for insured status to allow older workers to qualify for benefits. And it suggested raising the maximum taxable wage base, which both expanded revenue to the system and increased the size of the benefits for higher paid workers. It also proposed increasing the level of benefits paid both to workers and dependents, while keeping the program in actuarial balance.

A month later, the council released its second report, dealing with disability insurance. Here again, the majority supported the recommendations, but Folsom and Linton, concerned about the administrability and cost, objected to an insurance program for the disabled, preferring instead a means-tested program for that population. A few months later, the council published its report on public assistance, then on unemployment insurance.

As the advisory council was calmly and quietly deliberating, the election of 1948 was heating up. Truman found himself hemmed in on the left and the right. Henry Wallace had been Roosevelt's vice president during his third term, but Wallace's pro-Communist statements caused Roosevelt to drop him from the ticket and replace him with Truman in 1940. In 1947, many liberal Democrats were telling Wallace that he was the rightful heir of the New Deal and that Truman's policies toward Communist Russia were too bellicose. Many on the left objected, for example, to Truman's request for what appeared to be an open-ended commitment of aid to Greece and Turkey, in order to prevent the spread of Communism. On December 29, 1947, Wallace declared that he would run for president as a third-party candidate.

Meanwhile, many white southerners were unhappy with Truman for his stance on civil rights. Bluntly demanding that "[o]ur Bill of Rights [be] implemented in fact," Truman had established in 1946 the President's Committee on Civil Rights to recommend how to bring that result about. The committee's report, issued in October 1947, was sweeping. Strom Thurmond, the Democratic governor of South Carolina, joined with other southern governors in denouncing it.

Notwithstanding the opposition of southern leaders of the party, on January 7, 1948, in his State of the Union Address, President Truman proclaimed his intention to propose a comprehensive civil rights package. On February 2, he appeared before a joint session of Congress and called for strengthening civil rights laws, enacting legislation providing federal protection against lynching, protecting the right to vote, and establishing a commission to protect against employment discrimination. On his own, President Truman strengthened the civil rights division of the Justice Department, appointed the first African American judge to the federal bench, and, most dramatically, on July 26, promulgated an executive order integrating the armed forces.

In response, southern members of Congress boycotted the annual Democratic Jefferson-Jackson Day dinner, where Truman was a featured speaker. At a meeting of the solid South's Democratic governors, Fielding Wright, the governor of Mississippi, argued for the formation of a third party. Governor "Big Jim" Folsom of Alabama proposed that the southern states back a single favorite son, who would challenge Truman for the Democratic nomination and then could bargain with Truman for the positions they wanted. He added that he would be glad to be the one to run. Thurmond, the voice of reason in this crowd, proposed the adoption of a strongly worded resolution threatening that the South would fight back. Then, he recommended, they follow up with some behind-the-scenes negotiation to seek common ground. Thurmond's suggestion became the consensus position, and Thurmond became the unofficial spokesperson for the group. Though the southern politicians called themselves the States' Rights Democrats, a North Carolina editor found the name too long for his headline. He substituted "Dixiecrats," and the name stuck.

By the spring of 1948, as Truman was trailing farther and farther in the polls, a long parade of Democrats, from Claude Pepper to Strom Thurmond, visited Dwight D. Eisenhower and urged him to accept the Democratic nomination for president. Even President Truman himself met privately with Eisenhower and suggested that, if General MacArthur sought the Republican nomination for president, Eisenhower should join the Democratic ticket with Truman—with Truman in the number two spot of vice president. In recounting the off-the-record meeting in his diary, Truman wrote, "Ike & I could be elected and my family & myself would be happy outside this great white jail known as the White House." The much-decorated and revered hero of World War II declined to accept the many entreaties to run, to the disappointment of his Democratic suitors.

This was the confidence that Truman and his own party were feeling about his chances. The Republicans, meanwhile, out of the White House for 16 years, were trying to find their strongest candidate. They courted

Eisenhower also, but he turned them down as well. It took three ballots for New York Governor Thomas Dewey, the Republican nominee in 1944, to secure the nomination against Governor Harold Stassen of Minnesota (the first of his nine unsuccessful runs to be president), Senator Arthur Vandenberg and conservative Senator Robert A. Taft (R-Ohio), sometimes nicknamed "Mr. Republican." In what *Time* magazine called "a political bull's-eye," Dewey selected Earl Warren to be his running mate.

Conventional wisdom was that this was a dream team, sure to sweep to victory in November. In a July 5, 1948 report on the convention, *Time* magazine described the ticket: "The face of the Republican Party, as shown by its candidates, had never appeared so photogenic, so politically winning.... [I]t smoothly combined the cool self-assurance of Thomas Edmund Dewey, 46, with the genial Western affability of smiling Earl Warren, 57." *Time* confidently predicted, "Barring a political miracle, it is the kind of ticket that could not fail to sweep the Republican Party back into power."

The Democratic convention was marked by a pitched battle over a civil rights plank in the platform. Minneapolis mayor and Senate candidate Hubert Humphrey championed the liberal plank, proclaiming that the Democratic party should "get out of the shadow of states' rights and walk forthrightly into the bright sunshine of human rights." The Dixiecrats proposed a plank proclaiming allegiance to states' rights. When the liberal plank won by a vote of 651½ to 582½, the entire Mississippi delegation and half the Alabama delegation walked out. Although Truman won the party nomination, the angry southern delegates who had not joined the walkout refused to make the selection unanimous.

Despite their anger, the most senior southern Democrats in Congress did not want to lose seniority by leaving the Democratic party. As committee chairmen, they could block civil rights legislation, and they were not convinced that Dewey would be any more of a friend to the South. As Governor William Tuck of Virginia expressed it, "What's the sense of jumping out of a fourth-floor window, if it isn't going to save someone's life?" Even so, the States' Rights Democratic party nominated Strom Thurmond on July 17 to be its candidate for president of the United States.

President Truman ran against the "terrible 80th Congress." In a speech to the Greater Los Angeles Press Club, he lambasted the Congress, which he claimed had "not done very much for the benefit of the people." As part of a popular bill to increase the matching rate and maximum allowable benefit under the federal-state public assistance programs, Congress narrowed the definition of "employee" under the Social Security Act, excluding over a half million people from coverage. At a campaign stop, Truman vetoed the bill, declaring "If our Social Security program is to endure, it must be protected against…piecemeal attacks." Congress promptly overrode the veto. Congress also passed, over the president's veto, a bill that excluded newspaper and magazine vendors from Social Security coverage. Truman accused the Republicans of undermining Social Security and failing to adopt national health insurance.

On Tuesday, November 2, 1948, Harry S. Truman pulled off the biggest upset in American history. Virtually all the pundits had it wrong. A broadly smiling Truman holding a *Chicago Tribune* front page proclaiming "Dewey Defeats Truman" is the most famous image of the surprising result, but the *Tribune* was not the only one to make the mistake. *Life Magazine* also printed a picture of Dewey with the words "the next president."

To add to the sweetness of the victory for the Democrats, Congress fell back into Democratic control. The Senate went from having 51 Republicans and 45 Democrats to having 54 Democrats and 42 Republicans, a Democratic swing from −6 to +12. The result in the House of Representatives was just as dramatic. Republicans went from having 246 representatives to the Democrats' 188 to finding themselves with only 171 to the Democratic majority of 263, a change for the Democrats from −58 to +92. Because Truman had campaigned on the issue of Social Security, many saw the victory as a mandate for the program, though Dewey, a moderate, also supported Social Security.

On December 31, 1948, the advisory council forwarded its comprehensive report to the Senate Finance Committee. Ten days later, the recently reelected President Truman sent his annual message on the budget to Congress. In that message, he reminded Congress, "Public assistance was designed as a backstop, a second line of defense, eventually to be replaced in large measure by social insurance benefits." Arguing, "We have not made progress toward this objective in the last decade," he called upon Congress to take "[t]hree principal steps…to strengthen and complete the system of social insurance.…First, old-age and survivors insurance should be extended to nearly all the 25 million gainfully employed persons not now covered; the scale of benefits should be sharply raised....Second, disability insurance should be provided.... Third, a comprehensive national health program should be established." He forcefully concluded, "Action is long overdue."

About six weeks after the budget message, on February 21, 1949, the chairman of the House Committee on Ways and Means introduced two administration-drafted bills, based on the advisory council recommendations, one dealing with the old-age and survivors' program and a proposed disability insurance program and one dealing with public assistance and child welfare services

Hearings began in the House a week later. The committee heard 250 witnesses, including Slichter and Ball, who testified together on behalf of the council. In April, the committee went into executive session to consider the bill and held daily sessions, starting early each morning. Chairman Doughton was punctual and had no patience for members who arrived late. The unfortunate members who were on time were subjected to his tirades about members who were tardy. Those who were late had to tolerate Doughton interrupting committee action, turning and asking, with irritation in his voice, "Why weren't you here? We've got to get going."

Staffing the committee were Charlie Davis, who was the Ways and Means Committee clerk, and Fedele Fauri, who was on loan from the Legislative Research Service, Congress's research division of the Library of Congress, the world's largest library, with its 530 miles of bookshelves. Bob Myers sat in on the sessions to answer questions about the actuarial impact of proposed changes, and Wilbur Cohen sat in on many sessions to represent the administration. Before every member and every congressional committee started hiring large, permanent staffs in the 1970s, and the numbers of congressional employees mushroomed, Congress simply borrowed experts from the Library of Congress or the executive branch, as they were needed. Members of the executive branch routinely drafted committee reports and explained technical issues during committee mark-ups and conferences.

Myers, now the chief actuary of the Social Security Administration, worked so closely and so regularly with Congress that on some publications of the Ways and Means Committee, he was actually listed as "Actuary to the Committee," even though he never held that position nor ever received a penny in pay from the committee. Myers had built a reputation for straight dealing, and so was trusted by both sides of the aisle.

During the executive sessions of the committee, which lasted four months, Fauri explained every provision of the bill in great detail. When that was done, the committee started at the beginning of the legislation once more and discussed every provision in elaborate detail. Wilbur Mills (D-Ark) was young and had been a member of the committee for only six years, but he was smart, hardworking, and, as a result, extremely influential. Mills was "a sharp man and a very able guy," according to Fauri, "the kind of individual who would really get to the crux of an issue, and know in detail much of the complications…of a formula or cost…." Fauri concluded, "I was impressed…by the amount of attention and work on the part of the…members of Ways and Means,…like Senate Finance."

Doughton, too, was smart and hardworking. Then 86 years old, he would arrive at the office at 6:00 A.M. and work an 11-hour day, leaving the office around 5:30 P.M. Born in rural North Carolina, he was generally conservative, but he was also open-minded and willing to change his view, if persuaded.

He routinely was driven home to his apartment near the Mayflower Hotel by the committee clerk, Charlie Davis, who owned an old beat-up Plymouth. One night, Davis was unavailable to drive, so Fauri, who had only been at the committee a few weeks, took Doughton home. Fauri had a brand-new Buick, with which Doughton immediately fell in love, saying "My, this is a fine automobile." From that point on, Fauri was the designated driver.

Around 5:30 every evening, Doughton would come to Fauri and ask, "Are you ready to go?" Though Fauri never was, he would always respond, "Sure," drop the congressman off, and return to the office. During those trips, the two men would talk about the work of the committee. Doughton initially was opposed to expanding Social Security to cover loss of wages due to disability, but Fauri, who had worked as a welfare director in Michigan before coming to Washington, described some of the experiences disabled workers confronted in the welfare system. Gradually, as Doughton studied and thought about the issue, he became a strong advocate of the proposal.

On August 22, 1949, the committee voted the Social Security legislation out of committee. The bill extended the coverage of Social Security to regularly employed agricultural workers and domestic workers, some of the self-employed, as well as other groups. Also, it increased the level of benefits by about two-thirds. The bill dropped, however, the administration's proposal for health insurance. It also eliminated the authorization, put in the law six years before, for the use of general revenue in the event of a deficit. The committee report explained that "your committee is firmly of the belief that the old-age…insurance program should be on a completely self-supporting basis."

The bill gave disabled workers benefits under Social Security, as well as extending, to the disabled, coverage under the federal-state welfare program that had been established in 1935 for the elderly. During the committee deliberations, Doughton had complained privately to Fauri about the enormous pressure the medical profession had mounted against both the disability provisions and the health provisions.

The American Medical Association had testified at the hearings, "To initiate a Federal disability program would represent another step toward wholesale nationalization of medical care and the socialization of the practice of medicine." Only two years before, the AMA had supported disability insurance, stating in a report "Social Security measures to maintain income such as disability insurance, old age insurance, and public assistance are…of vital importance."

During the hearings, the Chamber of Commerce too had opposed the disability insurance provisions, and that also was a change from its earlier position. As recently as 1944, the Chamber's Committee on Social Security had recommended, "For workers totally and permanently disabled at or after age 55 a system of benefit payments, calculated on a basis consistent with that for Old Age and Survivors Insurance, should be provided."

As a result of all the opposition, the disability insurance provision had barely made it through committee. In advance of the vote, Davis and Fauri did an informal count and had predicted that the provision would win by a single vote. On the day of the vote, Davis looked around the room and realized that one of the supporters, Representative Albert Camp (D-Ga.), was missing. Realizing that Camp's vote might make the difference, Davis whispered hurriedly to Fauri, "Go find him. We need him." Camp, a husky, slow-moving southerner, had gone to buy a soda in the cafeteria. Fauri and Cohen, who had both been racing around the building looking for Camp, finally found him in the men's room and hustled him back to the committee meeting. Sure enough, the provision barely passed the committee.

Seven of the 10 Republicans voted, along with the Democrats, to report the bill out of committee to the full House. All 10 Republicans, however, filed a minority report objecting to certain features of the bill. The report pointed out that Social Security was intended as a basic floor of protection and argued that the benefit increase, including the action of raising the maximum taxable wage base, was inconsistent with the concept of a floor. The minority also objected to the inclusion of disability benefits as part of Social Security.

Congressman Carl Curtis (R-Neb.) filed Additional Minority Views, to which two other Republican members joined. Curtis complained, "The old-age and survivors insurance program is a grossly unsound and ineffective tool for the social-security purposes it attempts to accomplish," asserting "It is totally unmoral." He advocated that it be replaced by a universal program of uniform benefits financed by a revamped flat-percentage income tax. The general design was Townsend-like but the level of benefit was very low.

On October 5, 1949, the legislation passed the House by a vote of 333 to 14. The Senate Finance Committee did not consider the Social Security measure until the following winter, because Congress adjourned soon after the House action. After extensive deliberations, the Finance Committee reported the bill to the full Senate on May 17, 1950. Before voting the bill out of committee though, it struck the disability insurance provisions. All members of the committee joined the report except Senator Hugh Butler (R-Neb), who, like his Nebraskan counterpart in the House, Carl Curtis, advocated that Social Security be replaced by a very minimal, flat benefit not related to wages.

The Senate passed the bill on June 20 by a vote of 81 to 2. The conference committee dropped the House provision for disability insurance but retained the provision which extended welfare coverage to the disabled. The conference report passed the House on August 16, the Senate, the next day, and it was signed into law on August 28, 1950.

An advisory council had played a vital role in Social Security policy making, as it had in 1938, and as it would many times in the future. The advisory council setting, with its representation of business and labor, permitted proposals to be hashed out between the two groups. When business and labor reached agreement and were backed by leading independent experts, the job of Congress became much simpler.

The Social Security Amendments of 1950 have often been referred to as the "third start" for Social Security, the first two being the original enactment in 1935 and the substantial revisions enacted in 1939. This third start covered about 8 million more private sector workers under Social Security. In addition, employers of 2.5 million state and local employees not covered by public pensions and of nonprofit workers could now elect coverage. And the statute increased benefits by an average of 80 percent. While the increase was a little more than price inflation since 1937, it was only about two-thirds the rise in wages since that time. The bill also eased the eligibility rules for receiving benefits, thus permitting older workers to qualify for benefits more easily.

The legislation retained all the design features that had been in place since Social Security's origin. The program took a big step forward toward its goal of universal coverage, although a number of important groups of workers continued to be outside the system. Social Security remained free of a means test, instead providing benefits automatically, as a matter of right to workers and their families once the workers had worked enough time to achieve insured status. Benefits continued to be related to prior wages but weighted toward lower-income workers through use of a progressive benefit formula. And the self-financing aspect of the program was reinforced by the repeal of the general revenue guarantee in the event of a funding shortfall.

The coverage and benefit improvements had an immediate impact on the welfare rolls. Because more people qualified for Social Security benefits, and those who did received higher benefits, the welfare rolls promptly started to decline. For the first time ever, the number of seniors receiving Social Security exceeded the number receiving welfare.

The passage of the Social Security Amendments of 1950 substantially increased the workload of the Social Security Administration. Claims for benefits instantly doubled. Nevertheless, the increase was absorbed efficiently and rapidly. The 3 million beneficiaries received their recalculated, increased September benefit checks accurately and on time, a mere 36 days after the amendments became law.

Truman and Altmeyer both believed that disability insurance and medical insurance were necessary to truly provide security to workers and their families. In signing the 1950 amendments into law, President Truman proclaimed:

> We still have much to do before our social security programs are fully adequate.... Both the House Committee on Ways and Means and the Senate Committee on Finance have already announced that they intend to study proposals for further improvement.

Despite these sentiments, no one knew when, or even whether, Congress would again take up Social Security legislation. After all, during the entire decade of the 1940s, no important Social Security legislation was enacted. In January 1952, President Truman sent to Congress his Message on the State of the Union, his Economic Report, and his Budget Message. As they had the year before, all included several Social Security recommendations: an increase in the level of Social Security benefits to make them more adequate, a further extension of coverage, and the addition of disability protection.

At the request of the federal security administrator, within whose agency the Social Security Administration resided, Cohen began work on a bill providing hospital cost coverage for beneficiaries of Social Security. The Truman administration had decided to narrow its focus from universal health insurance to health insurance for the elderly and begun thinking of structuring the insurance as an additional Social Security benefit.

As a strategic matter, restricting health insurance to Social Security beneficiaries—or, at least, starting with them—might dilute some of the unrelenting opposition, the Truman administration hoped. In some ways, providing health insurance to children as a first step might have made more policy sense. If children survived illness, they had full lifetimes ahead of them and generally their medical costs were smaller. At the same time, the point of social insurance was to prevent economic dependence, and the elderly were more than twice as likely to need hospitalization as the rest of the population. Older Americans ordinarily had fixed or even declining incomes, and since they were generally not employed, they had little opportunity for group insurance. The cost of medical care could wipe out the savings and income of most elderly swiftly and completely.

In addition to Cohen's work on health insurance, he developed a proposal that could serve as a first step to disability insurance. The so-called disability freeze provided that people who were found to be disabled and unable to work would receive Social Security retirement benefits calculated on wages up to the point of disability rather than on wages up to retirement age. Social Security benefits were based on average wages. Without the freeze, an individual, who started working at age 20, was disabled at age 40, and did not have earnings beyond that date, would have wages earned between ages 20 and 40 averaged with all the years after the worker became disabled, during which there would be zero earnings. The worker's average wages would be artificially reduced by all the zero years, producing a very low average and therefore a very low monthly benefit at retirement age. In contrast, with the freeze, average benefits would be calculated based on the 20 years of actual work, before the onset of the disability.

Disabled workers would still have to wait for retirement age to begin receiving monthly benefits, but the disability freeze would allow them to retain their insured status and also have benefits based on the years they were able to work. The disability freeze was similar to a waiver of premiums under private insurance. Its effect would be to preserve for the worker the rights previously earned under the program.

In the spring of 1952, believing Congress would not take up Social Security again so soon after the amendments of two years before, Cohen decided to attend an International Labor Conference in Brazil and to accept an invitation to speak at a social work conference in California. Before departing, he provided Altmeyer with a memorandum describing his work on the disability freeze, the hospital insurance proposal, and the other matters he was working on.

Because Congress had so recently passed a major Social Security bill, because there had been virtually no change in Social Security between 1939 and 1950, a period of 11 years, and, on top of all that, because the United States was in the middle of the Korean War, Cohen left on his trip confident that he would miss little in Washington. To his astonishment, legislative developments forced him to cut short his trip and return home on the double.

The legislative developments that cost Cohen the California sunshine were the handiwork of his friend and colleague, Bob Ball. When the advisory council of 1948 had completed its work, Ball had returned to his former employment with the University-Government Center and resumed his writing and teaching. However, the center was unable to maintain its funding and closed shortly thereafter. A position of assistant director at the Social Security Administration was vacant, and Altmeyer offered Ball the job, which he accepted. The position, a substantial promotion from Ball's previous position in government, included developing legislative proposals and working closely with members of Congress.

Ball was concerned that benefits, not large to begin with, could keep pace with inflation and gains in the standard of living only if Congress acted. The obvious question was how to get Congress to act. As he reviewed actuarial projections developed by Myers, Ball saw the answer to the question. Because Myers calculated his projections using conservative assumptions, the program had produced a sizable surplus in just the two years since Congress had passed the 1950 legislation. Ball recognized that Congress could raise benefits—a popular move in an election year—without raising taxes.

The job of the Social Security actuary is to prepare the tables for the annual report of the trustees, which indicates the future health of the program. In addition, it is the actuary's responsibility to determine the costs of proposed changes to the program. Projecting the future is an extremely uncertain enterprise. One important element in the projection is the assumption about wage growth over time. What happens to wage levels in the future affects Social Security's cost significantly. Wage levels affect both the income and outgo of the program. The higher a worker's wages, the higher the taxes paid. On the other side of the equation, the higher the wages, the larger the benefits replacing those wages.

Though the growth in wages affects both the income and outgo of Social Security, it has a greater impact on income than outgo. The benefit formula is progressive—replacing a higher percentage of the wages of lower-income workers than higher-income wages—and with every salary increase, every worker becomes higher paid in relation to his or her prior pay. The phenomenon is analogous to what was called bracket creep in the federal income tax code, which led to indexing of the tax brackets in 1981. There, with every increase in salary, a worker paid progressively higher taxes and the government gained additional revenue without any new tax legislation. Under Social Security, the bracket creep resulted in beneficiaries earning less favorable returns on their contributions, thus costing the system less money.

Myers, of course, understood that wages were highly likely to increase over time, since historically they always had. Nevertheless, conservative by nature, he decided to assume otherwise. Assuming no wage growth in the future—a so-called static assumption—was a conservative approach, assuring that the program would operate in balance and almost guaranteeing that any imbalances that did arise would all be in the direction of unanticipated surpluses. The Myers method of static assumptions virtually guaranteed an overfunded program.

In the spring of 1952, Ball alerted Charlie Davis, the clerk of the Ways and Means Committee, that the projected Social Security surplus made a benefit increase possible without raising taxes in an election year. Davis, in turn, informed Chairman Doughton. No major tax bill was under consideration. Moreover, Doughton sensed an emerging consensus with respect to disability insurance. Consequently, he introduced a bill proposing a benefit increase as well as the disability freeze proposal.

In contrast to prior enactments, which had generated months of congressional hearings, the Ways and Means Committee reported out the Doughton bill in four days, without having held a single day of hearings. The bill included both a benefit increase and the disability freeze. In order to expedite the bill and avoid the lengthy step of obtaining a rule from the Rules Committee, Doughton moved that the bill be brought up for consideration by the full House under suspension of the rules. A suspension of the rules required a two-thirds vote, which Doughton believed would present no problem. To his shock, the Republican members of the Ways and Means Committee, who had supported the bill in committee, opposed the motion. The motion failed to attract the needed two-thirds, barely capturing a majority: 151 to 141.

Prior to the vote, the American Medical Association had sent telegrams to every member, asserting that the disability freeze amounted to "socialized medicine" and arguing that the proposal would give the executive branch "absolute power over certain medical activities." By necessity, the bill required a medical determination of total and permanent disability in order for an individual to qualify for the freeze. Physicians opposed what they feared would be a first little slide down what they saw as the slippery slope to socialized medicine. In response to the AMA argument, Doughton retorted during the floor debate that there was "no more socialized medicine in [the disability freeze] than there is frost in the sun," but to no avail.

A month later, another motion to suspend the rules to consider the Social Security amendments, with modified legislative language for the disability freeze, was before the House. The ranking Republican on the Ways and Means Committee, Daniel Reed, speaking in opposition, asserted, "[L]et no person on this floor be deceived. You have the same old [legislation previously considered] before you. While the socialized medicine advocates pretend to" change the bill, they have not, he argued. Instead, he insisted, "You have socialized medicine here stronger in this bill than was [in the bill] heretofore defeated."

Doughton responded that the modified provision had been taken verbatim from legislation introduced by a Republican member of the Ways and Means Committee. Quoting Reed's words back to him, Doughton pointed out that, prior to the AMA telegram deluge, Reed himself had said that the disability provision in the bill "is a very important improvement which preserves the insurance rights of persons permanently and totally disabled." In a passionate conclusion, the 89-year-old Doughton ended his remarks, "This is probably the last social security bill which I will ever introduce for, as you know, I am going out of Congress and what political motives could I have?" The next day, the House voted to suspend the rules, and the Social Security amendments were passed, including the disability freeze, 361 to 22, without a word more of debate.

The Senate Finance Committee dropped the disability freeze, arguing that insufficient time remained in the session to study the provision adequately. The bill passed the Senate without the disability freeze by a voice vote and was sent to conference. The conference was initially deadlocked over the disability freeze issue. The Senate held firm to its position. At the same time, Representative Doughton felt strongly it should be included, and the other House conferees wanted the provision as a tribute to Doughton, who was retiring at the end of the session.

With the conference unable to reach agreement, Representative Wilbur Mills asked Wilbur Cohen, who had returned from his trip and was sitting in on the deliberations, if he could suggest a way to break the impasse. Cohen's initial suggestion was for a one-year trial of the provision. When that was rejected, he offered a Catch-22 solution. Why not, he suggested, enact the freeze but not allow any applications to be filed until July 1, 1953, about a year away. Then, he continued, terminate the freeze provision on June 30, 1953, the day before anyone is permitted to file a request to have benefits frozen. Cohen's on-the-spot brainstorm proved acceptable to all. The Senate won on the substantive point, but the House paid tribute to Doughton and had the freeze on the books for a year, allowing administrative work to be done in anticipation of future disability legislation, and establishing a precedent for the future. The Social Security amendments passed both Houses on July 5, and Congress adjourned two days later in time to attend the Republican and Democratic conventions, both scheduled for later that month.

The 1952 amendments were not dramatic in themselves. The legislated increase in benefit levels simply kept the program current with wage and price increases. Coverage was not extended, and, ultimately, nothing was done about disability insurance. Nevertheless, the amendments represented a sea change. For the first time in the program's history, benefit levels were increased only two years after the previous increase. If there was any doubt that Social Security's third start would be its final start, the 1952 amendments made clear that Social Security was now an important focus of Congressional energy and was becoming a major and fundamental part of the nation's safety net.

Moreover, more members were becoming aware of the need to extend protection to those who became disabled. During the debate in the Senate, the chairman of the Finance Committee, Senator Walter F. George (D-Ga.), stated, "Speaking for myself, and not for the Committee, I would…go further than the House Committee….We must try to bring the permanent and totally disabled cases under old-age and survivors' insurance at an earlier age than 65." He went on to say that the Finance Committee would take the matter up, along with extension of coverage to state and local employees, in January.

The nation was now well into the election season. At the Jefferson-Jackson Day Dinner on March 29, 1952, Truman surprised the audience by stating firmly that he would not be a candidate for president. The Democrats might have once again tried to persuade Eisenhower to run as their standard-bearer, but he was already taken by the Republicans. With the withdrawal of Truman, the Democratic race drew many candidates. After three rounds of balloting, Illinois governor Adlai Stevenson emerged with the nomination.

Both platforms included strong planks in support of Social Security. The Republican platform said, "We favor amendment of the Old Age and Survivors Insurance system to provide coverage for those justly entitled to it but who are now excluded," although it also included the cryptic statement, "We shall make a thorough study of universal pay-as-you-go pension plans." The Democratic platform called for "further strengthening" of the program through "increasing benefits" and extending coverage.

On November 4, Eisenhower won handily, carrying every region of the country but the South. With the 1952 election, a Republican president occupied the Oval Office for the first time in 20 years. In addition to the White House, the election brought changed leadership to Congress. Republicans now controlled both houses of Congress in addition to the White House. No one knew what this change in party control would bring. Representative Curtis, the congressman, who two years before called Social Security "totally unmoral," was particularly looking forward to a Republican Congress and a Republican president for the first time in his political career. He hoped he might find a more receptive audience for his views.

## CHAPTER 10

# All American Program (Minus a Tiny Splinter Group)

Holding elective office for the first time in his career, President Dwight D. Eisenhower had never been required to make a public statement about Social Security. No one knew where he stood.

Representative Carl Curtis hoped that the new president would join his cause in limiting Social Security or even undoing it. Curtis was on record favoring the replacement of Social Security with a minimal flat benefit payable to every older American without regard to prior work. The Curtis plan was appealing because it would pay benefits immediately to all those senior citizens who had not qualified for Social Security and were therefore stuck on welfare. But supporters of Social Security saw that the proposal would completely undermine the insurance-based earned-right concept so integral to Social Security. Once a flat, minimal, universal benefit was in place, a means test was an easy step away.

Policy makers knew that the 1950 Social Security Amendments would result in more and more elderly qualifying for benefits, but this would take time. By 1953, only about one-third of the elderly received Social Security. So few received benefits that the worker-to-retiree ratio was still a low 16 workers supporting every beneficiary, a ratio consistent with the program still just starting up. That statistic would change rapidly, of course. In just a few years, the ratio would be halved to eight workers for every retiree. And in two decades or so, as the current seniors were replaced by retirees who had worked enough under covered employment to earn Social Security, the ratio would fall to three workers to every beneficiary, where it would remain for the rest of the century. But the eventual maturation of the program did not help those elderly who had worked hard all their adult lives and found themselves on welfare here and now.

Could Congress and the president withstand the political pressure—and the political appeal of these elderly left out of Social Security? The Townsend movement was still exerting its influence and still pushing for those universal, flat benefits. In the just-concluded election, the Townsendites had endorsed 173 victorious congressional office-seekers, 100 of those, Republican.

Disconcerting to Social Security supporters, the leadership of the new Republican-controlled Congress appointed Curtis to chair a special subcommittee instructed to "conduct thorough studies and investigations of all matters pertaining to our Social Security laws." In designating Curtis as chairman, the leadership had elevated the conservative congressman over a higher-ranking Republican, Representative Robert W. Kean of New Jersey, who was a strong supporter of Social Security. The U.S. Chamber of Commerce shared Curtis's views and hoped the new Republican president did so, too. The Chamber developed a proposal calling for Social Security coverage or "blanketing in" of all uncovered elderly, irrespective of their contributions to the program.

What did Eisenhower believe? The new president's first State of the Union Address to Congress did not resolve the mystery. In it, he stated, "The provisions of the Old Age and Survivors Insurance Law should promptly be extended to cover millions of citizens who have been left out of the Social Security System." This sphinx-like statement still offered no real hints of Eisenhower's thinking. It could be read as consistent either with the existing earned right system or the Chamber's and Curtis's universal coverage, meager flat-benefit system.

Eisenhower gave no clues when he appointed Oveta Culp Hobby to be the new federal security administrator, the position to whom the commissioner of Social Security reported. Hobby, the wife of the former governor of Texas, was a smart and talented woman. Trained as a lawyer, she had served as parliamentarian of the Texas House of Representatives and had authored a book on parliamentary law. During World War II, she helped form the Women's Army Auxiliary Corps which resulted in the first women, other than nurses, to serve within the ranks of the army. As its commander, she first met Eisenhower. After the war, she served as coeditor and publisher of the *Houston Post*. Accomplished as she was, she had no background in Social Security and had made no public comments about it.

Along with everyone else, the employees of the Social Security Administration were in the dark about what Eisenhower thought. But they knew there would be changes. Prior to the election, Altmeyer had announced that he would retire. He recognized that his close association with Roosevelt's New Deal and Truman's Fair Deal made it impossible for him to remain in his position. Though not unexpected, his retirement nevertheless was unsettling for the other Social Security employees. After all, he had been in charge for nearly two decades, even before day one.

In November 1952, as soon as Hobby was named, Altmeyer wrote her, offering to send her material and brief her. He sent her memoranda on January 7 and again on January 19, identifying major issues that might come to her attention in her first six months in office. He heard nothing back. Perhaps not trusting the career civil service or perhaps simply not liking Altmeyer, Hobby kept to herself in her new position and froze him out.

On March 12, the new administration sent to Congress a reorganization plan, under which the Federal Security Administration would be changed to the cabinet-level Department of Health, Education and Welfare. The commissioner *for* Social Security, the job Altmeyer held, would be renamed the commissioner *of* Social Security, a new position held by no one. That seemingly innocuous change in the preposition made all the difference. Although Altmeyer had announced that he would step down on May 8, when he turned 62, his departure date turned out not to be of his own choosing.

The reorganization plan went through Congress rapidly. The effective date, proposed by the administration to be May 11, three days after Altmeyer's sixty-second birthday, was changed to April 11. Consequently, a month before his sixty-second birthday, Altmeyer would be out of the job he had held for almost 20 years. Leaving before turning 62 would cause his wife to lose contingent survivors' benefits under the federal pension program. When the newspapers found out about the forced departure and the loss of benefits, they publicized the indirect firing, complete with editorial cartoons. One depicted Altmeyer, bruised and beaten, leaning on crutches, listening, to Eisenhower's words over the radio: "I expect my cabinet officers to be fair and just and decent in dealing with career people in government…!"

The forced departure was particularly embarrassing for the administration because no successor had been selected. As Altmeyer was literally cleaning out his desk, he received a call from Hobby offering him a 30-day position as a consultant—though not a continuation in his current position. Recognizing that he was being kept on not for his expertise, but so he could collect benefits and the administration could save face, Altmeyer declined the offer. Nevertheless, during his extremely short tenure in the Eisenhower administration, he performed one last exceedingly valuable service for Social Security.

Hobby had invited a handful of people outside of the executive branch to help her formulate Social Security policy. The group was weighted with opponents of Social Security—including Representative Carl Curtis and three members of the Chamber of Commerce. Altmeyer learned of the meeting when Hobby's assistant phoned his office and directed him to find someone to staff the meeting—though Altmeyer himself was pointedly not invited to attend. In what turned out to be an extremely shrewd decision, Altmeyer chose to send Bob Ball.

Ball knew many of the businesspeople from his work on the advisory council and outside government. After the informal group met twice, both meetings unannounced, Wilbur Cohen mentioned the sessions to his friend Nelson Cruikshank, who handled Social Security for the AFL. Soon a radio broadcaster on an AFL-sponsored program made the information public.

Because of the heavy representation by the Chamber of Commerce, the announcer dubbed the group the "Hobby Lobby." Other news outlets picked up the story. The articles noted that the Chamber had publicized its plans to convene a national conference, in order to have its plan "fully explained to the people back home." The Chamber hoped that the conference could generate "strong grass-roots support for the plan." The description of the Chamber's lobbying effort cemented the Hobby Lobby nickname.

The meetings looked particularly exclusive because Hobby had recently turned down a requested meeting with the AFL. Responding to the embarrassing press coverage, pressure from Congress and the demands of organized labor to be included, Hobby quickly invited representatives of labor and agriculture to join the group. Ball became, in effect, the staff director. As he had done with the 1948 advisory council, Ball looked for areas of agreement that could result in a strengthened Social Security. He recognized that both business and labor were in favor of expanding coverage, although the Chamber representatives wanted to extend coverage to those already retired and move away from a contributory system while labor representatives were in favor of the existing wage-related structure.

When the expanded group met, they agreed to issue an interim report confined solely to the expansion of coverage to current workers, not retirees. That agreement was, of course, consistent with the view of the labor representatives; at the same time, it was not necessarily inconsistent with the views of business. After five more meetings, the group submitted its report to Hobby, now the secretary of health, education and welfare. They recommended extending coverage to the major groups not then covered, which included about 3 million self-employed farm operators, 2.7 million sharecroppers, and about 500,000 self-employed professionals, all groups excluded from coverage in the 1950 amendments. In addition, the Hobby Lobby proposed that state and local employers be permitted to elect coverage for groups of employees.

With respect to the blanketing in of those elderly not receiving Social Security—the original agenda of the Chamber—the report stated:

> [O]ur recommendations for extension of coverage at this time do not include the blanketing-in of persons already age 65 or over....We have excluded this group from consideration in this report because their inclusion would involve very substantial modifications of the present program which would require careful and prolonged study.

On August 1, 1953, the administration sent to Congress proposed Social Security legislation along the lines of the recommendations of the Hobby Lobby. In the message accompanying the transmittal, Eisenhower reminded Congress, "In my message...on the State of the Union, I pointed out that there is urgent need for making our social security programs more effective." The citizen-president from Kansas spoke of values:

> Retirement systems, by which individuals contribute to their own security according to their own respective abilities...are but a reflection of the American heritage of sturdy self-reliance which has made our country strong and kept it free....The Social Security program furnishes, on a national scale, the opportunity for our citizens, through that same self-reliance, to build the foundation for their security.

The commander-in-chief and former commanding general of the victorious Allied Forces in World War II concluded by talking about security:

> There are two points about these proposals which I cannot stress too strongly. One is my belief that [enactment of the proposed amendments extending coverage] would add immeasurably to the peace of mind and security of the individual citizens...; the second is my belief that they would add greatly to the national sense of domestic security.

Congress recessed a few days after the legislative submission and so took no action.

Gradually over the months that Ball and Hobby worked together, a sense of mutual respect and admiration had developed between them. Ball was now becoming a trusted adviser. However, he had one more hurdle to jump.

In November, Curtis was planning to hold subcommittee hearings at which he hoped to embarrass Social Security by publicizing examples of sympathetic individuals denied benefits, as well as anomalies and inconsistencies in the program's design. Curtis was interested in attacking the program, not the new administration. As a result, Secretary Hobby chose not to send anyone close to the administration, but instead to send Ball. As Ball later recalled, "Instead of supporting me, she in effect told me to go on up and testify and she would...make up her mind about me depending on how I made out."

In addition, Altmeyer, now a private citizen, received a letter from Chairman Curtis requesting that he testify. Recognizing the purpose of the hearing was to embarrass, Altmeyer declined the invitation. On September 24, he was served with a subpoena at his home in Madison, Wisconsin, compelling him to testify.

As the hearing date arrived, the diplomatic, soft-spoken, and unflappable Ball decided to be as low-key as possible. He had good instincts about when to be monosyllabic in his answers and when to elaborate; when to give technical, dry responses and when to highlight the program's philosophy. Ball testified for six grueling days.

Altmeyer's testimony was similar, though there were a few more fireworks. Curtis's staff person, who was conducting some of the questioning, asked Altmeyer over and over again to read aloud lengthy statements the former commissioner had made and material he had written. Finally, one of the Democratic members interrupted and asked Altmeyer whether he had "a pair of Oregon boots on." Altmeyer had no idea what the congressman was talking about, although he learned later that "Oregon boots" were worn by prisoners to prevent escape. The congressman then angrily shouted, "Bringing a man like you here under subpoena! Mr. Chairman, you ought to be ashamed of yourself." Curtis and the other congressman exchanged words, Curtis trying to maintain order, the other member, at one point demanding that Curtis stop banging "that damned gavel." In the final transcript, the exchange remained, but the word "damned" was expunged.

As a result of the Curtis hearings, Social Security had to endure a day or two of bad press when the proceedings highlighted the number of Social Security checks going to foreign countries as the result of beneficiaries who lived abroad. But Ball succeeded in being as boring as possible, and even the occasional fireworks with Altmeyer were not enough to raise pulses for very long. The press quickly lost interest, and the story died. At some points, it looked as if Curtis himself was bored by the proceedings. His staff had prepared detailed questions for him to ask, which included specific instructions recommending alternative follow-up questions depending on the answers. At times Curtis, reading straight from the staff document, accidentally recited the stage directions into the record. Before it was cleaned up, the transcript read, at parts, if the witness answers so-and-so, then you say this.

By now, Hobby was convinced of the program's merit. The administration proposal that had been submitted to Congress in August had dealt only with coverage, the area on which the Hobby Lobby had reached agreement. Hobby wanted a review of the benefit provisions, in order to develop a more comprehensive Social Security proposal to submit to Congress on its return in January. At the time the Hobby Lobby submitted its report on coverage, the secretary had indicated she would use the group to consider other changes. She came to understand that the group would be incapable of developing a comprehensive bill because its disagreements were so fundamental. Consequently, she turned to her undersecretary of health, education and welfare, Nelson Rockefeller, and the Hobby Lobby disappeared into history.

To help him with the assignment, Rockefeller contacted a partner at the well-known Wall Street law firm, Debevoise & Plimpton. Rockefeller wanted the attorney to come to Washington for the assignment. Unwilling to relocate, the senior partner proposed that a young lawyer with the firm, Roswell B. Perkins, be hired to do the work, which, the senior partner promised, he would supervise with occasional trips to Washington.

Rockefeller offered the position to Perkins, who accepted. Perkins spent the next few weeks exhaustively studying Social Security and consulting intensively with Ball and other experts in and out of government. He came to the same conclusion as Rockefeller and Hobby, "Social Security…was fundamentally…sound." He spent the next months developing legislation for the administration and was subsequently appointed assistant secretary of health, education, and welfare.

Eight days after Congress reconvened in January, the president proposed a more comprehensive set of amendments of Social Security than he had done the previous August. In an accompanying message, President Eisenhower made unmistakable his understanding and support for the program: "I am determined to preserve [Social Security's] basic principles. The two most important are: (1) it is a contributory system (2) the benefits received are related in part to the individual's earnings. To these sound principles our system owes much of its wide national acceptance."

With these statements, the president signaled his unequivocal preference for the system as it had evolved and implicitly rejected the Chamber of Commerce blanketing-in proposal. The administration proposed expanding Social Security to include about 10 million workers left out of the previous enactments. These included self-employed farmers, certain categories of farm workers and domestic workers not covered by the 1950 legislation, self-employed professionals also exempted from the 1950 act, and public employees, not covered by the 1950 legislation, whose employers elected coverage.

In addition, the president recommended increasing the level of Social Security benefits: "For [Social Security] to fulfill its purpose of helping to combat destitution, these benefits are too low." He also proposed increasing the maximum taxable wage base for workers. He explained, "The maintenance of a relationship between the individual's earnings and the benefits he receives is a cornerstone of the [Social Security] system." He pointed out that "statistical studies reveal that in [1938] 94% of full-time male workers protected by [Social Security] had their earnings covered by the program.… Today, the earnings base…covers the full earnings of only 40% of our regular male workers." Eisenhower concluded, "It is clear, therefore, that another revision of this base is needed to maintain a reasonable relationship between a worker's benefits and his earning."

He also advocated that the program be made more progressive by allowing more years of low or no earnings to be dropped in calculating a worker's average earnings. He explained that "a worker may earn little or nothing for several months or several years because of illness or other personal adversity beyond his power of prevention or remedy." In that case, he said, "the level of benefits is reduced below its true relation to the earning capabilities of the employee." His proposal was aimed to address this unfairness.

Finally, Eisenhower proposed enactment of the disability freeze that was the subject of the Cohen-inspired Catch-22 in the 1952 legislation— the provision that expired before it started. The president believed, "One of the injustices in the present law is its failure to make secure the benefit rights of the worker who has a substantial work record in covered employment and who becomes totally disabled." At the same time, Eisenhower hoped that if the disability freeze was enacted, disabled workers who applied for the freeze could then be identified and provided rehabilitation services.

The main groups opposing the administration's bill were, by now, the usual suspects: business and insurance groups, the American Medical Association, and supporters of the Townsend plan. Labor, for its part, sought greater liberalizations. The Ways and Means Committee made some relatively minor modifications to the administration plan and reported it to the floor, where it passed on June 1, 1954, by a vote of 356 to 8. In the Senate, the chief issue was the coverage of farm operators and self-employed professionals, particularly physicians. The bill, which passed the Senate on a voice vote and was sent to conference, excluded these two groups from coverage, though it did include farm workers not included in 1950.

The American Farm Bureau, the largest and wealthiest of the farm organizations, opposed coverage though it made its opposition known only through a short letter, arguing that there was not enough evidence to assure the practicality of covering farmers. The Farmers' Union favored coverage, but was small in size and limited geographically to a few western states. The oldest farm organization, the Grange, had no public position on Social Security coverage.

For the period that Ball was out of government before becoming executive director of the 1948 advisory council, he had from time to time spoken to various groups who were excluded from coverage, and he always tried to convince them of the benefit of Social Security. He spoke with people at the Department of Agriculture and he also spoke with Herschel D. Newsom, the president of the Grange, who had an office, as fate would have it, only a few doors away from his. During the time they were professional neighbors, Ball would explain to Newsom what coverage under Social Security would mean for his members. Ball gradually convinced him of the benefits that coverage would bring.

When the 1954 amendments were considered by Congress, Ball asked Newsom for a telegram setting forth the organization's support for coverage. At the right moment in the conference committee meeting, Ball handed the telegram to Wilbur Mills. Surprisingly, the Senate conferees yielded to the House version. None of the agricultural groups had been actively lobbying to be included. The largest farm group was on record as opposed. Normally, in those circumstances, Congress would take the line of least resistance and do nothing. In this case, the members chose the statesman-like path of enacting the proposal. The conference report passed Congress on the day of its adjournment, August 20, 1954. Altmeyer, hearing about the successful inclusion of farmers, remarked, "It really is a miracle to get farm coverage. I am still amazed."

With Eisenhower's public statements about Social Security and his proposals to expand it, people now knew that he was a strong supporter of the program. What people did not know was that his public statements actually understated his support.

In a private letter to his brother Edgar, dated November 8, 1954, he was direct: "There is a tiny splinter group…that believes you can [abolish Social Security]. Among them are H. L. Hunt [wealthy founder of the Hunt Oil Company]…, a few other Texas oil millionaires, and an occasional politician or business man from other areas. Their number is negligible and they are stupid."

Roosevelt's landslide victory of 1936, Truman's successful run against the Republican Congress, which he accused of "piecemeal attacks" against Social Security, and the widespread congressional support for Social Security improvements backed Eisenhower's assessment that those opposed to the program were "a tiny splinter group." While some of the "negligible" number may have been stupid, others were unquestionably very smart.

William F. Buckley, Jr., had gained some prominence a few years before with the publication of *God and Man at Yale*, a critique of his undergraduate education and the way that he believed it undermined American values. In 1953, he had become the first president of the Intercollegiate Society of Individualists, founded by Frank Chodorov, whom Buckley described as "the gentle, elderly anarchist, friend…a fine essayist whose thought turned on a single spit: all the reasons why one should be distrustful of state activity." In 1955, Buckley would found the *National Review*, which, according to neoconservative Irving Kristol, "continued the polemic against the New Deal that characterized American conservatism…throughout the 1930s and 1940s."

Another prominent conservative, economist Milton Friedman, who had similar views about government and Social Security, was making his mark at the University of Chicago. A decade before, Friedman had joined a group of 35 other like-minded scholars who had founded the Mont Pelerin Society. Friedman was later to write that the meeting "marked the beginning of my active involvement in the political process." Although neither man would play a prominent role in Social Security's history, they were both to support and inspire a future generation that would.

A few weeks before Eisenhower penned his letter, the country had completed its 1954 midterm election. As was true throughout most of American history, the party out of power gained seats. Eisenhower, still extremely popular, barely lost his Republican majority. The Senate went from a Republican majority of 2 (48 Republicans, 46 Democrats and 2 others) to a minority of 1 (48 Democrats and 47 Republicans). In the House of Representatives, the Republicans went from a majority of 8 seats (221 to 213) to a minority of 29 votes (203 to 232).

In addition to the electoral changes, key people were on the move. Wilbur Cohen, who had spent the first two decades of his adult life working in government, went to the University of Michigan, where he accepted a tenured position offered by his friend Fedele Fauri, who had left the Library of Congress's Congressional Research Service to become dean of the School of Social Work several years earlier. Ball also briefly considered a job offer to be director of social welfare in California, but, to the relief of Hobby, chose to stay in Washington. When she heard that

Ball had decided to stay where he was, she told him that it was "her good news for the day." Then, in July 1955, Hobby herself resigned, and Marion Folsom agreed to move over from Treasury to replace her.

One of Folsom's actions was to bring in, he later explained, "the top office management experts from some of the largest companies in the country, including insurance companies" to survey the operation of Social Security and report to him on inefficiencies. Administrative costs were only about 2 percent of outgo (today they are less than 1 percent), but Folsom wanted to see if there was room for improvement. The private sector administrative experts "came back with a very glowing account, saying that they had found very little of which they could criticize," Folsom remarked afterward. "They made a few suggestions which the Administration adopted right away.... Some of these people came to me individually afterwards and said, 'You know, we learned a lot more here than we were able to contribute.'"

The Democrats, once again in control of Congress, believed that disability insurance should finally be added to Social Security. Discussion of disability insurance provided through Social Security dated back to the 1934 Committee on Economic Security. Protection against loss of wages due to disability had been recommended by advisory council after advisory council. The protection was widespread in Europe, where invalidity insurance (as the Europeans called disability insurance) had generally appeared in the original legislation, together with old-age and survivors' insurance.

Although the administration had favored the disability freeze, it opposed insuring against the risk outright. Much of the business community was hostile to government-provided disability insurance. Many in the private sector believed the program was unworkable and argued that when private sector insurance companies offered this form of insurance, costs proved very difficult to estimate accurately. Supporters of disability insurance contended that the poor experience of the private sector arose because employers used the disability insurance as a form of early retirement for employees who were no longer productive, and the insurance companies did not want to challenge their clients. Nevertheless, the administration was concerned about controlling costs.

The president and his advisers believed strongly in rehabilitation and returning people to work. They wanted to use the disability freeze to identify people who had become disabled and provide them with rehabilitation services. Their goal was to return as many people to work as possible, not provide them with benefits replacing wages.

Despite the opposition of the administration, many in Congress were interested in enacting disability insurance. Senator Robert Kerr (D-Okla), who planned to introduce a bill on the subject, asked Folsom to assign Ball to his staff to help in its drafting. Folsom agreed, reasoning that the country was best served if a bill was more expertly drafted, whether or not the administration favored it.

Soon after the start of the new Congress, the Ways and Means Committee took up the matter of disability insurance. To limit the cost, the committee restricted the program to workers aged 50 and over, who were permanently and totally disabled. The bill also included a provision permitting women to retire early, at age 62. The bill passed the House by a vote of 356 to 8 on July 18, 1955.

The administration opposed both provisions in testimony before the Senate Finance Committee. Delivering the testimony was the secretary of health, education and welfare, Marion Folsom. Wanting testimony that reflected the administration's position but not wanting to foreclose options, he asked Ball and Perkins to draft the testimony jointly, despite, and perhaps because of, their opposing views on the subject. With a speech writer arbitrating, Ball and Perkins stayed up all night arguing over virtually every thought, sentence, even word. They finished just as Folsom was heading to Capitol Hill to testify and handed him the testimony as he walked out the door.

The Finance Committee reported out a bill that included Social Security improvements, but not the disability provisions. On the floor of the Senate, Senator Walter George (D-Ga) offered the disability insurance provisions as an amendment. The vote was a nail-biter. Majority leader Lyndon Johnson was, in his renowned way, twisting arms, grabbing lapels, buttonholing members, draping his arm around shoulders, and using his legendary persuasive powers to convince wavering senators to vote for disability insurance. He told everyone that "this is one of our most important positions." As the tension was building in the chamber, lobbyists for the AMA and for organized labor were grabbing members in the hallways just before they entered.

A number of members voted against the bill but had informed the leadership that if their votes were necessary, they would switch. On the other side, a few extremely conservative senators, including Joseph McCarthy (R-Wis.), were ready to vote for the bill, even though they opposed it, if it would result in a tie. They knew that if a tie occurred, Vice President Richard Nixon, as president of the Senate, would be forced to break it by casting the deciding vote against the bill. Recognizing that the disability bill was politically popular, the conservatives, whose views were well to the right of Nixon's, figured, that a vote by the vice president defeating the measure would damage his support when he inevitably ran for the presidency. The conservatives wanted to slow that train if they could.

When the final tally was read, the amendment had passed by a vote of 47 to 45—one vote, since Vice President Richard Nixon, as president of the Senate, would have defeated the legislation in the event of a tie. When the vote was concluded, there was pandemonium in the galleries. Nelson Cruiksshank, the chief labor lobbyist remembered sitting in the Senate gallery and relishing the victory with Ball, also there watching.

The 1956 presidential election was a reprise of 1952. Eisenhower, perhaps even more popular, once again handily defeated Adlai Stevenson, this time with Estes Kefauver as his running mate. Though television had been invented in 1926, its use exploded in the 1950s. By 1955, half of all the homes in the United States had televisions. Not surprisingly, the election of 1956 saw the first use of television campaign ads and televised conventions.

With a disability insurance program now in place, attention began to turn to health insurance. Insurance against the medical costs of ill health was a standard component of European programs of social insurance. It had been a goal of progressives since the days of Wisconsin Professor John R. Commons in the early twentieth century.

A number of hopeful developments were unfolding for health insurance. The 1950s were a decade of rapid growth in employer-provided pension plans and health insurance, thanks to union efforts on behalf of their members, coupled with a tight employment market. In 1957, two years after the AFL merged with the CIO, the executive council of the AFL-CIO voted to make enactment of government-provided health insurance the organization's top priority, in order to secure this protection for all workers. The American Hospital Association, which in the past had been opposed to the concept, was concerned about the financial pressure its member hospitals were experiencing and began to consider whether government-provided health insurance might be the answer.

Moreover, while the AMA's rallying cry against "socialized medicine" was still powerful, it had proven, in the last few years, to have chinks. Despite the charge of 'socialized medicine," Congress had enacted first the disability freeze, and then disability insurance itself. The same accusation of "socialized medicine" had been unsuccessful, in 1955, in an attempt to derail a Democratic proposal to distribute to all American children, free of charge, the newly discovered polio vaccine.

The vaccine's discovery was a major source of relief and a tremendous cause for celebration by the parents of the nation. The Administration proposed providing it free only to low-income children; Senator Lister Hill (D-Ala.), the Democratic chairman of the Senate Labor and Public Welfare Committee, proposed providing the vaccine free to everyone. In hearings before his Committee shortly before Hobby announced her resignation, she provoked unfavorable headlines when, prompted by Senator Barry Goldwater, she declared that the popular proposal of free vaccines for all American children would be "socialized medicine."

Now in the rhythm of enacting Social Security bills every two years, Congress passed legislation providing a benefit increase and extending benefits to families of disabled workers, and President Eisenhower signed it into law on August 28, 1958. The Social Security provisions had provoked little controversy. The biggest question was how large the benefit increases should be.

During consideration of the measure, Senator Wayne Morse (D-Ore) offered an amendment to add health insurance to the legislation, but the amendment lost on a voice vote. In the House, Representative Aime Forand (D-RI) introduced a health insurance bill for senior citizens. Wilbur Cohen had been among those advising Forand on the proposal. In response to the proposed legislation, the AMA quintupled its lobbying budget. The bill did not emerge from committee, but hearings were held. These developments marked the start of the newest and most serious drive yet for government health insurance.

In the 1958 midterm election, the AFL-CIO pushed the issue of health insurance. In November, the Democrats made sizable gains, picking up 15 seats in the Senate and 49 seats in the House. Pressure for action on health insurance was mounting.

A few months before the 1958 election, Eisenhower named Arthur Flemming to be the new secretary of health, education and welfare. Flemming, an experienced administrator and educator, was a proponent of health care for the elderly. He spent the next two years developing plans and attempting to sell them to the president.

Another who made a cameo appearance to urge Eisenhower to champion the cause of health insurance was Robert P. Burroughs, a New Hampshire businessman active in Republican politics. An early and active supporter of Eisenhower, Burroughs had traveled to Europe to meet with the future president, then the first Supreme Commander of NATO forces. Burroughs had been one of the first to urge Eisenhower to accept the Republican presidential nomination, and had been an informal adviser as Eisenhower sorted through his options. Eisenhower felt deep gratitude to Burroughs, who from then on always had immediate access to the president.

Eisenhower had, several years before, appointed Burroughs to serve on a Social Security advisory council; he and Ball became friends. As luck or fate would ordain, Ball had a summer home in New Hampshire, and the two men started to get together over the summers. Ball spoke about health insurance and Burroughs became interested. On October 16, 1959, Burroughs met privately with Eisenhower. At the meeting, Burroughs presented a draft plan, that Ball had largely drafted, to provide health insurance through Social Security, and argued that Eisenhower should "take the lead in bringing this protection to retired people." Although Eisenhower did not embrace the idea, he did urge Burroughs to work with Secretary Flemming. For his part, Flemming, who had been trying to interest the president in the issue, did a delighted double-take when Burroughs showed up on his doorstep, sent by the president himself.

That same year, a new Senate Subcommittee on Problems of the Aged and Aging conducted public hearings that focused increased attention on the problems of health care costs. So did a subcommittee of the Senate Committee on Labor and Public Welfare. Media coverage of the hearings spotlighted stories of elderly Americans unable to pay for the medical care they needed, and the press accounts caught the attention of the public. As a result, health insurance was becoming a major issue nationwide.

In 1960, like clockwork, another Social Security bill was before Congress. Included in the legislation was a provision to extend disability benefits to all workers regardless of age. Other improvements were included, as well. But the primary focus of the legislation was health care for the aged.

The powerful Democratic leaders, Speaker of the House Sam Rayburn and Senate Majority leader Lyndon Johnson, were determined to make progress. Johnson, his eye starting to gaze at the coveted presidential nomination of the Democratic party, was especially motivated.

Flemming and Ball sought to convince Eisenhower that it was in his and the nation's best interest for the administration to get behind a plan. Flemming developed a new, more modest alternative, which called for federal grants to states so that the states could provide subsidies for private health insurance for those with low income. Vice President Nixon, who was gearing up for his own presidential run, decided to embrace the Flemming plan and do what he could to win Eisenhower's support. The combination of forces resulted in the Flemming approach becoming an administration proposal.

The stage was set. The liberal Democrats favored a federal Medicare program that provided health insurance as part of a worker's retirement benefits, but the Ways and Means Committee defeated the social insurance approach by a vote of 17 to 8. The administration bill, which the Democrats saw as wholly inadequate, went down to defeat, as well. Wilbur Mills, who had become chairman of the House Ways and Means Committee in 1958, personally opposed the idea of adding health insurance to Social Security. He was concerned about jeopardizing the solvency of the rest of the Social Security system. At the same time, he was under tremendous pressure from Rayburn and Johnson. He looked for a compromise.

With the help of the ubiquitous Wilbur Cohen, Mills worked out a new approach. In 1935, when Congress had enacted welfare programs for the aged and for families with dependent children, the legislation contained one very progressive step forward. Up until that time, welfare payments, when they were provided outside of the poorhouse, generally were payments to grocers or other vendors for goods. The 1935 legislation mandated that the states, as a requirement of receiving federal matching money, pay recipients directly with cash, not indirectly with vendor payments.

Prohibiting demeaning vendor payments was good public policy and a big advance in humane welfare policy. The problem was that it prohibited states from paying doctors and hospitals. The Mills legislation carved out an exception from the vendor payment restriction, so that states could provide low-income recipients with medical care. In addition, the proposal provided for a new category of recipients. Middle-class people who had large medical payments that would force them into welfare—the so-called medically indigent—would be able to have their medical bills paid, as well.

At this point, the AMA realized that continuing to oppose everything was no longer a successful strategy. If the AMA saw health insurance for all the elderly as socialism, it saw health benefits targeted to those with low income and those in dire medical straits as socialism-lite, as some have quipped. Nevertheless, the physician group hoped the less filling socialism-lite approach might satisfy sufficiently to take away some of the steam from the push for more widespread health insurance. Consequently, the AMA consulted with Mills in drafting the legislation and supported it. With the AMA's backing, the bill flew through the House of Representatives.

In the Senate, Robert Kerr was acting as chairman of the Finance Committee because Chairman Harry Byrd was ill. Kerr did not approve of the health insurance approach, recognizing "I'd lose every doctor in the state," but wanted legislation that would help the elderly in Oklahoma. After working with Cohen and consulting with Mills, the Kerr-Mills bill was reported to the full Senate.

In August 1960, the Senate held a high-drama, post-presidential convention session to consider the Social Security legislation. The Democratic nominee for president, Senator John F. Kennedy, and his running mate, Senator Lyndon B. Johnson, attended as senators. Republican presidential nominee, Vice President Richard M. Nixon, attended as president of the Senate.

First, the administration plan was considered and defeated on a straight party-line vote. Next, the approach favored by the liberal Democrats—to add hospital insurance to Social Security—was defeated by a coalition of Republicans and supporters of the Kerr-Mills bill. Finally, the Kerr-Mills approach carried by a vote of 91 to 2. President Eisenhower signed the Social Security Amendments of 1960—which included the Kerr-Mills amendment—into law on September 13, 1960, about six weeks before Americans would choose their next president.

The cards seemed to be falling into place for health insurance at least for the elderly. The Kennedy-Johnson ticket was on record in support of expanding Social Security to include health care. Republican Presidential nominee Richard Nixon, too, had recognized the need to help the elderly pay their medical bills. After a half century of effort, the question of health insurance was beginning to look like when, not whether.

## CHAPTER 11

# Visible Gains, Subterranean Tremors

M ixed metaphors notwithstanding, Camelot and the New Frontier arrived with the new decade. John Fitzgerald Kennedy was the first American president born in the twentieth century. Dashingly handsome, a war hero with a strikingly beautiful and cultured wife, the new president projected the glamour of a Hollywood star, combined with the vigor of an athlete playing fun-filled football on brisk, clear autumn days.

Acting quickly after his inauguration, the new president sent a message to Congress on February 9, 1961, stating "Twenty-six years ago this nation adopted the principle that every member of the labor force and his family should be insured against the haunting fear of loss of income caused by retirement, death or unemployment...but there remains a significant gap that denies to all but those with the highest incomes a full measure of security—the high cost of ill health in old age."[1] The proposal outlined a plan to expand Social Security benefits to include payment for the cost of hospital care.

Perhaps Kennedy could achieve what had eluded the others. A half century earlier, John Commons, Arthur Altmeyer, Barbara Armstrong, and other social reformers had pushed for social insurance to cover health costs. President Roosevelt had considered including it in the Social Security Act of 1935 but had changed his mind, concerned that it could bring down the whole package of needed reforms. Truman had recommended it.

Eisenhower, too, saw the need for government help with health care costs, though he did not support a compulsory program of social insurance.

No one believed success would come easily. The day after Kennedy's message to Congress, the *New York Times* ran a front-page article headlined "Kennedy Submits Aged Care Plan; Stiff Fight Likely." In case the casual reader still had some illusions about an easy victory for the new administration, the article was subtitled "Republicans Openly Hostile—Some Key Democrats Are Cool to Program."

The battle lines had been drawn. Although the American Medical Association had supported government health insurance in 1917, it reversed course in 1920 and had never looked back. Now, with a new, popular president pushing for government-provided health care for the elderly, the AMA was in full fight mode. A May 8, 1961, *Newsweek* article quoted an AMA officer: "The surest way to total defeat is to say that the AMA should try to sit down and negotiate."

The AMA announced "an all-out effort" aimed to defeat "the most deadly challenge ever faced by the medical profession" and launched a nationwide television, radio, and newspaper ad campaign. Washington bureaucrats, the ads warned, would be right there with Americans in "the privacy of the examination room." Patients would lose the "freedom to choose their own doctor," and doctors would lose the ability "to treat....patients in an individual way."

Nor was the AMA fighting alone. Representing business were the Chamber of Commerce and the National Association of Manufacturers. The Health Insurance Association of America, which in 1993 would sponsor the Harry and Louise television commercials that so successfully galvanized opposition to President Bill Clinton's health insurance plan, represented 260 heath insurance companies in their opposition. The Pharmaceutical Manufacturers Association joined the fight, as did a variety of other powerful lobbies. And these groups had plenty of resources. To help defeat the president's priority legislation, the AMA established the American Medical Political Action Committee, or AMPAC.

On his side, the president had the American people. The Senate subcommittee charged with investigating the problems of the aged had spotlighted the burden of medical costs in hearings it conducted around the country. Millions of families had experienced firsthand the increasing hospital costs of the past decade. Gallup surveys revealed that two-thirds of all respondents would willingly pay higher taxes to finance old-age health insurance.

But widespread support among the electorate did not always translate into votes in Congress. The Democratic president had won the election by a razor-thin margin, and the Republicans had gained 22 seats in the House. In addition, Kennedy had plenty of opposition in his own party. The bill had to get through the Ways and Means Committee, chaired by the increasingly powerful Wilbur Mills. Sixteen of the committee's 25 members were opposed to the administration proposal, including Mills himself. On the bright side, if Mills could somehow be persuaded to support the measure, the other members would almost certainly follow his lead.

Spearheading the campaign for the administration was Wilbur Cohen, who had returned to government for the fight. Over the past years, between faculty responsibilities at Ann Arbor, he had assisted Democratic members of Congress with policy proposals and speeches. Two of those whom he had helped in their Senate days were President Kennedy and Vice President Lyndon Johnson.

In 1960, the Kennedy campaign had asked Cohen, at the senior age of 46, to become a leader of Senior Citizens for Kennedy, and he had agreed. After the election, the group was renamed the National Council of Senior Citizens for Health Care Through Social Security. New leadership took over, and Cohen moved to Washington. Asked what would be his dream job in the new administration, Cohen had responded, and was appointed, assistant secretary of legislation for the Department of Health, Education and Welfare.

He was aided in his fight for health insurance by organized labor. He was also joined by his longtime friend and ally Bob Ball. Since 1953, Ball had been running, at first unofficially, then officially, the Bureau of Old Age Survivors Insurance, the part of the Social Security Administration responsible for Social Security (as opposed to the Bureau of Public Assistance, unemployment insurance, and other programs). At the beginning of the Kennedy administration, some consideration had been given to naming Ball commissioner, but Cohen and Ball both wanted the job to be seen as nonpartisan, not necessarily changing with every new president. Consequently, Commissioner William L. Mitchell, another who had started with the program in the 1930s, stayed in the job until his retirement the following year.

When Mitchell decided to retire, Ball was quickly picked to replace him, becoming the fifth person in the program's history to hold the position of commissioner. In the swearing-in ceremony, Cohen spoke of Ball's "great ability, great sense of social responsibility, and great dignity." The outgoing commissioner praised his "intellectual capacity, integrity, industry, and resourcefulness."

Cohen, Ball, and others in the administration knew that they did not have the votes to win in 1961. Their strategy was to continue moving the process along and to maintain pressure on Congress. They recognized that health insurance for the elderly would be a popular issue in the 1962 midterm election, if no action was taken prior to that. Taking the long view, they hoped at the worst to achieve victory in 1963 or 1964, after the midterm election, if they were not successful before.

At the end of July and early August, the Ways and Means Committee held nine days of contentious hearings on the administration proposal. The hearings left no doubt that the issue remained highly charged. At the end of the hearings, Speaker Sam Rayburn told reporters that there were insufficient votes to bring the bill out of committee. Consistent with those comments, the *New York Times* reported that the Ways and Means Committee planned to do nothing more on the proposal that session.

The story attracted little notice, except from those directly involved. (It would have been an "inside the beltway" story, but the first section of that highway encircling the capital would not be opened until December.) Everyone was focused on Europe, where the Soviet Union was spending the month of August building the Berlin Wall.

Knowing that its Medicare proposal was a nonstarter in 1961 and concerned about the recession the country was experiencing, Kennedy had also proposed Social Security legislation recommending a variety of targeted improvements. Unlike the health care proposal, these changes flew through Congress, which, by this time, had developed substantial expertise on the subject. Kennedy signed the Social Security Amendments of 1961 into law a month before the Ways and Means Committee held its hearings on the administration's health proposal.

A month after the completion of the Ways and Means Committee hearings, Kennedy wrote the chairman of the Senate Special Committee on Aging, which was created that year to replace the Subcommittee on Problems of the Aged. In the letter, Kennedy related that he planned to make Medicare his "highest priority" in the 1962 congressional session. Soon after, the secretary of health, education and welfare, Abraham Ribicoff, announced that the administration would mount "a great fight across the land" to secure a Medicare bill. In late October, the White House sponsored 14 regional conferences. Behind the scenes, Cohen headed a task force designed to find common ground with Mills and others in order to develop legislation that could pass Congress.

Kennedy decided to seek recorded votes on Medicare in both the House and the Senate in 1962. Assistance for the hospital costs of the elderly was increasingly popular with the electorate, and the president wanted members to be on record. Kennedy planned to spotlight Medicare in the upcoming midterm election as an essential element in his New Frontier.

Rhetoric became more high-pitched and, if possible, even more adversarial in 1962. Proponents of reform charged that opponents were using "scare tactics," that they were "desperate men" engaged in "irrational tirades." For its part, the opposition accused the administration of engaging in a "propaganda blitz" for "partisan political gain." The federal Treasury, according to the opponents, was being "looted" in the process.

On May 20, 1962, Kennedy spoke at New York's Madison Square Garden to a crowd of almost 20,000 and to an additional 20 million people watching on television. In the speech, he set out the problem:

> [T]ake...a family which may be found in any part of the United States. The husband has worked hard all his life and he is retired. He might have been a clerk or a salesman...or worked in a factory....He's always wanted to pay his own way....His...children are now on their own. He and his wife are drawing social security....He has a pension from where he worked....He owns his own house. He has twenty-five hundred... dollars in the bank. And then his wife gets sick...First goes the twenty-five hundred dollars....Next he mortgages his house....Then he goes to his children, who themselves are heavily burdened....Then their savings begin to go.

In his speech, the president explained his proposal and asked for support. As part of a coordinated effort, other administration officials gave similar speeches in 45 cities around the country at the same time, including Cohen, who flew to San Diego to address a rally.

The AMA sought free television time to respond but was turned down, so the group purchased a half hour of paid time on NBC. The president of the AMA spoke at an empty Madison Square Garden, to highlight its "grossly unfair disadvantage." He denounced the administration's bill as "a cruel hoax and a delusion."

Despite the public posturing, progress was being made behind the scenes. Several Republicans introduced bills addressing the issue of health care costs for the elderly. The AMA signaled, through a magazine interview of its executive director, that the organization might accept health insurance for low-income elderly. Most important, Cohen was making headway in informal talks with several Ways and Means Committee members. Nevertheless, Mills remained determined not to report a bill out of the Ways and Means Committee. The Senate Finance Committee was no more help. It had voted 10 to 7 in January against even holding hearings. Nevertheless, a number of senators outside the committee were strong proponents, and they wanted to be on record before the election, showing their support for the popular measure.

With the administration's approval, two senators, one from each party, co-sponsored a health care amendment to an unrelated bill being considered on the floor. On July 17, the galleries were packed as the roll call began. The outcome was too close to predict. Every single senator was present. The first senator voted against the administration. Seesawing back and forth, the vote was tied after 26 senators had voted. The administration had a slight edge as the vote got to what *Time* magazine dubbed "the 'murderers' row' of Conservatives at the end of the alphabet." When the final vote was cast, the amendment had been defeated, 48 to 52. The outcome represented just a one-vote difference, because Senator Carl Hayden (D-Ariz.), had agreed in advance to vote for the measure if his vote had been needed to produce a tie.

An hour after the vote, President Kennedy staged a televised press conference, where he decried that "this is a most serious defeat for every American family." He pointed out, "Nearly all the Republicans and a handful of Democrats joined with them to give us today's setback." He closed by forcefully urging "I hope that we will return in November a Congress that will support a program like Medical Care for the Aged....With your support in November, this bill will pass in 1963."

Kennedy was reportedly most upset by the Democrats who opposed him. They included a number of the most powerful senators from the South. One, George Smathers (D-Fla.), had been Kennedy's best man when he married Jacqueline almost a decade before. Notwithstanding their friendship, Smathers voted regularly against the president, causing White House aides to quip, "He hasn't stood up for Jack since the wedding."

The Democratic National Committee, organized labor, and the AMA all campaigned hard on the issue of Medicare, but the election was dominated by foreign affairs. Just before the election, on October 22, 1962, Kennedy announced to the nation and the world that he was ordering a naval blockade of Cuba. Six days later, on October 28, Soviet premier Nikita Khrushchev agreed to remove the missiles that the Soviet Union had erected there.

The midterm election of 1962 brought no dramatic change. Democrats lost four seats in the House but retained control, with a dominating 259 Democrats to 176 Republicans. In the Senate, Democrats gained four seats, increasing the party's already lopsided control to 67 Democrats, 33 Republicans. The election did produce two open Democratic seats on the all-important Ways and Means Committee. The House Democratic leadership, which had resolved to place members on the committee only if they supported health insurance or at least promised not to block it, filled the two vacancies with members sympathetic to Medicare.

The new year delivered more grassroots activity. The AMA unveiled "Operation Hometown," a new effort to stir up opposition to what it saw as socialized medicine. The National Council of Senior Citizens grew in membership to 1.5 million. And the Senate Special Committee on Aging continued to hold publicity-drawing hearings.

The president sent modified Medicare legislation to Congress at the start of the new year, but the action was all behind-the-scenes. Cohen spent most of his time courting the critics, particularly Mills, trying various proposals to meet every objection raised. He was at his desk on November 22, 1963, in the middle of modifying the administration's proposal to meet some of those criticisms, when he learned that President Kennedy had been assassinated.

At the moment Kennedy was shot, Vice President Johnson was in another limousine in the motorcade on that hot, sunny day in Dallas, Texas. As the shots pierced the air, Secret Service agent Rufus Youngblood hurled Johnson to the floor of the car and protected him with his own body as the motorcade sped to Parkland Memorial Hospital.

The country fell into a unified period of mourning for its fallen leader. The next hours, days, and months witnessed President Johnson seek to calm and heal a traumatized nation, while steadily gathering the reins of power. Five days after the assassination, Johnson addressed a joint session of Congress and the entire nation. He enumerated President Kennedy's dreams, including the "dream of conquering the vastness of space…the dream of a Peace Corps…the dream of education for all of our children…the dream of jobs…the dream of care for our elderly…and above, all, the dream of equal rights for all Americans." He committed to the nation that those dreams "must and will be translated into effective action."

For more than half his life, Johnson had lived and breathed Washington politics. He had known personally all four of the presidents who preceded him in office. He understood the personalities, procedures, and customs of Congress and was more capable than anyone of getting legislation enacted.

Johnson's legislative skill and the nation's shock and grief combined to transform Kennedy's enumerated dreams into reality. On July 2, 1964, Johnson signed into law the landmark Civil Rights Act of 1964, which prohibited discrimination in employment and public accommodations. On August 20, he signed into law the Economic Opportunity Act of 1964, which created, among other programs, Head Start, Job Corps, and VISTA or Volunteers in Service to America. The question was, would this be Medicare's year, as well?

Johnson sent a message on health care to Congress on February 10, 1964. He declared that "too many Americans still are cut off by low incomes from adequate health services. Too many older people are still deprived of hope and dignity by prolonged and costly illness." And he threw down the gauntlet: "[O]ur remaining agenda…will be unfinished until each American enjoys the full benefits of modern medical knowledge."

On July 7, 1964, the Ways and Means Committee reported to the House of Representatives an election-year increase in Social Security benefits, but with no Medicare. A few days later, Congress recessed for the Republican National Convention, which was convening on July 13 at the Cow Palace in San Francisco.

The event was a coronation for conservative senator Barry Goldwater. Having lost by so tiny a margin in 1960, Richard Nixon might have been the frontrunner for the Republican nomination had he not, in effect, eliminated himself from contention two years before. Not only had he lost his

1962 bid to be governor of California, but he had petulantly lashed out at the press after the results were in, angrily declaring "You won't have Nixon to kick around anymore." Now it was Goldwater's turn.

In 1960, Goldwater's *Conscience of a Conservative* had been published. The slim, 120-page volume, ghostwritten by *National Review* editor and speechwriter L. Brent Bozell, criticized both Democrats and Republicans. Goldwater quoted disapprovingly Truman's secretary of state, Dean Acheson, for writing that the New Deal "conceived of the federal government as the whole people organized to do what had to be done." Goldwater objected equally to the words of Eisenhower-confidant Arthur Larson, who wrote that "if a job has to be done to meet the needs of the people and no one else can do it, then it is the proper function of the federal government."

"Here we have," Goldwater criticized, "an unqualified repudiation of the principle of limited government." Sounding like Herbert Hoover at the 1936 Republican National Convention, Goldwater complained of the two quotes, "There is no reference...to the Constitution." The book then discussed a variety of public policies, starting with "States' Rights."

In a chapter entitled "The Welfare State," Goldwater lumped together, undifferentiated, Social Security and public assistance. He claimed that "collectivists" had been unsuccessful in bringing about "Nationalization," or "a State-owned and operated economy." But, he warned, "The collectivists have not abandoned their ultimate goal—to subordinate the individual to the State—but their strategy has changed. They have learned that Socialism can be achieved through Welfarism quite as well as through Nationalization."

His bottom line was that Social Security and welfare should be provided by the private sector or, if government involvement was absolutely necessary, by state and local governments, but under no circumstances by the federal government. Rather, Social Security and programs like it inevitably, according to Goldwater, lead to "unlimited political and economic power...as absolute...as any oriental despot." The recipient of these programs, according to Goldwater, is transformed by them "into a dependent animal creature."

The book became an overnight hit, selling millions of copies and attracting an army of followers. One of the book's owners was George W. Bush, then a student at Phillips Academy, an exclusive prep school in Andover, Massachusetts. In addition to owning the book, Bush had the opportunity to hear Goldwater in person when the Arizona senator spoke to the Andover students at an evening assembly during Bush's senior year.

Goldwater's nomination as the Republican candidate for president was the culmination of an extensive grassroots movement that had begun in the summer of 1961, soon after *Time* magazine featured Goldwater on its cover. In that June 23 issue, *Time* gushed, "Barry Morris Goldwater, 52, traveling tirelessly about the land to champion the cause of the Republican Party, U.S. conservatism and his own variety of rugged individualism, is the hottest political figure this side of Jack Kennedy."

Later that summer, a group of men who had been leaders of the nationwide Young Republicans organization formed what would become the Draft Goldwater Committee. Also actively supporting Goldwater was another organization of young conservatives, the Young Americans for Freedom, which had been created in the fall of 1960 on the Sharon, Connecticut, estate of William F. Buckley, Jr., conservative founder and publisher of the *National Review*. In 1962, the YAF had held a rally in Madison Square Garden at which Goldwater addressed a crowd of 18,500 people.

The campaign had faltered slightly in the New Hampshire primary. In response to a reporter's question about Social Security, Goldwater had responded, "I would like to suggest…that Social Security be made voluntary, that if a person can provide better for himself, let him do it." The ramifications of Goldwater's proposal were instantly apparent. The headline the next day in the *Concord Monitor* read, "Goldwater Sets Goals: End Social Security" Not surprisingly, Goldwater lost the primary.

Advising Goldwater was Milton Friedman, who shared the candidate's views on Social Security. In 1962, Friedman had published *Capitalism and Freedom*, which was a compilation of lectures that Friedman had delivered a half dozen years earlier. In a chapter entitled "Social Welfare Measures," Friedman asserted, "The 'social security' program…involves a large-scale invasion into the personal lives of a large fraction of the nation without, so far as I can see, any justification that is at all persuasive."

Recovering from the New Hampshire loss, the Goldwater campaign got a big boost in California. A co-chairman of Californians for Barry Goldwater was asked to speak at a fundraiser at the Coconut Grove in Los Angeles. The speaker gave an electrifying address, which was repeated on nationwide television a week before the election.

The speaker, well-known actor Ronald Reagan, voiced similar themes about Social Security. "[C]an't we introduce voluntary features that would permit a citizen to do better on his own, to be excused upon presentation of evidence that he had made provisions for the nonearning years?" And then Reagan repeated the same strident attack against Social Security that opponents had been making since the 1930s:

> [I]n 1936, Mr. Democrat himself, Al Smith, the great American, came before the American people and charged that the leadership of his Party was taking the Party of Jefferson, Jackson, and Cleveland down the road under the banners of Marx, Lenin, and Stalin. And he walked away from his Party, and he never returned til the day he died—because to this day, the leadership of that Party has been taking that Party…down the road in the image of the labor Socialist Party of England.

Goldwater won the California primary, helped in large measure by his chief competitor, Nelson Rockefeller, who flew home to New York every weekend to be with his pregnant second wife. Rockefeller's advisers warned him that these trips simply reminded voters of his scandalous remarriage. A mere 18 months after divorcing the mother of his five children, Rockefeller had married "Happy" Murphy, a woman with whom he had been conducting a five-year affair. To add to the scandal, Happy had given up custody of her own four children in order to secure her own divorce. To the objections of his advisers, Rockefeller responded that his second wife was more important to him than the presidency.

In politics, timing is everything. In unfortunate timing, Happy gave birth to their son, Nelson Rockefeller, Jr., just days before the California primary. Rockefeller flew to be by his wife's side while the Goldwater campaign unleashed a flood of new ads questioning Rockefeller's morality and emphasizing Goldwater's close traditional family. Although Goldwater won just that one contested primary, and attracted only 51.6 percent of the vote there, he was unstoppable from that point on.

Unlike earlier Republican conventions where the winning candidate sought to unify the party, Goldwater made no such effort, picking fellow conservative Bill Miller for his running mate rather than a more moderate member of the party. In accepting the nomination, Goldwater galvanized the delegates, but frightened moderates, when he asserted, "[E]xtremism in the defense of liberty is no vice. And…moderation in the pursuit of justice is no virtue." And the divisive mood of the convention was not helped by the boos and catcalls Goldwater delegates let fly at Rockefeller, drowning out his words, when it was his turn to speak.

After the convention, Congress returned to Washington. The House of Representatives took up the Social Security benefit increase that the Ways and Means Committee had reported to the House just before recessing for the Republican convention. The House passed the Social Security Amendments of 1964 by a vote of 388 to 8. In the Senate Finance Committee, several amendments were offered to add hospital insurance to the bill. All failed. The bill, raising Social Security benefits but including no health provisions, was reported out of committee on August 21.

Then the Democrats were off to Atlantic City, New Jersey, to convene from August 24 to August 27. There they nominated Lyndon Johnson and Hubert Humphrey as the Democratic ticket in the upcoming election.

Back in Congress after the convention, the proposed Social Security Amendments of 1964 were the pending business before the Senate. Al Gore, Sr. (D-Tenn.), offered an amendment, on August 31, which increased further the proposed level of Social Security benefits and added hospital insurance to the program. The vote was a cliffhanger, as it had been the year before. Five moderate Republicans voted for the program. Sixteen Democrats, all but one from the South, voted against. Republican nominee Goldwater interrupted a campaign trip to fly back to Washington in order to vote against the amendment. By a vote of 49 to 44, the Gore amendment passed.

After years of congressional deliberations, a half century after the American Association for Labor Legislation drafted its model bill, the Senate passed government-provided health insurance for the elderly. But there was little time for supporters to savor their historic victory. The next day, the entire bill passed the Senate by a vote of 60 to 28; then it was time for proponents to match wits with Wilbur Mills.

Seeking to ensure that the health insurance proposal emerge from the conference committee as part of the report, the administration flirted with an effort to have the full House of Representatives vote to instruct the conference to yield to the Senate version. Though the health insurance provision appeared to have majority support in the House, the tactic did not, and the idea was dropped. Sure enough, the House conferees voted 3 to 2 against the Senate health provision; the Senate conferees voted 4 to 3 to accept a bill only if Medicare were included.

As with the Clark amendment in 1935, the conference was hopelessly deadlocked. Ordinarily, with just weeks to go before the election, the conferees would have dropped the health care provisions and agreed to the Social Security benefit increase. However, both sides recognized that an increase in the contribution rate to support larger Social Security benefits could complicate the future enactment of health insurance paid for through wage contributions and payroll taxes. Seeing the increasing probability that Medicare would be enacted, its opponents pushed for raising Social Security benefits substantially. Unwilling to compromise on even the normally noncontroversial benefit increase, the conferees remained deadlocked. On October 2, Mills announced that the conference committee was unable to reach agreement.

On the surface, it appeared that Medicare, in the words of a *New York Times* editorial, faced "the limbo of perennial issues." Nevertheless, subtle and not-so-subtle signals to the contrary abounded. Mills himself, in speaking to an Arkansas Kiwanis Club shortly before the unsuccessful conclusion of the conference committee, remarked, "I have always thought there was great appeal in the arguments that wage earners, during their working lifetime, should make payments into a fund to guard against the risk of financial disaster due to heavy medical costs....I am acutely aware of the fact that there is a problem here which must be met."

Still, not everyone was convinced. A week before the election, Ronald Reagan asserted, in a televised address in support of Goldwater, "[N]o one in this country should be denied medical care because of a lack of funds. But I think we're against forcing all citizens, regardless of need, into a compulsory government program."

But the electorate apparently was in favor of being forced. Johnson won in a landslide, garnering almost 61 percent of the popular vote. The president barely missed carrying Goldwater's home state of Arizona. The only other states that Goldwater carried were five southern states, embittered by Johnson's support for civil rights. And the congressional wins were just as big. The Democrats gained 38 House seats, resulting in 295 Democrats to 140 Republicans, and 1 additional Senate seat, increasing their margin to 68 Democrats to 32 Republicans. Because Johnson had made clear that Medicare would be a top priority if he won reelection, many saw the vote as a mandate for it.

After the election but before the new Congress convened, Mills signaled his willingness to support the health insurance proposal. Speaking to the Little Rock Lions Club on December 2, 1964, Mills explained, "I can support a payroll tax for financing health benefits just as I have supported a payroll tax for cash benefits."

Cohen consulted with Ball and began to develop a modified hospital insurance bill for the administration. Myers worked on the actuarial aspects of the proposal. This was the beginning of long days and nights of drafting, consulting, and negotiating for Cohen and Ball—a period that, they both realized, would probably result in the enactment of the legislation that they had been working on for so long. Seeing the package as a train leaving the station, the two men loaded it up. The AMA was supporting an expansion of the 1960 Kerr-Mills proposal, in an effort to forestall the enactment of more broad-based insurance for the elderly. Building on the AMA idea, the administration bill, in addition to including Social Security benefits for hospital costs, provided for the expansion of Kerr-Mills so that it paid the health costs of all low-income people, not just the low-income elderly.

Meanwhile, Wisconsin Congressman John Byrnes, ranking Republican on Ways and Means, worked on a Republican alternative. Modeled on the plan offered to federal employees, it provided for a voluntary arrangement, financed partly through premiums and partly through general revenue. It had one big selling point over the administration's plan: It covered doctors' fees, not just the hospital costs covered under the administration's approach. The Republicans were fond of pointing out that the Democratic plan was not nearly as generous in its coverage.

In the new Congress, the Social Security health insurance proposal was the first bill introduced and, accordingly, was assigned the number H.R. 1 in the House of Representatives and S.1 in the Senate. Mills now became a leader in pushing the legislation. He immediately convened the committee and began to hold marathon-length sessions, considering every detail of the complicated legislation.

One afternoon, the committee was intensely debating the pros and cons of the administration's approach of using taxes on employers and employees to finance new Social Security benefits paying hospital costs versus the Republican alternative, which would establish voluntary insurance purchased with subsidized premiums and paying all medical costs, versus the AMA approach, which focused exclusively on the low-income population. In the middle of the discussion, Mills posed a simple question for which no one had a good answer: Why not do everything? Why not include the AMA plan and Byrnes's plan and the administration plan?

Sure enough, the bill that emerged from committee contained Medicare Part A, a mandatory federal program financed by employer and employee payroll contributions and covering hospital costs; Medicare Part B, a voluntary federal program financed by premiums and general revenue and covering physician services; and Medicaid, a joint federal-state program, financed from general revenue and covering low-income nonelderly, as well as elderly. On April 8, 1965, the House of Representatives made history by passing the bill by a margin of 313 to 115. The Senate passed its own version on July 9 by a vote of 68 to 21. The conference report was passed by both chambers of Congress at the end of July.

President Johnson flew to Independence, Missouri, to sign Medicare and Medicaid into law on July 30, 1965, in the presence of former President Harry Truman, who had been the first president to advocate national health insurance. Truman put the matter plainly:

> This is an important hour for the Nation, for those of our citizens who have completed their tour of duty and have moved to the sidelines.... These people are our prideful responsibility....Not one of these, our citizens, should ever be abandoned to the indignity of charity....Mr. President, I am glad to have lived this long.

Then it was Johnson's turn.

> No longer will older Americans be denied the healing miracle of modern medicine. No longer will illness crush and destroy the savings that they have so carefully, put away over a lifetime so that they might enjoy dignity in their later years. No longer will young families see their own incomes, and their own hopes, eaten away simply because they are carrying out their deep moral obligations to their parents....And no longer will this Nation refuse the hand of justice to those who have given a lifetime of service and wisdom and labor to the progress of this progressive country.

With the passage of Medicare and Medicaid, the Social Security Administration went about the massive job of implementing the complicated legislation. Medicare alone involved the staffs of approximately 6600 hospitals, about 250,000 physicians, around 1300 home health agencies, numerous Blue Cross, Blue Shield and other health insurance companies, over 100 group practice prepayment plans and scores of agencies acting as fiscal intermediaries. In the first 60 days, hospitals saw a million Medicare patients. Yet as it had done throughout its existence, Social Security, now under the stewardship of Bob Ball, efficiently and successfully implemented the three new medical programs, Medicare Part A, Medicare Part B, and Medicaid.

As a reward for his important contribution, as a means of keeping him from returning to the University of Michigan, and as a mark of his value, Johnson appointed Wilbur Cohen to the position of undersecretary of health, education and welfare, the second highest position in the department. Confirmed without controversy, Cohen laughingly told friends that Robert Weaver, soon to be appointed secretary of housing and urban development, "called me up and said [the lack of controversy] must be because I am getting too conservative."

With Medicare and Medicaid now law, attention turned to the retirement, disability, and survivor parts of Social Security. Democrats and Republicans both recognized the value of keeping those cash benefits up to date. The arguments arose at the margin, whether the relatively low level of benefits should be made more adequate or whether that job should be left for individuals and their employers to handle.

Between 1958 and 1965, no general across-the-board benefit increases were enacted. Congress passed a 7 percent increase in 1965, but it was insufficient to make up for the preceding seven years of inflation and wage growth. In 1967, Johnson requested a 15 percent increase along with other more targeted improvements. In the Ways and Means Committee, the increase was reduced to 12.5 percent, but in the Senate, the benefit increase was restored to the administration-recommended 15 percent. The conference committee settled on a 13 percent increase.

The next year, 1968, brought another presidential election. The Vietnam War was in full swing and the nation was convulsed with protests, demonstrations, and marches. Senator Eugene McCarthy (D-Minn.), running as an antiwar candidate, decided to challenge Johnson for the Democratic presidential nomination. McCarthy garnered 42 percent of the vote in New Hampshire on March 12 and won the Wisconsin primary outright two days later. Two days after that, Senator Robert F. Kennedy (D-N.Y.) threw his hat in the ring, as well. In a March 31 televised address to the nation, President Johnson shocked everyone when he announced:

> With America's sons in the fields far away, with America's future under challenge right here at home, with our hopes and the world's hopes for peace in the balance, I do not believe that I should devote an hour or a day of my time to any personal partisan causes....Accordingly, I shall not seek, and I will not accept, the nomination of my party for another term as your President.

The secretary of health, education and welfare had departed in January, and Cohen had been acting secretary since that time. In the spring, Johnson appointed Cohen to that cabinet post, a position he held for the remainder of the Johnson presidency.

The Democratic National Convention in Chicago was a television news anchor's dream, a politician's nightmare. As television footage outside the convention hall caught Chicago police clubbing antiwar protesters, cameras inside the hall showed Chicago mayor Richard Daley cursing Senator Abraham Ribicoff as, from the podium, the Connecticut senator denounced the police tactics.

By contrast, the Republican nomination process was calm and orderly. Richard M. Nixon, in a remarkable comeback from 1962, handily won the nomination in a campaign emphasizing law and order. But below the calm surface, the ground was shifting.

The same army of supporters who had championed the Goldwater candidacy had worked, two years later, to elect Ronald Reagan to the office of governor of California. During the 1968 convention, these Young Americans for Freedom breakfasted with a member of the organization's advisory board who was running for the Senate and they brunched with William Buckley. They also mounted a losing campaign to nominate Governor Reagan for president.

In addition to Democratic candidate Hubert Humphrey and Republican candidate Nixon, the segregationist former governor of Alabama, George Wallace, was also on the ballot. On November 5, Wallace got 13.5 percent of the vote, Humphrey received 42 percent, and Nixon won with 43.2 percent.

After the election, the Young Americans for Freedom group turned its energy to campus politics. In 1969, the Young America's Foundation was formed to become, in its words, "the principal outreach organization of the Conservative Movement." Still around was the Intercollegiate Society of Individualists, whose first president, back in 1953, had been William Buckley. Now renamed the Intercollegiate Studies Institute, it channeled money to conservative students who were starting and running college newspapers with a conservative slant.

Both the Democratic and Republican party platforms that year called for automatic adjustments for Social Security, though the Democratic platform called for first raising the benefit levels "to overcome present inadequacies." As has often happened throughout the history of Social Security, conservatives and liberals agreed on the same sets of reforms for strikingly different reasons. For this policy fight, observers would need a scorecard.

Ball favored the so-called automatics because he was concerned that recipients experienced drops in their standards of living while waiting for Congress to raise benefit levels in response to changes in inflation and wage growth. The Social Security population was elderly, many beneficiaries in their 80s and 90s with relatively short life expectancies, and he did not want to delay updating their benefits. Myers supported automatic increases for completely different reasons. He was concerned about the congressional tendency to respond to election-year pressure by significantly expanding benefits rather than just updating them.

Cohen disagreed with his longtime colleagues. He thought it was helpful to the program to have frequent congressional action. Congress generally enacted other improvements in the same legislation. Also, the constant legislating produced knowledgeable members. Economist Arthur Burns, a Nixon adviser who would become chairman of the Federal Reserve Board, opposed the idea of automatic increases on economic grounds. He was concerned about the impact on the economy of larger benefits in inflationary times, when spending should be curbed, and no increases in deflationary times, when spending should be encouraged. He also was concerned about a measure that he feared would institutionalize inflation by insulating the elderly from its effects.

Elected officials were no more uniform in their views. Representative John Byrnes, the ranking minority member on the Ways and Means Committee, and Representative Melvin Laird (R-Wisc.), the ranking member on the Social Security subcommittee of the House Appropriations Committee, both favored the idea of automatic adjustments. But powerful Wilbur Mills did not. He liked the political control and credit that came with legislating increases.

To add to the political complexity, President Nixon was contemplating a major reform in two other parts of the Social Security Act of 1935. When Congress enacted Social Security in 1935, it had also enacted the Old Age

Assistance (OAA) program and Aid to Families with Dependent Children (AFDC). These programs provided matching funds to states giving financial assistance to low-income elderly and to families of low-income children, respectively. AFDC was particularly complicated to administer and controversial. The original intent in 1935 was to provide benefits in situations where a parent's support was lost as a result of death, disability, or abandonment. But issues arose if the father was absent, but another man was living in the home. Was that a qualifying situation or not? Over time, states used the eligibility requirements as a pretext to control what administrators saw as immoral behavior on the part of the children's mothers. In 1960, 23,000 children were kicked off the Louisiana rolls because their mothers had borne other children outside of marriage.

Former Harvard professor Daniel Patrick Moynihan, a domestic adviser to Nixon, developed a new program, the Family Assistance Plan, which would replace both OAA and AFDC with a completely federal program providing a uniform benefit nationwide. Many conservatives, who objected on philosophical grounds to guaranteeing a person's income opposed the proposal. Liberals objected to the low level of benefits that were proposed.

To ease its passage, Nixon decided to combine the controversial Family Assistance Plan with a one-time 10 percent across-the-board increase in Social Security benefit levels and automatic increases thereafter. On September 25, 1969, the president sent the comprehensive Social Security legislation to Congress. In an accompanying message, Nixon said, "This nation must not break faith with those Americans who have a right to expect that Social Security payments will protect them and their families. The impact of an inflation now in its fourth year has undermined the value of every Social Security check."

Instead of acting on the comprehensive package, however, the Ways and Means Committee reported out of committee just an ad hoc increase of 15 percent, jointly cosponsored by Chairman Mills and ranking minority member Byrnes. The 15 percent increase flew through the House, passing unanimously. In the Senate, Russell Long (D-La.), son of Huey Long and now the chairman of the Senate Finance Committee, attached the same increase to the Tax Reform Act of 1969, then being considered in the Senate. President Nixon signed the bill into law on December 30.

The next year, in a replay of what happened the year before, Mills had his Ways and Means Committee report out a simple ad hoc benefit increase of 5 percent. This time, Representative Byrnes offered an amendment on the floor to recommit the bill to committee with instructions to add the automatic increases and report the bill back to the full House. In a rare defeat for Mills, a coalition of Democrats and Republicans passed the amendment, and the bill was sent to the Senate containing the automatic adjustment formula.

The Senate version of the bill also included the automatic adjustment provision, making final passage appear a certainty. Though it appeared Mills had lost, he was not done fighting. The Senate Finance Committee, as is the custom, appointed conferees and formally asked the Ways and Means Committee for a conference to reconcile differences in the two measures. In a creative, eleventh-hour move, Mills refused the request. The unconferenced legislation died when Congress adjourned, notwithstanding that the House and Senate versions each contained the proposal.

At the beginning of the new Congress, the first bill introduced in the House, H.R. 1, was Nixon's comprehensive reform containing his welfare proposal and his proposal for automatic annual adjustments for Social Security. But this time, rather than blocking its passage, Mills was its sponsor.

As Ball had watched the unfolding congressional action, he decided to see what he could do to change the outcome in the next session. A majority of Congress and the administration wanted the measure, but one man, Wilbur Mills, was single-handedly blocking the road. On his own initiative, Ball met with Mills and suggested a modification in the automatic-adjustment legislation that would address the chairman's concerns. If the automatic adjustments were a fail-safe mechanism, taking effect only if Congress failed to act, Ball advised, Mills could preempt the automatics any time he chose, simply by acting first. Mills liked the idea and jumped on it.

On May 18, the Ways and Means Committee reported H.R. 1 to the floor with both the historic welfare and Social Security changes included. As Senate deliberations on the Family Assistance part of the bill dragged on through all of 1971, Mills developed a new ambition. He decided he wanted to seek the Democratic nomination for president. With an eye toward the New Hampshire and Florida primaries, both states with large numbers of Social Security recipients, he had an idea that might help him win votes.

Though the proposal adjusting Social Security benefits automatically was temporarily stalled with the controversial welfare reform proposal, he knew that it would be enacted that term. He also saw that once it was enacted, the Social Security actuaries would have to switch from static assumptions about wage growth to dynamic ones, since the program would not depend on legislative action but would increase benefits automatically. And once the switch was made, there would be a projected surplus, for the same reasons there had always been one every year or two in the past.

This time, because of the one-time switch from static to dynamic assumptions, the projected surplus would be large. Mills asked Ball how large. The change to dynamic assumptions, Ball told the chairman, supported a whopping 20 percent increase in benefits. (Ball and Elliot Richardson, the secretary of health, education and welfare, had earlier tried to sell the White House on proposing the 20 percent increase, but to no avail.)

That was all Mills needed to hear. The year before, on March 12, 1971, Senator Long had successfully attached a 10 percent increase, retroactive to January 1, to a veto-proof bill increasing the debt limit of the federal government. Mills decided to use the same approach, since the administration objected to so large an ad hoc increase. On June 30, 1972, Congress enacted the ad hoc increase together with the automatic adjustments, starting in 1975, and Nixon signed the veto-proof legislation on July 1, 1972.

On October 30, the president signed into law the Social Security Amendments of 1972. In the legislation, the controversial Family Assistance Plan had been modified and narrowed to cover only the most sympathetic poor—the poor aged, blind, and disabled. The new program, Supplemental Security Income, is often confused with Social Security because both programs are administered by the Social Security Administration, they serve overlapping populations, and they have similar sounding names. But that is where the similarities end. Completely separate and independent from Social Security, the Supplemental Security Income program is a means-tested welfare program funded from general revenues.

The election was just days away. As in 1968, the main issues in the 1972 election were the Vietnam War and the sound-bite concept, law and order. George Wallace once again declared his candidacy, this time as a Democrat, but was paralyzed in an assassination attempt while addressing a crowd in Laurel, Maryland, on May 15, 1972. The Democratic candidate, Senator George McGovern, ran as an antiwar candidate.

Mills's 20 percent benefit increase, enacted over the summer was ready to be included in the monthly Social Security checks in the fall before the election. Traditionally, increased benefits were accompanied by simple straightforward notices employing formulaic language, which simply stated that Congress had passed and the president had signed into law the enclosed increase. This time, in anticipation of the upcoming election, Chuck Colson, the Nixon aide who famously remarked, "I'd walk over my own grandmother to re-elect Richard Nixon," saw an opportunity. He decided that a message with red, white, and blue coloring, Nixon quotes, his signature, and perhaps even his photograph, with words implying that he alone was responsible for the increase that he in fact had opposed, would be just the thing.

This kind of politicizing of the program was unprecedented. Ball complained to Secretary Elliot Richardson. The secretary asked Richard Darman, a Harvard Business School graduate on his staff, to intervene with the White House. At the same time, Ball upped the ante, indicating that if the Democratic Congress got word of the ploy, they would likely pass a law prohibiting the action, generating considerable unfavorable publicity for the administration. He also threatened to resign in protest. In the end, the White House backed down, and the standard notice was used.

Even without the benefit check inserts, Nixon won in a landslide, receiving almost as high a percentage of the popular vote as Johnson had in 1964 and losing only Massachusetts and the District of Columbia. After the 1972 election, Nixon decided to replace Ball with a commissioner of his own choosing.

Because Ball had run the Social Security Administration efficiently and smoothly, successfully implementing the extremely technical, complicated Medicare program, the Nixon administration had kept him as commissioner of Social Security for the first term. That decision had angered Myers. As a consequence, Myers had left government in 1970 two years into Nixon's first term. But he had not gone quietly.

During the Eisenhower years, Myers believed that career civil servants "funnelled information to liberals in Congress," although he pointed out that "this was done in a way that didn't leave individuals' fingerprints." Myers had decided at the end of the Eisenhower administration that if he "was around to see another Republican in the White House," he would "blow the whistle" on the "expansionists," as he called Ball and other liberals interested in expanding Social Security.

As soon as Nixon took office in 1969 and decided to retain Ball as commissioner, Myers had sought meetings with high-ranking members of the administration to voice his concerns. Everyone had listened politely but had taken no action. In speeches to professional actuarial groups, business organizations, and senior citizen groups, Myers began to talk publicly about what he believed were the subversions going on in the bureaucracy, and the newspapers began to cover the remarks.

With the administration still taking no action against Ball, Myers had approached *Reader's Digest* with a proposed article about his charges, and the high-circulation magazine had agreed to print it. After the article appeared, the altercation came to a head. Myers had been invited to give several speeches out of town, but the date conflicted with a meeting of an advisory council. Ball insisted that Myers attend the meeting. As Myers described it, "I sent [Ball] back a note the same day, telling him, essentially, to take a long walk in a cold rain," and went on the trip. That was the end of Myers's civil service career.

By spring of 1973, as President Nixon's second term got underway, neither Ball nor Cohen nor Myers worked for the government. But none was retired. And none was out of the business of Social Security policy making. Still, an era had passed. Ball had spent 33 years in the government working on Social Security. He had risen from a GS-3, the lowest-level job given a college applicant, to commissioner of Social Security, an office requiring a presidential appointment and Senate confirmation. Myers had devoted 36 years to government service. Twenty-three of those years were in the crucial position of chief actuary. And Cohen had worked in the government for 29 years, his last position, the secretary of health, education and welfare, a position in the cabinet of the President of the United States.

In a foreshadowing of things to come, the same year that Ball left government, a new player, the Heritage Foundation, joined the Washington policy-making scene. Its self-described mission was "to formulate and promote conservative public policies based on the principles of free enterprise, limited government, individual freedom, traditional American values, and a strong national defense." The values that the Heritage Foundation exposed are, of course, all ones that virtually all Americans embrace. Somehow, in the minds of members of Eisenhower's tiny splinter group though, the values of free enterprise, limited government, and individual freedom always seemed to mysteriously morph into opposition to Social Security.

CHAPTER 12

# The Sky Is Falling
# and Social Security
# Is Bust

Nineteen seventy-three was not a good year for confidence in government, the economy, or retirement income. That summer, Americans were glued to their television sets, watching a procession of witnesses testify before the Senate Watergate Committee, which was investigating the scandals swirling around President Richard Nixon.

On Yom Kippur, Egypt and Syria attacked Israel. The Organization of Petroleum Exporting Countries (OPEC) announced that its members would ship no oil to the United States or any other country supporting Israel in the war and would quadruple the price of oil worldwide. An already-sluggish U.S. economy and already-high inflation intensified, as lines at gas stations grew long, sometimes snaking for miles, and prices on everything seemed to skyrocket. The price of food jumped 20 percent. Inflation climbed to 11 percent, with some months reaching annualized rates of over 16 percent. At the same time, unemployment rates soared. By 1975, unemployment reached 8.5 percent, the highest it had been since before the nation's entry into World War II.

That same year also witnessed unsettling news stories about income Americans were counting on for retirement. Congress was nearing the end of a decade-long struggle to enact legislation aimed at protecting the rights of American workers in employer-promised pensions. The struggle was punctuated by sensational hearings and books highlighting the many ways people failed to get pensions they counted on.

Charlie Reed, a coal miner with Jones and Laughlin Steel Corporation, worked in the mines for 23 years until he was laid off. When Reed turned 65, he applied for a pension. He learned that he had failed to meet the plan's vesting requirements, and he was left with nothing. Joseph Vojnarowski worked 42 years with Haws Refractories in Johnstown, Pennsylvania. On the eve of his retirement, at age 64, he, too, was left with no pension because the pension trust had been inadequately funded and was bankrupt. People read news stories like these and thought about their own pensions.

And in 1973, for the first time in the 38-year history of Social Security, the trustees of the program's trust funds reported that the program projected a deficit. The automatic increases enacted under President Nixon followed the design of the ad hoc increases that had come before. Never before, however, had the nation undergone the double-digit inflation, sluggish wage growth, and high unemployment it was now experiencing.

Inflation had caused benefit levels—outgo—to increase more rapidly than anticipated, and unemployment and slow wage growth had caused Social Security income to be lower than projected. To make matters worse, the formula enacted in 1972 was extremely sensitive to the exact economic conditions the country was experiencing. The formula worked fine for adjusting the benefits of those already retired. It would have worked fine for workers just starting to retire had the same conditions that had existed over the life of the program continued. It did not work fine, though, in this period of rapid inflation and lethargic wage growth. For those just applying for benefits, the formula produced larger and larger benefits as a percentage of final pay. If the formula were unchanged and the economic conditions had remained what they were, eventually it would have provided people more in monthly Social Security benefits than they took home in paychecks while working.

The problem with the formula became painfully obvious soon after it was enacted into law. The annual trustees' reports began showing higher costs and lower income each year. In the 1975 report, the trustees forecast that the funds would be exhausted by 1979.

Opponents of Social Security wasted no time seeking to capitalize on the deficit, an action the responsible press noted and criticized. "Thirty-five years after issuance of the first benefit checks by the Social Security System, critics of this widely and deservedly admired program are doing their utmost to undermine confidence in both its fairness and its actuarial soundness," informed a 1975 *New York Times* editorial. The *Times* connected the contemporary critics with those of the past. "The criticisms are of a kind Congress rightly rejected at the birth of Social Security, but recession-fed anxieties about every aspect of the economy tend to give them exaggerated credibility now."

In response to the projected deficit, President Gerald Ford, who had succeeded the scandal-battered Nixon when he resigned, sent a Special Message to Congress on February 9, 1976, proposing corrective measures. The correction was intended, like the original 1972 indexing provision, to mirror what had been done historically on an ad hoc basis every few years.

Recognizing that the goal of retirement programs is to replace wages at the end of a worker's career, the Ford administration developed a formula that would replace the same percentage of final pay for workers over time. High-salaried workers earning at the maximum taxable wage base would receive benefits equal to around 27 percent of final pay, whether they retired in 2010, 2050, or 2100. Average-income workers (earning the equivalent of around $35,000 today) toward the ends of their careers, would receive, at retirement, a benefit equal to around 41 percent of final pay; and low-income workers (earning the equivalent of around $16,000 today), would receive from Social Security approximately 55 percent of final pay.

These percentages were set at about the level that benefits were at after the 1969 amendments. They are about the levels the 1939 amendments assumed they would be. In addition to the formula change, Ford recommended an increase in the Social Security payroll tax contributions of just 0.3 percent on employers and employees each—an amount costing workers, at most, $1 a week.

About his proposals, Ford pointed out, "Their prompt enactment will demonstrate our concern that lifetimes of sacrifice and hard work conclude in hope rather than despair." He declared, "Maintaining the integrity of the system is a vital obligation each generation has to those who have contributed to it all their lives." And he pledged, "I strongly reaffirm my commitment to a stable and financially sound Social Security system."

But it was an election year. Despite Ford's best intentions, Congress was unwilling to do anything that would reduce future benefits or raise the payroll tax by even the small three-tenths of 1 percent the program needed.

And indeed the election was heating up. Ronald Reagan had announced that he would challenge Ford for the Republican nomination.

Reagan emphasized that he was an outsider to Washington, in contrast to Washington-insider Ford, who was first elected to Congress in 1948, almost three decades earlier. Consistent with the outsider theme, a Reagan campaign brochure from 1976 began:

> Reasons for Reagan:
>     He'll work to return government to the people.
>     The federal bureaucracy didn't make America great. The people did. And as the bureaucracy grew larger and more cumbersome—as government slipped out of the hands of the people—America became less and less able to cope with its problems.

The Ford campaign, directed by Ford's chief of staff, Richard B. Cheney (today, President Bush's vice president), won the Florida primary when it made an issue of Reagan's stand on Social Security. In an unspoken comparison, a widely distributed Ford campaign brochure stated that the president would "preserve the integrity and solvency of the Social Security system." Despite his Florida win, Ford barely captured the Republican nomination with a delegate count of 1,187 to Reagan's 1,070.

Also running as an outsider to Washington—a message that played well with the voters in light of Watergate—was the Democratic standard bearer, Jimmy Carter. In his speech accepting the Democratic nomination for president, Carter said, "As a governor, I had to deal each day with the complicated and confused and overlapping and wasteful federal government bureaucracy." Fueling sentiments of cynicism and distrust, Carter pointedly remarked, "It is time for the people to run the government, and not the other way around." The theme played well enough to give Carter the victory in November.

The summer after the election, the Carter administration's proposal to solve Social Security's fiscal problems was introduced in Congress by James Burke (D-Mass.), the chairman of the Social Security Subcommittee of the Ways and Means Committee. When Wilbur Mills was chairman of the committee, he had not operated with subcommittees, preferring to keep greater power to himself by considering all business in full committee sessions. But in October 1974, Washington had awakened to an embarrassing scandal involving the powerful chairman.

In the wee hours of the morning, D.C. police stopped his limousine, which was driving without lights, and found a drunk and bloody Mills. Out of the car jumped an enebriated Fanne Fox, a local stripper—her stage name, "the Argentine Firecracker"—who dove into the nearby Tidal Basin in front of the stately Jefferson Memorial. The congressman's regular driver, Walter Little, who was off that night, was particularly upset, believing that had he been driving, he could have prevented the scandal. Although Mills won reelection the next month, the scandal forced him to resign his chairmanship, and Representative Al Ullman (D-Oreg.) took over as chairman. Mills did not seek reelection in 1976 and retired in 1977.

The Carter administration proposed the same correction of the benefit formula that the Ford administration had proposed in 1976. Because the change was sound public policy and had been supported by both Republican and Democratic administrations, Congress passed the proposal without controversy. The benefit formula enacted in 1977 was much like all the other benefit formulas enacted and amended over the years and followed the same basic principles. Over a worker's career, wages were recorded for purposes of determining his or her benefit or "primary insurance amount." Since 1939, average monthly wages were calculated and used in determining benefit levels instead of the cumulative wages, that the 1935 legislation had originally called for. In 1977, one additional change was made. Instead of the actual wage amounts being averaged, the amounts were first brought up to date to reflect recent wage levels, and then averaged.

The reason for that was to achieve an approximation of a worker's final pay. The goal of retirement income is to replace workers' wages so that workers may maintain their standards of living in retirement, once wages are gone. The best private pension plans, offered by the largest and most successful corporations, generally peg benefits to the last five years of earnings or some variation of that.

Policy makers wanted Social Security to provide, as private pensions did, benefits geared to the replacement of final pay. Because Social Security covers the entire population, however, policy makers wanted the system to be fair in every situation. They did not want someone who became unemployed just prior to retiring, for example, to have an artificially low final pay because the average would reflect a year of zero earnings. On the other hand, the decision makers wanted to avoid fraud and collusion between employers and employees to create deceptively high final salaries. Use of final pay might invite employers and employees to game the system by deferring salary until right before retirement. More fundamentally, policy makers believed it more equitable to take into account a lifetime of earnings, in determining benefits, not just an average of a few.

To get a measure of final pay, while addressing all of these concerns, policy makers decided to base benefits on a worker's career earnings, as Social Security had always done, but have those career earnings replicate, as closely as possible, final pay for purposes of determining the amount on which to base benefits. All of these goals were met and problems avoided by indexing earnings to growth in average wages.

To illustrate, wages were about three times higher in 1977 than they were in 1954. Workers who retired in the late 1970s and earned $3000 in 1954 would have their average wages calculated not by using the 1954 amount of $3000, which would bear no relationship to the current pay. Instead, the $3000 would be increased threefold to $9000 for purposes of figuring out average pay. (The example is highly simplified—the indexed amount would have been $9094—and does not take into account, as it should, the exact year of retirement, the age of the beneficiary and so on, but the concept is the same.) Once the workers' wages were indexed in this manner, they would be, as they had been since 1939, averaged and converted into a monthly amount. That monthly amount, the Average Indexed Monthly Earnings (AIME), was plugged into a formula, just as it always had been. The benefit formula enacted in 1977 was:

90% of the first $180 of AIME; plus
32% of the AIME over $180 through $1085; plus
15% of the AIME in excess of $1085.

As the formulas have been since 1935, the higher the average lifetime monthly earnings, the higher the benefit in absolute terms but the lower the benefit as a percentage of wages.

To ensure that the progressivity of the benefit formula was maintained and to keep workers receiving the same percentage of final pay irrespective of the year in which they retired, the legislation provided that the percentages in the formula would remain unchanged, but the dollar amounts—the places where the wage amounts are broken or bent into categories, referred to by Social Security specialists as "bend points"—would be indexed each year to the rise in average wages nationwide. Finally, Social Security contributions were still assessed, as they had been since the beginning, on wages up to a maximum level. The maximum level would be indexed in the same way that the wages and formula would be. The indexing of these three items—the wages, the maximum taxable wage base, and the bend points of the formula—together produced stable replacement rates of preretirement earnings.

A Republican and Democratic president each proposed this same solution, known colloquially as wage indexing, and Congress passed it, for the simple reason that it made the most sense. The formula enacted in 1972—where the percentages of a different formula were indexed to inflation and unindexed wages determined the average monthly wage—inadvertently caused replacement rates to rise in times of high inflation. The 1977 solution was much more preferable than other options considered and rejected. For example, indexing wage records to prices, known colloquially as price indexing, causes replacement rates to fall drastically and over time to result in less progressivity, as well as lower and lower benefits, as a percentage of final pay, for everyone. In order to keep stable replacement rates, wage indexing was proposed by Ford and Carter and adopted by Congress.

Once a worker was retired and receiving benefits, that benefit amount would be protected against inflation through annual increases based on the consumer price index. In that way, the value of the income did not decline during retirement years, which otherwise would have caused a drop in a retiree's standard of living. Not even the most generous private pension plans provide this unlimited inflation protection. Consequently, beneficiaries of private plans suffer a decline in the value of their pension income, which purchases less the longer they are retired.

In the past, Social Security benefits were kept up to date with wage growth and inflation as a result of congressional enactments every few years, usually election years. To permit regular, predictable increases and to discourage Congress and the president from overdoing the increases in the heat of an election campaign, Nixon had proposed, and Congress had adopted—once Wilbur Mills hopped on board, at least—the automatic adjustments. With the immediate-course corrections proposed by Ford and Carter and enacted by Congress, President Nixon's idea now worked.

In addition to correcting the formula, Congress confronted two additional problems in the legislation. The correction of the formula would take care of the future, but more short-term revenue was needed to get Social Security out of the hole the economy and the flawed formula had put it in. Also, by this time, the demographic shift in the population was clear. The

baby boom generation, brought into being by the high birth rates following the end of World War II, had all been born by 1964. In the decade since
then, fertility rates had dropped substantially, resulting in a baby bust. In
addition to the short-term deficit, Social Security was showing a long-term
shortfall as a result of the projected aging of the population.

To make up the shortfall, the administration proposed two fundamental changes in the program. President Carter proposed taxing employers
on the entire payrolls, while employees still paid taxes up to a maximum
taxable wage base. In addition, the administration proposal provided for
general revenue financing in times of high unemployment. Congress
rejected both ideas. Instead, it financed Social Security's shortfall through
the traditional method of increasing the maximum taxable wage base and
raising the payroll tax equally on employers and employees. The enactment went a significant way toward eliminating the long-range deficit
but, in a break from the past, did not put the program in actuarial balance
for the subsequent 75 years, the estimation period consistently employed
since 1965 by the trustees in their reports assessing the long-term health
of the program. Without Wilbur Mills at the helm, Congress, for the only
time in its history, enacted a financing package, fully aware that subsequent trustees reports would continue to report deficts.

The Social Security legislation was the most controversial ever
enacted, but experts believed the changes would solve the short-term
financing problem. Accordingly, the 1978 annual trustees' report stated,
"The Social Security Amendments of 1977...restore the financial soundness of the cash benefit program throughout the remainder of this century and into the early years of the next one."

Simultaneous with Social Security's financing woes, a major change in
the world of private pension arrangements was gaining momentum. The
universe of pension plans, public and private, can be divided into two
broad categories, defined benefit plans and defined contribution plans. In
contrast to defined benefit plans like Social Security, which promise a
monthly percentage of pay as a lifetime benefit, defined contribution plans
like 401(k)s make no promises down the road. Employers contribute, for
example, 5 percent of a worker's salary in an account, but make no promises about—and bear no responsibility for—the funds that might (or might
not) be available at retirement. The employer implicitly says, Here's a percentage of your pay; good luck investing it. Although these arrangements
are called retirement plans, because they do provide income in retirement,
they are more appropriately thought of as savings plans.

Although private defined benefit plans are better as vehicles of retirement planning because their benefits are pegged to final pay, the amount needed to maintain a certain standard of living, they are not as secure as their private defined contribution counterparts. The employer making the promise can, among other disasters, go bankrupt or inadequately fund the plan. These and other concerns were a major reason that Congress passed pension reform legislation in 1974. The law addressed many of the insecurities, requiring, for example, that employers set aside in trust sufficient funds in advance to satisfy the future promises and that the plans purchase insurance in the event of insufficient funds to pay promised benefits

The pension legislation was an important reform, but all the safeguards imposed substantial additional costs on employers—and private pensions are voluntary arrangements. Defined contribution plans are much cheaper for the employer to provide. All the employer has to do is put some money in an account. If the investment goes sour, that is the employee's problem, not the employer's. Employers largely stopped establishing defined benefit plans after pension reform was enacted, and switched to offering defined contribution plans instead.

Employer-provided defined contribution plans had been around for a century, but they got a big boost as a byproduct of the new costs now imposed on defined benefit plans. Despite the many inherent weaknesses of defined contribution plans as a mechanism for accumulating retirement income, many workers preferred them, or at least did not object to the change. Defined contribution plans are often better for the young, mobile worker. A 30-year old who quits Employer A for a job with Employer B will not get much retirement income from Employer A's pension plan, no matter how generous it is, when he or she is ready to retire in 35 years upon turning age 65. Even if Employer A were to provide 80 percent of final pay, the 80 percent would be calculated on the unindexed salary that the retiree had earned as a 30-year-old, three and a half decades earlier. As part of the pension reform law, Congress enacted individual retirement accounts for those who had no pension plan. This new device introduced even more people to the concept of savings accounts as retirement income vehicles.

Defined contribution plans—already exploding as a result of the added costs the pension reform legislation had imposed on defined benefit plans—went through the roof when Congress added subsection (k) to section 401 of the Internal Revenue Code. Although enacted in response to a seemingly narrow question raised by some proposed regulations promulgated by the Department of the Treasury, employers quickly saw the possibilities in the new section 401(k), which permitted employees to elect whether to take cash wages or tax-deferred compensation placed in an account. Section 401(k), which took effect on January 1, 1980, became an overnight sensation. Within two years, almost half the large companies in the country had either started a 401(k) plan, often as a supplemental plan, or were actively exploring doing so.

These new investment vehicles became familiar to many Americans. Employees with 401(k) plans and everyone with individual retirement accounts received regular statements and could watch their contributions and earnings grow. Opponents of Social Security saw in these private vehicles an opportunity to finally, finally get rid of the hated government program.

Two other developments filled the opponents with hope. Public confidence in the future of Social Security, so high in the past, dropped precipitously and remained low. In 1975, 63 percent of those polled answered that they felt very confident or somewhat confident in the future of Social Security; 37 percent replied that they felt not too confident or not at all confident. In just three years, the numbers had just about reversed, with only 39 percent responding that they felt very or somewhat confident and 60 percent answering that they felt not too confident or not at all confident.

Some of this reflected a drop in confidence in government generally. In 1964, 75 percent of Americans believed they could trust the government in Washington. The numbers started to slip into the low 60s and 50s along with the escalation of the Vietnam War. Watergate caused the numbers to take a nose-dive, from which they have never recovered. In 1974, only 36 percent of those polled responded that they trusted their government. (Opinion polls showed a new all-time low in 1995, when only 15 percent reported that they trusted the government.)

A promise to provide a benefit 40 years in the future requires trust. In the past, most people had trusted the government. It resonated with Americans when Franklin Roosevelt said, in his 1936 Madison Square Garden speech responding to Landon's attacks on Social Security, "When [the opponents of Social Security] imply that the reserves...created [to fund Social Security] will be stolen by some future Congress, diverted to some wholly foreign purpose, they attack the integrity and honor of American Government itself." By the late 1970s, after the experiences of Vietnam and Watergate, many citizens no longer believed that the American government had much integrity and honor left.

The combination of anxiety over Social Security as a result of the projected shortfalls, general distrust of the government, and the growth in individual retirement accounts and later, 401(k)s, presented new opportunities for opponents of Social Security. The libertarian Cato Institution, which was founded in 1977, began publishing books and articles critical of the program. In 1979, it published a piece by Carolyn L. Weaver advocating Social Security "choice," with the provocative title "Social Security: Has the Crisis Passed?" The following year, it published a book by Peter Ferrara, *Social Security: The Inherent Contradiction*, and two years after that, his *Social Security: Averting the Crisis*. Both books claimed that Social Security was a bad deal and should be privatized.

Attacking Social Security became the trendy, fashionable pursuit within the circle of academic economists. These academics began to publish analyses comparing how much beneficiaries got from Social Security in contrast to what they might have received if they had invested their contributions in private investment accounts. Along with these analyses of whether Social Security beneficiaries got their money's worth, critics also began to publish plans to privatize Social Security.

During these same years, General Augusto Pinochet and Chile became part of the American Social Security debate. On September 11, 1973, General Pinochet launched a bloody coup d'état against the democratically elected Salvador Allende, who died in the government takeover. Two years later, Milton Friedman traveled to Chile, where he delivered lectures at the university in Santiago and met privately with Pinochet.

With Friedman's encouragement, Pinochet employed the Chicago-based private sector approach to fix the serious economic problems confronting his country. A group of Chilean exchange students had done graduate work in economics in the United States, mainly at the University of Chicago, where they had studied with Friedman. Known as the Chicago boys, they returned to Chile after their studies. Pinochet appointed the Chicago boys to high-level positions in his government and gave them the green light to work their private sector magic.

Pinochet appointed one of the Chicago boys (although so-labeled, he had actually studied at Harvard), José Pinero, to be his minister of labor. During his tenure from 1978 to 1980, Pinero substituted a system of private accounts for Chile's Social Security system. As soon as it was in place,

Pinero and his supporters in the United States began to write articles about its wonders.

Myers, now out of government, spent his time writing and lecturing. Meticulously careful and precise in all his work, he read with dismay the blizzard of articles attacking Social Security and promoting private accounts, including the just-created Chilean system. At times he appeared to be playing an academic version of the arcade game Whack-A-Mole. As fast as he would respond to the misinformation in one article, another would pop up. As fast as he wrote, he could not keep up with the deluge of articles containing errors, misunderstandings, and plain misrepresentations. Ball and other supporters of the program found themselves similarly engaged.

Myers and the others diligently and respectfully critiqued the arguments about money's worth on the terms presented by their authors. Those arguments were often loaded with misleading numbers, including for example questionable assumptions about interest rates and inflation, and frequently ignored survivors' and disability benefits. At the same time, he and other students of Social Security saw that the arguments were academic exercises, based on simplified economic models to permit analysis and comparison, but inapposite to the real world in which Social Security resides. Social Security offers benefits that do not exist in private plans. The program protects benefits completely against inflation, whether inflation is slow or galloping. Workers' spouses and former spouses are protected whether a worker has been married to one spouse for life or has been married and divorced multiple times, and children are protected, like spouses, with supplemental benefits. Those supplemental benefits are in addition to those received by workers and in no way reduce the size of the benefits workers earn for themselves. Moreover, all Americans are benefited by living in a society where senior citizens have independent sources of income and are not dependent on adult children or welfare. And finally, Social Security has historically provided the security and peace of mind of benefits guaranteed by the United States of America. As the famous Mastercard commercial goes: Benefits that are priceless. For everything else, there's Mastercard.

While criticizing Social Security became the new academic sport, another favorite American sport, politics, was in full court press. Senator Edward Kennedy (D-Mass.) challenged President Carter for the Democratic nomination. Though Carter won the battle for the nomination, he lost the war. The combination of a stagnant economy and the Iran hostage crisis, where 66 Americans had been seized on November 4, 1979, fueled Carter's unpopularity. After four years as president, he was now the Washington insider. During the second debate of the presidential campaign, Carter accused Republican nominee Ronald Reagan of advocating a voluntary Social Security system. Reagan implicitly disavowed his earlier view and said, "I, too, am pledged to a Social Security program that will reassure these senior citizens of ours that they are going to continue to get their money." One year to the day after the American hostages had been seized in Iran, Reagan captured 489 electoral votes to Carter's 49. With that decisive victory, the Reagan Revolution hit Washington. Ronald Reagan became president of the United States, and Republicans gained control of the Senate for the first time since the 1952 election.

That same year, the Social Security trustees forecast that the program unexpectedly was once again in financial trouble in the short term. The trustees projected that the trust funds would be exhausted, unable to pay benefits on time, starting in 1983. Instead of improving, the economy had grown worse since the 1977 amendments. Inflation ran in double digits consistently, hitting 13.5 percent in 1980. Wages decreased, declining 4.9 percent in 1980, and unemployment climbed close to 8 percent. To add to Social Security's troubles, the 1977 amendments had delayed the effective date of the benefit formula change. The delayed effective date together with the combination of high inflation, negative wage growth, and high unemployment caused a new, headline-grabbing shortfall in Social Security.

Unsettling stories began appearing in the press once again. The *New York Times* ran one on November 30, 1980, headlined "Social Security is Still Not Secure," in which it reported that Social Security "remains in deep financial trouble." As soon as the new Congress convened, Representative J. J. Pickle (D-Tex.), the new chairman of the Social Security Subcommittee of the Ways and Means Committee, instructed his staff to develop legislation. Pickle was attracted to the idea of raising the retirement age. Though Ball opposed much of Pickle's approach, he nevertheless consulted with him and helped the staff develop, in Ball's words, "the best provisions of an approach that I didn't fully approve of." With bipartisan support, Pickle introduced his bill on April 9, 1981.

While Pickle was hard at work on Social Security, so was the new administration. Bob Myers had helped with the transition between the election and the inauguration and then had been appointed by the president to be deputy commissioner of Social Security. Myers soon discovered, however, that despite the president's promised support for the program in the election, some of those who served Reagan had other ideas.

President Reagan appointed Representatve David Stockman (R-Mich.) to be the director of the Office of Management and Budget (OMB). Stockman saw Social Security, which he called "closet socialism," as simply one more part of the overblown welfare state. As part of the transition, Stockman prepared a memorandum entitled "Avoiding a GOP Economic Dunkirk." He recommended that in Reagan's first 100 days in office, the president propose an economic package consisting of both tax reductions and substantial cuts to Social Security and other programs in the federal budget, which he claimed had "become an automatic 'coast-to-coast soup line.'"

On Stockman's recommendation, the administration proposed $2.5 billion of Social Security cuts as part of its omnibus budget bill. It included, for example, the elimination of the so-called student benefit. Benefits for dependent children had been in the law since 1939. As an increasing number of children began to attend college, Congress in 1965 extended the dependent benefits up to age 22 for children who were still in school. The idea behind the benefit was that it was paid because of the loss of a parent's support. Just like their younger siblings, children in college are still in need of support, which working parents generally furnish. Social Security, proponents of the student benefit reasoned, was substituting for that parental support, which was lost as a result of death or disability.

Reasonable arguments could be made for and against the student benefit. But Stockman's decision to propose its elimination and the other Social Security changes as part of a general omnibus budget package represented a sea change that had been set in motion in 1968. In that year, President Lyndon Johnson altered the presentation of the federal budget, so that all receipts, irrespective of source, and all expenditures, irrespective of destination, would be combined in one unified budget. The seemingly innocuous decision, which followed the recommendation of a blue-ribbon commission, had the felicitous result, for Johnson, of diverting attention away from the size of the deficit in the general fund, out of which most expenditures, including those to support his budget-busting Vietnam War, were made. As Johnson intended, the new presentation combined that deficit in the general fund with surpluses in the Social

Security trust funds. In addition to the recognized consequence of masking the size of the general fund deficit, however, the change in how the budget was presented had the unintended consequence of altering perceptions about Social Security.

When Stockman assessed federal expenditures, they appeared to him to be each in competition for scarce federal dollars. Social Security possessed no greater claim on federal revenue than any other program. To him, federal receipts were fungible, and all claims had to be justified in competition with every other national need. This was not an idiosyncratic view, nor one limited to conservative Republicans. The Carter administration had unsuccessfully proposed as part of its fiscal year 1980 budget many of the same changes to Social Security that Stockman had advocated and had done so out of the same general concern about overall budget expenditures.

In contrast, Ball, Myers, Cohen, and other students of the program historically saw Social Security in very different terms. To them it was a pension program, to which people contributed with the expectation of receiving benefits in the event of an insured event—death, disability or old age. Through this lens, the federal government was simply an instrument to collect, disburse, oversee and make rules regarding Social Security's funds. Those who perceived the program in this way believed changes to Social Security should be made not as part of a budget bill, whose goal was to save federal tax dollars, but as part of a bill like Pickle's, where Social Security contributions and benefits were balanced in the context of the long term. Unlike general fund expenditures, Social Security had its own source of funding, contributions authorized by the Federal Insurance Contributions Act, whose use was restricted to payment for Social Security benefits.

It was as if policy makers were staring at the famous optical illusion that has in the center of a drawing the outline of a candlestick, while the sides of the candlestick form two silhouetted profiles facing each other. The observer tends to see either the candlestick in the middle or the two faces staring at each other, but not both. For the history of Social Security, people saw the candlestick—a program of social insurance that the government created, similar in spirit to a private pension trust established by an employer. Stockman could see only the two faces staring at each other—Social Security payroll taxes pouring into the Treasury, along with income taxes, estate taxes, and all other federal receipts; and federal monies for defense spending, food stamps, environmental protection, and Social Security pouring out.

The different way of understanding Social Security is not a harmless optical trick. Rather, it has serious policy implications. In analyzing alternative ways to squeeze money from Social Security, Stockman remarked, "I'm just not going to spend a lot of political capital solving some other guy's problem in 2010." He saw only money going in and money going out. It was enough for him to worry four or five years down the road. To Ball, Cohen, and Myers, Social Security deficits in 2010 were not, in any way, "some other guy's problem." These are words that Cohen, Myers, or Ball would never have thought, much less uttered.

They understood that, in addition to providing tangible cash benefits, Social Security provides an extremely important intangible benefit, security and peace of mind. People value Social Security because they understand that they are contributing to it in anticipation of receiving benefits at a time when they suffer a loss of wage income and need lost wages replaced. If Social Security competed with other federal programs as part of an annual appropriations cycle, the benefit of security would be gone and the whole understanding of the program would be lost. Budgeteers assume that people would gladly keep paying Social Security contributions, even if the withheld wages were not used to support Social Security. That is the true optical illusion.

Although Pickle's bill called for an increase in the retirement age and other proposals that reduced the cost of Social Security, Stockman was hostile to the proposal. "If it succeeded, a once-in-a-century opportunity would be lost," he feared. Stockman believed that "what was needed was something far more radical" for Social Security. He termed the Pickle bill "a tepid and inadequate palliative."

Though the administration's budget bill cut federal outlays, it did not restore Social Security's solvency over the long run. Consequently, in addition to its budget bill, the administration also developed its own Social Security financing bill. Although Myers was in on the meetings developing the Social Security plan, he noted, "It was clear from the beginning that the shots were being called by OMB and the Executive Office of the President." Stockman would have served the president better if he had bothered to listen to Myers who had been a student of Social Security since 1934.

The administration's Social Security reform package contained eight items. Many were controversial, but one, reducing early retirement benefits, set off an explosion. If workers choose to retire early, before the statutorily-designated normal retirement age, they receive Social Security benefits that are actuarially equal to the benefits they would have gotten if they had retired later. In other words, workers who retire at age 65, and live exactly the number of years actuarial tables predict, receive from Social Security precisely the same value over their lifetimes that those workers would if they had chosen to retire at age 62 instead. If they begin collecting benefits at age 65, those workers receive larger monthly benefits than if they had chosen to retire at age 62, but if they retire at age 62, they receive the benefits for three additional years. The present value of both sets of benefits is equal.

The Reagan proposal would have reduced the benefits for people who retired early more than the actuarial reduction warranted. Specifically, the law provides that people who retire at age 62 receive the actuarially equivalent 80 percent of the monthly amount received by people who retire at age 65. The administration proposed to reduce the percentage to 55 percent of the age 65 benefit.

As Myers explained, "This 80 percent reduction factor...comes at the end of a mathematical analysis, which, in fact, I did." In contrast, "The 55 percent was just drawn out of the air." According to Myers, the administration "figured out how much money they wanted to save and worked their way back from that."

The proposal was particularly unfair to low-income workers in physically demanding jobs who had no other means of support with which to evade the punitive reduction. Wealthier workers who had private pensions or other resources on which to live, could avoid the penalty by simply not applying for benefits until they reached normal retirement age. In addition to that and the many other substantive problems with the proposal, Stockman and the others designing it were completely insensitive to the manner in which the benefit cut would take effect. Their goal was to maximize the number of dollars saved, so, instead of phasing in the change, the administration proposed that it be effective almost immediately. A worker who was turning age 62 the following year, in 1982, and was expecting $248 each month would, if the Reagan administration proposal were enacted, receive only $170 each month.

Although the president had signed off on the proposal and the secretary of health and human services, Richard Schweiker, had opposed it, Chief of Staff James Baker, who recognized the political explosiveness of the issue, insisted that Schweiker, not the president, announce the package to the press. On May 12, in accordance with Baker's demand, Schweiker unveiled the package at a press conference.

Riding to Capitol Hill the next morning, the Democratic Speaker of the House, Tip O'Neill, read about the proposal in the newspaper, arrived at his office, and called his own press conference. "For the first time since 1935 people would suffer because they trusted in the Social Security system," O'Neill angrily explained. When a reporter asked about the politics, O'Neill shot back, "I'm not talking about politics. I'm talking about decency."

And the phones started ringing. Representative Carroll A. Campbell, Jr. (R-S.C.), commented, "I've got thousands of sixty-year old textile workers who think it's the end of the world. What the hell am I supposed to tell them?"

The Senate had no problem with the congressman's question. The senators knew just what to say. On May 20, the Senate voted 96 to 0 for a resolution stating unequivocally that they would never enact any change in Social Security that would "precipitously and unfairly penalize early retirees."

At first, the administration thought it could forge a compromise. On May 21, the president sent a letter to the leaders of Congress warning that "the Social Security System is teetering on the edge of bankruptcy." Acting in the role of the good cop, Reagan continued, "I have today asked Secretary Schweiker to meet with you...to launch a bipartisan effort to save Social Security."

In the role of bad cop, Stockman employed scare tactics to pressure Congress to act. "Unless both the House and the Senate pass a bill in the Congress which can be signed by the President within the next 15 months, the most devastating bankruptcy in history will occur," Stockman charged in testimony before the Social Security Subcommittee of the House Ways and Means Committee. Stockman helpfully pointed out to the elected representatives that the "bankruptcy...will occur" and, therefore, the Social Security checks would stop, "on or about November 3, 1982," the day after the upcoming election.

In private, Stockman made clear that he was interested not in Social Security's future but rather in big budget cuts. "I still think we'll recover a good deal of ground....The [need to reduce Social Security's projected deficit] will permit the politicians to make it look like they're doing something *for* the beneficiary population when they are doing something *to* it which they normally wouldn't have the courage to undertake," Stockman confided privately to *Washington Post* writer and editor William Greider.

Despite the administration's hope for bipartisan congressional action, rhetoric remained heated throughout the summer. Supporters of Social Security objected to the administration's characterization of the program as in "crisis" and on the edge of "bankruptcy." On June 17, 1981, the *New York Times* ran a story headlined "Reagan Accused of Overstating Social Security System's Woes." The accuser was not a partisan opponent of the president, but a Republican ally, Senator John Heinz of Pennsylvania, chairman of the Senate Select Committee on Aging. According to the paper, Heinz "accused the Reagan Administration yesterday of overstating the need for drastic action to save the Social Security System from bankruptcy."

Nevertheless, cries of "crisis" and "bankruptcy" became the common way of speaking about the program. On July 16, for example, the *New York Times* printed an op-ed entitled "Social Insecurity." The very first sentence began, "To many people, the Social Security crisis is a matter of...."

In a Senate Finance Committee hearing on the state of the trust funds, Senator Moynihan lashed out at the administration: "[A] two-page [administration] press release uses the word 'crisis'—page 1—'crisis,' 'crisis,' bankrupt'—you turn over, 'crisis,' 'crisis.' Four crises, one bankrupt and two pages," Moynihan highlighted. The senator charged that the administration was engaged in "political terrorism, " and "terrifying older people," in an effort to stampede Congress into making benefit cuts. Senator Bill Bradley (D-N.J.) accused Schweiker of trying to make the shortfall appear worse than it really was by keeping "two sets of books," a pessimistic set for Social Security and a rosy one, when that served the administration's purposes.

Moynihan and Bradley were understandably angry. Bankruptcy is a meaningless concept when applied to the federal government as a whole or any of its programs. As long as the federal government has, under the Constitution, "Power To lay and collect Taxes" and the authority to issue and sell Treasury bonds, it and its programs will not go bankrupt. It is instructive to note that the reference to potential bankruptcy would be impossible to claim if Congress simply reinstated the authorization, present in the law from 1943 to 1950, to pay any shortfall in Social Security out of general revenue.

Out of all federal programs, Social Security was being singled out for alarmist claims about bankruptcy because it operated under the conservative principles of a balanced budget and long-range projections. No one ever pointed out that if deficit spending were the definition of bankruptcy in a federal program, then the entire federal government—other than Social Security—had been bankrupt for 20 years. During the prior two decades, the government had run deficits every year with the exception of 1969.

Despite the raging battle over the administration's Social Security package, Congress that summer enacted the Omnibus Budget Reconciliation Act of 1981, which included the elimination of student benefits and other more minor Social Security cuts. In early September, Pickle's Social Security Subcommittee of the Ways and Means Committee held hearings on the administration financing plan. Pickle's own bill had gotten lost in the strong reaction to the president's plan.

Notwithstanding the passage of the budget bill with its Social Security cuts, the administration had no desire to push its financing package that had caused such a firestorm. Although the subcommittee requested that Schweiker and Stockman appear, the administration sent Myers instead. Myers was asked to explain Schweiker's and Stockman's absence. He told the committee, "As I understand it, the secretary [Schweiker] had another engagement." As Myers recalled later, "That was pretty lame, but the excuse that came from Stockman's office was breathtaking. They said that they lost the invitation....They may as well have said the dog ate their homework."

A few weeks later, Reagan sought to save face, while implicitly admitting defeat. On September 24, in a nationwide televised address from the Oval Office, the President castigated the Democratic majority in the House for the failure to achieve a Social Security reform package and announced that he would form a bipartisan commission to study Social Security's finances and make recommendations.

The commission was to consist of 15 members, 5 appointed by the leadership of the House of Representatives, 5 by the Senate, and 5 by the White House. The appointees covered the political spectrum. They ranged from liberal Lane Kirkland, president of the AFL-CIO, a Senate appointee, to four business leaders appointed by the White House. No one thought that the business representatives, some of them very conservative, would ever agree with the head of organized labor.

In an unusual move, 7 of the 15 appointees were sitting members of Congress. They not only ran the political gamut, but they held powerful positions in their respective bodies. They included, from the House, liberal Democrat Claude Pepper of Florida, champion of the elderly and chairman of the House Select Committee on Aging, as well as two Republicans, conservative Texan Bill Archer, ranking minority member of the Social Security Subcommittee of the Ways and Means Committee, and more moderate New Yorker Barber Conable, ranking minority member of the Ways and Means Committee.

The Senate members included Senator Robert Dole (R-Kan), powerful chairman of the Senate Finance Committee, Senator Bill Armstrong (R-Colo), chairman of of the Social Security Subcommittee of the Senate Finance Committee, Senator Daniel Patrick Moynihan, ranking minority member of the Social Security Subcommittee of the Senate Finance Committee, and Senator John Heinz, chairman of the Senate Special Committee on Aging.

President Reagan named Alan Greenspan, at that time working in the private sector in New York, as the chairman. Speaker Tip O'Neill chose Bob Ball as one of his appointees. Bob Myers became the executive director.

The initial reaction to the composition of the commission was that its membership included individuals who were too far apart in views to reach consensus. Moreover, if the diversity of views did not block agreement, appointing sitting members of Congress almost surely would. Members of Congress are willing to take political heat on controversial proposals when their votes are decisive and when they believe the vote is in the best interests of their constituents and the country. But none of them could be expected to sign onto controversial proposals and take political heat as part of an academic exercise. After all, the commission had the power only to make recommendations to the president and Congress. Nothing it decided would have the force of law.

From the outside, it looked as if a number of appointees had agreed to serve on the commission simply to block it from agreeing to something they hated. It certainly did not look like a group that could find common ground. President Reagan directed the commission to report its recommendations by December 31, 1982. Even if the diverse membership was unlikely to solve Social Security's financing shortfall, it might be successful in an unspoken goal. Perhaps, the White House might be hoping, the commission could keep the volatile Social Security issue off the political table through the midterm election, to be held a comfortable two months before the commission was required to report.

## CHAPTER 13

# Aging Gracefully

Harvard University's Kennedy School of Government was packed with people. Every seat on the floor of the wide-open, three-story atrium was taken. Students were hanging over the multi-tiered balconies that lined the staircases. Professors of public policy were talking quietly among themselves, waiting for the program to begin.

The date was October 31, 1985, 50 years after the enactment of Social Security and 3 years after the successful conclusion of the bipartisan National Commission on Social Security Reform, better known as the Greenspan commission. The commission had accomplished what many had thought was the impossible. It had issued a report containing a package of highly controversial amendments, and its recommendations had flown through Congress in record speed. At the start of the commission, few watching from the outside would have bet that the commission would have reached consensus, much less that Congress would have adopted the commission's recommendations virtually without change.

Professors at Harvard and elsewhere were busily studying the commission, trying to understand how it had pulled off this miracle. And tonight, a packed crowd of Harvard students and professors were gathered to see if they could gain insight from Bob Ball, Wilbur Cohen, and Bob Myers, three men who had devoted their careers to Social Security.

Upstairs, in the rooftop terrace reserved for receptions and dinners, the dean of the Kennedy School of Government, Graham Allison, and his guests kept watching the door. The three featured speakers had agreed to attend a dinner and reception in their honor. The gathering had begun at 6:00. At 7:30, none of the three had arrived, and the program was scheduled to start in just 30 minutes.

Finally, at 7:45, there was nothing to do but head downstairs and hope that they made the program. Thomas Eliot, who had tangled with Barbara Armstrong in 1934 and subsequently, as general counsel for the Social Security Board, had helped defend the constitutionality of Social Security in a landmark case before the Supreme Court, was set to make the introductory remarks. At 7:55, still glancing nervously at the door, he and the moderator (the author of this book) assumed their places on the risers strategically set to provide the audience with the optimal view of the speakers.

All of a sudden, at 7:58, the three men, ties askew, coats flying, briefcases swinging, came bursting in. Laughing apologetically, they hastily explained that they had been sitting on a runway at Washington National Airport since 4:00 that afternoon, watching the minutes tick by, and the hour hand grow increasingly close to the appointed time of the program. Quickly taking their places on the risers , the panel of three, all in their 70s but with the enthusiasm and spirit of college students, commenced a lively and energetic discussion of the past, present, and future of Social Security. As part of their remarks, they related the story of the commission.

Its start had been inauspicious. Within two weeks of the naming of its members, the White House issued a press release stating that the president did not want a solution that included tax increases. Instead, the commission should "eliminate abuses and duplications," which the Democrats took to be code words for cuts in benefits. Various administration officials made similar comments in informal discussions with the press.

In response, Congressman Pepper sent Reagan a letter accusing the administration of trying to dictate policy to the commission. He suggested that Reagan rename the group "the National Commission on Cutting Social Security Benefits" and sternly demanded that the commission be allowed to operate without preconditions.

Underneath the rhetoric was a basic question whether the liberals and conservatives could establish enough trust to even attempt to reach a consensus. Fortuitously working in the commission's favor were some longstanding friendships that bridged the ideological divide. The conservative chairman, Alan Greenspan, was longtime friends with two of the liberal members, Lane Kirkland and Pat Moynihan. In addition, Greenspan's assistant (the author of this book), happened to be old friends with Ball's assistant and was friendly with Speaker O'Neill's top strategist, as well.

Also working in the commission's favor was the chairman's view of his role. Greenspan was more conservative in his personal views than many of the members. Nevertheless, he recognized that if the commission was to have any chance at success, he had to seek common ground, in accordance with the president's wishes, rather than simply reflect his own personal viewpoint. He believed he had special obligations, was more constrained than other members, because of his position as chairman, and could not simply act on his own predilections, as he might have, had he not been in that role.

On January 30, before the commission's first meeting, Greenspan invited Ball to a private breakfast at the Watergate Hotel, where Greenspan stayed when he was in Washington. Even at this early date, Ball was the informal leader of the five Congressionally appointed Democrats. The five had decided, following their appointments, to form a coalition and to meet regularly to plan strategy and coordinate positions. Although seven Democrats had been named to the commission, two were White House appointees, and their views were closer to the administration's than to the other Democrats on the commission, so the five Congressionally-appointed Democrats excluded the other two from their private caucuses. Ball had been advising Speaker O'Neill for several years, had O'Neill's confidence, and knew best, of all the members of the commission, what the Speaker would be willing to accept in a Social Security financing package. Ball's expertise in the field, together with his close ties to O'Neill, had made Ball the obvious choice to lead.

Greenspan and Ball had never met before their Watergate breakfast. After exchanging pleasantries, Ball raised the subject of the administration's comments to the press and told Greenspan that the Democrats were beginning to doubt that the administration was interested in making the commission work. Ball warned that if the administration continued saying that it would accept only benefit cuts, the Democrats would announce that they would accept no cuts, deadlocking the commission before it even started.

Greenspan was conciliatory. He agreed that the public rhetoric was counterproductive and said he would seek an end to the administration's divisive public comments. Ball's next point was that he wanted three people appointed as staff to the commission. Greenspan readily agreed, requesting only that, in the spirit of cooperation, the staff be unified under one executive director and not follow the congressional model of Democratic and Republican staff.

Ball recommended that the commission begin by seeking to establish a consensus on the size of the problem to be addressed, and he discouraged theoretical discussions. Numerous examples from the history of the program showed liberals and conservatives agreeing to the same policy but for totally different philosophical reasons—from the 1939 decision to scale back the trust fund to the relatively recent decision to index benefits. Greenspan thought that the approach Ball outlined made sense.

The breakfast meeting was a positive start to what looked like a long, difficult road ahead. Commission meetings were held about once a month, either in a hotel or in a Capitol Hill meeting room. The commission staff was housed in an historic town house on Jackson Place, facing Lafayette Square, catty-corner to the White House. The town house, with its high ceilings, cornices, marble fireplaces, crystal chandeliers, and views of 1600 Pennsylvania Avenue, had been a temporary residence for Theodore Roosevelt when the president's official home was undergoing some repairs.

In accordance with Ball's suggestion, the initial meetings were educational, since commission members had varying degrees of knowledge about the program. As Moynihan liked to say, "Everyone is entitled to his own opinion, but not his own set of facts." Having settled the initial controversy over administration comments about no benefit cuts, the commission enjoyed a smooth beginning. It was the calm before the storm.

On May 5, Senator Pete Domemici (R-N.M.), chairman of the Budget Committee, announced that his committee's budget plan included $40 billion in unspecified Social Security savings, which had received the administration's endorsement. The Democrats interpreted this development as a new attempt to dictate the outcome of the commission. The budget plan was for the very year the commission was seeking a negotiated package of reforms. A furious Moynihan rushed to the floor to denounce the statement. In the best tradition of Shakespeare's Marc Antony speaking at the funeral of Julius Caesar, Moynihan assured, "I do not want to speak of a breach of faith," while nevertheless clearly implying that a breach of faith was exactly what he thought was the proper characterization of Domenici, the Budget Committee, and the White House.

The next day, the five congressionally-appointed Democrats on the commission released a statement to the press, contending that "the integrity of the Social Security Commission is seriously jeopardized and its status as a bipartisan commission is a subject of grave concern."

The following day, Moynihan introduced a Senate resolution rejecting the Budget Committee's plan. An angry debate ensued. Democrats accused Republicans of balancing the budget on the backs of the elderly. Republicans accused Democrats of election-year grandstanding.

In unfortunate timing, the next public meeting of the commission was scheduled for May 10, just three days later. When the members gathered in Room 5150 of the high-ceilinged Dirksen Senate Office Building, television cameras were waiting. Heinz, expressing weariness at hearing the Democrats' Republican-bashing rhetoric, announced that he planned to introduce a bill removing Social Security from the overall budget process, in hopes that the move would halt "a lot of political posturing."

Moynihan angrily retorted that Heinz's proposal was fine for the future, but "we are facing a crisis of the present." Moynihan continued that the Budget Committee "ordered the Commission to cut $40 billion." Pepper, speaking in support of Moynihan, claimed, "This Commission has been compromised," and demanded that Greenspan reject the Budget Committee action.

Moynihan jumped in again, charging that the administration had "terrorized older people into thinking that they won't get their Social Security." That charge infuriated Armstrong, who denounced Moynihan as "engag[ing] in the most outrageous statements on the floor of the Senate," adding that he "has demagogued this issue from front to back and top to bottom, and he is trying to do the same thing here." Pepper leaped to Moynihan's defense, demanding that Greenspan rein in Armstrong. "If one member can make an assault on another, we become a brawling group," Pepper decried.

Trying to retain some semblance of order, Greenspan offered his hope that "we can keep the rhetoric down to an absolute minimum." He then added, "Gentlemen, may I request that this particular discussion be moved to another forum?" But the members were not quite done.

Dole dryly commented, "I want to apologize to the non-Congressional members of the Commission. We carry on like this all the time on the floor of the House and the Senate." He then joined the fracas. After the elected members had made their points for the cameras and after the press had its story, the commission proceeded to its scheduled business.

During these early days, some progress was made in private. As an initial matter, Greenspan hoped to reach agreement with Ball on the size of the short-term problem. Using very pessimistic assumptions about the economy would project a greater shortfall than perhaps might actually materialize. Nevertheless, Greenspan saw that using pessimistic assumptions and defining Social Security's revenue needs to be very large would paradoxically both make the commission's task more difficult and facilitate agreement. If a massive amount of revenue was required, tax increases alone or benefit cuts alone would be too substantial to be acceptable. Rather, a mix of the two would be necessary, and that was the recipe for compromise.

Greenspan asked his assistant to have lunch with Ball and see if she could get a reading of where the Democrats stood. She reported back that Ball also wanted the commission to rely on very pessimistic assumptions about the economy in defining the short-range problem. Ball was deeply concerned about the drop in public confidence in the program. He did not want a repeat of 1977 when political leaders hailing a 50-year fix only to find that the economy did not cooperate.

Ball knew that the 1990s would be a favorable time for Social Security. The generation of workers born during the Depression would be reaching retirement. That had been an era of low birth rates. At the same time, the post–World War II baby boom generation would be at the peak of its productivity and earnings potential. But getting through the next eight years to the flush 1990s, especially if the rocky economy of the 1970s continued, would be a challenge.

Greenspan wanted to give the commission the best possible opportunity for compromise; Ball wanted to avoid another round of financing shortfall. The way to achieve both goals was through the use of very pessimistic assumptions. The two men had a meeting of the minds

But both wanted to do more. Although the 1990s would be well financed, the first baby boomers, those born in 1946, would turn 65 in 2011. The two men wanted to make sure that the program was in balance in the next century. Here they reached easy agreement, because the benchmark for solvency was well defined.

Each year, the actuaries at the Social Security Administration project program costs and revenues for the subsequent 75 years. In preparing their annual long-range projections, the actuaries develop dozens of assumptions concerning unemployment, retirement rates, immigration, men's and women's labor force participation, birth rates, wage levels, inflation, mortality, and myriad other trends. Each one of these factors substantially affects the long-range outlook.

The actuaries make three sets of assumptions: a high-cost set, a low-cost set, and an intermediate set. As Myers describes it, "[T]he further out in the future we would project, the softer the numbers become. It's just like the pattern fired by a shotgun: the farther away from the barrel you get, the more spread out the pellets are. So projecting costs 75 years in the future means that you'll get a range, sometimes a wide range and our best guess lies somewhere between the two extremes."

Policy makers routinely judged solvency based on the intermediate set of assumptions. If the commission could put Social Security in long-range actuarial balance for the entire 75-year valuation period, the program would be in balance into the late 2050s. By that time, the youngest boomers would be in their nineties. Even if the actuaries' projections proved too optimistic, Congress would have decades to make midcourse corrections.

With the approach of summer and the midterm election not far behind, the commission continued to have its formal monthly meeting, but everyone recognized that not much progress was likely with the election looming. Myers had calculated that in the three years preceding the start of the commission, Congress and various advisory groups had held a total of 211 hearings, in which 2,539 witnesses had testified about the Social Security financing issue. Nevertheless, as the work of the Commission slowed to a crawl, a number of experts were asked to present their views. So many conservative economists and think tanks were pushing private accounts as a substitute for Social Security that among the witnesses was Stanford University professor Michael Boskin who was invited to discuss his privatization plan. Notwithstanding that nod to the privatizers, not even the most conservative members of the commission proposed, at any time, replacing Social Security with private accounts or any other radical reform of the program.

As much as the Republicans hoped that the commission might provide cover during the election season, Democrats had very different ideas. Pepper, so closely identified with the rights of the elderly—and 82 himself—traveled to 22 states in an effort to get Democrats elected. Then, just before the election, the Democrats discovered a Republican fundraising letter sent out about six weeks earlier. The solicitation, in the form of a public opinion poll on Social Security, requested that recipients check one of three options for reforming Social Security and return the form. One of the choices involved making the program voluntary; the others contained benefit cuts. The *New York Times* described the mailing as "political manna from heaven" for the Democrats, and that is how the Democrats treated it. The Democratic National Committee sent out letters, produced ads and made speeches warning that the fate of Social Security might ride on how the electorate voted.

The Democrats gained 26 seats in the House. Republican congressman Robert Michel, who had represented his district of Peoria, Illinois, for 26 years and had risen to the powerful position of minority whip, barely won reelection. After the election, he said, "There will have to be some adjustments, some modifications in the things we are doing, no question about it."

But the Democrats saw the need to compromise, as well, if progress was to be made. Tip O'Neill commented, "There has to be some bending on both sides." President Reagan echoed the theme: "There have been concessions and compromises in both directions on all the major issues, and we expect to continue to work with the Congress in that way."

A week after the election, the commission held a three-day retreat at a Ramada Inn just outside Washington, in Old Town Alexandria, Virginia. The three days away from competing demands would permit the commission to focus on developing final recommendations. A sense of drama was in the air. The election was over, and the Democrats had increased their hold of the House, softening up the White House for compromise.

About 100 reporters and 10 television cameras packed the meeting room. Outside, the Gray Panthers—a radical group of senior citizens whose name was a play on the 1960's radical group the Black Panthers— picketed, chanting "No ifs, ands or buts, no Social Security cuts!" The sunshine laws put in place in the early 1970s required the commission meetings to be held in public, and the November meetings were indeed open, but the real action was offstage. All the television cameras caught was Bob Myers droning on about various arcane aspects of the law. Occasionally, if a camera were turned just right, it might catch one member stand up, stroll over to another, bend down, and whisper something. Then the camera would film the two members walk out a side door together.

The better-organized group of five liberal Democrats led by Ball started the behind-the-scenes negotiation. They had decided in their separate caucus to offer a benefit cut—a delay of a few months in the cost-of-living adjustment—as a carrot for the conservatives and a signal of good faith. As Myers recited and explained the myriad ways Social Security's projected deficit could be closed, Ball leaned over and whispered to Dole, seated next to him.

The two men slipped out of the meeting room and took an elevator to one of the hotel bedrooms. The other Democrats in the Ball group soon joined them. As discussions progressed, Dole returned to the meeting, whispered to Greenspan, who, although chairing the meeting, nevertheless left the room to join the two, leaving Myers to filibuster for the television cameras.

Greenspan listened to what was being discussed. Heartened by the progress, he left the room and called Reagan's chief of staff, James Baker. Meanwhile, Ball retreated to another room to touch base with O'Neill. But an impasse soon developed. The Democrats were not willing to concede more without some movement from the other side. And the other side had not developed a clear position of what was acceptable and what was not. The negotiations soon reached a dead end.

Meanwhile, commission member Alexander Trowbridge had, for some time on his own initiative, been circulating possible compromise packages. The president of the National Association of Manufacturers, he was a moderate Democrat and a supporter of Social Security. He wanted to contribute to finding an acceptable compromise, but had no allies. He was too conservative to be part of the Ball group, and without clear direction from the White House, there was no organized Republican group. Nevertheless, be began, on his own, to develop and circulate proposals. For his part, Ball was in close contact with O'Neill and could negotiate for him, but now it was the administration's move. The White House had to become more active if a compromise package was to develop.

The commission held its final meeting on December 10, 1982. Everyone knew Social Security legislation was imperative, if benefits were to continue to be paid on time. The Social Security trust funds were less than a year away from exhaustion. The law was silent about what happened to benefits if the funds became completely depleted, and no one wanted the courts and lawyers deciding the question. It was in no one's interest to have the distribution of benefit checks interrupted, but with no real progress beyond what was done in November, the December meeting had an empty agenda. The meeting, the briefest of the year, lasted just 15 minutes.

Following the December meeting, Greenspan asked for an extension of the life of the commission and told the White House it was time for action. Shortly after that final meeting, Ball received a call from Richard Darman, an assistant to President Reagan. Darman and Ball had worked together a decade earlier in the Nixon administration, when Ball had been commissioner and Darman had been an assistant to Elliot Richardson, then secretary of health, education and welfare. Darman had been helpful in persuading Nixon's aide, Chuck Colson, not to send out the political check stuffer in 1972—the episode over which Ball had threatened to resign as commissioner. The two men had always respected and trusted each other.

In true Washington style, Darman began the conversation with Ball by asking "Can we have a meeting that never took place?" When the two men "never" met on December 17, Darman made clear that the White House wanted a deal. Reagan recognized that it was in everyone's interest to have a proposal developed in private through the commission, rather than in the public glare and amid the grandstanding of Congress. Darman pulled out a paper and showed it to Ball. The paper was one of Trowbridge's draft plans, which now contained Reagan's handwritten notations. Darman was under the misimpression that the Ball group had endorsed the Trowbridge plan. Startled, Ball quickly explained that Trowbridge was not part of his group.

As Ball studied the document, he saw that the plan was not even close to what his group would accept. Over the next several hours, Ball outlined for Darman where he saw the sticking points and the areas where he thought compromise might be possible. At the end of the meeting, Darman promised to see if there might be any more give by the White House.

The next move occurred in early January. On January 3, the *New York Times* printed an op-ed entitled "Reagan's Faithful Allies," authored by Dole. Its thrust was that, although the media had reported that relations between the White House and the Republicans in Congress had "become frayed," the reports were wrong: The Republicans in Congress wanted to work with the president. The op-ed contained a paragraph in the middle about Social Security, which, Dole explained, was "a case in point." Stating that "Social Security overwhelms every other domestic priority," he pointed out that its deficit could be closed "[t]hrough a combination of relatively modest steps." He asserted that when a financing package was enacted, "the credit, rightfully, will belong to this President and his party."

Moynihan later related that he read the op-ed, approached Dole on the Senate floor later that day, and suggested that, if Dole really believed what he wrote, "why not try one last time" to get a compromise through the commission? The two men called Ball, then the three contacted Greenspan and the White House.

After a handful of clandestine meetings, the media got wind that something was up, despite the group's best efforts. On January 7, the *Washington Post* ran a story reporting that Darman and White House Chief of Staff Jim Baker would be meeting secretly about Social Security with some commission members, in a house just outside Washington. Reporters concluded that the meeting must be at Ball's suburban Virginia home. That morning, Ball woke up to see a reporter lounging against a car across the street from his house. Within two hours, the street was bustling with reporters, photographers, television cameras, and sound crews.

As it turned out, the *Post* had been incorrect. But only about the location. The negotiators were scheduled to meet in the basement of Baker's fashionable home on Foxhall Road, located within the city. Still, Ball was in a quandary. If he emerged from the house and drove away, he would lead a parade of media to the private, off-the-record meeting. A journalist had rung the doorbell and asked Ball's wife if there was to be a meeting there. Mrs. Ball had responded truthfully, asking if she looked as if she were expecting company, while pointing to the jogging suit she was wearing. But the so-called fourth branch of government did not budge.

In desperation, Ball called Darman. Behind Ball's house was an extremely steep slope, covered in snow, which led through a thickly wooded area to the George Washington Parkway, a major high-speed thoroughfare. Darman dispatched a White House car while the 68-year-old Ball darted out the back door and gingerly sidestepped down the slope to the waiting car. The press missed the out-the-back-Jack escape.

Meetings continued over the next days. The location shifted to the historic Blair House, across the street from the White House and around the corner from the commission offices. The scene was one of high drama: banks of cameras and lights outside all three locations, teams of expectant reporters and high-level officials scurrying in and out.

The negotiation was a complicated dance. Ball was on the inside, unofficially representing the interests of the Speaker and the House Democrats, labor, and the elderly. He was well prepared, because he had spent the year engaged in extensive discussions with the other members of the group of five and O'Neill. Representing the White House were Baker, Stockman, Darman, and Greenspan. Baker, the chief negotiator, consulted with Reagan frequently to ensure that the president would sign off on any agreement that was reached. Barber Conable represented the House Republicans, and Dole and Moynihan sat in as the Senate representatives.

The negotiations almost broke down numerous times. Concerned about balance between benefit cuts and tax increases, negotiators sometimes balked at the size of each. Ball kept offering creative solutions. He proposed, for example, that some of the revenue come from taxing benefits, the proceeds of which would be dedicated to Social Security. He argued that taxation of benefits could be viewed either as a tax increase or a benefit cut. The solution proved acceptable to both sides.

Both business and labor objected to the proposal to speed up already scheduled tax increases. Lane Kirkland, as president of the AFL-CIO, was particularly concerned with an increased tax on workers. Robert Beck, chairman of the board and chief executive officer of the Prudential Insurance Company, strenuously opposed any break with the parity of contributions paid by business and labor, a parity that had been in the law since the program's origin in 1935. During a sleepless night, Ball once again came up with an acceptable compromise: a two-step tax increase, one offset by a tax credit, to ease the burden on workers; the other a standard increase with no offset. Both parties reluctantly agreed.

While the insiders were meeting at Blair House, conservative Senator Bill Armstrong (R-Colo.) decided to hold his own meeting. From the beginning, Myers had mused, "Armstrong didn't seem to like the idea of this commission, didn't like the mix of people appointed to it and didn't even like being a member of it himself." As the negotiators were reaching the final stages, Armstrong urged the five most conservative members of the commission, none of whom had sat in on the Blair House discussions, to oppose the compromise on the grounds that it relied too much on taxes. The six, led by Armstrong, began to develop a conservative alternative.

Baker heard about the development and instantly recognized the political problem. The president would not want to be outflanked on the right. On the other hand, if the president did not accept the Blair House compromise, the battle in Congress would be messy and public. Baker and Dole believed that together they could persuade three of the six in Armstrong's group to break ranks. Slipping out of the ongoing Blair House meeting, Baker and Dole met with those three in the White House to persuade them of the importance of going along with the compromise. When conservative Robert Beck, a White House appointee to the commission, was still unmoved, Baker brought him in to the Oval Office to meet with Reagan directly. The "Great Communicator," living up to his billing, proved persuasive. Beck was now safely onboard.

Saturday morning, January 15, the negotiators reached final agreement. Now they had to make sure their troops were still behind them. Greenspan walked to the commission offices through a phalanx of question-shouting reporters and briefed those members in attendance. Meanwhile, Ball remained at Blair House and strategized. Even though the five in his group were by no means united in their position, Ball, as he had been doing throughout his career, had kept the group together and found common ground. Though they had experienced their share of policy disagreements, the five understood that it was crucial to remain united. Now it was show time. Kirkland and Pepper, the two people whose endorsement would be crucial to Democratic support and eventual passage of the proposal, were the two most likely to be opposed. Figuring that Pepper would be the most difficult to persuade, Ball called Kirkland to get him on board first. Kirkland told Ball that if Pepper signed on, Kirkland would too. Taking a deep breath, Ball phoned Pepper and described the details of the final package. Pepper had serious reservations, but, finally persuaded by Ball and Pepper's aide, Richard Lehrman, who was participating in the call, the congressman reluctantly agreed to the deal.

That evening, the commission members met at the office on Jackson Place to approve the final package. But there was one more snag. The White House had a new condition, this time about the public announcement. Reagan, perhaps concerned about being outfoxed by the wily O'Neill, wanted an identically worded joint press release issued by the White House and the Speaker, rather than the customary separately-worded releases.

O'Neill, meanwhile, was in California, participating in a celebrity golf tournament. When reached, he was irritated by the suggestion and in no mood for last-minute changes, even on something trivial. "Not in my lifetime; there's not going to be any joint statement," the Speaker stormed, throwing in some colorful language to underscore the point.

O'Neill dictated his own press release, strongly endorsing the compromise, and let the White House know that he was issuing the release on his own, adding "Take it or leave it." The White House took it, deciding that separate press releases with a common theme would work. That settled, Greenspan convened a meeting of the commission, described the compromise, and asked for a show of hands for and against. All voted for the package, with the exception of Armstrong and his two conservative allies, Democrat Joe Waggonner, the amiable former congressman from Louisiana and Republican Congressman Bill Archer. Armstrong had sat in on the last few negotiating sessions at Blair House. At one point during a break in the negotiation, Armstrong had told Ball, "I disagree with everything you are doing, but I certainly admire the way you are doing it."

The recommendations of the commission were highly controversial. It recommended, for example, that Social Security benefits be subject to taxation for the first time in history, with the proceeds dedicated to the trust funds. A recent Congress had voted overwhelmingly—the Senate unanimously, the House with only one dissenting vote—for a resolution that benefits should remain tax-free. These votes were taken not in response to any legislative proposal, but rather in reaction to an advisory council recommendation on the topic.

The commission also proposed that new federal workers and all members of Congress be covered under Social Security as of January 1, 1984, and that states and localities that opted into the program be prohibited from later withdrawing. Coverage of public employees was a bread-and-butter issue for their unions. In the past, the employee groups had successfully and resoundingly defeated all attempts to bring public workers under the program on a mandatory basis.

To make up part of the cost of the baby boom's retirement, the commission proposed two alternatives, between which Congress could choose. The five members of the Ball group proposed a modest tax increase in 2010; eight commission members recommended raising the retirement age, phased in gradually, starting in the next century.

A proposal to raise the retirement age, like the other recommendations, had long been viewed as anathema. In 1977, President Carter's secretary of commerce, Juanita Kreps, had merely mentioned in an interview her view that the retirement age under Social Security should be gradually increased. She had no direct policy-making authority for Social Security. Nevertheless, her comments sparked an uproar. The *Washington Post* ran a story the next day, "Full Social Security At 68, Not 65, Eyed," and congressional offices started receiving phone calls. Kreps had been forced to quickly explain that the Carter administration was considering no such proposal.

Raising the retirement age is so controversial because it is indistinguishable from an across-the board benefit cut for retirees. Social Security has a "normal retirement age," but that is of significance only in calculating benefits for disabled workers and for survivors, whose benefits are calculated as if the worker had reached normal retirement age. For retirees, the program essentially has a band of retirement ages, starting at age 62. Regardless of whether a worker chooses to begin to collect Social

Security benefits at age 62, age 65 or age 70, the worker gets the same lifetime benefit, because the size of the benefit is adjusted. The financial impact of increasing the retirement age is to provide a lower monthly retirement benefit at every age than would be received without the change—i.e., an across-the-board cut.

Related to issues about retirement age are questions about life expectancy. Many people are under the mistaken impression that Americans receive retirement benefits for considerably longer than they did when the program was created. The misconception results from looking at life expectancies from birth, which have changed dramatically because of the medical success achieved in conquering childhood diseases. But those numbers reflect changes in the numbers of those who survive to retirement, not what happens thereafter. The statistics regarding children distort the overall average. Bob Myers is fond of talking about the man who drowned in a lake that, on average, was only half a foot deep; it is important to look more closely at the data, he would caution.

For Social Security purposes, the correct question is not how many live to age 65, but rather how long those reaching age 65 live thereafter. Here the numbers are not as dramatic. In 1940, men who survived to age 65 had a remaining life expectancy of 12.7 years. Today, a 65 year old man can expect to live not quite three years longer than he might have in 1940, or 15.3 years beyond reaching age 65. For women, the comparable numbers are 14.7 years beyond age 65 in 1940; 19.6 years in 1990.

Sound policy or not, controversial or not, consideration of these proposals now shifted to Congress. On January 15, 1983, the commission submitted its recommendations to President Reagan, Speaker O'Neill, and Senate majority leader Howard Baker. Senator Dole was the first off the mark, introducing the commission recommendations as S.1 in the Senate. Ball thought that if Senator Ted Kennedy would cosponsor the legislation, the bipartisan nature of the compromise would be highlighted. Kennedy hesitated, wanting to retain the option to offer amendments to liberalize the provisions. Once Ball explained that the package was a delicately balanced compromise and that any changes might bring the entire bill down, Kennedy was persuaded and signed onto the Senate bill.

On February 1, the House Ways and Means Committee started its hearings. In keeping with the bipartisan nature of the recommendations,

Ball and Greenspan testified together at the expedited hearings. The two men agreed in advance that Greenspan would answer the questions posed by Republicans, while Ball would handle the questions of Democrats. They also agreed that their united position would be that any change could unravel the entire package.

When the bill was debated in the House, the Rules Committee permitted only one set of amendments, the commission's proposed choice between raising the retirement age or the tax rate, as the way to put the program in long-range financial balance. On the House floor, Congressman Pickle, who had proposed a financing bill two years before, offered an amendment gradually raising the retirement age to age 67. The amendment carried by a vote of 228 to 202. Pepper then moved to substitute a tax rate increase in 2010 for the change in retirement age. The Pepper amendment lost by a vote of 132 to 296. The entire bill then immediately passed the House by a vote of 282 to 148.

The next day, March 10, President Reagan praised the House for its speedy action. "I want to take this opportunity to express my admiration—and the gratitude of the American people—for the responsible, bipartisan spirit the House of Representatives has demonstrated," and he reiterated his support for the commission's work, calling the package "a fair, workable plan."

The very next day, the Senate Finance Committee reported the bill to the floor of the Senate. On March 29, the Senate passed the bill by a vote of 88 to 9. The Senate bill addressed the long-term shortfall by increasing the retirement age by just one year and cutting initial benefits by 5 percent. In conference, the House position prevailed.

Only two months had passed between the introduction of the package in Congress and its final passage. That was faster action than had occurred on any other set of Social Security amendments in the history of the program. The commission had, in effect, acted as a congressional conference committee, but, in this case, it had met and reached agreement before the congressional committees had acted. The Republican president and the Democratic Speaker had agreed on the legislative proposal; labor, business, and the elderly were on board; and major players in the Senate had signed off—all before any formal congressional consideration. Greenspan's and Ball's urging that the proposal be treated as a unified whole and be voted up or down as a package added to the commission's report having the kind of deference and power usually granted only to conference committee reports.

Wilbur Cohen had followed the work of the commission closely; Myers had served as executive director of the commission with skill, efficiency, and dedication; and Ball had masterminded the successful, bipartisan outcome. In a few years, the three men would speak to a full house in the cavernous atrium at the John F. Kennedy School of Government. There, they would educate the Harvard faculty and students about the history of Social Security and celebrate the fiftieth anniversary of a program that they had all begun working on as young men.

Ball, who had been so centrally involved in the successful conclusion, felt a sense of great pride as well as a sense of relief. He considered his work on the commission as perhaps the most important accomplishment of his career. Reflecting on the work, Ball noted, "There have been a few times when the program was at very crucial stages. One was the '37–'38 Council; and another, the '47–'48 Council, where a lot really hung in the balance. And then the Greenspan Commission."

On April 20, 1983, President Reagan signed the Social Security Amendments of 1983 into law, in a high-profile, well-attended ceremony in the Rose Garden. With members of Congress, the commission, and the press in attendance, President Reagan said:

> This bill demonstrates for all time our nation's ironclad commitment to social security. It assures the elderly that America will always keep the promises made....It assures those who are still working that they, too, have a pact with the future....
>
> [T]his legislation will allow social security to age as gracefully as all of us hope to do ourselves...
>
> Our elderly need no longer fear that the checks they depend on will be stopped or reduced....Americans of middle age need no longer worry whether their career-long investment will pay off....And younger people can feel confident that social security will still be around when they need it to cushion their retirement.
>
> These amendments reaffirm the commitment of our government to the performance and stability of social security.

The next trustees' report, issued on June 27, 1983, announced that Social Security "will be able to pay benefits on time" for the full 75-year period, through 2057—the year in which the youngest baby boomers, those born in 1964, would turn 93.

## CHAPTER 14

# A Leninist Strategy

"So, today we see an issue that once divided and frightened so many people now uniting us," proclaimed President Reagan, on April 20, 1983, as he signed the Social Security Amendments of 1983 into law. The president would have been more accurate if he had said "now uniting *most* of us." While the nation's leaders were basking in the achievement of putting Social Security back on track, a few diehard opponents were gnashing their teeth.

Within months of the signing ceremony, the libertarian Cato Institute published in its fall journal an article entitled "Achieving a 'Leninist' Strategy." In the article, Stuart Butler and Peter Germanis, both with the conservative Heritage Foundation, asserted that "we must...prepare the political ground so that the fiasco of the last 18 months is not repeated," a reference to the Social Security amendments and the Greenspan commission that led to them. In true Leninist fashion, the authors proceeded to outline the steps necessary to achieve "a radical reform of Social Security." The radical reform the authors contemplated was individual accounts, as detailed in Peter Ferrara's two Cato-published books and one Heritage-published work. The Leninist strategists labeled the books a "manifesto."

As the title of their article suggests, the authors considered themselves revolutionaries, seeking to overthrow Social Security, just as Lenin had plotted against capitalism. Butler and Germanis urged their fellow revolutionaries to "be prepared for a long campaign." They argued that the ground for radical reform was to be seeded by weakening support for Social Security. This was to be achieved, in true revolutionary style, through "guerrilla warfare against both the current Social Security system and the coalition that supports it."

The Leninist strategists argued that the population be "divided into the young, the middle-aged working population, and the retired or those nearing retirement. Of these," the authors reasoned, "the young are the most obvious constituency...for the private alternative." They pointed out, "The overwhelming majority of people in this group have stated repeatedly that they have little or no confidence in the present Social Security system." Those retired or near retirement, though, were a problem. The Leninist "strategy must be to propose moving to a private Social Security system in such a way as to detach, or at least neutralize" these older Americans.

In addition to the tactic of weakening support for the traditional program, the authors laid out a second element of their Leninist strategy. They urged building support for "the IRA [individual retirement account]-based private system that Ferrara has proposed," by putting together a "coalition that will gain from its implementation." These included, according to the authors, "the banks, insurance companies, and other institutions that will gain from providing such plans to the public." The authors pointed out, "Not only does business have a great deal to gain from a reform effort...but it also has the power to be politically influential."

"Achieving a 'Leninist' Strategy" concluded with a plea for patience, stating that "it could be many years before the conditions are such that a radical reform of Social Security is possible." The revolutionaries reminded their adherents, "as Lenin well knew, to be a successful revolutionary, one must also be patient and consistently plan."

Those wanting to get rid of Social Security were just waiting for the right politician to champion their cause. While they waited, they kept the revolutionary flame alive and growing through a series of books, articles, and conferences. "I wrote about [privatizing Social Security] through the 1980s for every conservative think tank," Ferrara explained. "The idea was to spread ownership of the idea and make it a movement proposal."

The conditions looked good for radical reform despite the 1983 amendments. Even though the 1983 trustees' report showed Social Security in surplus through the year 2057, the last year of the valuation period, confidence in the program remained low. Public opinion polls showed people believed there to be a serious problem, and younger workers believed they would not receive benefits.

Over the subsequent years, confidence in Social Security never returned to the levels it was at in the early 1970s and before, just as confidence in the government never did. Only 35 percent felt "very confident" or "somewhat confident" in the future of Social Security in 1985, two years after Congress had enacted the amendments. In that same survey, a whopping 61 percent reported that they were "not too confident" or "not at all confident" in the program's future, even though the survey was preceded by three consecutive years of reassuring trustees' reports.

Looking forward, Ball decided to create an institution that could serve as a network for existing experts and a magnet to draw new professionals to the study of Social Security. He hoped that these people would share his devotion to the well-being of his fellow citizens, understand the importance of social insurance, and aid policy makers when concerns and issues arose. In 1987, the Ball-conceived National Academy of Social Insurance, a nonpartisan organization that today consists of over 700 of the country's leading experts on social insurance, admitted its first members.

That same year, as proponents of the Leninist strategy held conferences and circulated papers, Social Security lost a leader, a champion, and perhaps the one person most responsible for the enactment of Medicare. In May, Wilbur Cohen, who was then teaching at the LBJ School of Public Affairs at the University of Texas, left his home in Austin and flew to Washington, D.C., where he attended some meetings and discussed with Ball steps that might be taken to get needed health insurance to all Americans. He then boarded a plane for Seoul, Korea, where he had been invited to speak at a symposium on aging and welfare. He checked into the Plaza Hotel in Seoul. In the middle of the night, he suffered a massive heart attack and died.

Cohen had left simple instructions for his remains. He wished to be cremated and his ashes to be spread over his wife's ranch in Texas, where they were living at the time of his death. His brother, Darwin, wanted something more, however. Darwin had a stone placed in the family plot in Milwaukee with the following inscription:

> In honor, Wilbur Joseph Cohen, born Milwaukee, Wis., June 10, 1913, for his contributions to improve the health and well being of the nation; the seventh secretary of Health, Education, and Welfare; architect of social security and father of medicare; distinguished educator, administrator and counsellor to presidents; an eloquent voice for the progressive vision of America; a man of insight and compassion who gave much of himself because he

cared deeply for others; remembered by his friends with affection, his associates with respect, his country with gratitude, and his family with love.

Those who shared Cohen's values and beliefs missed him deeply but continued on. Myers, Ball, and other supporters of Social Security were increasingly concerned about public confidence, but were powerless to restore it. Those who wanted radical reform of Social Security continued to spread the private accounts concept contained in their manifesto.

In 1988, a presidential candidate, who shared the views of the Leninist strategists about Social Security, appeared on the scene. Former Delaware governor Pierre S. "Pete" du Pont IV, an heir to those who had thrown money at any Roosevelt hater they could find, sought the Republican nomination for president and ran on a platform of private accounts to replace Social Security.

But unfortunately for the revolutionaries, George H. W. Bush won the Republican nomination and the election that year. As president, he showed his understanding of the program, when he said, "In my budget plan, I say we've got to control the growth of…mandatory programs, but set Social Security aside. It's not a welfare program.…It's sacrosanct."

Though Bush's popularity was high at the end of the Persian Gulf War, he lost support when he raised taxes despite his "Read my lips; no new taxes!" stand in the 1988 election. He was also hurt by an economic recession that lasted much of his term in office. The 1992 election was a three-way contest, with Ross Perot garnering almost 19 percent of the popular vote. William Jefferson Clinton won with 370 electoral votes and just under 43 percent of the popular vote.

With a Democrat in the White House, adherents of the Leninist strategy saw that they would have to continue to be patient. In 1994, the House of Representatives returned to Republican control for the first time in over 40 years, the first time since Eisenhower was president. The Republicans had run in support of the "Contract with America," drafted and promoted by Congressman Newt Gingrich (R-Ga.). The contract was wide-ranging, proposing, for example, reform of welfare, a crackdown on crime, reduction of the size of congressional staffs, and extension of all federal laws to Congress itself.

Unfortunately for those opposing Social Security, the Contract with America expressed implicit support for the program by proposing only minor modifications. Under the heading "The Senior Citizens Fairness

Act," it proposed changing only a few Social Security provisions that were unpopular. These included repealing a 1993 tax on Social Security benefits and increasing the amount that beneficiaries could earn and still receive benefits.

The so-called earnings limitation or, more accurately, retirement test, had been an unpopular feature of Social Security ever since its enactment. The concept was that Social Security was intended to replace wages lost to retirement. The dilemma was to devise a reasonable method for the Social Security Administration to determine whether someone was retired or not. In the original 1935 legislation, retirement was defined to mean total cessation of work. An older person could not earn a single dollar and receive a benefit. This was too restrictive, denying benefits to retirees who worked a few hours to supplement their benefits. Sure enough, the 1939 amendments changed the test of retirement—the amount that could be earned without loss of benefits—to $14.99 a month.

Throughout the history of the program, older people resented losing benefits as a result of work, and liberalizing the retirement test was always a popular provision in Congressional enactments. A further liberalization of the retirement test was included in the politically-savvy Contract with America. (In 2000 the retirement test was repealed entirely for people at or above normal retirement age.)

The anti-Social Security forces did get one break from the Clinton administration. In 1994, as the law had required since 1956, the secretary of health and human services appointed 14 members to serve on Social Security's quadrennial advisory council. Ball was interested in serving and was appointed. In addition, however, several proponents of private accounts were named to the council, including Carolyn L. Weaver, who had advocated Social Security "choice" in a January 1979 Cato policy report.

Not surprisingly, given the wide range of views, the advisory council could not agree on a single set of recommendations for future reform to Social Security, but instead lined up behind three separate packages. Though council members were unable to reach agreement on reforms, their report did contain important information. The trustees had begun to project a long-term deficit in Social Security's financing occurring somewhere more than 35 years in the future. Included in the report was an appendix, entitled "Developments Since 1983," which addressed the causes of the projected shortfall.

The appendix began by debunking the myth that the inexorable tide of aging baby boomers had anything to do with the projected deficit. "The usual popular explanation," the statement in the appendix noted, "has been to repeat" the change in worker-to-beneficiary ratio. While acknowledging that the ratio "is the main reason why Social Security will be more expensive in the future than it is today," the report stated that the change in the worker-to-beneficiary ratio "has almost nothing to do with why there is a...deficit. The estimate of the future relationship between beneficiaries and workers was just about the same in 1983 when the program was last in balance." The report clarified: "In other words, the fundamental ratio of beneficiaries to workers was fully taken into account in the 1983 financing provisions and, as a matter of fact, was known and taken into account well before that."

The report then explained that the shortfall resulted from a variety of factors. The actuaries had adopted slightly more pessimistic economic assumptions and improved their methods of estimating costs. The actuaries assumed higher rates of disability and lower rates of recovery than earlier projections. And because of the assumptions about the increasing longevity of the elderly population and because the 75-year valuation period moved through time, every new valuation included a more expensive year at the end of the valuation period.

The appendix summarized the new projected deficit: "The current deficit...result[s] from an accumulation of relatively small annual changes in the actuarial assumptions and in the method of making the estimates." It also noted, "Curiously, changes in demographic assumptions over the last 12 years have had the effect of reducing, not increasing, the deficit."

The very fact of a new projected deficit, whatever the cause, was a positive development for those who wanted to undermine public support for Social Security. In another fortunate development for the adherents of the Leninist strategy, 401(k) plans continued to be hot. By the time the advisory council reported, almost 31 million workers participated in 401(k) plans, which contained assets of over $1 trillion. As the stock market went up and up in the 1990s, these arrangements became more and more popular.

In a similar development, between 1982 and 1986, IRAs were made universal, available to all workers irrespective of income or employer-provided plans. The so-called universal IRAs had resulted in a huge increase in deductible contributions to those plans. At their peak in 1985, taxpayers contributed $38.2 billion to these vehicles. When the eligibility was once again restricted in 1986, contributions fell back and leveled off. Still, in 1996, Americans made tax-deductible contributions of $8.6 billion to IRAs. More and more Americans were becoming used to private accounts for retirement income. Although they were labeled retirement income, 401(k) plans generally permitted withdrawals for medical emergencies and other hardships, so how much of the saved sums would truly provide retirement support was unclear.

Nevertheless, these developments were heartening to the Leninist strategists. Cato formed the Project on Social Security Privatization on August 14, 1995. A cochairman of the project was José Pinero, the Pinochet minister of labor who had designed the Chilean system of private accounts. Just as supporters of private accounts had been doing since almost the moment Chile had privatized its Social Security program, Cato touted the Chilean system as a model for the United States, despite its decidedly mixed results. As the *New York Times* was to report:

> [N]ow that the first generation of workers to depend on the new system is beginning to retire, Chileans are finding that it is falling far short of what was originally advertised under the authoritarian government of Gen. Augusto Pinochet.
>
> [T]he government continues to direct billions of dollars to a safety net for those whose contributions were not large enough to ensure even a minimum pension....
>
> Even many middle-class workers who contributed regularly are finding that their private accounts—burdened with hidden fees that may have soaked up as much as a third of their original investment—are failing to deliver as much in benefits as they would have received if they had stayed in the old system.

The new Cato project fueled privatization talk with publications and conferences. In less than a decade, the project could proudly boast that it had "published more than forty books, articles, and reports" criticizing Social Security and advocating private accounts.

During these years, Social Security produced large surpluses, as it had been projected to do when the 1977 and 1983 amendments had been enacted—but the federal budget produced record deficits. Senator Moynihan, once a strong supporter of the 1983 Amendments, the legislation that was the reason for the surpluses, became concerned that the government was increasingly financed by the Social Security payroll tax, through the general fund borrowing of Social Security's assets, rather than by the more progressive income tax. He decided that Social Security should operate on a pay-as-you-go basis, taking in no more money than was needed to pay current benefits. The problem was that the surplus building up in the 1990s would be needed to pay the benefits of the baby boom generation when its members retired. In response, Moynihan developed a proposal of benefit cuts and tax increases designed to keep Social Security in long-range balance without the surplus.

Not content to simply cut the payroll tax down to the amount needed to cover current benefits, Moynihan decided to propose a voluntary 401(k)-type arrangement on top of Social Security. He hoped that the voluntary-account proposal would help to restore confidence, particularly among younger Americans who, he claimed, "had concluded they themselves would never get Social Security." Apparently having heard the drumbeat of the Leninist revolutionaries, he noted, "As the 1990s arrived, and the long stock market boom, the call for privatization of Social Security all but drowned out the more traditional views."

Washington was becoming thick with Social Security plans. Moynihan had his plan. Ball continued to refine a plan he had begun when he was a member of the 1994–96 advisory council. Cato and the other conservative think tanks were pushing privatization. Not to be outdone, the Clinton administration was developing its own approach.

On January 27, 1998, President Clinton delivered his sixth State of the Union Address. He pointed out that there were "barely 700 days left in the 20th century." He spoke of the fiscal discipline he and Congress had finally achieved—a discipline that Moynihan doubted would ever arrive. "Tonight, I come before you to announce that the federal deficit, once so incomprehensively large that it had eleven zeros, will be simply zero." He added, "If we maintain our resolve, we will produce balanced budgets as far as the eye can see."

Then Clinton posed a question. "What should we do with this projected surplus?" His answer was simple: "Save Social Security first." In the following year's State of the Union Address, delivered on January 19, 1999, he elaborated about his vision for Social Security.

He began by reminding listeners of the reason behind the program. "When President Roosevelt created Social Security, thousands wrote to thank him for eliminating what one woman called the 'stark terror of penniless, helpless old age.'" He pointed out, "Even today, without Social Security, half our nation's elderly would be forced into poverty."

He then made clear what should not be done. "The best way to keep Social Security a rock-solid guarantee is not to make drastic cuts in benefits; not to raise payroll tax rates; and not to drain resources from Social Security in the name of saving it." Rather, the president proposed, just as Altmeyer had suggested over 60 years earlier in response to Senator Vandenberg's concerns, "investing a small portion [of Social Security's surplus] in the private sector just as any private or state government pension would do." In addition, he called for taking steps to reduce poverty among elderly women, whose poverty rates were almost double the rates of elderly men, and to eliminate the limit on what those past retirement age could earn and still receive benefits.

Clinton proposed that a portion of the government surplus be used partly to ensure Medicare's fiscal soundness and partly to add a much-needed drug benefit. He proposed help for the costs of long-term care. In addition, the president proposed a new pension initiative, which he labeled universal savings accounts or USA accounts, which would use a part of the budget surplus to match wages that workers chose to save and invest.

The response of the advocates of the Leninist strategy was immediate and negative. Seventeen days after Clinton's 1999 address, the Heritage Foundation—where Stuart Butler, the first named author of "Achieving a Leninist Strategy" was now vice president of domestic and economic policy studies—issued a scathing executive memorandum that complained, "[T]here is little in the President's proposal that could serve as the basis for serious Social Security reform."

Heritage did not need to worry, though. Most Americans were not focused on Social Security. Nine days before Clinton's 1998 State of the Union Address where he proclaimed, "Before we do anything with that surplus, let's save Social Security first," Matt Drudge's scandal-mongering *Drudge Report* revealed a titillating morsel: *Newsweek* magazine had killed an article that would have detailed a Clinton affair. Just three days later, just six days before the State of the Union speech, the *Washington Post* reported the existence of recorded conversations between White House intern Monica Lewinsky, with whom Clinton was alleged to have had that affair, and her confidante, Linda Tripp.

From that point on, the melodrama dominated the newspapers. On January 19, 1999, Clinton once again was before Congress and the nation to deliver an address outlining the state of the nation. But the speech, which built on his "Save Social Security First" remarks, and outlined specific proposals for reform was overshadowed by the salacious scandal.

Exactly one month before President Clinton's 1999 State of the Union Address, the House of Representatives voted articles of impeachment. A few hours before Clinton delivered the address, White House counsel Charles Ruff gave the defense's opening statement in the president's impeachment trial.

On October 27, 1999, then–minority leader Richard Gephardt (D-Mo.), joined by Representative Charles Rangel (D-N.Y.), the ranking minority member on the Ways and Means Committee, Representative Robert Matsui (D-Calif.), ranking minority member on the committee's Social Security Subcommittee, and a number of other Democrats introduced in the House President Clinton's Social Security reform package. This time the Heritage Foundation wasted even less time mounting its attack. It issued an executive memorandum the next day, "Clinton's Newest Social Security Plan: From Bad to Worse." Again, Heritage did not need to worry. A new presidential election season had begun, and the Republican-controlled Congress showed no interest in Social Security legislation.

On March 7, 1999, the wealthy governor of Texas had announced that he was forming a committee to explore a run for the presidency. Despite his limited political experience and his weaknesses as a speaker, he had one huge asset. He happened to be the son of a former president, and the two men shared the same first and last names, George Bush. Name recognition in politics is invaluable. When Senator Robert Dole ran for president, he quipped that his name was a household word in Hawaii. George Bush immediately became the candidate to beat.

Here was the answer to the prayers of adherents to the Leninist strategy. Well before Bush formed his exploratory committee, he had been thinking about the presidency and had been thinking about Social Security, as well. He had a long history of hostility to the program. As a student at the Harvard Business School in the early 1970s, he had railed against Social Security and other New Deal programs. In his losing bid for a congressional seat in 1978, he had ventured that "people [should] be given the chance to invest [Social Security] the way they feel."

In September 1997, just three years into his first term as governor—a full year and a half before he even established his exploratory committee—Bush had dinner in the governor's mansion with the head of the Cato Institute and José Pinero, the Chilean-privatizer-turned-Washington-insider. The three men discussed the privatization of Social Security.

A half year later, in the spring of 1998, as Bush was running for a second term as governor, he met with a group of public policy experts and conservative economists, including Michael Boskin, the author of a privatization proposal that he had presented to the Greenspan commission in August 1982. One of the other participants recalled, "On the day we talked about Social Security, [Bush] said, 'We have to find a way to allow people to invest a percentage of their payroll tax in the capital markets.'"

Despite Bush's interest in privatizing Social Security, it was not an issue that he chose to highlight in his bid for president. Rather, he emphasized tax cuts and educational policy. On September 18, 2000, with the election less than two months away, the director of Cato's Project on Social Security Privatization published "Memo to George W. Bush: Social Security is a Winning Issue." In the open memo, the Cato director wrote, "If George W. Bush wants to revive his struggling campaign, he should make this a campaign about issues, and one issue in particular—Social Security."

Bush chose not to take Cato's advice, and Cato's director of the Project on Social Security Privatization admonished him in a postelection analysis: "Bush often seemed defensive about the issue, struggling to reassure seniors and counter Gore's charges, rather than highlighting the advantages of his approach." Given that Florida has the highest percentage of elderly residents of all the states, that it was the deciding state in the 2000 Electoral College vote, and that resolving the result in Florida took 36 days and a highly politicized Supreme Court opinion, it had probably been a politically astute decision for Bush to eschew Cato's counsel.

But the patience of the anti-Social Security forces seemed to have paid off. They finally had a president who seemed to see the world their way. Despite Social Security's absence from the campaign, President Bush established a presidential commission, on May 2, 2001, to study and make recommendations about Social Security. Unlike most presidential commissions, which are given broad guidelines within which to work, this commission was to be tightly constrained. Among the stipulations dictated by Bush was that the commission's recommendations "must include individually controlled voluntary personal accounts." It was not a commission to consider what should be done; rather, it was a commission to advise the president how to do what he had already made up his mind to do.

One of the administration's favorite ploys seemed to be devising appealing names as tools in political fights. During its first term, the administration proposed, for example, "The Clear Skies Act," a bill that many environmentalists argued hurt the environment, and permitted pollution of the air, and "No Child Left Behind," an initiative that many educators thought hurt children's education. An early foray into this public relations world of political spin was the name the president chose for his commission. Established to recommend private accounts as a substitute for Social Security, a proposal that Ball, Myers, and other experts on Social Security thought would destroy the insurance program, the Bush group bore the program-friendly title, "President's Commission to Strengthen Social Security."

Naturally, the members consisted only of people who were in favor of private accounts. At the President's request, Pat Moynihan, who had just retired from the Senate after four terms, agreed to serve as a co-chair of the panel. In light of Moynihan's credentials as both a Democrat and a champion of Social Security, the former Senator's service lent the commission a veneer of credibility and bipartisanship. Notwithstanding its appearance, several people who worked for the late Senator contend that he disagreed with Bush about Social Security. John Hambor, a staff aide who advised the late Senator on Social Security, wrote a letter to the editor, which appeared in the *Washington Post* on March 18, 2005 under the heading, "Twisting Mr. Moynihan's Social Security Views." In the letter, Hambor expressed weariness at "seeing [Moynihan's] views distorted for political purposes by Republican supporters of individual Social Security accounts," and contended, "The attempt to transform the late senator into a supporter of the Republican plan to undermine Social Security does a disservice to [Moynihan's] memory." Senator Moynihan passed away on March 26, 2003, and can no longer speak for himself on the question of his views.

On September 11, 2001, four months after the president created the commission, Osama bin Laden's terrorist organization attacked the United States. The commission filed its final report a few months later, in December, but no one outside of those who worked in the area of Social Security paid attention. Nevertheless, the quiet, negative drumbeat continued.

Prior to the midterm election in 2002, Republicans pollsters discovered that the terms "privatization" of Social Security and "private accounts" did not play well. Frank Luntz, a Republican pollster and consultant, drafted a memorandum entitled "The 14 Words Never to Use." The second word and phrase on the list were "privatization" and "private accounts." Luntz urged that politicians favoring those arrangements describe them as "personalization" and "personal accounts." He explained, "Personalizing Social Security suggests ownership and control over your retirement savings, while privatizing it suggests a profit motive and winners and losers."

Good advice, though a little late, since privatization had already become part of the anti-Social Security vocabulary. Cato in 1995 had named its policy center on Social Security the "Project on Social Security Privatization." In keeping with the 2002 Republican directive, Cato changed the name to the "Project on Social Security Choice" that same year.

Countless embarrassing incidents ensued. Representative Chris Chocola (R-Ind.), for example, said on November 1, 2000, "Eventually, I'd like to see [Social Security] privatized." After the Republican language police spoke in 2002, Chocola said, "I do not support the privatization of Social Security." When his Democratic opponent ran political ads using the earlier quote about privatization, Chocola claimed that he was "misrepresented."

On the September 14, 2002, television program *Capital Gang*, Mark Shields pointed out, "In an Orwellian abuse of the language, conservatives...insist that they're now for Social Security choice, not for dreaded privatization." In response, conservative columnist Robert Novak quickly asserted, "I'm still for privatization."

Perhaps he responded too quickly. Just six weeks later, on October 28, Novak cohosted *Crossfire*, along with Paul Begala. Their guests were two political strategists, one Democrat and one Republican. When the Democratic strategist asserted that Republicans wanted to "privatize Social Security," Novak once again quickly interrupted, this time to say "That's a Democratic term."

Although no longer using the word "privatization," the Bush administration nevertheless appeared to be doing everything it could to dampen confidence in the future of Social Security. Though trustees' reports between 2001 and 2004 grew slightly more optimistic, with the projected year of exhaustion of the funds receding slightly further into the future, Social Security Administration publications became more alarmist. No longer confirming that Social Security faced "no immediate crisis," the publications now warned that the program was "unsustainable," and "underfinanced."

A Social Security pamphlet entitled "The Future of Social Security," published in 2000, the year before President Bush took office, opens with the reassuring "Will Social Security be there for you? Absolutely." The

2004 version of the same pamphlet no longer contained those confidence-building words. Instead, the booklet now read: "Social Security must change to meet future challenges." In the same public document, where the heading "Social Security Is an Economic Compact Among Generations" appeared in 2000, the pamphlet by 2004 had been altered to the frightening "Current Social Security System Is Unsustainable in the Long Run."

Most disturbing was the change in the annual statement sent to all of the 125 million workers, age 25 and over, who pay into the trust funds. This statement, completely unsolicited, simply arrives in each worker's mailbox. The 2001 statement proclaimed, "Will Social Security be there when you retire? Of course it will." This reassurance was gone by 2002, and in 2005, the unsettling remark "Congress has made changes to the law in the past and can do so at any time" was now in the mailing, just in case workers were feeling too secure.

The Social Security Administration made an even more subtle but highly suspicious change in its Web address. Social Security's Web site came online in May 1994 with the unsurprising address "*SSA.gov.*" The address was consistent with other government Web addresses: *DOJ.gov* for Department of Justice, *DOL.gov* for Department of Labor, *aoa.gov*, for Administration on Aging, and so on.

If users made the inadvertent but common mistake of typing "*SSA.org*," rather than "*SSA.gov*," they realized the error immediately. *SSA.org* is the home page of the Soaring Society of America, and its site carries a screen-filling photograph of an airplane and the large-lettered word "Soaring."

In May 2003, however, Social Security's Web address was changed to "*Socialsecurity.gov.*" (One can still reach the Web site with the old address, but *ssa.gov* is not publicized. *Socialsecurity.gov*, not *SSA.gov*, is the address listed on the Web site home page, provided by the recorded message on the hotline, and listed in official publications, including the annual statement that is mailed, unsolicited, to almost every home in the country.) After the change, people searching for the Social Security Administration official Web site who inadvertently type in "*Socialsecurity.org*" rather than "*Socialsecurity.gov*" find themselves on the pro-private accounts Project on Social Security Choice, sponsored by the Cato Institute.

Everyone with children knows that the address "*whitehouse.com*" was grabbed by pornographers, hoping to catch visitors who were seeking the

Web page of the White House, home of the president. But the prospect of unsuspecting Americans finding themselves on Cato's Web site was not the result of the think-tank's cleverness. Cato's Web address for its Project on Social Security Choice had been well established at the time the Bush administration decided to change the Social Security Administration's Web address. Cato's Web page, with the Web address *socialsecurity.org* was launched in 1997, two years after its Project on Social Security Privatization was created. The administration's shift to the Web address *Socialsecurity.gov* came six years later, in 2003.

Perhaps the administration had simply been extremely careless to switch to a Web address so easily confused with a very similar private sector site. On the other hand, Cato's Project on Social Security Choice has close dealings with the administration. Several of its employees staffed the president's commission, and several others were members of the commission. At least one Cato employee was given a high-level position in the Social Security Administration itself.

Although the administration seemed to be setting the stage for private accounts, the play was just not opening. During his first term, President Bush proposed and secured five large tax cuts. Those cuts, coupled with the huge costs of the wars in Iraq and Afghanistan, produced enormous federal deficits. A number of the advocates of radical reform of Social Security had wanted the president to push the proposal in his first term while the government was projecting a $5.6 trillion surplus over 10 years. Private accounts would be extremely costly. They constituted, in essence, a new expensive spending program. Even if the idea was to phase out the traditional program, Social Security could not realistically be phased out for many, many decades. But despite the fervent desire of the most radical of the Leninist strategists, Bush opted for the always-popular tax cuts.

With monstrous deficits stretching to the horizon, Ball, Myers, and other supporters of Social Security thought that even the most irresponsible politician would not propose private accounts. Bad as the deficits might be for the country, they provided a measure of protection for the program upon which so many Americans depended. After a lifetime of service, Robert M. Ball and Robert J. Myers, now in their 90s, thought that perhaps they could finally retire, believing that Social Security was safe from those intent on destroying it. They were in for a shock.

## CHAPTER 15

# The Drumbeat
# Finds a Drummer

Though Ball and Myers, now in their 90s, had spent their careers making sure that others could retire, they could not yet retire themselves. While the liberal Democrat Ball and the conservative Republican Myers were distressed, another nonagenarian, 92 year-old libertarian Milton Friedman, was heartened as he sat in his San Francisco high-rise overlooking the Pacific Ocean and the San Francisco Bay. He looked westward but enjoyed what he visualized to the east in Washington, D.C.

For the first time in any of the three men's long lifetimes, a president wanted to undo Social Security. Republican presidents, as well as Democratic presidents, had all appreciated the value of the program. President Eisenhower had proclaimed that Social Security "should remain, as it has been, the cornerstone of the government's programs to promote the economic security of the individual." President Nixon had declared, "This nation must not break faith with those Americans who have a right to expect that Social Security payments will protect them and their families."

President Ford called the program "a primary goal of our Government" and noted on another occasion, "Its value is no longer debatable." President Reagan spoke of "our nation's ironclad commitment to Social Security," asserting that "those who are still working...have a pact with the future." Even President Bush's own father, President George H. W. Bush, valued Social Security, as his predecessors had. "And there's one

271

thing I hope we can agree on," the elder Bush told Congress and the nation in his 1990 State of the Union Address. "To every American out there on Social Security, to every American supporting that system today, and to everyone counting on it when they retire, we made a promise to you, and we are going to keep it.... [T]he last thing we need to do is mess around with Social Security."

Every president, irrespective of party, had understood the value of the program. Until now. On November 2, 2004, George W. Bush retained the presidency by winning 286 electoral votes to Senator John Kerry's 252. Though Bush haters were upset, telling themselves that Bush had once again stolen the election, this time in Ohio, he nevertheless was the president for four more years.

Social Security had barely been mentioned in the lengthy, smear-filled campaign and certainly the program had not been emphasized. Neither candidate nor almost any of the voluminous number of political ads that had been run focused on it. Bush gave the briefest of nods to Social Security and private accounts in his 2004 State of the Union Address and his acceptance speech at the Republican National Convention. If they listened closely, some of the electorate fleetingly heard the candidates' views on Social Security at the third presidential debate, held on October 13 at Arizona State University in Tempe.

Bob Schieffer, anchor of *CBS Nightly News* and moderator of the debate, asked President Bush about Social Security and private accounts about halfway through the 90-minute debate. In response to Schieffer's direct question, Bush made general comments about benefit checks continuing to be paid, as they had in his first term, how there was "a problem for our youngsters," and asserted, "I believe that younger workers ought to be allowed to take some of their own money and put it in a personal savings account." He also said, "I called together a group of our fellow citizens to study the issue. They came up with a variety of ideas for people to look at."

In contrast to the President's vague generalities at public forums, Bush told supporters at a private luncheon in September, according to a *New York Times Magazine* article, that if reelected, he would "come out strong...with fundamental tax reform, tort reform, privatizing of Social Security." Hoping to capitalize on the leaked private comment, the Kerry campaign released a new ad on October 17. With the words "January Surprise" flashing on the television screen, a narrator asserted that once

Bush was inaugurated for a second term, he would seek to privatize Social Security. The Bush campaign immediately denounced the leak as a "made-up" quote and the Kerry ad as "a false, baseless attack."

On a campaign stop in Wilmington, Ohio, on October 25, Vice President Cheney was asked whether the administration planned to privatize Social Security. Cheney's answer was reassuring: "No, the Social Security program is in good shape for the current generation of recipients and probably for the next generation of recipients, too. But we got a problem down the road...for...people now in their 20's and 30's." He explained that voluntary 401(k)-type accounts were "one of the things that we've talked about" for "somebody like my kids." But, he reassured, "There's obviously a lot of work that needs to be done, a lot of questions would have to be answered in connection with that."

Then he branded the Kerry campaign talk a scare tactic by a campaign in trouble: "When you get down to the tail end of the campaign and our opponent is in trouble, they always trot out, 'oh, what about Social Security—the Republicans are going to do it in.' Not true. Won't happen."

As it turned out, the Kerry ad was inaccurate. There was no "January Surprise." The surprise came in November. It was a two-days-after-the-election bombshell, to be exact. At a press conference on Thursday, November 4, President Bush announced that "reforming Social Security will be a priority of my Administration." Although just 10 days earlier, Cheney had confided that a proposal advocating private accounts required "a lot of work that needs to be done, a lot of questions... answered," apparently that work had been completed and those questions resolved as the votes were counted.

On February 2, 2005 at 9:00 P.M. Eastern Standard Time, in the grand wood-paneled chamber of the U.S. House of Representatives, the floor packed with members of Congress, justices of the Supreme Court, and the president's cabinet, the president had the eyes of the nation. As his State of the Union Address was broadcast across the country and around the world, Bush made his Social Security proposal the centerpiece of his discussion of domestic issues.

His opening swipe was that Social Security was out of date. "Social Security was a great moral success in the 20th century," he said, subtly emphasizing that the program was outmoded by referring, in the very next phrase, to "this new century." He then asserted, to angry boos by the Democrats, that Social Security "is headed toward bankruptcy."

To hammer home both points, the President continued: "Our society has changed in ways the founders of Social Security could not have foreseen. In today's world, people are living longer and, therefore, drawing benefits longer."

Bob Myers watched Bush on television from his home right outside Washington and stared in disbelief. In 1934, not only could Myers foresee the world as it changed, he had forecast those changes with great specificity. He was the one who had crunched the numbers for President Roosevelt's Social Security proposal. Myers and Otto Richter, the senior actuary with whom he had worked, had been extremely farsighted. Myers knew, in 1934, that people in the twenty-first century would live longer and draw benefits longer.

As it turned out, Myers and Richter were a shade too conservative in their projections, believing the percentage of the population that would be elderly in the future would actually be higher than it turned out to be. Specifically, in 1934, he and Richter projected that, in year 2000, 12.7 percent of the population would be age 65 or older. How accurate were they? According to the 2000 census figures, the percentage of those aged 65 and over was 12.4 percent of the population.

Not content simply to rewrite history, Bush followed up with something much worse. To the consternation of Myers, Ball, and every other Social Security expert watching that night, Bush sought to prove the point that Social Security was unsustainable through the use of a terribly deceptive and misleading factoid. The president announced, "And instead of sixteen workers paying in for every beneficiary, right now it's only about three workers."

"Sixteen workers paying in for every beneficiary" is a meaningless statistic that never affected policy in the slightest. The 16-to-1 ratio is a figure plucked from 1950, the year that Social Security expanded to cover millions of theretofore uncovered workers: farm workers, domestic workers, and others. Those 1950 amendments followed the recommendations of the 1948 advisory council—the advisory council that catapulted Bob Ball's already-stellar career into the stratosphere.

Myers, Ball, and every other pension expert know that all pension programs that require a period of employment for eligibility, private as well as public, show similar ratios at the start, because all newly covered workers are paying in, but no one in the newly covered group has yet qualified for benefits. The president could just as accurately have said that in 1945, the ratio of workers to beneficiaries was 42 workers paying in for every one beneficiary or the equally accurate but misleading ratio from 1937, 26 million workers paying in for about a dozen beneficiaries.

When Franklin Roosevelt, Frances Perkins, and Henry Morgenthau were arguing about the funding of Social Security, they were talking about the late 1960s and beyond, when the program reached maturity, not 1935. Roosevelt, Dwight Eisenhower, Richard Nixon, Wilbur Mills, Russell Long, and the other policy makers throughout Social Security's 70-year history, were careful to leave Social Security in long-range actuarial balance.

They all knew, as President Bush should know, that what is important is not the worker-to-beneficiary ratio at the start of the program but the ratio when the program reaches maturity. Consistent with the meaninglessness of the 16-to-1 factoid, the worker-to-beneficiary ratio was halved to eight workers for every beneficiary within five years, and by 1975, the ratio was where it is today. The 1994–1996 advisory council had not agreed on much, but it made one very valuable contribution. Its report included the appendix that stated that "the fundamental ratio of beneficiaries to workers was fully taken into account in the 1983 financing provisions and, as a matter of fact, was known and taken into account well before that."

But the myth that the aging baby boomers would wreck Social Security was such a good sound bite. It was so much punchier than the shortfall's true cause, explained by the 1994–96 advisory council: "The current deficit…result[s] from an accumulation of relatively small annual changes in the actuarial assumptions and in the method of making the estimates."

Despite the deceptiveness of the ratio, it became the administration's mantra. The ratio was cited in every speech by the president, the vice president, the secretary of the treasury, and every other member of the administration talking about Social Security. A pictograph showing 16 little men equaling 1 little man in 1950, 3⅓ little men equaling 1 man today, and 2 men equaling 1, labeled "When Younger Workers Retire," was prominently displayed on the White House Web site.

Even worse, when visitors went to the Social Security Administration's Web site, their eyes would be caught by an item labeled "About Social Security's Future," which appeared in font several times larger than the font of the items above and below—font larger, for example, than "Social Security announces help for disability applicants." When visitors to the site clicked on "About Social Security's Future," they were once again treated to the 16-to-1 factoid. The ratio was so drilled into people's consciousness that comedian Jon Stewart on *The Daily Show* used it as a focus of a joke, showing decreasing numbers of workers seeking to hold aloft extremely obese older people.

It was clear that the administration sought to make people believe that the traditional Social Security program was unworkable and fundamentally flawed. Callers to the Social Security 800-number hotline were routinely placed on hold. While waiting to speak to a live voice, the captive listener was bombarded with a variety of "facts" designed to undermine confidence in the program. Callers, of course heard, the now familiar, 16 to 1 factoid repeated. In addition, callers were subjected to rhetorical questions, including, "Did you know that the 76 million-strong baby boom generation will begin to retire in about ten years? When that happens, changes will need to be made to Social Security." A few minutes later, a voice informed the person waiting on hold that "the percentage of older Americans will about double between now and 2030....Long-run changes will need to be made."

Listeners were not told that in 1983, Congress put the program into balance through 2057—the year the youngest boomers, those born in 1964, will turn 93. Nor were callers told that other demographic factors concerning mortality and fertility have been more favorable for the program than were projected in 1983 and that the current deficit has nothing to do with the number of people born between 1946 and 1964. Moreover, the recording did not inform the public that Social Security employed three sets of assumptions about the future and that one set produced a slight surplus over the 75-year period.

The same hotline recording also informed people that they do not have accounts into which their monies are kept until retirement. The recording failed to note that neither do workers who are entitled to benefits from the private defined benefit pension plans of General Motors, General Electric, Ford, or other private employers. Like Social Security, these blue-chip plans provide guaranteed benefits that replace wages. The benefits are paid from pooled resources held in trust and invested by the employer. Only defined contribution funds, like those held in 401(k) plans, are allocated to separate accounts, because the employer has no obligation beyond the contribution to the account. Rather, workers are on their own, bearing the total risk, entitled only to whatever has accumulated. Most important, the hotline recording certainly did not relay the fact that Social Security has paid every benefit promised on time every single month throughout its 70-year history. Nor did it remind people that they cannot outlive Social Security, in contrast to 401(k)s or other private savings, since it is paid every month even if the beneficiary lives until age 120.

The selective facts pounding innocent callers were all aimed in a single direction. The subliminal message was that the program was broken and could not be easily repaired. It was, the hotline recording implied, unworkable and in desperate need of revamping. The recording sounded like the sultry voice of Tokyo Rose during World War II, seductively whispering "Have no confidence in Social Security; don't count on it."

All the talk about the unsustainability of Social Security and the president's desire to "strengthen" it hid the reality. Bush's desire for individual accounts was part of the same ideological battle, rooted in the same animosity toward the program, that motivated William Randolph Hearst and other Landon supporters in 1936, Carl Curtis and his supporters in the 1940s and 1950s, and Milton Friedman, Barry Goldwater, and their disciples.

But reality is hard to conceal. Despite the obvious tactic to convince people that the traditional Social Security program was fundamentally flawed, the true motives of those who wanted change kept leaking out.

A memorandum from the president's director of strategic initiatives, dated January 3, 2005, and marked "not for attribution," put in writing what was patently obvious to anyone who knew much about the history of Social Security. The memo drew the battle line, stating that "this will be one of the most important conservative undertakings of modern times," and outlined the plan of attack. The first step, according to the leaked document, was to convince the American people that "the current system is heading for an iceberg." The memorandum concluded with a startling but refreshingly frank assessment: "For the first time in six decades, the Social Security battle is one we can win."

A second leak occurred a few weeks later, for those who found the first one too subtle. The Senate and House Republican leadership handed out a joint "Guide to Social Security Reform," to all Republican senators and congressmen at a retreat during the last weekend in January at The Greenbrier, an upscale resort in West Virginia. The 100-page document resembled a playbook for a football team rather than a serious policy analysis for necessary reforms of a complicated statute.

The guide contained talking points and helpful political reminders, such as to be sure to use: "'[p]ersonalization' not 'privatization.'" Sounding as if written by well-coached adherents of the Leninist strategy, the guide cautioned, "You will face the unique challenge of recruiting the support of both current and future retirees—two groups with very different views on Social Security's reliability....A number of helpful messaging techniques have already been tested in the field."

On page 6 was a graphic of workers holding up retirees, suspiciously resembling the facetious cartoon of *The Daily Show*, as if the authors had concluded that *The Daily Show* version was punchier than the more boring equation of little men found on the White House Web site. To make sure all Republicans conveyed a uniform message, the guide furnished a PowerPoint presentation, sample speeches, and a model letter to constituents.

When the Congressional readers turned to "Case Studies," they might have thought that they were finally getting to something policy-worthy—how the president's proposal will affect ordinary Americans struggling for economic security. The cases were indeed about security and survival, but not about economic survival of everyday Americans. Rather they told tales of political survival, recounting stories of those brave Republicans who had dared to propose radical reform of Social Security and had not gotten thrown out of office but had indeed managed to survive politically.

Nervous Republicans could be consoled by such heartwarming stories as that of Senator Elizabeth Dole (R-NC), who "'never ran away from her support of Social Security reforms' and won 54%–45%," and Senator John Sununu (R-NH) who successfully fended off his opponent's charges of "supporting 'privatization' of Social Security" with "an articulate advocacy of voluntary individual investment accounts as part of Social Security—modernization."

But the administration and the congressional leadership could stiffen their colleagues' backbones only so much. The Republicans held majorities in both the Senate and the House of Representatives, so they could enact what they wanted. But they would all be up for reelection eventually. They, like most politicians, have a strong sense of self-preservation—as the decision to include politically comforting case studies in the guide clearly acknowledged. Constituents, not just Republican officeholders, would have to be sold.

The dilemma for the administration was not simply getting Congress to vote the right way but getting it to vote at all. The last two major Social Security bills had been passed in 1977 and 1983, both odd-numbered, nonelection years. In those two instances, doing nothing would have left the Social Security trust funds unable to pay full benefits on time in a matter of months. Congress seemed to act only when faced with this kind of action-forcing, real-world event.

The Bush administration recognized that action on Social Security must occur immediately, in 2005, because Congress was unlikely to tackle the politically charged subject in 2006, an election year. And the experience of 1982 indicated that if opponents of Social Security allowed the program to be an election issue, it was likely to be bad for the opponents and good for the program's supporters.

The administration embarked on a strategy that could, if successful, both motivate quick Congressional action and undermine American confidence in Social Security, weakening support for Social Security—the first prong of the Leninist strategy. Soon after the election, Bush launched a campaign to convince the public that Social Security was in crisis, and that pressure must be brought on Congress to act at once. If the President could convince Americans that the program faced a crisis, perhaps the American people, alarmed about the Social Security lifeline that so many depended on, would demand that Congress act.

In over a dozen speeches, statements, and press conferences between his election in November and the start of Congress on January 4, Bush asserted that "the crisis is now" for Social Security. In meetings with supporters, he used vivid language to make his point: If "we don't start moving on [Social Security reform] now…the system will be flat broke," and "bankrupt," and "flat bust." But the boy had cried crisis one too many times before.

The president had labeled medical malpractice lawsuits a "crisis in America." He had called the blocking of the confirmation of judges by Democrats "a vacancy crisis." Most notoriously, he had built support for the preemptive war against Iraq by convincing Americans that a crisis of national security loomed. In his State of the Union Address just prior to the Iraq invasion, President Bush had warned:

> Year after year, Saddam Hussein has gone to elaborate lengths, spent enormous sums, taken great risks to build and keep weapons of mass destruction.…Imagine those 19 hijackers…this time armed by Saddam Hussein. It would take one vial, one canister, one crate slipped into this country to bring a day of horror like none we have ever known.

This time, the Democrats called the president on his scare tactics. Social Security, retorted Harry Reid, Senate minority leader, "is a crisis created in the minds of the White House because they want to take care of the fat cats on Wall Street." Jokes and cartoons about the president's use of crisis language began to appear.

Seeing that its ploy was not working, the administration backed off the references to crisis. On February 9, in a question-and-answer session on Social Security, in Raleigh, North Carolina, Bush remarked that "step one of my strategy is to continue saying…we have got a serious problem. In other words, sometimes they say, is it serious, is it a crisis—look, whatever you want to call it."

Part of the difficulty that the administration had faced in convincing people of a crisis was that Social Security's trustees projected that the program would be in actuarial balance until the early 2040s. The nonpartisan Congressional Budget Office showed the program to be in balance for even a decade longer, until the early 2050s. It was a hard sell to convince people that a potential problem, more than 35 years away, required Congress to act precipitously before the end of the current year.

Seeing the obvious difficulty, Bush tried to make the case that the "crisis" or "serious problem" or "whatever you want to call it" really arrived sooner. The president and his supporters latched onto 2018, which helpfully moved up the "crisis" by over 20 years. That was also a hard sell, because 2018 was still 13 years in the future, and, more to the point, nothing happened in that year. The trust funds would not even start dipping into principal until 2028. In 2018, outgo was still projected to remain less than the income of the funds, just not less than one part of the income, the income from taxes. In addition to income from taxes, the funds have, since their creation, had interest income on the Treasury bonds held in trust.

In order to make the case that the "crisis" or "serious problem" or "whatever you want to call it" would really, truly occur in 2018, Bush borrowed a tactic from the election of 1936. He and his allies sought to convince Americans that Social Security was simply an accounting gimmick holding no true assets, just a bunch of worthless IOUs in the form of Treasury bonds. Accordingly, the president staged a photo op in Parkersburg, West Virginia, where Social Security's Treasury bonds are kept. Standing in the room where the bonds are stored, Bush declared, "There is no trust fund—just IOUs that I saw firsthand."

Was the president anticipating a vault overflowing with gold coins, bills, gold bricks, emeralds, and diamonds, like the kind pictured in the comic books featuring Scrooge McDuck? Unlike cartoon renditions, the vaults of the wealthy are overflowing with paper, just like the Social

Security trust funds. But, of course, not just any pieces of paper. And certainly not worthless paper.

The Social Security trust funds, as the president correctly pointed out, are jam-packed with pieces of paper, all right—pieces of paper granting rights legally enforceable in a court of law. Treasury bonds are just as much an asset as those other pieces of paper the president kept touting—stock certificates—or, for that matter, gold coins and dollar bills. It would be surprising if the wealth of multimillionaire Bush did not consist primarily of pieces of paper or perhaps simply electronic records in computers.

Bush's claim that the Treasury bonds are worthless pieces of paper worked better when Landon used it in 1936. Because of the concern that the Supreme Court would more likely hold Social Security unconstitutional if funds were paid into and out of a trust fund, Congress initially had Social Security contributions simply credited to a reserve account. Consequently, Landon had a point that the program's reserves would be "cash which the Treasury gives the Treasury." It was only after the Supreme Court found the Social Security program to be constitutional that the Roosevelt administration and Congress gave the stronger protection of a trust fund with a set of appointed trustees, legally responsible for the conduct of the trust. The very first Social Security amendments following the Supreme Court decision—the Social Security Amendments of 1939—created the trust fund.

If most people were told that a trust arrangement had been created for them and that the trust held trillions of dollars' worth of Treasury bonds, or even millions of dollars' worth, they would feel—and be—very wealthy. No financial planner would tell them that the Treasury bonds being held in trust for them were worthless pieces of paper.

Moreover, not only are the assets contained within the trust valuable, the trust itself provides important protection to the beneficiaries of Social Security. All trustees, by virtue of that position, are held to very high standards under the law. They are fiduciaries and must act, at all times, in the exclusive interest of their beneficiaries. The 1939 amendments named the secretary of the Treasury, the secretary of labor and the predecessor of the secretary of health and human services as the trustees. In a 1983 effort to increase public confidence, Congress expanded the board to include two public trustees. In 1994, the commissioner of Social Security was named as a sixth trustee.

The government officials who are on Social Security's board of trustees wear two hats; they are in charge of their departments and they are trustees.

If a conflict arises between the two roles, the trustees must resolve it in favor of the trust beneficiaries. This is not just a matter of legal theory. The Social Security trustees were sued on this very point in the fall of 1985.

At that time, President Reagan and Congress were fighting about raising the debt ceiling. The debt ceiling was created by Congress in 1947 to cap federal borrowing. If the government wants to borrow beyond the cap, it must raise the ceiling, a politically unpopular move. In 1985, Congress and the administration were arguing about the budget and the debt ceiling as the government was running out of money.

The Treasury Department and the Social Security trust funds have well-established, complicated arrangements to ensure that transactions are neutral between the two entities. Secretary of the Treasury James Baker had the legal obligation, as managing trustee, to protect the Social Security trust funds. Instead, he acted to forestall the closing of the government, at the expense of the trust funds. In September and October, he was required to transfer to the trust funds monies collected by the Internal Revenue Service. When he did not do so, the trust funds had to dip into reserves, which cost the program $10 million a day in lost interest.

When the conflict arose between his two roles, Secretary of the Treasury James Baker was obligated under the law to act in the interest of the trust beneficiaries. When he did otherwise, AARP, the Save Our Security Coalition (an advocacy group begun in the 1970s by Bob Ball and Wilbur Cohen), several beneficiaries, including Ball and Cohen, and a number of members of Congress hired a lawyer—the distinguished Elliot Richardson, former attorney general of the United States under President Nixon—who immediately went to court. Richardson filed a lawsuit, Civil Action No. 85-3466, in the United States District Court for the District of Columbia, on behalf of the plaintiffs, against the then-five Social Security trustees. The suit charged that, among other wrongdoing, "Defendant Trustees have violated and continue to violate their fiduciary obligations to the beneficiaries of the Trust Funds." The Justice Department filed a motion to dismiss the complaint, which was denied by U.S. District Court judge Thomas F. Hogan. The government resolved its debt ceiling controversy the same day, and the lawsuit became moot.

When President Bush visited Parkersburg, West Virginia, where trillions of dollars' worth of Treasury bonds are held in trust for the beneficial interest of the beneficiaries of Social Security, he declared, "A lot of people in America think there is a trust.... There is no trust 'fund.'" That would be a shock to Judge Hogan, who became chief judge of the District Court in 2001, to the lawyers at the Department of Justice who litigated the case, and to Elliot Richardson, if he were still alive.

When Social Security receives interest income or redeems Treasury bonds in order to pay benefits, the United States must cover the cost of the obligations by drawing money from the general fund or issuing and selling more bonds, as it must when required to pay any of its debt obligations. The arrangement is confusing because those paying into the trust funds and those paying taxes to the general fund are overlapping, though not identical, populations. But the argument that the trust funds are merely part of the Treasury lending money to itself overlooks the legal character of a trust.

Parents who create trusts for their children are not simply engaged in a sleight of hand. The children have claims enforceable in a court of law on the funds set aside in the trusts. They would not have such legal claims if the funds are not in trust but remain in the parents' bank accounts, even though the funds originate with the same two parents.

As Altmeyer and others pointed out in the 1930s, if Social Security were not holding the Treasury bonds, others would, because government spending apart from Social Security exceeds income. Banks in Japan, China, and Great Britain currently hold over half of all privately-held U.S. treasuries. The terms and conditions of all the outstanding bonds are essentially identical, and there is no reason in law or logic that would make instruments held by those foreign banks more worthy of being honored than the bonds held by Social Security.

Moreover, states have unemployment insurance funds invested, just as Social Security is, in U.S. Treasury bonds. Are these investments secure, as presumably the Treasuries held by foreign banks are, or are they, in Bush's language, "just IOUs"—impliedly worthless—like those held by Social Security? They are not held by the federal government, but they are held for the beneficial interest of American workers. Just like the bonds held by Social Security, the interest and principal of the Treasury bonds held by the states must be satisfied by many of the same taxpayers who paid into the unemployment insurance trust funds in the first place.

Calling the Treasury bonds "just IOUs" served several of the president's purposes. It bolstered his claim that "the crisis is now." In addition, it also worked to undermine confidence in Social Security. If confidence was undermined, support for the program might erode, just as the authors of "Achieving a 'Leninist' Strategy" had sought.

Not content to undermine confidence in the future of Social Security in a general, scattershot way, the president decided to divide, target, and conquer. Early in the push for private accounts, Bush met with 24 African American clergy and business leaders. He told them that Social Security was unfair to African Americans because of their shorter life expectancies. The shorter life expectancies, higher infant mortality rates, and overall poorer health of African Americans when compared to European Americans are national scandals. But instead of proposing a solution aimed at the underlying causes, President Bush instead attempted to capitalize on this reprehensible state of affairs.

Bush's political ploy did not play well. First, many pointed out that the Social Security system is fair to all races. Although African Americans get a lower percentage of retirement benefits due to their shorter life expectancies, they get a higher proportion of disability and survivor benefits. African Americans constitute about 12 percent of the population, but about 23 percent of all children receiving survivors' benefits are African American, as are 17 percent of all disability beneficiaries. Moreover, the weighted benefit formula and the dropout years in calculating benefits favor lower-income workers, who are disproportionately African American.

But what really provoked outrage was the opportunistic nature of the argument. The administration advocated no programs to improve the health and longevity of African Americans. Even worse, it proposed cuts in Medicaid, one of the few government programs that might improve the poorer health of African Americans.

Another way the administration sought to weaken the support for Social Security was to try to keep its most vocal defenders, those aged 55 and older, out of the debate. This was a play taken right from the Leninist strategy playbook. The authors of the 1983 article advised, "The... strategy must be to propose moving to a private Social Security system in such a way as to...neutralize" those at or near retirement. Otherwise, they continued, "the retired (or nearly retired) population will continue to strongly oppose any package that threatens to significantly reduce their benefits."

The advocates of private accounts believed that they could splinter support for the traditional Social Security program by convincing those aged 55 and over that they would not suffer benefit cuts. Consistent with this approach, the president emphasized repeatedly that those older Americans would experience no change in the benefits they received from the program. But those older citizens refused to leave the debate, much to the exasperation of Bush supporters.

At yet another retreat at the fancy, well-toned Greenbrier resort, pollsters and focus group analysts gave senior congressional staffers the bad news. Senior citizens, the staffers were told, were not willing to sit out the debate, despite the assurances that their benefits would not be cut. Hearing the polling results, a Senate aide resolved to "continue to make our case to the American people that Social Security will be fine for those that are at or near retirement."

Supporters of private accounts seemed determined to believe that those aged 55 and over simply did not understand what the president had been saying repeatedly. But polling data showed that they understood exactly what Bush was saying. They understood it, but they remained in the debate, opposed to the administration reform. Many elderly explained that they were not worried about their own benefits, but they cared greatly about the benefits their children and grandchildren might or might not get. These concerned grandparents wanted to make sure that their grandchildren had the security of a guaranteed retirement, not the gamble and uncertainty of individual accounts. Typical was one 69-year-old who summed up his generation's view: "I'm a parent as well as a grandparent....It's everybody's concern what happens to this country."

Another prong of the Leninist strategy was to build support for private accounts as an alternative to Social Security. Frank Luntz, a Republican pollster and consultant, warned the Republicans once again, as he had in 2002, about the use of language in the Social Security fight. In the appendix of a playbook summarizing the lessons learned from the 2004 election, Luntz included his 2002 memorandum, "The 14 Words Never to Use," which contained the stern warning, typed all in capital letters, "BANISH PRIVATIZATION FROM YOUR LEXICON." Bush apparently took Luntz's advice to heart. On March 15, 2005, as part of a 30-minute interview with a handful of regional newspaper reporters, the president charged, "Privatization is a trick word" used by those "basically trying to scare people."

But the problems with the proposal went far beyond the language. The administration had offered some general descriptions of the private accounts proposal but few details. Even without details, analysts could see that the proposal had serious defects. The administration had announced that the accounts, funded by a portion of a worker's Social Security contibbutions, were voluntary. But workers all paid the same Social Security taxes. The administration realized that it could not give workers who opted for private accounts the same Social Security benefits as everyone else and, in addition the full amount of the private accounts. If that were the structure, the voluntary nature of the account would be in name only. It would make no sense not to sign up for a private account if all workers paid the same amount of taxes, everyone qualified for the same benefits, and the only difference was that workers who signed up got individual accounts in addition. To make the accounts voluntary, workers who opted for them either had to pay back to Social Security the taxes that they had used to fund their individual accounts or receive lower Social Security benefits.

At first, the administration's description of its proposal sounded like account holders would be treated as if they borrowed their Social Security taxes in order to deposit the monies in private accounts and would, at retirement, have to pay the loans back with interest of 3 percent above inflation. A *Washington Post* story that appeared the day after the president's State of the Union Address and purported to explain the Bush plan was headlined: "Participants Would Forfeit Part of Accounts' Profits." The article quoted an "administration official" who explained, "Basically, the net effect on an individual's benefits would be zero if his personal account earned a 3 percent real rate of return."

The White House quickly corrected the record. Since the White House had stressed that people "owned" their accounts, the same reduction would come from the Social Security benefit otherwise earned, rather than the private account. Later that day, the *Post* published a correction: "The original story…should have made clear that, under the proposal, workers who opt to invest in the new private accounts would lose a proportionate share of their guaranteed payment from Social Security plus interest."

But the correction had serious implications and raised unanswered questions. Even if the workers came out the same at the time of retirement, whether the retirement income came from the Social Security fund or the private account—a questionable proposition—10 years into retirement would be quite a different story. The portion from the private account might have lost considerable value since the private account benefit presumably would not have been protected against inflation.

Much more serious though, the corrected approach would have an extremely different impact on spouses, divorced spouses, and children. About 14 million people, mainly women, receive Social Security benefits based partly or totally on a spouse's work record. Currently, 3.1 million children are entitled to monthly Social Security checks, totaling about $9 billion. The administration never explained the impact of the private accounts proposal on these benefits.

Under current law, the Social Security trust funds can support benefits paid to workers' dependents as additional add-on benefits, not reducing the amount received by the worker. Monthly Social Security checks paid to divorced spouses and children from prior marriages do not affect in any way benefits paid to workers, their current spouses, or their new families. But the president proposed replacing part of the traditional benefits with a fixed sum from private accounts. If some of Social Security were coming from a fixed amount in a private account, would divorcing spouses for the first time have to fight over this pot of retirement income? Would all children continue to receive full benefits (up to a family maximum), or would larger families be forced to divide up the private accounts, because their traditional benefits would be reduced?

Among the many more technical questions, would dependents' benefits be subject to the offset, based on the earnings in the private accounts or just the worker's own benefit? If the answer was that only the worker's benefit was subject to the offset and the offset disappeared when the worker died, surviving spouses could wind up receiving higher benefits as widows or widowers than the couple received jointly when both were alive and the worker's benefits were offset. To avoid that anomaly, a current spouse's benefit could be subject to the offset, but then an ex-spouse not subject to the offset might receive a higher benefit than a current spouse. To resolve that odd result, all spouses, current and former, could have their benefits offset. But the offset was to be based on a fixed dollar amount equaling the part of the Social Security taxes diverted to the private accounts plus imputed interest. Therefore, the more benefits among which the fixed offset was to be divided, the smaller the impact on each benefit. Workers who hopped in and out of marriage every 10 years would have smaller offsets and thus do better than the couple that stayed together.

No technocrat can easily unravel these problems and countless others. They all come from trying to mesh a defined contribution plan for individuals with a defined benefit program of social insurance, which protects families through add-on benefits. The two conceptually different approaches cannot be reconciled coherently. Moreover, in addition to problems of plan design, the administrative costs were likely to be exhorbitant and the administrability itself, perhaps impossible.

But no one was looking at the details. The widespread opposition to the president's proposal was more fundamental and profound. Most people simply did not want to trade the guarantee of Social Security's promised benefits for the risk to the individual from investing in the stock market. In addition, because the proposal for private accounts required essentially a new spending program, it would cost trillions of dollars. The proponents of private accounts called these new expenditures "transition costs," although most people think of transitions as lasting but a few years. This "transition" would last many, many decades, if not the entire 75-year valuation period.

Supporters of the current program also pointed out that individual accounts would do nothing to close the projected long-range deficit of Social Security. In early January, about ten weeks after the election, "several Republicans close to the White House" had reportedly disclosed that the administration favored a controversial change in the indexing of Social Security. Interest groups immediately denounced the proposal, after projecting just how large the benefit cuts would be and how they would affect individuals. By the time of the State of the Union Address, the deflated trial balloon was simply one of a list of possible reforms. For the next few months, President Bush answered every question about what he would do to close the projected deficit by saying: "All ideas are on the table, except raising the payroll tax rate," a sentiment that displayed an open mind though not much leadership.

Most frustrating to the private account proponents, younger workers—the group the Leninist strategists predicted would be the proposal's strongest supporters—were not flocking to the cause. Even though younger workers continued to express skepticism about their own chances of receiving benefits, they nevertheless opposed the president's plan. Just like their grandparents who were focused on the future security of their grandchildren, the grandchildren were concerned about their grandparents. Around 150 college student body presidents signed a petition opposing the president's proposal for private accounts.

To the shock and dismay of the Republicans, the Democrats formed a solid wall against the president's private accounts scheme and refused to negotiate on the issue of long range solvency until he dropped the idea. Bush and his supporters latched onto any Democrat they could find. President Clinton and the late Senator Moynihan were mentioned in President Bush's State of the Union Address, and their names became stock lines in Bush's speeches. Representative Charles Rangel had a simple response. "If you're talking about bipartisanship, you have to be talking to people who are alive and elected," Rangel helpfully explained.

President Bush and his supporters also sought to wrap themselves in the cloak of yet another popular Democrat, Franklin Roosevelt. Another of President Bush's mantras, in addition to his favorite ratio 16 workers to 1 beneficiary, became "Franklin Roosevelt did a wonderful thing when he created Social Security." Apparently he had changed his mind since his days as a student at the Harvard Business School when he had called President Roosevelt a "socialist" for creating Social Security and other New Deal programs. Opponents of the traditional Social Security program used Roosevelt's picture and his name in television ads pushing private accounts. Roosevelt's grandson had an angry response: "I have written a letter of protest....It is just a disgrace. And it's an insult to his memory."

Of course, President Bush did not need Democratic support. The president was Republican, and his party controlled both houses of Congress. They had not sought bipartisanship when they enacted, over strong Democratic objections, their prescription drug bill. They had not sought bipartisanship when they intervened to have a feeding tube reinserted in Terri Schiavo, a brain-damaged woman in Florida. And the party leadership had certainly not sought bipartisanship when President Bush, after the election, renominated his most controversial choices for judgeships and when Senate Republican leader Bill Frist had sought to end the possibility of filibusters over judicial nominations in order to ram the choices through the Senate, despite strong Democratic opposition. But in this fight that a Republican president had started over Social Security, the Republicans sought bipartisan cover.

To stir up support and put pressure on the Democrats, the president announced that he would begin a campaign-style speaking tour, with "60 stops in 60 days" to push his plan for private accounts. "The President's road show" a PBS correspondent reported, "is using the same techniques that were successful in his reelection bid, carefully choreographed events in front of handpicked, sympathetic, largely Republican audiences, there by invitation only."

Just as during the campaign, stories started appearing of people thrown out of these forums on the smallest pretext, if someone even thought they might make trouble. In Fargo, North Dakota, more than 40 local residents were kept from the event. In Denver, Colorado, three well-dressed attendees who carried no signs, made no comments, and had tickets from the local Republican congressman, were forcibly ejected because they were seen getting out of a car with the bumper sticker "No more blood for oil."

Most attending the events were not allowed to speak. Rather, several people, usually a retiree and a young worker, perhaps a housewife or an African American, were handpicked and were required to rehearse the night before the event. In Little Rock, Arkansas, a 31-year-old insurance agent who had gone to college with the Republican governor's son was asked to participate. Once he agreed, he received a number of phone calls from the White House questioning him about his background, family, and views on Social Security. The White House thought about using his mother as well, until the administration discovered that she had questions about private accounts. Then the rehearsals began. The participants met the evening before the event with a stand-in for the president. Bush's advance team did five run-throughs with the participants in order to prepare them fully.

The White House was not looking for true discussion. These were staged events, designed to garner favorable coverage on local television and other media. As *USA Today* informed, "Presidential visits are rare in most communities, and they're often covered like a combination of a rock concert, a Hollywood premiere and the Super Bowl." Coverage would typically start a few days before the president arrived.

In response to these press-generating events, the supporters of Social Security worked the media as well as they could. An organizer for a coalition of pro-Social Security groups explained, "As soon as we find out where the president is going, we reach out to our local grass-roots groups and start organizing." Members from the grass-roots organizations contacted local reporters, distributed press releases, and staged events that sought to get some of the coveted television and print coverage. Groups opposing the president's efforts staged counterrallies at almost every one of Bush's stops.

Interest groups on both sides of the issue had mobilized for the battle as soon as the president had announced his plans, just after the election, to fundamentally change Social Security. The supporters of Social Security were generally easy to identify. Well-known AARP, the membership organization for people age 50 and over, began running full-page newspaper ads defending the program against administration attacks. Similarly, the AFL-CIO, the longtime federation of organized labor, was an organization everyone knew. But other groups, whose names concealed their true interests, joined the fight. Notwithstanding its deceptive name, the Alliance for Worker Retirement Security represented not workers but business. Founded by the National Association of Manufacturers, it is a coalition of over 40 organizations including the U.S. Chamber of Commerce, the Business Roundtable, and Pfizer Co., a major pharmaceutical company with revenues of $52.5 billion in 2004.

Another group with shadowy support was the United Seniors Association, which the *Washington Monthly* described as "a soft-money slush fund for a single G.O.P.-friendly industry: pharmaceuticals." The United Seniors group sought to use many of the smear tactics that had appeared in the recently ended presidential campaign. The United Seniors Association hired the same people who assisted the self-named Swift Boat Veterans for Truth with the very effective, mud-slinging ad against Democratic candidate John Kerry. This time the target was the well-respected and popular AARP.

The United Seniors group ran an attack ad claiming that AARP backed gay marriage and opposed American soldiers, but the ad did not fare quite as well as the anti-Kerry smear. Comedians quickly made jokes about the odd juxtaposition of homosexuality and a senior citizens group, a population most Americans do not exactly associate with steamy sex. When the president of the United Seniors Association said of AARP, "They can run, but they can't hide," Maureen Dowd, a syndicated columnist with the *New York Times*, remarked that the image of senior citizens scurrying away to hide did not fit most people's picture of "the walker-and-cane set."

As the president trudged through his carefully choreographed campaign of "60 stops in 60 days," he discovered that there was one aspect of his orchestrated trips that he could not control. Support for his Social Security plan fell the longer he was on the road. According to a *Newsday* April 27 story appearing just days before the end of the 60 days, "A majority of Americans favored the concept [of private accounts] before the tour. A slim majority in a new poll opposes it." Even more unsettling for the president, when the 60-day campaign began in March, 56 percent reported that they disapproved of his handling of Social Security; two months later, 64 percent reported that they disapproved. When the 60 days came to an end, Bush decided to extend the tour. In response to the falling support and the extension of the campaign-style trips, Democratic senator Richard Durbin (D-Ill.) remarked, "If [Bush is] going out to push for privatization, let's help him pack!"

Meanwhile, back in Congress, Republican leaders were engaged in a bit of an Alphonse-Gaston routine, no one eager to make the first move on developing a Social Security package without cover from the president. On April 26, Senator Chuck Grassley (R-Iowa), chairman of the Senate Finance Committee, scheduled a hearing on Social Security in which a panel of experts testified. Included was Robert Pozen, a Boston businessman who had been a member of President Bush's commission investigating private accounts as a substitute for part of Social Security's guaranteed protection. He described a proposal, which he appealingly labeled "progressive indexing." The proposal would preserve the levels of Social Security benefits for those who had career average earnings of $20,000 or less, while the 70 percent of workers above that level would have benefits, measured as a percentage of preretirement earnings, decline over time. Eventually, benefits would reach an almost flat, minimal level, largely unrelated to prior wages.

Two days after the hearing, the president held the fourth prime-time television press conference of his presidency. He picked the first night of network television's hotly contested May sweeps week, during which ratings determine advertising rates for the season. And the press conference was on the first night, a Thursday, the most coveted air time of the week.

The administration informed the networks the night before that the president wanted his press conference televised, starting at 8:30 P.M. Eastern Standard Time. Aware that a president had authority to preempt programing only in the case of a national emergency, the networks first checked to make sure that President Bush had no plans to launch another war, and that it was indeed their choice whether or not to air the press conference. The networks then contemplated the boatloads of money riding on their decision. CBS, confronted with preempting its popular *Survivor, CSI: Crime Scene Investigation*, and *Without a Trace*, turned the White House down. NBC, faced with not showing its popular *Apprentice*, also announced it would not be televising the press conference. FOX followed suit. Only ABC, which had planned to show the movie *Sweet Home Alabama*, agreed to televise the press conference.

Faced with so many networks turning their backs on the press conference, the White House caved and moved it a half hour earlier. With that switch, NBC and CBS agreed to air the press conference. Learning of the decision of the other networks, FOX, now the odd-station out, buckled and aired the press conference, as well. But like Cinderella at the stroke of midnight, the networks switched immediately at 9:00 from the press conference to more popular programming, not waiting for the responses to the last few shouted questions.

At the time of the press conference, the Democrats were continuing to maintain a solid wall of opposition to the president's proposal and public opinion polls showed that most Americans opposed Bush's handling of Social Security. Nevertheless, instead of signaling a willingness to compromise, Bush, in the words of the *Washington Post* the morning after the press conference, "doubled-down on his bet."

At the press conference, using the now-familiar factoid, "In 1950, there were 16 workers for every beneficiary, today there are 3.3 workers for every beneficiary," the president embraced the Pozen proposal, which would cause Social Security benefits to erode over time into a very minimal, almost flat benefit, largely unrelated to income, except in the case of the lowest-paid American workers.

In reporting about the press conference, news stories focused on the size of the future benefit cuts that the president's indexing proposal would produce and on who would suffer them. Survivors' benefits and disability benefits are generated from the same common formula that the president was proposing to alter. The administration now acknowledged that benefits for surviving spouses and children would be cut. In the past, Bush had asserted that benefits for survivors and the disabled "won't change. We're talking about the retirement aspect of Social Security."

While the administration now confessed that benefits for the survivors of deceased workers would be cut along with the benefits for retirees, it continued to asert that benefits for the disabled would remain unchanged. But that is much more difficult to do than to say. Under current law, when disabled workers reach retirement age, they move seamlessly, without even realizing it, from disability benefits paid from the Disability Insurance Trust Fund to retirement benefits paid from the Old-Age and Survivors Insurance Trust Fund. This can be done because benefits are coordinated and the change is simply a matter of bookkeeping.

But a plan that reduces retirement benefits yet leaves untouched the benefits for workers who become disabled would produce one of two unintended but harmful results. One possibility is that workers receiving disability benefits would incur substantial reductions in benefits at the moment they reached retirement age. Alternatively, if disability benefits were not reduced at retirement age, someone who became disabled the day before retirement would receive substantially higher benefits than the benefits a coworker with the same earnings record and the same birthday would receive the very next day on retirement.

White House spokesman Trent Duffy recognized that there was a problem with the White House approach. "Any plan that maintains current disability benefits will need to address the transition to retirement," he admitted, although he provided no details about how this could possibly be done. The problems of coordinating different disability and retirement benefits are numerous and impossible to fix easily. As just one more of many examples, would children whose working parents become disabled be better off financially than those children whose parents die? Would the children of those disabled workers suffer a benefit cut if the parents subsequently did die?

If the president was trying to force the Democrats to announce a solvency package of their own by finally announcing a complete package himself, he failed. When asked by a reporter the day after the press conference whether the Democrats would counter with a plan of their own, Congressman Rangel pointedly responded that he spoke to many groups about Social Security and the only ones asking for a plan from the Democratic minority were the press and the White House. He then said what the Democrats had been saying for months: The Democrats would be happy to develop a bipartisan package once the president took private accounts off the table.

And many Republicans were expressing concern about the Pozen indexing proposal, as well. Former majority leader Trent Lott (R-Miss) explained, "I'm not overjoyed about [the indexing proposal], because I think it does begin to move [Social Security] toward a welfare system." Republican member of the Ways and Means Committee, E. Clay Shaw, Jr. (R-Fla.), expressed similar concern. "Means testing would change the whole nature of Social Security, which is supposed to be an earned benefit that you pay into. I'm a little skeptical," Shaw confided, adding that the Bush indexing proposal "is landing kind of flat."

Chairman Thomas of Ways and Means announced the day after the press conference that his committee would develop a "retirement package for aging Americans" that looked at private savings, pensions, and long-term health care, as well as Social Security, and was financed by a new tax on consumption. Thomas told the press that he would hold regular hearings with the goal of legislation by early June. A Thomas spokeswoman modified the comments, telling the press that action would occur in the summer, not early June. While majority leader DeLay supported Thomas in his efforts, Republican Speaker Dennis Hastert preferred, according to congressional staff, that the Senate act first.

Senator Grassley also planned to continue the work of the Senate Finance Committee with a bill by August, although he faced his own problems. Moderate Repub-lican Olympia J. Snowe (R-Me.) said that she would not support the president's private accounts proposal. But another Republican member of the committee, Senator Jon Kyl (R-Ariz.), said he would only support a package that contained it.

Grassley's comment that he might leave the private accounts proposal out of the package and permit the issue to be decided on the Senate floor proved controversial. House Republican leader DeLay believed private accounts were essential, according to an aide, as did many right-wing supporters of the president. Steve Moore, president of the Free Enterprise Fund, pleaded, "Republicans in the House must rescue the Social Security debate from the clutches of the bean counters who have bewitched the administration and most moderate Senate Republicans into obsessing over solvency."

Finding little support for Bush's proposal, four Republican members of the House Subcommittee on Social Security, the Chairman of the House Republican Policy Committee, and two Republican Senators unveiled another variation on a theme on Wednesday, June 23, 2005. With some fanfare, the Republican leaders announced that instead of diverting a portion of the Social Security payroll tax into private accounts, they would instead divert Social Security's annual surplus into those accounts—never pointing out the smoke-and-mirrors quality of the proposal, that the surplus comes from revenue raised by the payroll tax. The president's plan would divert payroll tax receipts at the moment they were collected by the Internal Revenue Service. The new proposal would wait the one day it took the IRS to transfer the funds to Social Security before diverting them. Though the press reprted about the proposal as if it were a serious new idea, the proposal was distinct from the president's plan, but not different—except in the few ways that it was worse.

Unlike Bush's private account plan, these private accounts only had a source of funding for 10 years, until Social Security's surplus ran out. Republicans hoped that focus on preserving the surplus through individual accounts would prove popular. Democrats quickly pointed out that

President Clinton, with his charge to "Save Social Security First," had preserved the surplus until the Republicans had gotten control of it. Representative Earl Pomeroy (D-NC) offered a simile, "It's kind of like if someone robbed your house, and then came around and wanted to be your banker. Remember this is the group that took the surplus to begin with."

On July 14, Chairman Thomas revised his timetable for acting on Social Security, acknowledging that his committee would not get to the reform package until September, at the earliest. Like his counterpart in the House, Grassley told reporters that he did not know when his committee would take up Social Security.

With nothing newsworthy happening, the issue of Social Security slipped from the front pages. Having spent months arguing that the problem confronting Social Security was very serious, it was hard for the president or his supporters simply to drop it. And the Democrats saw that if the issue was still alive in November 2006, perhaps they could convince voters to restore them to power so the program could be fixed properly.

Meanwhile, those who had worked on the program for decades watched from the sidelines. Ball received a call from Rod Perkins, with whom he had worked during the Eisenhower administration but had not spoken to in decades. Republican Perkins expressed his distress over what the president of his party was doing. Perkins and Myers decided to co-author an op-ed column expressing their support, as two lifelong Republicans, for Social Security and their opposition to the president's plan. By the time they submitted it, though, few newspapers were running op-eds on the subject.

With all the frenetic posturing about Social Security among politicians, interest groups, and the media, no one seemed to see the obvious solution, which was in plain sight. Just like those pesky glasses or set of keys that you cannot see even though they are right there on the kitchen table, the optimal way to close the Social Security deficit was in plain sight for anyone who truly wanted to end the "crisis," or "serious problem," or "whatever you want to call it." For the last decade, Bob Ball had been polishing it in his paper-strewn living room.

## CHAPTER 16

# The Ideal, Pain-Free (for Almost Everyone) Way to Strengthen Social Security

Of all the problems facing the nation, Social Security's projected shortfall several decades away is one of the easiest to solve. Unlike the threat of terrorism, the war in Iraq, the protection of the environment, or the provision of health care insurance, Social Security is a straightforward equation involving monies coming in and monies going out.

Bob Ball's proposal, which the author strongly endorses, cuts no one's benefits. And ninety-four percent of all American workers will experience no tax increase under the proposal. The 6 percent whose Social Security taxes are affected will simply have deductions from pay made at the same rate for at most a week longer into the year. The proposal is spelled out in detail in this chapter. To better understand it, a few general points are covered first.

The Ball/Altman proposal brings Social Security into "close actuarial balance" over the next 75 years. First employed in 1957, *close actuarial balance* is a test that the trustees have used to determine whether to recommend legislative changes in Social Security's financing. The test introduces some leeway from exact balance in recognition of the uncertainty of estimates covering as many as 75 years. Close actuarial balance is met if income is within plus-or-minus 5 percent of outgo over the next 75 years. Both Ball and the author believe that, given the high degree of uncertainty with such a lengthy estimate, close actuarial balance is the appropriate benchmark for judging the sufficiency of Social Security's financing. However, they suggest three additional changes for these policy makers who want to move beyond close actuarial balance and instead leave the program with a projected surplus.

The Ball/Altman proposal defines the long range as 75 years, the standard valuation period for Social Security. It is a much longer valuation period than generally used for private pensions and generally longer than used for public programs of other countries. Nevertheless, for the American program of social insurance, the trustees have concluded that it is a reasonable length of time to consider the long-term financial operations of the trust funds, since 75 years covers the working lifetime plus the retirement period of most workers. Workers who are age 20, just starting their working lives this year, will be age 95 (if still alive) in the last year of the valuation period.

The chapter expresses the long-range deficit, as well as the savings from recommendations for change, in terms of "percentage of taxable payroll," the standard method used by policy makers. Because the main source of Social Security's financing is from taxable payrolls, expressing the projected deficit and recommendations in that form shows at a glance how much of a shortfall is expected over the next 75 years and how much in the way of savings is obtained from individual proposals. (This will become clearer to the reader as the chapter progresses.)

All of the estimates used in this chapter were made by the Office of the Actuary in the Social Security Administration, based on the assumptions underlying the middle-range estimates of the 2004 trustees' report. The 2004 report assumptions are used because shifting to the 2005 report is a complicated process that had not been completed at the time of this writing. Very little change will result from using the 2005 figures instead of the 2004 figures, because the projectons for the two years are very close. The middle-range assumptions, as the name implies, are in the middle of the three sets of assumptions that the actuaries use in making estimates, and are the ones generally used by policy makers.

The 2004 projected long-range deficit is 1.89 percent of taxable payroll. In other words, the projected deficit would be eliminated with a contribution rate increase of 0.95 percent on employees, matched by a tax of 0.95 percent on employers' payrolls. The example of increasing the tax rate is cited merely to give the reader a sense of the magnitude of the shortfall. It is not proposed that the rate be changed; there are much better ways to eliminate the deficit than by raising the payroll tax rate.

What Bob Ball and the author are convinced is the ideal, pain-free (for almost everyone) way to strengthen Social Security consists of three elements: (1) conversion of the 2009 residual estate tax to a dedicated Social Security tax, starting in 2010; (2) the gradual restoration of the maximum taxable wage base, so that, as in the past, 90 percent of all earnings in covered employment would be taxed and counted for benefits; and (3) diversification of the trust fund portfolio to include both stocks and bonds. Here are the details.

## 1. Convert the Residual Estate Tax to a Dedicated Social Security Tax, Starting in 2010

In 2001, a spouse could bequeath an entire estate to a surviving spouse without the payment of an estate tax and could bequeath up to $675,000 to other heirs tax-free, as well. Amounts over $675,000 not left to a spouse were taxed at a rate of 50 percent. That meant that a father and mother could each shelter $675,000 from taxation and leave children (or other heirs) a total of $1,350,000 tax-free. Above that amount, half the assets were inherited, half went to the government.

In 2001, Congress enacted legislation that gradually phases out the federal estate tax, which was first enacted in 1916. The 2001 law provides for the transition to no estate tax by gradually increasing the excluded amount and gradually reducing the tax rate. In 2005, the amount excluded is $1,500,000, (or $3,000,000 for a husband and wife together), and the rate of taxation is 47 percent. In 2009, the exclusion is scheduled to rise to $3,500,000 ($7,000,000 for a husband and wife), and the tax rate drops to 45 percent. In 2010, the estate tax is scheduled to be zero on all estates, no matter the size. Then, so the overall federal budget deficit would not look so large, Congress has the estate tax come back to life in 2011. In that year, in the unlikely event that the estate tax survives—the president has proposed killing it off for a second time, but with no transition; and the House has passed the legislation, which is pending in the Senate at the time of this writing—the estate tax would revert to the way it was in 2002 (assets in excess of $1,000,000 not left to spouses, would be taxed at a 50 percent rate).

The Ball/Altman proposal provides that instead of the estate tax disappearing in 2010, it is frozen at the 2009 level and converted into a dedicated Social Security tax. The excluded amount would remain at the 2009 level, $3,500,000 ($7,000,000 for a husband and wife together), $2,000,000 more than it is in 2005, $2,500,000 more than it would be if it really were resuscitated in 2011. The rate remains at the 2009 rate of 45 percent, rather than the 2005 rate of 47 percent or the 2011 rate of 50 percent.

Under this proposal, almost all estates would be exempt from taxation. In 2003, when the estate tax exclusion was $1,000,000, fewer than 1.3 percent of all estates paid any estate tax. Even with respect to those estates that would be required to pay the tax, heirs would inherit a larger percentage of those estates than they do today. Requiring Paris Hilton, Donald Trump, and other very wealthy individuals, once they have passed away, to contribute a portion of their wealth to the common good, while still passing more than half of their estates to their heirs, seems the minimum that is reasonable to ask of those who benefited from the commonwealth (common wealth) so greatly while they were alive.

Moreover, dedicating the residual estate tax to Social Security reduces a burden unfairly placed exclusively on workers. Early on, policy makers decided that workers nearing retirement age should receive meaningful benefits even though those workers would not have time under the system to pay their own way. (In the private sector, employers, when starting up defined-benefit pension plans, generally do something similar, grandfathering-in older workers even though most of those workers' employment occurred prior to the time of establishing the plan.) Social Security currently pays for the grandfathering-in, or "legacy debt," solely through Social Security's tax on wages. But wages are a narrow base on which to finance the entire legacy debt. It would be much fairer to spread this start-up cost more widely, having a portion of that legacy debt financed through a tax on assets—the estate tax. After all, everyone benefits from having a Social Security system, and all of us should join in to pay the cost of getting the system started.

Some have expressed concern about the impact of the estate tax on family farms and small, family-owned businesses. But the vast majority of these enterprises would be completely exempt from payment of a tax under the proposal. Based on estate tax returns filed in 2004, three scholars with the Tax Policy Center (a joint venture of Brookings Institution and the Urban Institute), determined that with a $3,500,000 exemption, "[o]nly about 30 small businesses and farms would continue to pay the tax, contributing 0.2 percent of total estate tax revenues."

And even those 30 could, through estate planning, reduce their liabilities substantially. Family farms and small, family-owned businesses receive favorable estate tax treatment under current law. For example, a special formula may be used to reduce the valuation of the real estate of farmers and small business owners, as long as their heirs continue to use the property as a family-owned farm or business and do not sell it to a nonrelative for 10 years or more. The formula can result in reductions of the valuation of the real estate from between 40 and 70 percent. In addition, if more than 35 percent of an estate's assets consist of farms and business assets, the estate is permitted to pay any estate tax due in installments payable over 14 years, at reduced interest rates. And with careful estate and gift planning, the tax liability could be reduced or eliminated completely. The Ball/Altman proposal would leave all of that unchanged. Given the proposed high exclusion, the special favorable tax treatment, and the fact that many of the 30 would have other assets from which to pay the estate tax, it is doubtful that a single family farm or small business would have to be sold in order to pay the tax liability.

The estate tax is highly progressive. Those with the top 5 percent of the income in the country pay 40 percent of the income tax; under the Ball proposal, that 5 percent would pay 99.6 percent of the estate tax, which would be dedicated to Social Security. (The top 1 percent would pay 97.4 percent of the dedicated estate tax under the Ball/Altman proposal.) None of them would have to pay the tax, however, until they had passed on to greater rewards.

The estate tax proposal raises 0.51 percent of taxable payroll. Consequently, it reduces the total deficit of 1.89 percent to 1.38 percent of payroll (i.e., 1.89 minus 0.51).

## 2. Gradually Restore the Maximum Taxable Wage Base

When Social Security was enacted in 1935, all covered wages below a maximum level of $3000 were taxed. The $3000 limit—the maximum taxable wage base—covered 92.5 percent of all wages paid to workers covered under Social Security. Before automatic indexing, Congress raised the base from time to time as part of legislative increases in benefit levels. In 1977, when Congress modified the automatic indexing formula, which was so sensitive to the prevailing economic conditions, it also enacted ad hoc increases to the wage base, over and above the automatic adjustments, so that the base would cover 90 percent of all wages.

By 1977, the wages covered by the maximum taxable wage base had fallen to 85 percent of total wages, so the Ways and Means Committee decided to restore the percentage. The report accompanying the legislation explained:

> Your committee's bill provides for increasing the contribution and benefit base...to a level where about 90 percent of all payroll in covered employment would be taxable for social security pur-

poses....Your committee believes that it would be desirable to move toward taxing a higher proportion of total payroll in covered employment than the 85 percent that is now taxable.

The 90 percent level was reached in 1983. In the decades since then, however, the earnings of high-paid workers have increased much more rapidly than the wages of low-paid workers. As a result, more and more wages have risen above the maximum taxable wage base. Today, once again, only about 85 percent of wages in covered employment are below the maximum taxable wage base, although Congress has taken no action to bring about that result. Indeed, the last two times Congress acted, in 1977 and 1983, it once explicitly and once implicitly (by taking no contrary action) endorsed the 90 percent benchmark. The switch from coverage of 90 percent of wages to 85 percent was not a conscious policy decision, but a byproduct of whose wages grew the fastest over the last few decades.

This reform would raise the maximum taxable wage base very slowly and gradually above the increases automatically scheduled in the law, so that the base once again covers 90 percent of wages in covered employment. Indeed, the adjustment is so gradual that the 90 percent mark would not be reached until about 2043.

Specifically, on top of the current-law automatic annual increase in the maximum taxable wage base to match the growth in average wages, this proposal would provide for an additional 2 percent increase in the base, until the base once again covers 90 percent of all wages paid to covered workers. For example, in 2005, the maximum taxable wage base is $90,000. For 2006, on top of whatever the annual percentage growth in wages is, the base would increase an additional 2 percent, or $1800 (i.e., 2% of $90,000). The additional tax paid by the 6 percent of workers at or above the base in 2006 would be $111.60 (i.e., $1800 × 6.2%)

The 94 percent of workers earning under the maximum taxable wage base would have their taxes unchanged. Those earning at or above the maximum taxable wage base would have the same tax rate provided under present law deducted from wages a bit longer in the year—one additional week a year, at most. (The Federal Insurance Contributions Act (FICA) tax is withheld from covered workers' paychecks until the maximum taxable wage base is reached.)

Those workers paying increased Social Security contributions would receive higher benefits in the event of disability or upon reaching retirement age and their families would receive higher survivors' and other dependent benefits. Because of the progressive benefit formula and the timing of receipts and disbursements, the proposal would nevertheless generate net income for the trust funds. Specifically, the return to the 90 percent standard reduces the projected shortfall by 0.61 percent of taxable payroll.

### 3. Diversify the Portfolio

The final element of the proposal involves the way that Social Security trust fund assets are invested. The fundamental rule of every investment strategy is a diversified portfolio. Almost all public and private pension funds invest in both stocks and bonds. Public funds that invest in the stock market include the Federal Railroad Retirement Plan, the Federal Reserve Board pension plan, and the plan covering the Tennessee Valley Authority employees. Unlike these plans, Social Security is restricted by law to investment in United States' obligations or in entities whose principal and interest are guaranteed by the United States

This proposal authorizes a portion of the Social Security trust fund assets to be invested in a broadly diversified, indexed equity fund or funds. A variety of safeguards would be imposed to ensure no interference with the market or with the entities in which the funds are invested. This proposal recommends, for example, that the amount to be invested be strictly limited. In addition, the proposal suggests that a Federal Reserve-type board, with staggered, lengthy terms, be appointed and be responsible for two key decisions. First, the board would select the indexed fund or funds in which to invest Social Security assets. Second, the board would hire the fund managers, who would be chosen by competitive bid from among experienced professionals.

Under the Ball/Altman plan, Social Security would be prohibited from voting any stock or in any other way influencing the policies or practices of any company or industry whose stock is held by the indexed fund. As Ball points out, "There is no more reason to expect government interference in the operation of equity markets under this plan than under the President's proposal giving government the responsibility for the selection of funds into which the proposed individual accounts must be invested."

The Ball/Altman proposal would allow 20 percent of assets to be invested in equities. One percent of assets would be invested at the end of 2006, 2 percent of assets at the end of 2007, increasing by 1 percent a year in this manner until 20 percent is reached in 2025. The proposal suggests a limitation on total trust fund investments equal to 15 percent of the total market value of all stocks.

Just as the Railroad Retirement Act in 1934 was called a "trail blazer" during the debate over it in Congress that year, so here, too, it may be pointing the way. In 2001, Congress created the National Railroad Retirement Investment Trust for the express purpose of investing some of that retirement program's assets in the stock market.

Individuals investing retirement funds in the stock market are taking quite a risk. They bear the entire risk of poor investment performance. In addition, they have the risk of being forced to sell when the market is down. They ordinarily will have to cash in their investments at or near the time of retirement, and, if they are to protect themselves from running out of money before they die, will need to purchase annuities. The time of their retirement may not time well with the ups and downs of the stock market.

Research by Gary Burtless of the Brookings Institution makes the problem vivid. His research reveals that workers with identical 40-year careers, identical wages, all retiring at the same age of 62 and all purchasing level annuities for retirement, can have dramatically different benefits based on nothing other than market timing. A worker retiring in 1980, for example, could purchase an annuity equal to 47 percent of past earnings; her younger sister, retiring just one year later, would cash in for 68 percent of past earnings; her neighbor, who turned 62 in 1993, would receive only 42 percent. The neighbor's younger sister would receive 72 percent just four years later in 1997.

In contrast, an adequately funded Social Security fund would never be in a position of having to reduce net assets at any particular time and so could ride the market's ups and downs. Investment risks would be spread over the entire population and be independent of the time a worker filed for benefits. Retirement income would continue to be based on earnings records, not the vagaries of the stock market

Of the projected deficit of 1.89 percent of taxable payroll, this proposal meets 0.37 percent. The three proposals taken together, taking into account interactions, brings the projected deficit down from 1.89 percent of taxable payroll to 0.41 percent of taxable payroll, well within the range of close actuarial balance, which is calculated to be about 0.70 percent of taxable payroll today.

For those who support Social Security, the Ball/Altman proposal is unquestionably superior to the president's plan on every dimension, as the following side-by-side comparison illustrates. Unlike the president's proposal, the Ball plan does not cut benefits. Nor does it increase the Social Security tax rate.

| President's Proposal | Ball/Altman Proposal |
|---|---|
| *Combine Wage/Price Indexing of Social Security Initial Benefits* | *Freeze Estate Tax at 2009 Level, and Convert to a Dedicated Social Security Tax, Starting in 2010* |
| *People affected:* 70% of workers and families | *People affected:* Heirs (other than spouses) of estates over $3.5 million ($7 million for couples) |
| *Impact on people:* Substantial and continuing reduction in current law benefits as a percentage of preretirement earnings | *Impact on people:* No benefit cuts for anyone; almost all estates exempt from tax, wealthiest heirs will inherit larger percentage of estate than today |
| *Impact on program:* Radically transforms philosophy (over time, benefits will become minimal, almost flat, largely unrelated to wages) | *Impact on program:* Philosophy and structure unchanged; current law benefits maintained; dedicated tax added |
| *Substitute Private Accounts*<br>• Government selects indexed funds. | *Diversify Trust Fund Portfolio*<br>• Same (government selects indexed funds). |
| • Risk concentrated on individual with winners and losers.<br>• Risk of having to sell in down market on retirement. | • Risk is pooled and greatly reduced.<br><br>• Can wait out down market. |
| • High administrative costs.<br>• Trillions of dollars of added cost.<br>• Does nothing for long-term Social Security deficit. | • Low administrative costs.<br>• No additional cost.<br>• Cuts long-term deficit significantly. |
| | *Raise Maximum Taxable Wage Base*<br>• Complies with 1977 and 1983 congressional intent.<br>• Corrects effect of growing disparity between high wage earners and other earners.<br>• Affects only 6% of all workers.<br>• People affected will have FICA withholding for no more than 1 additional week a year. |
| BOTTOM LINE:<br>CUTS BENEFITS FOR ALL BUT THE POOR | BOTTOM LINE:<br>PROTECTS BENEFITS FOR EVERYONE |

The Ball/Altman proposal brings Social Security into close actuarial balance. The proposal is presented with a great deal of specificity, but modifications can be made. For example, if the maximum taxable wage base piece were phased in faster, in about 10 years, for example, the first two elements, without regard to the stock market investment recommendation, would by themselves bring the program into close actuarial balance. Such a quick increase in taxes though would be difficult for earners just over the maximum taxable wage base.

Ball and the author believe that doing more is unnecessary, given the great uncertainty attached to the 75-year estimates. Nevertheless, if Congress wanted to bring the estimated costs and revenues into exact balance, Ball offers two additional reforms that would accomplish this goal. Like the other elements discussed above, these are sound policy independent of any financing shortfall, and the author strongly endorses them.

## 4. Adopt the more accurate consumer price index recently developed by the Bureau of Labor Statistics (the so-called chained index)

Once workers retire and begin to receive benefits, those benefits are protected against inflation by adjusting them annually to the Consumer Price Index (CPI). The CPI is a widely used measure of inflation, developed and calculated each year by the U.S. Bureau of Labor Statistics. In 2002, the bureau developed a modification of the Consumer Price Index for All Urban Consumers (CPI-U). The new measure, the so-called Chained CPI-U, is, many experts believe, a more realistic measure of the impact of inflation because it more accurately takes into account buying habits as prices go up.

The switch from the CPI-U measure to the chained-CPI-U would save 0.35 percent of taxable payroll.

## 5. Cover under Social Security all new state and local employees hired on or after January 1, 2010.

Currently, 75 percent of all state and local employees are covered by Social Security. The proposal would provide that starting in 2010, every newly hired state and local employee would be covered by Social Security just as virtually every other worker in the United States is. Advisory councils and policy makers have advocated universal coverage since the 1930s. This proposal would bring in the last remaining group of workers still outside the system and complete that goal of universality.

The reason for the 2010 effective date is to permit public employers whose employees are not currently covered by Social Security to have time to revise their own retirement plans to become supplements to Social Security. When a similar provision was enacted in 1983 with respect to federal civilian employees, current employees were provided the option of either remaining with the existing Civil Service Retirement Plan or switching to the new federal Thrift Savings Plan, which supplements Social Security for all new federal hires.

As good as many state and local pension plans are, they will unquestionably function better as supplements to Social Security. Nowhere other than Social Security can retirees receive complete protection against inflation. Those state plans that do protect against inflation generally provide only partial protection up to a maximum cap. Then too, young workers and their families will generally have more generous survivor and disability protection under Social Security than under their state and local plans. Moreover, the ability to carry the benefit from one employer to another is available only under Social Security.

This proposal saves 0.19 percent of taxable payroll. These two proposals together with the original three taking into account interactions, save Social Security 1.94 percent of taxable payroll. Since the projected deficit is 1.89 percent of taxable payroll, these five proposals give Social Security a slight projected surplus of 0.05 percent.

If policy makers want Social Security to project a surplus for decades beyond the 75-year valuation period, Ball offers an additional option to accomplish that. The adoption of this last proposal, again supported by the author, should prevent Leninist strategists from crying, "Crisis!" the next time the actuaries change assumptions.

### 6.  Schedule a 0.5 percent contribution rate increase on both employers and employees each, in 2023

The year 2023 is selected because it is the year, once the other changes are made, that the trust fund ratio begins to decline. The "trust fund ratio" is the ratio of trust fund assets at the beginning of the year to benefit payments that year. It measures the size of the reserve in relation to annual benefits payable. In 2005, the trust fund ratio is over three, or more than 300 percent of the year's outgo. The ratio will continue to go up, with the five reforms discussed above, until 2023, when, without this stabilizing tax rate, the ratio will begin to decline. With the additional Social Security tax in 2023, the trust fund ratio will continue to grow throughout the 75-year valuation period. In 2079, it will be 772, which means that it will be equal to about seven and three quarters years of benefit payments.

One thing is certain about the next 75-year period. The assumptions underlying the long-range cost estimates will change from time to time, causing the estimated cost of the system to go up and down. The 2023 tax rate increase can guard against any estimate in rising costs to be labeled a crisis. The tax rate could easily be moved forward or back, changed in amount, or eliminated as future projections warranted.

Taking into account interactions, the rate increase generates 0.60 percent of taxable payroll. Taken with all the preceding reforms, the proposals provide Social Security a surplus of 0.65 percent of taxable payroll over the 75-year valuation period and project a balance for the program for decades beyond the usual 75-year period.

The following table summarizes the impact of the recommendations as percentages of taxable payroll.

### Bringing Social Security into Long-Range Balance*

| | Percent of Payroll |
|---|---|
| *Starting point:* The 75-year deficit: | −1.89 |
| *Deficit-reduction steps:* | |
| 1. Convert the residual estate tax to a dedicated Social Security tax | +0.51 |
| 2. Gradually restore the maximum taxable wage base: | +0.61 |
| 3. Diversify the portfolio: | +0.37 |
| *Total for 1 to 3:* | +1.47 |
| *Deficit well within close actuarial balance* (about 0.70 percent of payroll): | −0.41 |
| Additional Options | |
| 4. Improve the accuracy of the Cost of Living Adjustment (COLA) | +0.35 |
| 5. Extend coverage to all new state and local employees, starting in 2010 | +0.19 |
| *Total for 1 to 5 (taking interactions of the above proposals into account):* | +1.94 |
| *75-year balance:* | +0.05 |
| 6. Schedule a 0.5 percent contribution rate increase on employees and employers each in 2023: | +0.60 |
| *Total for 1 to 6 (taking interactions of the above proposals into account):* | +2.54 |
| *Program kept in balance for many decades beyond the traditional 75 years* | +0.65 |

*The estimates in this table have been made by the Office of the Actuary, Social Security Administration, based on the assumptions underlying the middle-range estimates of the 2004 trustees' report. They reflect a 75-year valuation period.

As these recommendations indicate, no radical reform of Social Security is necessary. If Congress enacted the Ball/Altman plan, our policy makers could turn their time and energy away from Social Security and toward other more pressing national concerns. Then, all Americans could turn their attention away from Social Security and begin to regain their confidence that the checks which have arrived so dependably since the program began are payments they can count on.

## CHAPTER 17

# From FDR's Vision to Bush's Gamble

On June 28, 1934, the day before President Roosevelt signed the executive order establishing the Committee on Economic Security, he spoke to the nation on the radio in one of his famous fireside chats. Roosevelt explained his reason for proposing Social Security,

> [W]e must...look to the larger future....We seek the security of the men, women, and children of the Nation. That security involves...[using] the agencies of Government to assist in the establishment of means to provide sound and adequate protection against the vicissitudes of modern life—in other words, social insurance.

Seventy years later, Social Security provides that sound protection against life's vicissitudes. Americans can count on Social Security's dependable monthly benefit checks both in the normal course of their aging and in times of tragedy—even during a nationwide emergency, as the program's admirable response to the terrorist attack of September 11, 2001, so recently demonstrated.

Workers have no guarantee, of course, against tragedy itself. Today, according to the Social Security actuaries, an American worker age 20 has a 20 percent chance of dying before reaching retirement age. That same worker has a 30 percent chance of becoming disabled before retirement age. But tragedy no longer brings destitution, as it did Mrs. Rogalas and her five children when, in 1906, her husband Adam was killed in a work-place accident. Now, if a 30-year old worker making an annual salary of about $27,000 dies and leaves behind a wife and two young children, Social Security provides the family with about $380,000 of life insurance benefits. That same worker is holding, through Social Security, a disability insurance policy with a present value of over $365,000.

In addition, Social Security provides workers a foundation of support on which to build an adequate level of retirement income. The benefits were conceptualized as a floor of protection on which private pensions and individual savings would be built.

For many citizens who have little or no employer supplement and few savings, Social Security is the difference between destitution and some measure of freedom and independence in old age. For everyone, the program is a safety net, when all else fails.

John J. Pinto, a retired pilot, was entitled to a substantial pension from his employer, United Airlines. Pinto had earned the promise of retirement income by bargaining away some of his salary. But the airline declared bankruptcy and defaulted on its pension obligations. Pinto, who now is forced to look for a new job because he is beyond the mandatory retirement age for pilots, confessed, "The last thing I thought was that I would depend on Social Security for the cornerstone of my retirement."

The implementation of Roosevelt's vision—sound and adequate protection for workers and their families in the event of disability, aging, or death—has transformed society. The world of poorhouses and elderly parents moving in with adult children has been replaced by an era of financial independence and dignity in old age. Milton Friedman, the Cato Institute, and other libertarians who have opposed the program throughout its history claim that Social Security curtails freedom. In truth, it does the opposite.

People who have independent income have more freedom, not less. They can choose where they want to live rather than going, hat in hand, to family members. Social Security beneficiaries have the freedom from worry that comes with a stable source of income. Independence and financial security in the aftermath of misfortune and in old age are blessings that exist today largely because of Social Security.

According to a 2005 report of the Center on Budget and Policy Priorities, a nonprofit, nonpartisan research organization, "Leaving aside Social

Security income, nearly one of every two elderly people—46.8 percent— has income below the poverty line." That percentage is strikingly similar to the pre-Social Security numbers. Nationwide surveys were not con- ducted at that time, but some states had gathered data. In 1934, Roosevelt's Committee on Economic Security canvassed the available statistics and reported, "Connecticut (1932), New York (1929) and Wisconsin (1925) found that nearly 50% of their aged population (65 years of age and over) had less than subsistence income." But Social Security has changed that. With Social Security, only 1 out of every 12 elderly persons, or 8.7 percent, is poor.

Because of the security it provides and the freedom it offers, Social Security has the overwhelming support of all Americans, with the excep- tion of "a tiny splinter group," as President Eisenhower called those opposed to Social Security in his day. But now a member of that tiny splinter group—in ironic prescience, a group Eisenhower described as including "a few...Texas oil millionaires"— has become the president of the United States.

Breaking ranks with every former president, Republican and Democratic alike, President George W. Bush is engaged in a high-profile campaign to undo Social Security. He hopes to accomplish what has eluded his ideological brethren who fought for similar ends over the last 70 years. Like Representative Carl Curtis in the late 1940s and early 1950s, Bush seeks to curtail the benefits of all but the lowest-paid work- ers, so that all beneficiaries would receive meager, basically flat benefits, largely unrelated to earnings. Like the president's ideological predeces- sors in the 1930s and 1940s, he wants all but the poorest workers to be primarily on their own—this time with the added twist of individual pri- vate investment accounts. His revisions would fundamentally alter the philosophy that underlies Social Security, a philosophy that has guided the program's policy makers throughout its history and kept it strong.

Perhaps having learned from the past, President Bush has cleverly avoided attacking Social Security on ideological grounds. Rather, he has endeavored to sell the reduction in benefits as a reform that is progressive because it spares the benefits of the lowest-wage workers. He holds out the hope of large gains with his talk of individual investment in the stock market. He even praises Franklin Roosevelt, the person Bush once called a "socialist," for his creation of Social Security. Instead of a frontal assault on the ideology of the program, President Bush seeks to convince Americans that Social Security is outmoded and unsustainable.

While President Bush will most likely fail in his quest to restructure Social Security, he and the Leninist strategists who support him have already succeeded in undermining a fundamental benefit that Social Security is intended to provide: security. President Roosevelt envisioned much more than a program that would keep people out of poverty, or even one that provided wage replacement up and down the income scale when work was no longer possible. Roosevelt wanted beneficiaries of the program—virtually every man, woman, and child in the United States—to have the confidence and peace of mind that they would be financially secure at retirement and in the event of lost wages due to tragedy.

President Bush has toured the country delivering the subversive and erroneous message that Social Security is designed for the last century and unworkable for an aging population. The increased average life expectancy of Americans is one of the greatest accomplishments of human ingenuity and modern science. Yet President Bush and others seeking to shake confidence in Social Security refer to the increasing longevity of Americans as if it were an unwelcome burden.

The president's erroneous refrain that Social Security will be "bust" and "flat broke" has gone a long way in elevating anxiety and fear about the future of the program. A New York Times/CBS News Poll conducted June 10 to 15, 2005, found, "Fifty-one percent of respondents said they did not think Social Security would have the money to pay the benefits they expect when they retire." A whopping 70 percent of those under age 45 held that belief.

Klaus Meyer, who lost a part of his private pension when his employer declared bankruptcy, captured the concern of many of his fellow Americans when he said, "[P]art of the retirement [benefit] I was promised…is gone. And now my Social Security is at risk. Where does it all end? You feel brutalized by the system." Meyer's concern about Social Security is a product of the Leninist strategy; if Americans cannot count on Social Security, perhaps they can be convinced to gamble on their future security with the president's private accounts.

In proposing such a radical change in Social Security, President Bush has taken on a gamble himself, a political gamble. He seeks to convey an image of political courage when he says, "Social Security has been called the 'third rail of American politics....' But if you don't touch it, you can't fix it." What he misses is that Social Security has the reputation of political invulnerability because it embodies fundamental American values that have overwhelming support.

Those basic values are what have made Social Security so effective and so popular. In all the many amendments of Social Security, these basic principles and intrinsic values have remained unchanged. Social Security is a conservatively structured program. Hemmed in on the left by Dr. Townsend and his supporters who advocated unrealistically large grants to all the aged and on the right by many conservatives advocating only means-tested welfare, Social Security was created with basic American values in mind. Its financing has always been conservative, relying on a dedicated tax and equal contributions from employers and employees to keep costs in check. It was built on the premise of work. Only those who have worked long enough to gain insured status and those workers' dependents are eligible for benefits.

It has been prudently and conservatively managed. It has an early warning system through its annual trustees' reports and 75-year projections, so Congress knows well in advance if the program needs fine-tuning. And it is one of the most efficiently-run programs around, public or private, with 99 cents of every dollar collected paid out in benefits.

Social Security's protections extend beyond just the individual to the family, a point that those advocating individual accounts fail to acknowledge. Within four years of enactment, the Social Security Amendments of 1939 added protection for children and spouses. These provisions have prevented millions of children who have lost parents from being engulfed in poverty. They permit those who stay home to care for children, and so reduce their own earnings, to have reasonable standards of living when the workers on whom they depend grow old, become disabled, or die. And the provisions have been amended to provide the same financial protection to dependent spouses who become divorced after many years of marriage.

Though Social Security has prevented millions of people from falling into poverty, it is much more than a poverty program. It is a program of social insurance, which provides benefits as a matter of right, not as a result of need. Franklin Roosevelt envisioned a program in which all workers paid in during their working years and drew benefits out when they were no longer working.

In converting that vision into reality, the staff of Roosevelt's Committee on Economic Security and those who followed recognized that benefits had to be adequate for those at the bottom rung of the economic ladder. The program would be unacceptable if low-income workers paid in over their working lives and then received nothing more than what was being provided down the street at the welfare office. To provide a meaningful return for those workers while restraining overall costs, the original program was designed with a weighted benefit formula that provided a higher return on first dollars earned.

In addition to providing adequate benefits to low-wage workers, the founders recognized that Social Security had to offer a fair return to higher-paid workers, if the program was to last. Social Security accomplishes both goals. The finely balanced formula produces benefits that are a higher proportion of a low-paid worker's wages, but a higher absolute dollar amount for higher-salaried workers who have contributed more dollars to the program during their working years. In that way, Social Security embodies goals of equity as well as adequacy.

In order to remain equitable, benefits for higher-income workers should not be cut. The financing shortfall facing Social Security should be kept in perspective and not used as an excuse to cut benefits or, worse, dismantle the program altogether. As Chapter 16 explains, Social Security's projected long-range deficit can be eliminated without benefit cuts, without Social Security tax rate increases, and indeed without any tax increases for about 94 percent of American workers.

The current debate over Social Security contains many hopeful signs. People have united over their support for the program. The generations have come together in their mutual sense of concern. And Americans have been reminded of Social Security's value. If the outcome of the current controversy is to reinforce people's appreciation for this vital institution, the debate will have provided a useful public service.

As James Roosevelt recently reminded people, "My grandfather, President Franklin D. Roosevelt, founded Social Security for very simple but important reasons. He believed that the only enemy that could ever defeat the United States of America was fear itself. He and my grandmother, Eleanor, looked at America and found fear of want."

Bush's attack on Social Security is rooted in the politics of fear. But the history of Social Security should give every supporter of the program a sense of courage and confidence. Social Security has survived prior assaults on its integrity. Armed with proper insight and understanding, we Americans can assert our will and demand that the program envisioned by Franklin Roosevelt remain his enduring legacy. With that victory, Social Security can "provide sound and adequate protection against the vicissitudes of modern life" to our children, grandchildren, and all future generations.

# Acknowledgments

First and foremost, I gratefully acknowledge five New Dealers. In the pages of this book, you will learn of the many contributions to Social Security made by three of them—Robert M. Ball, Wilbur Cohen, and Robert J. Myers. I met all three when I was assistant to the chairman of the bipartisan commission that produced the 1983 Social Security amendments. Each of the three became my friend, and each made immeasurable contributions to this project.

During the Spring and Summer of 1982, as staff work at the commission slowed in anticipation of the November election, I spent memorable afternoons in Bob Myers's office, where he regaled and enlightened me with anecdotes from Social Security's rich past. Long before I ever began to write this book, Bob Myers had been one of my most important and generous teachers in the field.

Like Bob Myers, Bob Ball contributed, decades before I wrote the first word of the manuscript, in priceless ways to my education about Social Security. On the current work, he read the entire manuscript closely and gave me detailed comments. His suggestions always improved the work; his briefings on background matters were invaluable. On the smallest detail, when he would preface his remark with, "I am doing this from memory. I am not saying you are wrong; I am just suggesting that you double-check...", I came to learn that he always was correct.

Wilbur Cohen died five years after our first meeting, and so I knew him less well and for a shorter amount of time than I have had the privilege to know Bob Ball and Bob Myers. Nevertheless, Wilbur's ebullient personality made him an instant friend. I am still guided and inspired by his compassion, commitment and energy. As I hope shines through in the

319

pages of this book, my affection and respect for Wilbur Cohen, Bob Myers, and Bob Ball are immense.

The other two New Dealers I acknowledge with overwhelming gratitude and love are my parents, Norman and Sophie Altman. Norman Altman was a man of prodigious talent. Like many others in his generation, he came to Washington, D.C. as a young lawyer to work in the New Deal, and he remained in the nation's capital to become a distinguished member of the bar. He embodied the best qualities of his generation; my memory of him has animated this book in innumerable ways. His concern for the welfare of others, commitment to social justice, intellectual gifts leavened with hard-headed pragmatism, and ability to make complex issues comprehensible and interesting are attributes which motivated this project and which I hope infuse its content.

Sophie Altman, too, came to Washington as a young lawyer to work in the Roosevelt Administration. Enormously talented like her husband, she became a pioneer in broadcast journalism in the 1940s. She created, and today produces, the award-winning high school competition, "It's Academic," which the Guinness Book of World Records has recognized as the longest running television quiz show anywhere in the world. She influences me daily with her commitment to excellence, unflagging determination and drive, creativity, love of laughter, and perspective on life. Her extraordinary qualities have served as guideposts in the writing of this book. I am forever grateful for her unwavering confidence in me and her support for this project.

Many others also deserve thanks and credit for helping me convert this book from an unmaterialized intention to the work you find yourself reading. Larry DeWitt, the Historian of the Social Security Administration, has produced the most comprehensive, accessible, and valuable website any student of the history of Social Security could want. Whenever I sought additional information, I e-mailed Larry and he responded quickly and comprehensively.

Others helped with substance, as well, reviewing part or all of the manuscript for accuracy, providing technical information, offering insights into people or events that I was puzzling about, sending me articles or quotes and so on. These talented and generous friends include Larry Atkins, Ed Berkowitz, Tom Bethell, Karen Fergusen, Dan Halperin, Lori Hansen, Rod Perkins, David Podoff, Virginia Reno, Bob Rosenblatt, Bruce Schobel,

John Shutkin, and Neta Warren. In addition, a few strangers responded promptly and helpfully when I e-mailed them out of the blue, including Joan Wise, General Counsel to AARP, Bob Brooke, an expert on antique games, and Professor Neil Harl of Iowa State University, an authority on the federal estate tax and its impact on family farms.

My niece Lee Spragens, a wonderfully talented editor and writer at Warner Brothers Studios, worked closely with me over many hours and days in my effort to make the book punchy and readable. Working with her was part of the fun of producing the manuscript, and we spent much time laughing together, as we worked. My sister Susan Altman, author of eleven books, read the entire manuscript and offered numerous helpful suggestions to produce more fluid sentences, to make complicated passages more comprehensible, and to keep the story moving briskly

I owe a huge debt of gratitude to Bill Arnone, who contacted Debra Englander, executive editor of John Wiley & Sons, about my manuscript, and followed up with an extensive e-mail. Debra was a terrific editor to whom I am appreciative. I similarly thank Alexia Meyers, and others at Wiley who worked on the manuscript, production, and marketing of the book. When I first sought suggestions in finding a literary agent and publisher, a number of other friends and colleagues were quick to respond. These supportive allies include Henry Aaron, Mert Bernstein, Karen Friedman, Carol Glass, Ted Marmor, Nell Minow, Larry Mitchell, Alicia Munnell, Diane Remin, and Syl Schieber. Added to those names are my extended family and friends who, too, were supportive, encouraging allies.

To my extraordinary husband, Chip Lupu, I have everlasting gratitude. Gifted with an intellectually rigorous mind, he read the entire manuscript, a few parts multiple times, and offered excellent editing suggestions and turns of phrase that always improved the work. In addition, he helped me better understand the constitutional issues facing the drafters of Social Security in 1934 and 1935. Much more important, though, are the intangibles he provided. He was, as he always is, a steady and enthusiastic booster, encouraging, loving, and giving.

I owe never-ending gratitude to my closest of friends, Jennifer Altman-Lupu and Michael Altman-Lupu. Their contributions included computer assistance, trips to Kinko's and Office Depot on my behalf and much, much more. Infinitely more valuable to me than their substantial tangible help were their love, encouragement, and support during the writing of this book—and for that matter, always.

In writing this history, considerations of space forced me to omit mention of many people who made, and continue to make, extremely important contributions to Social Security. They are heroes, and I do not mean in any way to slight the significant role that they have played in creating, building and sustaining America's most important social program. Finally, I acknowledge with gratitude the protagonist of this book, Social Security itself, which has contributed so much to making our nation a more secure and civilized home.

# Notes

**CHAPTER 1**

Page 1:   "We're evacuating."
[Bea Disman, Essay from the magazine GOVEXEC.com, *www.govexec.com/features/0904-15/0904-15s1.htm*.]

Page 3:   "must include individually controlled"
[Guiding Principles, Presideant's Commission to Strengthen Social Security, *http://csss.gov*.]

Page 5:   "The only man I truly"
[Kitty Kelley, *The Family: The Real Story of the Bush Dynasty* (New York: Doubleday, 2004), p. 57.]

Page 5:   "Said Republicans: 'Wage"
["Grand Finale," *Time* magazine, November 9, 1938.]

Page 5:   "will be bust in 10 years unless"
[Richard W. Stevenson, "For Bush, a Long Embrace of Social Security Plan," *New York Times*, February 27, 2005.]

Page 6:   "an expert on Social Security"
[Edward D. Berkowitz, *Mr. Social Security* (Lawrence: University Press of Kansas, 1995), p. 144.]

Page 6:   "as wise a counsellor"
[Senator Daniel Patrick Moynihan, Introduction to Robert J. Myers, *Within the System* (Winsted, CT: ACTEX Publications, 1992), p. iii.]

Page 6:   "a national treasure"
[Ibid, p. vii.]

Page 6:   "wears out its workers"
[E. T. Devine, *Misery and Its Causes*, p. 125, in Abraham Epstein, *Facing Old Age* (New York: Alfred A. Knopf, 1922), p. 4.]

Page 6: "A man's productive, wage-earning"
[Report of the Committee on Economic Security, "The Economic Problems of Old Age," Part II, Old-Age Security, U.S. Social Security in America (Washington: U.S. Government Printing Office, 1937) p. 138.]

Page 7: "Children or relatives"
[Report of the Pennsylvania Commission on Old Age Pensions, 1919, p. 20, quoted in Abraham Epstein, *Insecurity: A Challenge to America* (New York: Harrison Smith and Robert Haas, 1933), p. 501.]

Page 7: "Worthy people are"
[Report of the New York State Commission on Old Age Security, 1930, pp. 395–96, quoted in Ibid, p. 508.]

Page 8: "After the age of sixty"
[L. W. Squier, *Old Age Dependency in the United States*, pp. 28–29, in Epstein, *Facing Old Age*, p. 21.]

**CHAPTER 2**

Page 9: "could not fit himself"
[John R. Commons, *Myself* (New York: Macmillan, 1934), pp. 11, 38.]

Page 12: "any man who honorably wore the federal"
[Donald Bruce Johnson and Kirk H. Porter, *National Party Platforms 1840–1972* (Urbana: University of Illinois Press, 1973), p. 82.]

Page 12: "in the third story of a rattle-shack"
[Commons, *Myself*, p. 43.]

Page 13: "born again...after five"
[Ibid, p. 95.]

Page 14: "Curious isn't it"
[Ibid, p. 139.]

Page 15: "encourag[ing] the study of labor"
[David A. Moss, *Socializing Security* (Cambridge, MA: Harvard University Press, 1996), p. 12.]

Page 16: "that I was going to go under Professor"
[Larry DeWitt, *Never a Finished Thing: A Brief Biography of Arthur Joseph Altmeyer—The Man FDR Called "Mr. Social Security*," Chapter 1, The "Wisconsin World View," Social Security Administration website, *http://www.ssa.gov/ history/bioaja.html*.]

**CHAPTER 3**

Page 23: "'sharply curtailed benefits and refusal'"
[U.S. Social Security Board, *Social Security in America* (Washington, DC: U.S. Government Printing Office, 1937), p. 158.]

Page 24: "Of the nearly one hundred"
[Paul Studensky, "Teachers' Pension Systems in the United States, 1920, Introduction," quoted in Abraham Epstein, *Insecurity: A Challenge to America* (New York: Harrison Smith and Robert Haas, 1933), p. 526.]

Page 25: "This marks a new era in the life"
[Daniel Jordy, Bonus March Episode (May 21, 2000), *http://wappingersschools.org/JohnJayHS/students/ap/ap33/.*]

Page 26: "incipient revolution in the air"
[*The American Experience*, "MacArthur," PBS Enhanced Transcript, Part 1, *www.pbs.org/wgbh/amex/macarthur/filmmore/transcript/transcript1.html.*]

Page 27: "launch the Sinclair revolution"
[Upton Sinclair, California Historical Society, *www.californiahistory.net/9_pages/politics_sinclair.htm.*]

Page 28: "By last week the flow of money"
["Townsend to Burst," *Time* magazine, October 15, 1934.]

Page 29: "I place the security"
[Franklin D. Roosevelt, Message to Congress, June 8, 1934.]

Page 31: "Although Hopkins was eloquent"
[Frances Perkins, *The Roosevelt I Knew* (New York: Viking Press, 1946), p. 284.]

Page 31: "You shall not wholly reap"
[Leviticus 19:9,10. Bible, King James Version.]

Page 33: "a spiritual transformation"
[Perkins, p. 29.]

Page 34: "In this way, men and women"
[Roosevelt, Annual Message to the Legislature, 1931, in Joseph P. Harris, *Brief in Defense of Old-Age Benefits as provided in the Social Security Bill*, Papers in Support of Old-Age Provisions of Bill, Volume II: Old Age Security. U.S. Social Security Board, *Social Security in America* (Washington, DC: U.S. Government Printing Office, 1937).]

Page 34: "insisted that…however much they"
[Perkins, p. 284.]

Page 34: "of every child being issued"
[Arthur J. Altmeyer, *The Formative Years of Social Security* (Madison: University of Wisconsin Press, 1966), pp. 4–5.]

Page 35: "I see no reason"
[Perkins, p. 282.]

Page 35: "report to the President not later"
[Executive Order 6757, June 29, 1934.]

## CHAPTER 4

Page 39: "to report upon all"
[Perkins, p. 286.]

Page 40:   "trail blazer"
[Phillip Longman, "The Great Train Robbery: How the Railroad Retirement System Swindles Taxpayers, Jobs, Younger Workers, and Derails Amtrak," *Washington Monthly* (December 1987).]

Page 41:   "Each one of us"
[Harold W. Dodds quotes, Brainy Quote, *www.brainyquote.com/quotes/quotes/h/haroldwdo133123.html*.]

Page 42:   "This is the real thing."
[Columbia University Oral History Collection, Reminiscences of Barbara Nachtrieb Armstrong (1965), p. 33.]

Page 42:   "The Committee [on Economic]" and "my principal qualification"
[Robert J. Myers, *Within the System* (Winsted, CT: ACTEX Publications, 1992), p. 81.]

Page 43:   "it would be highly desirable"
[Peter A. Corning, "The Evolution of Medicare…from Idea to Law, Chapter 2: The Second Round—1943 to 1950," written pursuant to contract with SSA's Office of Research and Statistics, 1969, on Social Security Administration History Web site: *www.ssa.gov/history/corning.html*.]

Page 45:   "Just a minute"
[Columbia University Oral History Collection, Reminiscences of Armstrong, pp. 67–68.]

Page 47:   "But you can't do"
[Ibid, pp. 74–76.]

Page 48:   "Well, of course, I"
[Ibid, p. 93.]

Page 48:   "Dear Tom: Somewhere you picked up"
[Ibid, p. 95.]

Page 51:   "Your Court tells us"
[Perkins, p. 286.]

Page 53:   "On some points it is possible"
[Franklin D. Roosevelt, Address to Advisory Council of the Committee on Economic Security on the Problems of Economic and Social Security, November 14, 1934, on Social Security Administration History Web site: *www.ssa.gov/history/fdrstmts.html#advisec*.]

Page 54:   "fix…that little wagon"
[Columbia University Oral History Collection, Reminiscences of Armstrong (1965), p. 89.]

Page 54:   "backfire"
Columbia University Oral History Collection, Reminiscences of J. Douglas Brown, (1965) p. 117.]

Page 54: "turndown"
[Edwin E. Witte, *The Development of the Social Security Act* (Madison: University of Wisconsin Press, 1963), p. 46.]

Page 56: "Whether we come to"
[Roosevelt, Address to Advisory Council of the Committee on Economic Security, emphasis added.]

Page 56: "that workers 'should not"
[Columbia University Oral History Collection, Reminiscences of J. Douglas Brown, (1965) p. 110.]

Page 56: "Well, we went out of that"
[Columbia University Oral History Collection, Reminiscences of Armstrong, (1965) p. 83.]

Page 58: "unyielding opposition"
[Corning, "The Evolution of Medicare…from Idea to Law."]

## CHAPTER 5

Page 64: "We will have to put it through"
[Perkins, p. 296.]

Page 64: "Why, this will mean permanent"
["After 65," *Time* magazine, January 28, 1935.}

Page 65: "Give all the aged"
["Simple Plan," *Time* magazine, January 14, 1935.]

Page 65: "Organizations promoting fantastic"
[Franklin D. Roosevelt, Address to Advisory Council of the Committee on Economic Security on the Problems of Economic and Social Security, November 14, 1934, on Social Security Administration History Web site: *www.ssa.gov/history/fdrstmts.html#advisec.*]

Page 65: "About 120,000 people in"
["Simple Plan."]

Page 70: "impose a crushing burden"
[Minority Views on the Social Security Bill of 1935, in House Committee Report No. 613, 74th Congress, 1st Session, April 5, 1935, to accompany H.R. 7200, p. 44.]

Page 71: "business and industry are already"
[Geoffrey Kollmann and Carmen Solomon-Fears, "Major Decisions in the House and Senate on Social Security 1935–2000" (CRS Legislative Histories, RL 30920), on Social Security Administration History Web site: *www.ssa.gov/history/reports/crsleghist3.html.*]

Page 71: "Why talk about wanting"
[Ibid.]

Page 71: "vote most strenuously"
[Ibid.]

Page 72: "Never in the history of the world"
[Altmeyer, pp. 37–38.]

Page 72: "The lash of the dictator"…"This bill opens the door"
[Ibid, p. 38.]

Page 73: "Isn't this Socialism?"
[Perkins, p. 299.]

Page 74: "the probable alternative"
[Edwin E. Witte, *The Development of the Social Security Act* (Madison: University of Wisconsin Press, 1963), p.103, n. 65.]

Page 75: "If I were a betting man"
[Thomas H. Eliot, "The Social Security Bill: 25 Years After," on Social Security Administration History Web site: *www.ssa.gov/history/tomeliotart.html.*]

Page 76: "ancient and forgotten lore"…"I will accommodate any"
[T. Harry Williams, *Huey Long* (New York: Alfred A. Knopf, 1969), p. 833.]

Page 76: "A lot of 'em thought"…"That would be unusual"
[Ibid, p. 834.]

Page 77: "end the progress of"
[Altmeyer, p. 41.]

Page 83: "are interdependent, and neither"
[Minority Views on the Social Security Bill of 1935, in House Committee Report No. 613, p. 43.]

Page 83: "We can never insure"
[Franklin D. Roosevelt, Presidential Statement Signing the Social Security Act of 1935, August 14, 1935.]

## CHAPTER 6

Page 85: "I am not a"
[The Floyd B. Olson Page, *www.geocities.com/CapitolHill/Senate/8713/.*]

Page 86: "that cripple in the White House"
[Arthur M. Schlesinger, Jr., *The Politics of Upheaval* (Boston: Houghton Mifflin Co., 1960), p. 521.]

Page 86: "In Georgia the white"
["Gene & Junior," *Time* magazine, September 7, 1936.]

Page 86: "great betrayer and liar"
[Father Charles E. Coughlin, at Social Security Administration website, History, at *http://www.ssa.gov/history/cough.html.*]

Page 87:   "We're not for you"
[T. Harry Williams, *Huey Long* (New York: Alfred A. Knopf, 1969), p. 845.]

Page 88:   "I don't understand"
[Altmeyer, p. 43.]

Page 88:   "based entirely upon"
[Ibid.]

Page 89:   "We got along"
["Saturday Night and After," *Time* magazine, September 2, 1935.]

Page 89:   "Those damned amendments"
[Ibid.]

Page 89:   "I object." and "You've done worse"
[Ibid.]

Page 89:   "I have nothing to … I'm just having"
[Filibuster and Long quotes from Williams, *Huey Long*, p. 842.]

Page 89:   "All I care is"
[Ibid.]

Page 89:   "whether or not, because"
[Ibid.]

Page 90:   "abortion" and "signed, sealed,"
[Ibid, p. 843.]

Page 90:   "God, don't let me"
[Ibid, 876.]

Page 90:   "I just can't understand"
[Perkins, p. 157.]

Page 91:   "It was perfect."
[Schlesinger, *The Politics of Upheaval*, p. 519.]

Page 91:   "a hybrid organization financed"
[Southern Committee to Uphold the Constitution, *http://coat.ncf.ca/our_magazine/links/53/scuc.html.*]

Page 91:   "The most brazen attempt"
["Hamlets," *Time* magazine, February 10, 1936.]

Page 92:   "A small group in"
["Party for Peace," *Time* magazine, June 16, 1934.]

Page 93:   "American institutions and American"
[Ibid.]

Page 93:   "These pirates have reached"
[Ibid.]

Page 93:   "When you're licked, you're licked"
["Morning After," *Time* magazine, November 19, 1934.]

Page 94:   "I should like to see"
[Ibid.]

Page 95:   "been relegated to the"
[FDR press conference, May 31, 1935, at: *http://newdeal.feri.org/court/fdr5_31_35.htm.*]

Page 95:   "the best-loved family"
[Schlesinger, *The Politics of Upheaval*, p. 538.]

Page 96:   "when do you want" and following dialogue,
[Quotation and dialogue: Thomas H. Eliot, "The Legal Background of the Social
Security Act (1961), at: *www.ssa.gov/history/eliot2.html.*]

Page 96:   "Missouri Delegates are Pledged"
["Kansas Candidate," *Time* magazine, May 18, 1936.]

Page 97:   "I belong to but"
[Schlesinger, *The Politics of Upheaval*, p. 546.]

Page 97:   "If you fail, then"
["No Man's Land," *Time* magazine, June 29, 1936.]

Page 97:   "Dante tells us, that"
[Franklin D. Roosevelt, 1936 Acceptance Speech at Democratic National
Convention, text at: *www.cfinst.org/eguide/PartyConventions/speeches/1936d.html.*]

Page 97:   "a loose working agreement"
["No Man's Land," *Time* magazine, June 29, 1936.]

Page 98:   "Why I Can Support"
[Ibid.]

Page 98:   "We must make our"
["Merger of Malcontents," *Time* magazine, July 27, 1936.]

Page 98:   "great betrayer and liar" and following
[Ibid.]

Page 98:   "Money changers"
[Ibid.]

Page 98:   "reasonable and decent"
[Donald Bruce Johnson and Kirk H. Porter, *National Party Platforms 1840–1972*
(Urbana: University of Illinois Press, 1973), p. 375.]

Page 98:  "other disabilities"
[Ibid, p. 364.]

Page 99:  "We hold these truths"
[Ibid, p. 360.]

Page 99:  "Society has an obligation"
[Ibid, p. 366–367.]

Page 99:  "it is encouraging"
["The Shape of Things," Editorials, *The Nation*, June 24, 1936.]

Page 100:  "Careful study of the"
[Eveline M. Burns, "Letters to the Editor," *The Nation*, July 11, 1936.]

Page 101:  "luckiest politician"
["Roosevelt Rainbow," *Time* magazine, September 21, 1936.

Page 101:  "write the Republican platform in advance"
["I Accept," *Time* magazine, August 3, 1936.]

Page 101:  "I'm for it. Every"
[Max J. Skidmore, *Social Security and Its Enemies* (Boulder, CO: Westview Press, 1999), p. 42.]

Page 101:  "must be along AMERICAN"
[Ibid, pp. 43–44.]

Page 101:  "We shall amend the Social"
["I Accept."]

Page 102:  "The worker's cash comes"
[Alfred Landon, address in Milwaukee, Wisconsin, September 27, 1936 (in author's files).]

Page 103:  "The Social Security Act"
[Larry DeWitt, "John G. Winant: The First Chairman of the Social Security Board," Special Study #6, Research Notes & Special Studies by the Historian's Office, Social Security Administration, at: *www.ssa.gov/history/mywinantarticle. html*.]

Page 103:  "[H]ow gladly he would give"
[Ibid.]

Page 104:  "Having seen the cruelties"
[Ibid.]

Page 104:  "greatly distresses me"
[Ibid.]

Page 104:   "Imagine the field opened"
[Schlesinger, *The Politics of Upheaval*, p. 546.]

Page 104:   "puts half the working people"
[Ibid, p. 636.]

Page 104:   "Under some social security"
[Skidmore, *Social Security and Its Enemies*, p. 44.]

Page 105:   "Do You Want"
[Altmeyer, p. 69.]

Page 105:   "You're Sentenced TO A WEEKLY PAY REDUCTION *for*
ALL YOUR WORKING LIFE. YOU'LL HAVE TO *SERVE THE
SENTENCE* UNLESS YOU HELP REVERSE IT NOVEMBER 3."
[Sylvester J. Schieber and John B. Shoven, *The Real Deal* (New Haven, CT: Yale
University Press, 1999) pp. 53–4.]

Page 105:   "Notice—Deductions"
[Altmeyer, p. 69.]

Page 105:   "Effective January 1937, we"
["Nicolaus Mills, Alf Landon and Social Security Reform," Dissent (Spring 2005),
at: *www.findarticles.com/p/articles/mi_qa3745/is_200504/ai_n13633418.*]

Page 106:   "The labor vote"
[Schlesinger, *The Politics of Upheaval*, p. 636.]

Page 106:   "the current pay-envelope"
[Franklin D. Roosevelt, Madison Square Garden address (October 31, 1936) at
*http://history.sandiego.edu/gen/text/us/fdr1936.html.*]

**CHAPTER 7**

Page 111:   "I will have to act"
[Altmeyer, p. 49.]

Page 111:   "I have a conscience, too!"
[Ibid.]

Page 112:   "Cheer up! The good"
[Ibid. p. 50.]

Page 112:   "too damned many New"…"members of your race"
[Ibid.]

Page 115:   "The system ought to"
[Perkins, p. 282.]

Page 116:   "How unique is your name?"
[Columbia University Oral History Collection, Reminiscences of J. Douglas Brown,
(1965) p. 82.]

Page 117:  "that the implications of this decision could"
[Franklin D. Roosevelt, Press Conference (May 31, 1935) at *http://newdeal.feri. org/court/fdr5_31_35.htm*.]

Page 117:  "This means that 120 million"
[Arthur M. Schlesinger, Jr., *The Politics of Upheaval* (Boston: Houghton Mifflin Co., 1960), p. 488.]

Page 117:  "If we understand correctly"
[Ibid, p. 489.]

Page 117:  "The American people should"
["The Elephant Show," *Time* magazine, June 22, 1936.]

Page 118:  "We pledge ourselves"
[Donald Bruce Johnson and Kirk H. Porter, *National Party Platforms 1840–1972* (Urbana: University of Illinois Press, 1973), p. 366.]

Page 118:  "Over against the hosannas"
[Arthur M. Schlesinger, Jr., *The Politics of Upheaval* (Boston: Houghton Mifflin Co., 1960), p. 580.]

Page 118:  "The Republican platform proposes"
[Johnson and Porter, *National Party Platforms 1840–1972*, p. 362.]

Page 118:  "although the lawyers go"
[Schlesinger, *The Politics of Upheaval*, p. 582.]

Page 119:  "distasteful idea"
[Ibid, p. 490.]

Page 119:  "have remained upon"
[Homer S. Cummings, "Reasons for President's Plan and the Remedy," Radio address, February 14, 1937, at: *http://newdeal.feri.org/court/cummings.htm*.]

Page 120:  "younger blood"
[Franklin D. Roosevelt, Message to Congress on judicial branch reorganization plan, February 5, 1937, at: *http://newdeal.feri.org/speeches/1937b.htm*.]

Page 120:  "Cleverness and adroitness"
["De Senectute," *Time* magazine, February 15, 1937.]

Page 121:  "I doubt the wisdom"
[Ibid.]

Page 121:  "We'll take their baby out"
[Ibid.]

Page 121:  "Boys, this is where"
[K. Daniel Glover, "FDR's Court-Packing Fiasco," Web posted July 12, 1999, at: *www.enterstageright.com/archive/articles/0799fdrcourt.htm*.]

Page 121:  "to pack the court."
[Ibid.]

Page 121:  "No people ever recognize"
["The Big Debate," *Time* magazine, March 1, 1937.]

Page 121:  "A packed jury"
[Ibid.]

Page 122:  "That would be socialism."
[Altmeyer, p. 89.]

Page 122:  "the need to meet"
[Franklin D. Roosevelt, Radio address, March 9, 1937, at: *http://web.utk.edu/~scheb/ fdrfireside.htm.*]

Page 123:  "On account of the"
[Chief Justice Charles E. Hughes, letter to Senator Wheeler, March 22, 1937, at: *http://newdeal.feri.org/court/hughes.htm.*]

Page 123:  "Our conclusion is that the"
[West Coast Hotel Co. v. Parrish, 300 U.S. 379 (1937).]

Page 124:  "In this case we are"
["Four 5–4; One 9–0," *Time* magazine, April 19, 1937.]

Page 124:  "The silent intake of"
[Ibid.]

Page 124:  "What is the matter with Roberts?"
["Justice Owen J. Roberts, Memorandum, November 9, 1945, at: *http://newdeal. feri.org/court/roberts.htm.*]

Page 125:  "as if it were yesterday" and "in an euphoric glow."
[Wilbur J. Cohen, "The Early Days of Social Security," at: *www.ssa.gov/history/ 50wc.html.*]

Page 127:  "forced the Democratic Social"
[Harold B. Hinton, "Congress Departs Quietly for Home; Minority Jubilant," *New York Times*, August 23, 1937.]

Page 128:  "We recommend the rejection"
[U.S. Senate Judiciary Committee Report 711, 75th Cong., 1st Session (1937), at: *www.phschool.com/atschool/primary_sources/adverse_report_judiciary.html.*]

Page 128:  "I think this cause"
["The Great Debate (l)," *Time* magazine, July 19, 1937.]

Page 132:  "The Special securities issued"
[Appendix of Report of the 1938 Advisory Council on Social Security, at: *www. ssa.gov/history/reports/38advise.html.*]

Page 133:   "Every ten minutes I'd"
[Columbia University Oral History Collection, Reminiscences of J. Douglas
Brown (1965), p. 75.]

Page 133:   "You told us this"
[Ibid, p. 76.]

Page 134:   "Speak up, young man"
[Altmeyer, p. 100.]

Page 134:   "the staggering and illusory"
[Ibid, p. 106.]

Page 136:   "exposing the 'dangers'"
["Big Michigander," *Time* magazine, October 2, 1939.]

**CHAPTER 8**

Page 137:   "Admiral W. H. P. Bland"
[Shirley Povich, "At Redskins-Eagles Game, Crowd Was Kept Unaware that War
had Begun," *Washington Post*, December 7, 1991.]

Page 138:   "old Dr. New Deal"
[Altmcycr, p. 135.]

Page 138:   "We are determined,"
[Franklin D. Roosevelt, Annual Budget Message to Congress, January 5, 1942.]

Page 138:   "In Britain there was"
["Arithmetic of Promise," *Time* magazine, January 18, 1942.]

Page 138:   "When so many Americans"
[Roosevelt, Annual Budget Message.]

Page 140:   "in their clubs denouncing"
["Leaders & Revolutionaries," *The Time 100* (2000), at: *www.time.com/time/time100/
leaders/profile/fdr2.html.*]

Page 140:   "My fortune is in"
[Randolph E. Paul, *Taxation in the United States* (Boston: Little, Brown and Company, 1954), p. 201.]

Page 140:   "The higher the tax rates"
[Roosevelt, Annual Budget Message.]

Page 141:   "As Senator George has so aptly"
["The Care of the Goose," *Time* magazine, January 19, 1942.]

Page 141:   "Your country needs you!"
["The New Pictures," *Time* magazine, February 9, 1942.]

Page 141: "Even hard-boiled Collectors"
["T-Day Dawns," *Time* magazine, March 23, 1942.]

Page 142: "The new taxes will be"
[Paul, *Taxation in the United States*, p. 297.]

Page 142 "the Senate apparently is in"
[Ibid, p. 317.]

Page 142: "changed its morning coat"
[Ibid, p. 318.]

Page 142: "a tax-avoidance mechanism"
[Tax Evasion and Avoidance: Hearings Before the Joint Committee on Tax Evasion and Avoidance, 75th Cong., 1st Sess. (1937), p. 291, statement of Hon. Charles T. Russell, Deputy Commissioner of Internal Revenue.]

Page 143: "Pension Trusts are Termed"
[Reprinted in Ibid, pp. 296–98.]

Page 143: "volumes of communications"
[Revenue Revision of 1942: Hearings on H.R. 7378 before the House Committee on Ways and Means, 77th Congress, 2d Sess., p. 2405.]

Page 143: "were obviously conceived to"
[Ibid, p. 2438.]

Page 144: "I oppose the use"
[Roosevelt, Annual Budget Message.]

Page 146: "not for the needy"
[Joe Thorndike, "Wartime Tax Legislation and the Politics of Policymaking," Tax History Project (2001), at: *www.taxhistory.org/thp/readings.nsf/0/ f9cb12c7ca3ccf9185256e22007840e7? OpenDocument.*]

Page 146: "An expanded social security"
[Franklin D. Roosevelt, State of the Union Address, January 11, 1944.]

Page 147: "Harry, the President is dead."
["Presidents: Harry Truman," QuickFacts, History Central, at: *www.historycentral.com/ Bio/presidents/truman.html.*]

Page 147: "I expect to communicate"
[Altmeyer, p. 153.]

## CHAPTER 9

Page 150: "Old age and survivors"
[Edward Berkowitz, "Social Security: Back to the Future or Forward to the Past?" Third Millennium's Conferences and Symposia, at: *www.thirdmil.org/program/ conferences/socsec_history_berkowitz.html.*]

Page 154:   "That is very interesting"
[Author discussions with Robert M. Ball, Spring 2005.]

Page 154:   "highly irregular"
[Ibid.]

Page 156:   "The Council has studied"
["Introduction and Summary, Part I—Old-Age and Survivors Insurance," 1948
Advisory Council Report, at: *www.ssa.gov/history/reports/ 48advise4.html.*]

Page 157:   "Our Bill of Rights [be] implemented in fact"
[Harold I. Gullan, *The Upset that Wasn't* (Chicago: Ivan R. Dee, 1998), p. 76.]

Page 158:   "Ike & I could"
[Harry S. Truman Diary (July 25, 1947), Truman Presidential Museum & Library,
at *http://www.trumanlibrary.org/diary/page23.htm.*]

Page 159:   "a political bull's-eye"
["To Make a Good Society," *Time* magazine, July 5, 1948.]

Page 159:   "get out of the shadow"
[Gullan, *The Upset that Wasn't*, p. 99.]

Page 159:   "What's the sense of jumping"
[Ibid, p. 103.]

Page 159:   "terrible 80th Congress"
[Altmeyer, p. 163.]

Page 160:   "not done very much"
[Gullan, The Upset that Wasn't, p. 85.]

Page 160:   "if our Social Security"
["Veto of Resolution Excluding Certain Groups From Social Security Coverage,"
June 14, 1948. *The Public Papers of the President, Harry S. Truman, 1948*, (Wash-
ington, U.S. Government Printing Office, 1964): 346]

Page 160:   "the next president"
[Zachary Karabell, *The Last Campaign* (New York: Alfred A. Knopf, 2000), p. 255.]

Page 160:   "Public assistance was designed"
[Harry S. Truman, Annual Message on the Budget to Congress, January 10, 1949.]

Page 161:   "Why weren't you"
[Columbia University Oral History Collection, Reminiscences of Fedele Fauri
(1966), p. 8.]

Page 162:   "a sharp man and"
[Ibid, p. 9.]

Page 162:   "the kind of individual"
[Ibid, p. 5.]

Page 162: "My, this is a"
[Ibid, p. 11.]

Page 162: "Are you ready"
[Ibid.]

Page 163: "your committee is firmly"
[Altmeyer, p. 175.]

Page 163: "To initiate a Federal"
[Ibid, pp. 185–86.]

Page 163: "Social Security measures to"
[Ibid, p. 186.]

Page 163: "For workers totally and"
[Ibid.]

Page 163: "Go find him. We"
[Columbia University Oral History Collection, Reminiscences of Fauri, p. 14.]

Page 164: "The old-age and"
[Additional Minority Views, House Report 1300 on H.R. 6000, Social Security Act Amendments of 1949, 81st Cong, 1st Sess., p. 173.]

Page 164: "It is totally unmoral."
[Ibid.]

Page 165: "We still have much"
[Harry S. Truman, Statement upon Signing the Social Security Act Amendments, August 28, 1950, at: *www.ssa.gov/history/hststmts.html#signing*.]

Page 169: "socialized medicine"
[Altmeyer, p. 196.]

Page 169: "no more socialized medicine"
[Ibid.]

Page 169: "[L]et no person on"
[Geoffrey Kollmann and Carmen Solomon-Fears, "Major Decisions in the House and Senate on Social Security: 1935–2000," March 26, 2000, CRS Legislative Histories, at: *www.ssa.gov/history/reports/crsleghist3.html*.]

Page 169: "is a very important"
[Altmeyer, p. 197.]

Page 170: "This is probably the"
[Ibid, p. 211.]

Page 171: "Speaking for myself"
[Ibid, p. 201.]

Page 171: "We favor amendment of"
[Quotes for both platforms Donald Bruce Johnson and Kirk H. Porter, *National Party Platforms 1840–1972* (Urbana: University of Illinois Press, 1973), p. 503.]

Page 171: "further strengthening" and "increasing benefits"
[Ibid, p. 484.]

## CHAPTER 10

Page 174: "conduct thorough studies"
[Altmeyer, p. 214.]

Page 174: "blanketing in"
[Ibid, p. 215.]

Page 174: "The provisions of the"
[Dwight D. Eisenhower, 1953 State of the Union Address, at *www.janda.org/politxts/State%20of%20Union%20Addresses/1953-1961%20Eisenhower/DDE53.html.*]

Page 176: "I expect my cabinet"
[Larry DeWitt, *Never a Finished Thing: A Brief Biography of Arthur Joseph Altmeyer—The Man FDR Called "Mr. Social Security,"* Chapter 7: "Death by Preposition," at: *www.ssa.gov/history/ajabioc7.html.*]

Page 176: "fully explained to the"
[Altmeyer, p. 215.]

Page 177: "[O]ur recommendations for"
[Ibid, p. 216.]

Page 177: "In my message…on"
[Dwight D. Eisenhower, Special Message to the Congress Transmitting Proposed Changes in the Social Security Program, August 1, 1953, at:*www.ssa.gov/history/ikestmts.html.*]

Page 177: "Retirement systems, by which"
[Ibid.]

Page 178: "There are two points"
[Ibid.]

Page 178: "Instead of supporting me"
[Edward D. Berkowitz, *Robert Ball and the Politics of Social Security* (Madison: University of Wisconsin Press, 2003), p. 89.]

Page 179: "a pair of Oregon boots"
[Altmeyer, p. 228.]

Page 180: "Social Security…was fundamentally"
[Columbia University Oral History Collection, Reminiscences of Roswell Perkins (1968) p. 11–12.]

Page 180:   "I am determined to preserve"
[Dwight D. Eisenhower, Special Message to the Congress on Old Age and Survivors Insurance and on Federal Grants-In-Aid for Public Assistance Programs, January 14, 1954, at: *www.ssa.gov/history/ikestmts.html#pubasst.*]

Page 182:   "It really is a"
[Berkowitz, *Robert Ball and the Politics of Social Security*, p. 94.]

Page 182:   "There is a tiny"
[Dwight D. Eisenhower to Edgar Newton Eisenhower, Docment #1147, The Papers of Dwight David Eisenhower, *Volume XV—The Presidency: The Middle Way*, at: *http://eisenhowermemorial.org/presidential-papers/first-term/documents/1147.cfm.*]

Page 183:   "the gentle, elderly anarchist"
[William F. Buckley, Jr., *Miles Gone By* (Washington, DC: Regnery Publishing, 2004), p. 58.]

Page 183:   "continued the polemic against"
[Irving Kristol, "American Conservatism, 1945–1995," at: *www.thepublicinterest.com/notable/article2.html.*]

Page 183:   "marked the beginning"
Milton Friedman and Rose D. Friedman, *Two Lucky People: Memoirs* (Chicago: University of Chicago Press 1998, p. 159.]

Page 184:   "her good news for"
[Berkowitz, *Robert Ball and the Politics of Social Security*, p. 96.]

Page 184:   "the top office management"
[Columbia University Oral History Collection, Reminiscences of Marion Folsom (1965), pp. 71–72.]

Page 185:   "this is one of"
[Edward D. Berkowitz and Wendy Wolff, "Disability Insurance and the Limits of American History," *The Public Historian* (Spring 1986): 68.]

Page 187   "socialized medicine"
[Mrs. Hobby Terms Free Vaccine Idea a Socialistic Step," *New York Times* (June 15, 1955).]

Page 188:   "take the lead in"
[Dwight D. Eisenhower, Memorandum, Document #1345, The Papers of Dwight David Eisenhower, Volume XX—The Presidency: Keeping the Peace, at: *www.eisenhowermemorial.org/presidential-papers/second-term/documents/1345.cfm.*]

Page 190:   "I'd lose every doctor"
[Edward D. Berkowitz, Mr. Social Security, Lawrence: University Press of Kansas, 1995) p. 128.]

**CHAPTER 11**

Page 191:   "Twenty-six years ago"
[John F. Kennedy, Special Message to the Congress on Health and Hospital Care, February 9, 1961, at: *www.jfklink.com/speeches/jfk/publicpapers/1961/jfk27_61.html.*]

Page 192: "Kennedy Submits Aged Care"
[John D. Morris. "Kennedy Submits Aged Care Plan," *New York Times*, February 10, 1961.]

Page 192: "The surest way to"
[Theodore R. Marmor, *The Politics of Medicare*, 2nd ed. (New York: Aldine De Gruyter, 2000), pp. 38–39.]

Page 192: "all-out effort"
[Peter A. Corning, "The Evolution of Medicare…from Idea to Law, Chapter 4: The Fourth Round—1957 to 1965," written pursuant to contract with SSA's Office of Research and Statistics, 1969, on Social Security Administration History Web site: *www.ssa.gov/history/corning.html*; and at LSU Law Center's Medical and Public Health Law Web site: *http://biotech.law.lsu.edu/cphl/history/general/corningchap4.html*.]

Page 192: "the privacy of the examination room" and following
[Marmor *The Politics of Medicare*, p. 39.]

Page 194: "great ability, great sense of"
[Edward D. Berkowitz, *Robert Ball and the Politics of Social Security*, (Madison: University of Wisconsin Press, 2003), p. 117.]

Page 194: "highest priority"
[Corning, "*The Evolution of Medicare…from Idea to Law*."]

Page 195: "a great fight across the land"
[Ibid.]

Page 195: "scare tactics" and following
[Ibid.]

Page 195: "[T]ake…a family which"
[Address at a New York Rally in support of the President's Program of Medical Care for the Aged, May 20, 1962, at: *www.ssa.gov/history/jfkstmts. html#rally.*]

Page 196: "grossly unfair disadvantage"
["Squared Off," *Time* magazine, June 1, 1962.]

Page 196: "the 'murderers' row' of"
["The Case for Subtlety," *Time* magazine, July 27, 1962.]

Page 196: "this is a most serious"
[John F. Kennedy, Statement on the Defeat of the Medical Care Bill, July 17, 1962, at: *www.ssa.gov/history/jfkstmts.html#defeat.*]

Page 197: "He hasn't stood up"
["The Case for Subtlety."]

Page 197: "Operation Hometown"
[Marmor, *The Politics of Medicare*.]

Page 198: "dream of conquering the"
[Lyndon B. Johnson, Address Before a Joint Session of the Congress, November 27, 1963, at *www.pbs.org/ladybird/epicenter/epicenter_ doc_speech.html*.]

Page 198:   "too many Americans"
[Lyndon B. Johnson, Special Message to the Congress on the Nation's Health, February 10, 1964.]

Page 199 :   "You won't have Nixon"
[John Calvin Batchelor, *Ain't You Glad You Joined the Republicans?* (New York: Henry Holt and Company, 1996), p. 304.]

Page 199:   "conceived of the federal"
[Barry Goldwater, *The Conscience of a Conservative* (Washington, DC: Regnery Gateway, 1990), p. 9.]

Page 199:   "if a job has to"
[Ibid.]

Page 199:   "Here we have,"
[Ibid.]

Page 199:   "The collectivists have not"
[Ibid, p. 63.]

Page 199:   "unlimited political and economic"
[Ibid, p. 66.]

Page 199:   "into a dependent animal"
[Ibid, p. 67.]

Page 200:   "Barry Morris Goldwater, 52"
["Salesman for a Cause," *Time* magazine, June 23, 1961.]

Page 200:   "I would like to"
[*http://blog.radioleft.com/blog/cmd=post_comment/article_id=501300/parent_id=262108*]

Page 200:   "Goldwater Sets Goals: End"
[Theodore H. White, *The Making of the President, 1964* (New York: Atheneum Publishers, 1965), p. 104.

Page 200:   "The 'social security' program"
[Milton Friedman, *Capitalism and Freedom* (Chicago: University of Chicago Press, 2002, p. 182.).

Page 201:   "[C]an't we introduce voluntary"
[Ronald Reagan, "A Time for Choosing" (1964), at: *www.americanrhetoric.com/speeches/ reaganatimeforchoosing.htm.*]

Page 201:   "[I]n 1936, Mr. Democrat himself"
[Ibid.]

Page 201:   "[E]xtremism in the defense"
[Barry Goldwater, 1964 Acceptance Speech, at: *www.washingtonpost.com/wp-srv/ politics/daily/may98/goldwaterspeech.htm.*

Page 203:   "the limbo of perenniel"
[Corning, "The Evolution of Medicare...from Idea to Law."]

Page 203:   "I have always thought"
[Corning, "The Evolution of Medicare...from Idea to Law."]

Page 203:   "[N]o one in this"
[Reagan, "A Time for Choosing."]

Page 204:   "I can support a"
[Corning, "The Evolution of Medicare...from Idea to Law."]

Page 205:   "This is an important hour"
[Harry S. Truman at the Signing of the Medicare Bill, July 30, 1965, at: *www.cms.hhs. gov/about/history/presidents/LBJ7_30_65.asp.*]

Page 205:   "No longer will older"
[Lyndon B. Johnson at the Signing of the Medicare Bill, July 30, 1965, at: *www.cms. hhs.gov/about/history/presidents/ LBJ7_30_65.asp.*]

Page 206:   "called me up and"
[Edward D. Berkowitz, *Mr. Social Security* (Lawrence: University Press of Kansas, 1995), p. 241.]

Page 207:   "With America's sons in"
[Lyndon B. Johnson, Television Address, March 31, 1968, at: *www. presidentialrhetoric.com/historicspeeches/johnson_lyndon/renunciation.htm.*]

Page 207:   "the principle outreach organization"
["Information about YAF Foundation" at: *www.yaf.org/whoweare.asp.*]

Page 208:   "to overcome present inadequacies"
[Donald Bruce Johnson and Kirk H. Porter, *National Party Platforms 1840–1972* (Urbana: University of Illinois Press, 1973), p. 736.]

Page 209:   "This nation must not break"
[Richard M. Nixon, Special Message to the Congress on Social Security, September 25, 1969.]

Page 212:   "I'd walk over my own grandmother..."
["Charles Colson," Wikipedia, at *http://en.wikipedia.org/wiki/Charles_Colson*]

Page 212:   "funneled information to liberals."
[Robert J. Myers with Richard L. Vernaci, *Within the System* (Winsted, CT: ACTEX Publications, 1992), p. 158.]

Page 212:   "was around to see"
[Ibid.]

Page 213:   "I sent [Ball] back"
[Ibid, p. 181.]

Page 213:    "to formulate and promote"
["Our Mission," The Heritage Foundation, at: *www.heritage.org/about/*.]

## CHAPTER 12

Page 216:    "Thirty-five years after"
["Time-Tested Security, *New York Times*, April 3, 1975, p. 36.]

Page 217:    "Their prompt enactment"
[Gerald Ford, Special Message to the Congress on Older Americans, February 9, 1976, at: *www.ssa.gov/history/fordstmts.html*.]

Page 218:    "Reasons for Reagan"
[1976 Campaign Brochure, at: *www.4president.org/brochures/reagan76.pdf*.]

Page 218:    "preserve the integrity and solvency"
[Lou Cannon, *Governor Reagan* (New York: Public Affairs, 2003), p. 420.]

Page 218:    "As a governor, I"
[Jimmy Carter, Democratic Convention Acceptance Speech, 1976, at: *http://home.att.net/~howingtons/jimmy1976.html*.]

Page 222:    "The Social Security Amendments"
[1978 Annual Report of the Board of Trustees of the Federal Old-Age and Survivors Insurance and Disability Insurance Trust Funds, May 16, 1978, p. 2.]

Page 224:    "When [the opponents of"
[Franklin D. Roosevelt, Madison Square Garden Address (October 31, 1936).]

Page 227:    "I, too, am pledged"
[Second 1980 Presidential Debate, October 28, 1980, at: *www.pbs.org/newshour/debatingourdestiny/80debates/cart4.html*.]

Page 227:    "the best provisions of"
[Edward D. Berkowitz, *Robert Ball and the Politics of Social Security* (Madison: University of Wisconsin Press, 2003), p. 275.]

Page 228:    "closet socialism"
[David A. Stockman, *The Triumph of Politics* (New York: Harper & Row, 1986), p. 182.]

Page 228:    "become an automatic"
[William Greider, *The Education of David Stockman* (New York: E. P. Dutton, 1982), p. 141.]

Page 230:    "I'm just not going"
[Ibid, p. 41.]

Page 230:    "what was needed was"
[Stockman, *The Triumph of Politics*, p. 183.]

Page 230:    "a tepid and inadequate"
[Ibid.]

Page 230:  "It was clear from"
[Robert J. Myers with Richard L. Vernaci, *Within the System* (Winsted, CT: ACTEX Publications, 1992), p. 14.]

Page 231:  "This 80 percent reduction"
[Ibid, pp. 19–20.]

Page 232:  "For the first time"
[Rick Shenkman, "When Did Social Security Become the Third Rail of American Politics?" History News Network, at: *http://hnn.us/articles/10522.html*.]

Page 232:  "I've got thousands"
[Stockman, *The Triumph of Politics*, p. 190.]

Page 232:  "precipitously and unfairly"
[Myers with Vernaci, *Within the System*, p. 21.]

Page 232:  "the Social Security System"
[Ronald Reagan, Letter to Congressional Leaders, May 21, 1981, at: *www.ssa.gov/history/reaganstmts.html#letter*.]

Page 232:  "Unless both the House"
[Social Security Financing Recommendations, Hearing before the U.S. House of Representatives Subcommittee on Social Security, May 28, 1981, testimony of David A. Stockman, Director, Office of Management and Budget, pp. 40–41.]

Page 232 :  "I still think we'll"
[Greider, *The Education of David Stockman*, p. 46.]

Page 233:  "[A] two-page [administration]"
["Social Security Financing and Options for the Future," Hearings before the Subcommittee on Social Security and Income Maintenance Programs, Committee on Finance, U.S. Senate, July 10, 1981 (Washington, U.S. Government Printing Office 1981) Part 1: 43.]

Page 233:  "two sets of books"
["Social Security Financing and Options for the Future," Hearings before the Subcommittee on Social Security and Income Maintenance Programs, Committee on Finance, U.S. Senate, July 7 and 9, 1981 (Washington, U.S. Government Printing Office 1981) Part 1: 43.]

Page 234:  "As I understand it"
[Myers with Vernaci, *Within the System*, p. 4.]

**CHAPTER 13**

Page 238:  "eliminate abuses and duplications"
[John Trout, "Master Negotiator at the Summit," (October, 1993) (unpublished manuscript, on file with author) p. 26.]

Page 240:  "a breach of faith"
[Congressional Record, U.S. Senate, May 6, 1982, S4645.]

Page 240: "the integrity of"
[John Trout, "Master Negotiator at the Summit," (October, 1993) (unpublished manuscript, on file with author) p. 35.]

Page 241: "a lot of political"
[National Commission on Social Security Reform, Transcript of Meeting, May 10, 1982, Neal R. Gross, Court Reporters and Transcribers, p. 7.]

Page 241: "we are facing a"
[Ibid, p. 8.]

Page 241: "This Commission has been"
[Ibid, p. 10.]

Page 241: "terrorized older people"
[Ibid, p. 8.]

Page 241: "engag[ing] in the most"
[Ibid, pp. 14a–15.]

Page 241: "If one member can"
[Ibid, p. 30.]

Page 241: "we can keep the"
[Ibid, p. 23.]

Page 241: "I want to apologize"
[Ibid, p. 23.]

Page 242: "[T]he further out in"
[Robert J. Myers with Richard L. Vernaci, *Within the System* (Winsted, CT: ACTEX Publications, 1992), p. 38.]

Page 244: "There will have to" and follows
[Quotes from "Trimming the Sails," *Time* magazine, November 15, 1982.]

Page 245: "Can we have a"
[Author conversation with Robert M. Ball.]

Page 246: "why not try one"
[Daniel Patrick Moynihan, "Social Security Saved!" *Harvard University*, March 16, 1998, p. 5.]

Page 248: "Armstrong didn't seem to"
[Myers with Vernaci, *Within the System*, p. 36.]

Page 249: "Not in my lifetime"
[Robert M. Ball, Interview #5, Social Security Aministration Oral History Collection May 22, 2001) at *http://www.ssa.gov/history/orals/ball5.html.*]

Page 249: "I disagree with everything"
[Ibid.]

Page 252:   "I want to take"
[Ronald Reagan, Statement on House of Representatives Approval of Social Security Legislation, March 10, 1983, at: *www.ssa.gov/history/reaganstmts.html#letter*.]

Page 253:   "There have been"
[Conversation with Robert M. Ball, Spring, 2005.]

Page 253:   "This bill demonstrates for"
[Ronald Reagan, Remarks on signing the Social Security Amendments of 1983, April 20, 1983, at: *www.ssa.gov/history/reaganstmts.html#letter*.]

## CHAPTER 14

Page 255:   "we must…prepare the"
[Stuart Butler and Peter Germanis, "Achieving Social Security Reform: A 'Leninist' Strategy," *Cato Journal* (Fall 1983), pp. 547–556, p. 548.]

Page 255:   "a radical reform of"
[Ibid, p. 556.]

Page 255:   "be prepared for a long"
[Ibid.]

Page 256:   "guerrilla warfare against both"
[Ibid, p. 552.]

Page 256:   "divided into the young"
[Ibid, p. 553.]

Page 256:   "The overwhelming majority"
[Ibid.]

Page 256:   "strategy must be to propose moving to"
[Ibid, p. 555.]

Page 256:   "the IRA [individual retirement account]-based private"
[Ibid, p. 548.]

Page 256:   "coalition that will"
[Ibid.]

Page 256:   "the banks, insurance companies"
[Ibid.]

Page 256:   "[N]ot only does business"
[Ibid, p. 553.]

Page 256:   "it could be many"
[Ibid, p. 556.]

Page 258:   "manifesto"
[Ibid, p. 548.]

Page 257: "In honor, Wilbur"
[Edward D. Berkowitz, *Mr. Social Security* (Lawrence: University Press of Kansas, 1995), pp. 312–13.]

Page 258: "In my budget plan"
[George H. W. Bush, Question-and-answer session in Atlanta, Georgia, October 20, 1992, at: *www.ssa.gov/history/bushstmts.html#qanda.*]

Page 258: "Read my lips; no"
[Wikipedia at: *www.answers.com/topic/read-my-lips-no-new-taxes.*]

Page 259: "The usual popular explanation"
[Appendix I: Developments Since 1983, Volume I: Findings and Recommendations, *Report of the 1994–1996 Advisory Council on Social Security*, at: *www.ssa. gov/history/reports/adcouncil/report/toc.htm.*]

Page 261: "[N]ow that the first generation"
[Larry Rohter, "Chile's Retirees Find Shortfall in Private Plan," *New York Times*, January 27, 2005.]

Page 261: "published more than"
["About the Project on Social Security Choice," at: *http://socialsecurity.org/about/index.html.*]

Page 262: "had concluded they themselves"
[Daniel Patrick Moynihan, "Social Security Saved!" *Harvard University*, March 16, 1998, p. 4.]

Page 262: "As the 1990s arrived"
[Ibid, p. 5.]

Page 262: "barely 700 days left"
[Bill Clinton, State of the Union Address, January 27, 1998, at: *www.janda.org/politxts/State%20of%20Union%20Addresses/1993–2000%20Clinton/Clinton. 998.html.*]

Page 262: "When President Roosevelt created"
[Bill Clinton, State of the Union Address, (January 19, 1999) *http:// www.janda. org/politxts/State%20of%20Union%20Addresses/1993-2000%20Clinton/ Clinton.999.html.*]

Page 263: "[T]here is little in"
[David C. John, "Clinton's Bait-and-Switch Social Security Plan," Executive Memorandum #570, The Heritage Foundation, at: *www.heritage.org/Research/SocialSecurity/EM570.cfm.* (February 5, 1999).]

Page 264: "Clinton's Newest Social Security"
[David C. John, Executive Memorandum #633, The Heritage Foundation, October 28, 1999, at *www.heritage.org/Research/SocialSecurity/EM633.cfm.*]

Page 264: "people [should] be able"
[Richard W., Stevenson, "For Bush, a Long Embrace of Social Security Plan," *New York Times*, February 27, 2005, section 1.]

Page 265:   "On the day we"
[Ibid.]

Page 265:   "Memo to George W. Bush"
[Michael Tanner, Cato Project on Social Security Choice, September 18, 2000, at: *www.socialsecurity.org/daily/09-18-00.html*.]

Page 265:   "Bush often seemed"
[Michael Tanner, "Election Lessons for Social Security," Cato Project on Social Security Choice, November 12, 2000, at: *www.cato.org/dailys/11-17-00. html*.]

Page 265:   "must include individually controlled"
[Guiding Principles, President's Commission to Strengthen Social Security, at: *http://csss.gov/*.]

Page 267:   "Personalizing Social Security suggests"
[Nancy Snow, "The Language Police: Gettin' Jiggy with Frank Luntz," February 26, 2005, at: *www.commondreams.org/views05/0226-27.htm*.]

Page 267:   "Eventually, I'd like"
[Robin Toner, "Social Security Issues Rattling Races for Congress," *New York Times*, June 4, 2002.]

Page 267:   "In an Orwellian..." and following"
[Capital Gang transcript, September 14, 2002.

Page 267:   "privatize Social Security" and "That's a Democrat term."
[*Crossfire* transcript, October 28, 2002.]

**CHAPTER 15**

Page 271:   "should remain, as it"
[Dwight D. Eisenhower. Special Missage to the Congress on Old Age and Survivors Insurance and on Federal Grants-in-Aid for Public Assistance Programs, January 14, 1954, at *http://www.ssa.gov/history/ikestmts.html*.]

Page 271:   "This nation must not break"
[Richard M. Nixon. Special Message to the Congress on Social Security (September 25, 1969) at *http://www.ssa.gov/history/nixstmts.html*.]

Page 271:   "a primary goal of"
[Gerald Ford. Message to Employees of the Social Security Administration on the 40th Anniversary of the Social Security Act (August 14, 1975) at *http://www. ssa.gov/history/fordstmts.html*.]

Page 271:   "our nation's ironclad commitment"
[Ronald Reagan. Remarks on signing the Social Security Amendments of 1983 (April 20, 1983) at *http://www.ssa.gov/history/reaganstmts.html#letter.*]

Page 271:   "And there's one thing"
[George H. W. Bush. 1990 State of the Union address, at *http://www.janda.org/politxts/State%20of%20Union%20Addresses/1989-1992%20Bush/Bush.90.html*.]

Page 272: "a problem for our"
[George W. Bush, Presidential Debate, Tempe, Arizona, October 13, 2004.]

Page 272: "come out strong"
[Ron Suskind, "Without a Doubt," *New York Times Magazine*, October 17, 2004.]

Page 273: "made-up" and "a false, baseless attack"
[Jim VandeHei and Chris L. Jenkins, "Kerry Warns of Social Security Changes," *Washington Post*, October 18, 2004.]

Page 273: "No, the Social Security"
[Vice President and Mrs. Cheney's Remarks in Wilmington, Ohio, October 25, 2004, at: *www.whitehouse.gov/news/releases/2004/10/20041026-7.html.*]

Page 273: "reforming Social Security will"
[George W. Bush, News conference, November 4, 2004, at: *www.iht.com/articles/2004/11/04/america/web.bushconftext.html.*]

Page 273:
[George Bush, State of the Union Address, February 2, 2005.]

Page 275: "the fundamental ratio"
[Appendix I: Developments Since 1983, *Volume I: Findings and Recommendations, Report of the 1994–1996 Advisory Council on Social Security*, at: *www.ssa.gov/history/reports/adcouncil/report/toc.htm.*]

Page 277: "this will be one"
[Peter H. Wehner, Memorandum, "Some Thoughts on Social Security," January 6, 2005, at: *www.eurolegal.org/greendogdem/gdd0105/20050110gdd.htm.*]

Page 277: "'[p]ersonalization' not 'privatization.'"
[House Republican Conference, Senate Republican Conference, "Saving Social Security: A Guide to Social Security Reform," January 27, 2005 (on file with author).]

Page 279: "Year after year"
[George W. Bush, 2003 State of the Union Address, January 29, 2003, at: *www.janda.org/politxts/State%20of%20Union%20Addresses/2001-2004%20Bush/ GWB.2003.htm.*]

Page 279: "is a crisis created"
[Jim VandeHei, "Bush Paints His Goals as 'Crises,'" *Washington Post*, January 8, 2005.]

Page 280: "step one of my"
["President Discusses Strengthening Social Security in North Carolina," BTI Center for the Performing Arts, Raleigh, North Carolina, at: *www. whitehouse.gov/news/releases/2005/02/20050209-8.html.*]

Page 280: "There is no trust 'fund'"
[Ibid.]

Page 282:   "Defendant Trustees have"
[Civil Action No. 85-3466, First Amended Complaint for Declaratory Relief, Mandamus and Injunctive Relief, U.S. District Court for the District of Columbia, p. 14.]

Page 282:   "A lot of people"
["President Participates in Social Security Conversation in West Virginia," West Virginia University at Parkersburg, (April 5, 2005), at *http://www.whitehouse.gov/ news/releases/2005/04/20050405-4.html*.]

Page 284:   "The...strategy must be"
[Stuart Butler and Peter Germanis, "Achieving Social Security Reform: A 'Leninist' Strategy," *Cato Journal* (Fall 1983), p. 555.]

Page 285:   "I'm a parent as well"
[Jonathan Weisman, "Skepticism of Bush's Social Security Plan Is Growing," *Washington Post*, March 15, 2005.]

Page 285:   "BANISH PRIVATIZATION FROM"
[Nancy Snow, "Gettin' Jiggy with Frank Luntz," *The Language Police*, March 10, 2005, at: *http://gnn.tv/articles/1184/The_Language_Police*.]

Page 285:   "Privatization is a trick"
[Tony Batt, "Bush Says Social Security Opponents May Pay Price," Arkansas News Bureau, March 16, 2005, at: *www.arkansasnews.com/archive/2005/03/16/ WashingtonDCBureau/318756.html*.]

Page 286:   "Basically, the net effect"
[Jonathan Weisman, "Participants Would Forfeit Part of Accounts' Profits," *Washington Post*, February 3, 2005.]

Page 286:   "The original story"
[Ibid]

Page 289:   "If you're talking about"
[Jonathan Weisman, "New Strategy on Social Security," *Washington Post*, January 24, 2005.]

Page 289:   "socialist"
[Yoshi Tsurumi, "Hail to the Robber Baron?" *Harvard Crimson*, April 6, 2005, at: *www.apomie.com/crimson.htm*.]

Page 289:   "I have written a"
[Transcript, "An Oversight Hearing on the Bush Administration's Plans to Privatize Social Security," Senate Democratic Policy Committee Hearing, January 28, 2005, at: *http://democrats.senate.gov/dpc/hearings/hearing18/transcript.pdf*.]

Page 289:   "The President's road"
["Selling Social Security," Online NewsHour PBS, March 4, 2005, at: *www.pbs.org/ newshour/bb/social_security/jan-june05/ss_3-04.htm.l*]

Page 290:   "Presidential visits are rare"
[Richard Benedetto, "Protesters of Overhaul Dog Bush," *USA Today*, May 24, 2005.]

Page 290:   "As soon as we"
[Ibid.]

Page 291:   "a soft-money slush"
[Nicholas Confessore, "Bush's Secret Stash," *Washington Monthly* (May 2004).]

Page 291:   "They can run"
[Maureen Dowd, "Swifties Slime Again," *New York Times*, February 24, 2005.]

Page 291:   "the walker-and-cane set"
[Ibid.]

Page 291:   "A majority of Americans"
[Craig Gordon, "Bush's Fix Falters," Newsday.com, April 27, 2005, at: *www.newsday.com/mynews/ny-usprez274234956apr27,0,880523.story? page=1*.]

Page 291:   "If [Bush is] going"
[Ibid.]

Page 293:   "doubled-down on his bet"
[Dana Milbank and Jim VandeHei, "A Gambler Decides to Raise the Stakes," *Washington Post*, April 29, 2005.]

Page 293:   "won't change. We're talking"
[Transcript, "President Discusses Social Security in Florida", Tampa Convention Center, Tampa, Florida, February 4, 2005, at *www.whitehouse.gov/news/releases/2005/02/20050204-13.html*.]

Page 294:   "Any plan that maintains"
[David Espo, "White House Leaves Disabled Benefits Open," Associated Press, May 13, 2005, at: *www.sacunion.com/pages/nation/print/4805/*.]

Page 294:   "I'm not overjoyed about"
[Judy Keen, "Bush Says He's Not Deterred on Social Security," *USA Today*, May 3, 2005.]

Page 294:   "Means testing would change"
[Michael A. Fletcher, "In Miss., Bush Touts Social Security Plan," *Washington Post*, May 4, 2005.]

Page 294:   "is landing kind of flat"
["Thomas Weighs Tax to Rescue Bush on Social Security," Bloomberg.com: U.S., at: *http://quote.bloomberg.com/apps/news?pid=10000103&sid= aBtMwRqPtgSU&refer=news_index*.]

Page 294:   "retirement package for"
[Carolyn Lochhead, "Republicans Broaden Strategies for Overhauling Social Security," *San Francisco Chronicle*, April 30, 2005.]

Page 295:    "Republicans in the House"
[Glen Johnson, "House Republican Split over Social Security Timetable," *Chicago Sun-Times*, May 2, 2005.]

## CHAPTER 16

Page 300:    "[o]nly about 30"
[Leonard E. Burman, William G. Gale, and Jeffrey Rohaly, "Options for Reforming the Estate Tax," *Tax Notes*, April 18, 2005, p. 383.]

Page 301:    "Your committee's bill"
[Social Security Financing Amendments of 1977, U.S. House of Representatives, Report of the Committee on Ways and Means to Accompany H.R. 9346, House Report No. 702, Part 1 (Washington, D.C.: U.S. Government Printing Office, 1977), p. 18.]

Page 303:    "There is no more"
["There is no more…" Robert M. Ball, "Fixing Social Security," Issue Brief, The Century Foundation (June, 2005) at *http://www.tcf.org/Publications/Retirement Security/ballplan.pdf*.]

## CHAPTER 17

Page 311:    "[W]e must…look to the larger"
[Franklin D. Roosevelt, Address of the President Delivered by Radio from the White House, June 28, 1934. at *http://www.historycentral.com/documents/FDRsfifthfirside. html*.]

Page 312:    "The last thing"
[Dale Russakoff, "Human Toll of a Pension Default," *Washington Post*, June 13, 2005.]

Page 312:    "Leaving aside Social Security"
[Arloc Sherman and Isaac Shapiro, "Social Security Lifts 13 Million Seniors Above the Poverty Line," Center on Budget and Policy Priorities, February 24, 2005, at: *www.cbpp.org/2-24-05socsec.htm*.]

Page 313:    "Connecticut (1932), New York (1929)"
["Old Age Security Staff Report to Mr. Witte," Final Staff Report, Old Age Security, Committee on Economic Security, at: *www.ssa.gov/history/reports/ces/ces2armstaff.html*.]

Page 313:    "a tiny splinter group" and "a few…Texas"
[Dwight D. Eisenhower to Edgar Newton Eisenhower, Document #1147, The Papers of Dwight David Eisenhower, *Volume XV—The Presidency: The Middle Way*, at: *http://eisenhowermemorial.org/presidential-papers/ first-term/documents/1147 cfm*.]

Page 313:    "socialist"
[Yoshi Tsurumi, "Hail to the Robber Baron?" *Harvard Crimson*, April 6, 2005, at: *www.apomie.com/crimson.htm*.]

Page 314:   "Fifty-one percent of"
[Robin Toner and Marjorie Connelly, "Poll Finds Broad Pessimism on Social
Security Payments," *New York Times*, June 19, 2005.]

Page 314:   "[P]art of the retirement"
[Russakoff, "Human Toll of a Pension Default." *Washington Post* (June 13, 2005).]

Page 314:   "Social Security has been called"
[Speech to Republican National Convention, August 3, 2000, at: *www. cnn.com/
ELECTION/2000/conventions/republican/transcripts/bush.html.*]

Page 316:   "My grandfather, President Franklin"
[Transcript, An Oversight Hearing on the Bush Administration's Plans to Privatize Social Security, Senate Democratic Policy Committee Hearing, January 28,
2005, at: *http://democrats.senate.gov/dpc/hearings/hearing18/transcript pdf.*]

# Recommended Reading

Aaron, Henry J. and Reischauer, Robert D. *Countdown to Reform: The Great Social Security Debate*. New York: The Century Foundation Press, 1999

Altmeyer, Arthur J. *Formative Years of Social Security*. Madison: University of Wisconsin, 1966

Baker, Dean and Weisbrot, Mark. *Social Security: The Phony Crisis* Chicago: The University of Chicago Press, 1999

Ball, Robert M. *Social Security: Today and Tomorrow*. New York: Columbia University Press, 1978

Ball, Robert M. and Bethell, Thomas N. (Editor), *Insuring the Essentials: Bob Ball on Social Security*. New York: The Century Foundation Press, 2000

Berkowitz, Edward D. *Mr. Social Security*, Lawrence, Kansas: University Press of Kansas, 1995

Berkowitz, Edward D. *Robert Ball and the Politics of Social Security* Madison: The University of Wisconsin Press, 2003; paperback 2005

Bernstein, Merton C. and Bernstein, Joan *Social Security: The System That Works*. New York: Basic Books, 1988

Brown, J. Douglas *Essays on Social Security*. Princeton: Industrial Relations Section, Department of Economics, Princeton University, 1977

Burns, Eveline M. *Social Security and Public Policy*. New York: McGraw Hill: 1956

Derthick, Martha *Policymaking for Social Security*. Washington, DC: Brookings Institution, 1979

Diamond, Peter and Orszag, Peter. *Saving Social Security: A Balanced Approach* Washington, DC: Brookings Institution Press, 2003

Edelman, Peter, Salisbury, Dallas L., and Larson, Pamela eds. *The Future of Social Insurance: Incremental Action or Fundamental Reform?* Proceedings of the Thirteenth Annual Conference, National Academy of Social Insurance. Washington, DC: The Brookings Institution Press, 2002

Epstein, Abraham *Insecurity: A Challenge to America*. New York: Random House, 1938

Ferguson, Karen and Blackwell, Kate, *Pensions in Crisis* New York: Arcade Publishing, 1995

Graetz, Michael J. and Mashaw, Jerry L., *True Security*. New Haven: Yale University Press, 1999

Kingson, Eric R. and Schultz, James B., eds. *Social Security in the 21st Century* New York: Oxford University Press, 1997

Marmor, Theodore R. and Mashaw, Jerry L. *Social Security: Beyond the Rhetoric of Crisis*. Princeton: Princeton University Press, 1988

Munnell, Alicia *The Future of Social Security* Washington, DC: The Brookings Institution, 1977

Myers, Robert J. *Social Security* 4th ed. Philadelphia: Pension Research Council and University of Pennsylvania Press, 1993

Schieber, Sylvester J. and Shoven, John B. *The Real Deal: The History and Future of Social Security*. New Haven: Yale University Press, 1999

Skidmore, Max J. *Social Security and its Enemies* Boulder: Westview Press, 1999

Steuerle, C. Eugene and Bakija, Jon M. *Retooling Social Security for the 21st Century: Right and Wrong Approaches to Reform*. Washington, DC: Urban Institute Press, 1994

Thompson, Lawrence H. *Older and Wiser: The Economics of Public Pensions*. Washington, DC: Urban Institute Press, 1994

# Index

357